D0097874

Allegories of Love

———————————

Allegories of Love

CERVANTES'S *PERSILES AND SIGISMUNDA*

Diana de Armas Wilson

PRINCETON UNIVERSITY PRESS

PRINCETON, NEW JERSEY

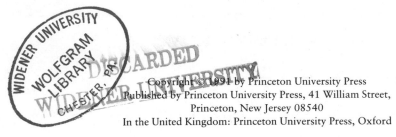

Copyright © 1991 by Princeton University Press
Published by Princeton University Press, 41 William Street,
Princeton, New Jersey 08540
In the United Kingdom: Princeton University Press, Oxford

All Rights Reserved

Library of Congress Cataloging-in-Publication Data

Wilson, Diana de Armas, 1934–
Allegories of love : Cervantes's Persiles and
Sigismunda / Diana de Armas Wilson.
p. cm.
Includes index.
1. Cervantes Saavedra, Miguel de, 1547–1616.
Trabajos de Persiles y Sigismunda. 2. Women
in literature. 3. Sex differences in literature.
I. Cervantes, Saavedra, Miguel de, 1547–1616.
Trabajos de Persiles y Sigismunda, 1991. II. Title.
PQ6327.P5W55 1991   863'.3—dc20   90-40841

ISBN 0-691-06854-2 (alk. paper)

Publication of this book has been aided by the Program of
Cultural Cooperation Between Spain's Ministry of Culture
and United States' Universities

This book has been composed in Linotron Sabon

Princeton University Press books are printed on acid-free paper,
and meet the guidelines for permanence and durability of the
Committee on Production Guidelines for Book Longevity of the
Council on Library Resources

Printed in the United States of America by Princeton University Press,
Princeton, New Jersey

2   4   6   8   10   9   7   5   3   1

For Douglas

Pars animae meae

CONTENTS

ACKNOWLEDGMENTS

MORE THAN ANYONE, Rachel Jacoff helped me to envision this book. Her critical and scholarly powers led me to formulate, particularly at the beginning stages of this project, what had earlier seemed an impossible dream. She has been, in Pliny's terms, "the witness of my life," and I owe her an inestimable debt.

Ruth El Saffar, my mentor and *comadre* in Cervantine studies, first showed me how to think about Cervantes as an iconoclast. Her work has contributed to what is best in this book. Without her expert criticism and timely encouragement—acknowledged in my epilogue—I would still be haunting the dusty library stacks.

The following generous friends and scholars have read and commented upon chapters of this book, often in their earliest versions, and helped me to assess the direction of my research: Edward Aylward, Andrew Bush, Anthony Cascardi, Leland Chambers, Marie Cort Daniels, Edward Dudley, Daniel Eisenberg, Mary Malcolm Gaylord, Eric Gould, Barbara Johnson, Andrea and Steve Nightingale, Patricia Parker, T. Anthony Perry, David Quint, Burton Raffel, Peter Rudnytsky, Celia Weller, and Michael Zappala. Two Golden Age Hispanists, H. Patsy Boyer and María Antonia Garcés, read more extended sections and offered helpful criticism on questions of language. I am also grateful to Robert E. Brown, my editor at Princeton University Press, who expedited the preparation of the manuscript with the grace and efficiency of a true professional. Princeton's anonymous readers rescued me from various conceptual errors and infelicities. My copyeditor, Annette Theuring, who read the final typescript with care and concern and gratifying expertise, found many last-minute inconsistencies. It is a pleasure to thank these friends and interlocutors.

I would like to express my special gratitude to Joseph Foote, whose close and energetic readings of my manuscript unpretzeled my prose and eliminated many, though regrettably not all, of my stylistic tics. Any *pedanterías* that remain are strictly my own.

I am indebted to Carol Taylor and Carolyn Bolden of the Faculty Computing Lab at the University of Denver—as well as to R. Daniel Wilzoch—for their invaluable help with my manuscript. Special thanks are due to my Chairman, Gerald Chapman, for enabling me to secure a quarter's released time from my teaching duties.

I wish to thank the National Endowment for the Humanities for three separate grants that enabled me to deepen my knowledge of Cervantes.

My early work on allegory was assisted by an NEH Summer Seminar at the Newberry Library in Chicago in 1982. The Endowment also granted me the directorship of a Summer Seminar on *Don Quixote* for secondary school teachers in 1985. Finally, the stimulus and the leisure needed to finish this book were provided by an NEH Grant for University Teachers. This last grant—a gift of time for which I am deeply grateful—freed me from teaching duties and allowed me to do research at the Biblioteca Nacional in Madrid. Finally, I wish to thank the University of Denver Research and Creative Work Fund for support in the preparation of the index, expertly freelanced by Miranda Wilson.

"Children are half one's soul," Cervantes wrote in a little-known play entitled *De la entretenida* (act 3), "but daughters are the most complete half" ("Mitades son del alma / los hijos; mas las hijas / son mitad más entera"). I am grateful, beyond thanks, for the love and support of my four daughters—Antonia, Andrea, Fiona, Miranda—who were always ready to discuss the progress of this book, to suggest cover designs, or to sustain me with their music during my long bouts at the computer. They are the women behind this text.

My closest reader, in all senses, is acknowledged in my dedication.

Versions of several portions of this book have appeared in print: "Cervantes on Cannibals," *Revista de estudios hispánicos* 22 (October 1988); "Contesting the Custom of the Country: Cervantes and Fletcher," in *From Dante to García Márquez: Studies in Romance Literatures and Linguistics Presented to Anson Conant Piper*, ed. Gene H. Bell Villada, Antonio Giménez, and George Pistorius (Williamstown, Mass.: Williams College, 1987); "Cervantes's *Labors of Persiles*: 'Working (in) the In-between,'" in *Literary Theory/Renaissance Texts*, ed. Patricia Parker and David Quint (Baltimore: Johns Hopkins University Press, 1986); "Uncanonical Nativities: Cervantes's Perversion of Pastoral," in *Critical Essays on Cervantes*, ed. Ruth El Saffar (Boston: G. K. Hall and Co., 1986); "Cervantes' Last Romance: Deflating the Myth of Female Sacrifice," *Cervantes* 3 (Fall 1983).

INTRODUCTION

CERVANTES'S LAST ROMANCE—the work he twice heralded as "el gran *Persiles* [the great *Persiles*]"—was regarded by many of his contemporaries as his *obra maestra*. Yet it has been eclipsed for nearly four centuries by the vastly more popular *Don Quixote*, a work that justly exhibits a pride of place in the European canon.[1] Published posthumously in 1617, the *Persiles* is a text that challenges our ability to read figuratively. "We read well, and with pleasure," Annette Kolodny reminds us, "what we *already know how* to read."[2] We read *Don Quixote* with knowledge and pleasure, thanks, in part, to its countless novelistic imitations. But the *Persiles*, a work that should be read side by side with *Don Quixote*, if only for the retrospective logic it brings to that earlier novel, remains to this day an underread text, quietly barred from the canon of the great European Master discourses.

Now that readers may freely question the partialities and repressions that have gone into the canonizing of masterworks, it is instructive to ask why the politics of Cervantine canon formation have, since about 1630, repressed a text that its author so highly favored. The *Persiles* would be either "the worst" or "the best" book of entertaining fiction written in Spanish, Cervantes claimed, in a teasing binary that he instantly exploded: he regretted having said "the worst" because the opinion of his friends assured him otherwise.[3] "Whatever Cervantes's friends thought, or at least said," Wyndham Lewis thundered centuries later, "it takes a stout heart today to plough from end to end through *Persiles y Sigismunda*, a labyrinth-novel twice as large and complicated as *La Galatea*."[4]

What neither Cervantes nor his friends could foresee was that the *Per-*

---

[1] Cervantes's prepublication advertisements were made in chapter 4 of the *Viaje del Parnaso* (1614) and in the dedication to *Ocho comedias y ocho entremeses* (1615).

[2] Annette Kolodny, "Dancing Through the Minefield: Some Observations on the Theory, Practice and Politics of Feminist Literary Criticism," *Feminist Studies* 6 (Spring 1980): 12; emphasis added.

[3] In the dedication to *Don Quixote*, pt. 2 (1615), Cervantes speculates that the *Persiles* will be "o el más malo, o el mejor que en nuestra lengua se haya compuesto, quiero decir de los de entretenimiento: y digo que me arrepiento de haber dicho el más malo, porque según la opinión de mis amigos, ha de llegar al estremo de bondad posible." See Miguel de Cervantes Saavedra, *El ingenioso hidalgo Don Quixote de la Mancha*, ed. Luis Andrés Murillo, 2 vols. (Madrid: Clásicos Castalia, 1978), 2:39. Because of the many editions in use, however, I have chosen to refer to passages from *Don Quixote* by part and chapter number, preceded by the initials *DQ*. Unless otherwise stated, all translations are my own.

[4] This statement, perhaps confessional, introduces Lewis's short and inaccurate précis of the *Persiles* in *The Shadow of Cervantes* (New York: Sheed and Ward, 1962), 187.

siles would be a little-read work—an "obra poca leída," as one modern editor laments.[5] Some three centuries after its publication, one of its rare admirers tried to challenge the mystique of a canon that could so serenely ignore its creator's own judgment: since Cervantes believed, unfalteringly, that the *Persiles* was his obra maestra, José Bergamín wondered, not unreasonably, whether a time might come when criticism recognized it as such.[6] Although the *Persiles* will never—*should* never—usurp the place of *Don Quixote*, certainly the time has come when exclusivist or irreducible notions of "master narratives" no longer terrorize readers. Criticism should recognize the *Persiles*, if only because it is the last work of a writer who gave to early modern Europe its most generative critique of reading.[7]

In the ongoing reassessment of Cervantes, still a site of enormous cultural power, critics have variously described the *Persiles* as an "encyclopedic" work, as "one of the most ambitious intellectual feats ever attempted by a novelist," and as "the culmination of a lifetime of writing."[8] The author of this last phrase, Ruth El Saffar, elsewhere adds a wise caveat to prospective readers of the *Persiles*: "So long as we are caught in the dichotomies that entangled the Cervantes of 1605, we will not be able to read his late romances. But I think we are arriving at a time when that will be possible."[9] We have at least arrived at a time when it is possible to

---

[5] Emilio Carilla, ed., *Los trabajos de Persiles y Sigismunda*, by Miguel de Cervantes (Salamanca: Biblioteca Anaya, 1971), 12.

[6] José Bergamín, *Laberinto de la novela y monstruo de la novelería*. For a discussion of eighteenth- and nineteenth-century readers who regarded the *Persiles* favorably, see Rudolph Schevill, "Studies in Cervantes: I. 'Persiles y Sigismunda': Introduction," *Modern Philology* 4 (1906–1907): 1–24. By and large, however, Continental criticism has responded to the work with a long silencing tradition.

[7] Among the critics who have made it possible to regard the *Persiles* as worthy of sustained scholarly attention are Rafael Osuna, whose prescriptive essay laments its "forgetting" ("El olvido del *Persiles*," *Boletín de la real academia española* 48 [1968]: 55–75); Juan Bautista Avalle-Arce, whose Spanish edition has superseded all others (*Los trabajos de Persiles y Sigismunda* [Madrid: Clásicos Castalia, 1969]); Tilbert Diego Stegmann, whose German monograph includes a massive bibliography (*Cervantes' Musterroman* Persiles: *Epentheorie und Romanpraxis um 1600* [Hamburg: Hartmut Ludke Verlag, 1971]); Alban K. Forcione, whose two studies serve as a quarry for much contemporary work on the *Persiles* (*Cervantes, Aristotle, and the* Persiles [Princeton: Princeton University Press, 1970], and *Cervantes' Christian Romance: A Study of* Persiles y Sigismunda [Princeton: Princeton University Press, 1972]); and Ruth El Saffar (*Beyond Fiction: The Recovery of the Feminine in the Novels of Cervantes* [Berkeley: University of California Press, 1984]), 127–69.

[8] Alban K. Forcione, *Cervantes' Christian Romance*, 60n; Edward Dudley, "The Wild Man Goes Baroque," in *The Wild Man Within: An Image in Western Thought from the Renaissance to Romanticism*, ed. Edward Dudley and Maximillian E. Novak (Pittsburgh: University of Pittsburgh Press, 1972); Ruth El Saffar, *Beyond Fiction*, 169.

[9] "The Truth of the Matter: The Place of Romance in the Works of Cervantes," in *Romance: Generic Transformations from Chrétien de Troyes to Cervantes*, ed. Kevin Brown-

read the *Persiles* in English, thanks to a new translation by Celia E. Weller and Clark A. Colahan, the first since Louisa Dorothea Stanley's now unreadable 1854 version.[10]

Among other obstacles to reading Cervantes's last romance, as the history of its reception reveals, has been a steady aversion—even a repugnance—to the "erotic pangs" ("*erōtika pathēmata*") Cervantes chose to explore in his avowed imitation of the Greek romancer Heliodorus. Apart from our entanglement in dichotomies, then, some of the expectations and interpretive strategies that we bring to Greek romance have been tainted by Nietzsche's deprecation of the genre as the quintessence of Alexandrian decadence. Others have been colored, ironically, by Cervantes's own advertised subversion of chivalric romance in *Don Quixote*. But in our postmodern search for new modes of fiction, Cervantes's last romance offers a surprising radicality. It not only rewrites Don Quixote's pathogenic quest for the ideal woman, but, what is even more "novel," it tries to articulate the unrepresented: the female unknown that Don Quixote, perhaps out of *terror feminae*, had signified as "Dulcinea." Unlike *Don Quixote*, which set the mold for subsequent Western prose fiction, the *Persiles*, which set few or no molds, may be read as an early poetics of sexual difference, an issue which Cervantes, unlike many of his critics, never elides, denies, or universalizes.

What I propose here, then, is an "alternative" Cervantes: an interpretation of what has been called his "final statement on the human condition"[11] based on the concept of gender as a category of analysis. Although significant critical attention has been given to the religious allegory of Cervantes's last romance (its orthodox Christian meaning),[12] I believe it is the erotic interpolations within the *Persiles*—some dozen episodes of antiromance—that reveal the text's peculiar susceptibility to our historical moment. In these episodes, which I discuss as framed "exemplary novels," women and other marginalized "others" are allowed to participate in the production of knowledge about themselves. This study addresses not only those feminine psychic needs that Cervantes so presciently explores, in their weaknesses as well as their strengths, but also the male libidinal economies that intersect, often violently, with them.

---

lee and Marina Scordilis Brownlee (Hanover, N.H.: University Press of New England, 1985), 251.

[10] Celia E. Weller and Clark A. Colahan, trans., *The Trials of Persiles and Sigismunda* (Berkeley: University of California Press, 1989).

[11] Dudley, "Wild Man Goes Baroque," 116.

[12] Alban Forcione's admirable study, as he himself explains, "by no means exhausts the thematic substance of the *Persiles*," which he allows "can be read in a variety of ways." As an example of a different approach, Forcione cites his own earlier study, *Cervantes, Aristotle, and the* Persiles, in which he read the *Persiles* for its literary theory (*Cervantes' Christian Romance*, 60n).

"There used to be a comfortable belief," Kenneth Clark recalls, "that great artists grew old in a kind of haze of benevolence, but a theory which does not apply to Dante, Shakespeare, Milton, Tolstoy, Beethoven, Michelangelo and Rembrandt is not really of much value."[13] The theory does not apply to Cervantes, either, who seems to have grown old in a haze of experimentation. The *Persiles* helps us to understand the literary evolution of Cervantes. The language of this work in the original Castilian, as I trust my quotations will show, is at times so innovative, so gnostic in its stance toward authority, that it disrupts the signifying order, expanding the boundaries of the possible. A greater familiarity with the *Persiles* would contribute substantially to the way we look at the late Cervantes, at *Don Quixote*, and at the cultural codes of the Renaissance in relation to our own.

To read the *Persiles* is also to reassess the intersections of novel and romance, including the differences *within* romance forms that move us here to adopt Peter Dunn's compelling view of Cervantes's best fiction as "intergeneric."[14] The adequacy of our theoretical distinctions between "novel" and "romance" is pointedly questioned through Michael McKeon's recent documentation, in *The Origins of the English Novel*, of "the persistence of romance, both within the novel and concurrently with its rise."[15] The "intergeneric" structures of the *Persiles* lead us to face an even more vertiginous problem, perhaps an exclusively Cervantine one, given the way the mimetic episodes in the *Persiles* accommodate romance elements: namely, the persistence of romance within the novels within a romance.

The "encyclopedic" nature of the *Persiles* renders the text itself resistant to any totalitarian critical approach. My own, an avowedly eclectic one, includes a range of contemporary and traditional Cervantine criticism, of Renaissance imitation theories, of theories of allegory, of old and "new" historicism, of theories of the gendered subject, and of psychoanalytic insights in and out of a feminist context. A word is perhaps in order here on my tempered use of Freudian theory, which programmatically excludes the author as a locus of study. "Turn to the poets," Freud concluded his 1932 lecture on the *terra incognita* of woman, "if you want to know more about femininity."[16] As psychoanalysis, now under

---

[13] Cited in *Shakespeare's Late Plays*, Program for the National Theatre of Great Britain (Summer 1988).

[14] Peter Dunn writes in the context of the picaresque and "the criticism that has kept it in place" ("Cervantes De/Reconstructs the Picaresque," *Cervantes* 2 [1982]: 131).

[15] Michael McKeon, *The Origins of the English Novel, 1600-1740* (Baltimore: Johns Hopkins University Press, 1987), 3.

[16] *The Standard Edition of the Complete Psychological Works of Sigmund Freud*, trans. James Strachey, 24 vols. (London: Hogarth, 1953–1974), 22:135. Further references to the

trial,[17] turns the question of femininity back to literature, at last heeding
Freud's own advice, literature will be held to a fuller accounting of earlier
representations of love and sexuality. A poet writing in prose, Cervantes
has much to tell us about femininity, and most of it in the *Persiles*. But
the role played by woman in Cervantes does not sustain Freud's essen-
tialist theory of gender, in which masculinity is the measure of the feminine. When we turn to Cervantes, we find femininity represented as dis-
rupting the hierarchical gender dualism that Freud affirmed, with its
fetishized notions of male primacy. Cervantes's pre-Cartesian model of
the psyche, as my study shows, displaces hierarchy with mutual but nondominant difference, with *learned* relations of complementarity and ad-
jacency. Like Freudian psychoanalysis, Cervantes's writing explores how
sexual identity is constituted, how differentiation itself comes about. Unlike Freud, however, Cervantes represents gender identity as inhabiting
language, as culturally instituted and maintained. The language of literature, as Don Quixote's madness documented for all time, creates as well
as interprets sexual sensibilities.

I have used a variety of interpretive tools to look closely at the cultures
that Cervantes represents in the *Persiles*, a text whose cast of characters
includes English, Scottish, Spanish, Portuguese, French, Italian, Irish,
Danish, Lithuanian, Polish, Norwegian, Icelandic, and Arabic subjects.
Many of the discussions in this book have a Renaissance cross-cultural
dimension, as, for example, the pages addressing John Fletcher's imitation of the *Persiles*; or Spenser's deployment of allegorical subcharacters;
or Shakespeare's theater of exorcism; or Inca Garcilaso's chronicles of
human sacrifice; or Montaigne's plug for polygamy; or Pope Innocent
VIII's bull on "incubi and succubi"; or Leone Ebreo's dialogues of love,
the Italian text of a sephardic Jew expelled from his native Spain that
would be reintegrated, thanks to an American *mestizo* translator, back
into the Spanish language. This web of cultural relations may show my
commitment to a comparative perspective in this book. I have wished,
above all, to build some small bridges between Renaissance Spain and the
English-speaking critical world that has, perhaps remembering the Armada, neglected Hispanic literature, a problem recently and sensitively
articulated by the editors of *The Comparative Perspective on Literature*:
"We regret . . . the lack of an essay treating Hispanic literature, an area
swiftly becoming more and more prominent in comparative studies—in
striking contrast to the situation of the sixties and early seventies."[18]

Standard Edition will be parenthetically documented in the text by volume and page number, preceded by the initials *SE*.

[17] See *The Trials of Psychoanalysis*, a special issue of *Critical Inquiry* (13 [Winter 1987]).

[18] Clayton Koelb and Susan Noakes, eds., *The Comparative Perspective on Literature*
(Ithaca: Cornell University Press, 1988), 4.

Chapter 1 of my study ("Kidnapping Romance") focuses on the romance that Cervantes used as his avowed model for the *Persiles*, Heliodorus's *Aethiopica*. In remotivating the "star-crossed lovers" of Greek romance, Cervantes manipulated the ascendant, even nascent, idea of married love in the Renaissance, a crucial period in the formation of contemporary sexual values. This chapter, which reexamines the relationship between Cervantes and Heliodorus in the light of both sixteenth-century imitation theory and contemporary genre theory, tries to disabuse readers of the notion that the *Persiles* is "a poetic novel of chivalry."[19] It also poses one fundamental question: why would Cervantes, whose avowed intention in *Don Quixote* was to topple romance, wish, at the close of his life, to "kidnap" it back again?

Chapter 2 ("Canonizing Romance") reexamines the Canon of Toledo's blueprint for the ideal romance in order to distinguish it from the quest for the "Holy Skirt," to use Cervantes's own playful travesty of chivalric romance. After exploring the process by which Cervantes makes us conscious of his fiction as an enterprise distinct from both history and lying, as well as a body deformed from its Greek model, I question the canonization of good and evil as the main organizational category of romance criticism. The equally ancient dualism of male/female generates, I suggest, a far less inert reading of the *Persiles*.

Chapter 3 ("Some Versions of Allegory") centers on the figure/mode of *allegoria* in a variety of historical manifestations, from Plutarch to Paul de Man, in order to situate the polemical issue of allegory in the Renaissance. Minding Sir John Harington on the subject of "infinite Allegories," I have wished—perhaps vainly, considering the subject—to "avoid tediousness" (*Orlando Furioso*, 1591). What Cinquecento critics intoned on the matter of allegory is followed by what Cervantes's characters have to say about it. Throughout this chapter and in anticipation of the next, my study stresses the importance of Platonist thinking in understanding and appreciating Cervantes's darker fictions. The chapter closes with a showcase study of Cervantes's own allegorical praxis in the *Persiles*: his personification of libido ("SENSUALIDAD") within a dream narrative, a technique that has much to tell us about the specific historical shift from religious to sexual allegory.

Chapter 4 ("Cervantes and the Androgyne") focuses on the organizing metaphor for Cervantes's romance, the androgyne, a structure that figures a reconciliation of opposites. This figure subtends the entire textual body of the *Persiles* and even divides it into two disturbing halves, the

[19] Manuel Durán's phrase in "Cervantes's Swan Song: *Persiles and Sigismunda*," in *Cervantes*, ed. Harold Bloom (New York: Chelsea House Publishers, 1987), 79. In this same essay, Durán later admits that the *Persiles* is "much more in tune with history, geography, and common sense than the romances of chivalry" (96).

"split" text traditionally lamented by critics. My discussion here addresses the nature of this shaping metaphor in the *Persiles* as well as its place in the discourse of the Renaissance. Cervantes's use of such a metaphor, with the play of difference and division it (en)genders, creates a surplus of meaning in his text, even opening it, as my citations document, toward a scandalous interchangeability of gender. Unlike Don Quixote, both heroes of the *Persiles* are able to cross what Foucault calls "the clearly defined frontiers of difference."[20] The close of this chapter is a discussion of Leone Ebreo's generative retailoring of the Platonic androgyne, in the *Dialoghi d'amore* that Inca Garcilaso de la Vega translated into Spanish for Cervantes's age. For the philosophical treatment of love in his last work, Cervantes turned, once again, to the Hebrew Neoplatonist he had earlier acknowledged, in the prologue to *Don Quixote*, as the only resource needed for writing about "amores."

"Cervantes on Cannibals," chapter 5, relates the structures and events of the first six chapters of the *Persiles*, its great allegorical *foci*, where Cervantes fictionalizes the psychogenesis of sexual difference. For the germinal staging of his allegory, Cervantes invents a Barbaric Isle: an all-male fantasy island fueled by a messianic ideology of World Conquest. At the threshold of the *Persiles*, Cervantes encodes a culture in which imperial and libidinous discourses intertwine under the imperatives of a "Barbaric Law." This emblematic narrative represents a North Sea culture of domination and submission that communicates in terrorizing "signs," cannibalizes alien males, and traffics in "vendible" women. Although Cervantes's poetical fiction has given rise to more than one allegorical meaning, it would seem difficult *not* to read a gendered narrative in this representation of a violent and sacrificial *mapa mentis*. I interpret (with a nod to Montaigne) Cervantes's narrative on cannibals as an ironic commentary on the commercial inflections of his own—and not only his own—culture of power relations, scapegoating, and conspicuous consumption. Cervantes's literalization of his cannibals as empire-builders falls squarely in the ironic tradition we have come to expect from the creator of *Don Quixote*. My reading aligns Cervantes's cannibalism with Freud's cannibalism of the "primal horde," in order to speculate on the curiously revealing differences between the two patriarchal visions. As models for Cervantes's parodic barbarians, however, I nominate Pliny's Essenes, an all-male community of refugees living on the shores of the Dead Sea "sine ulla femina" (*Natural History*). But in this chapter I also glance at various commentaries on cannibalism in the New World that bear directly on the Spanish imperialist project, most especially the com-

---

[20] Michel Foucault, *The Order of Things: An Archaeology of the Human Sciences* (New York: Vintage Books, 1973), 46.

prehensive text that many of these chronicles pour into, Inca Garcilaso de la Vega's *Comentarios reales* (1609).

Moving from the *Persiles*'s violent beginnings into the text itself, then, chapter 6 ("Plot and Agency") offers an overview of the main plot followed by reflections on the biblical undermeaning detectable through its Exodus typology. In discussing the much-maligned protagonists of the *Persiles*, I stress the conventional personhood of allegorical characters, their "frozen" agency and their collective voice. Sophisticated criticism now available on the heroes of Spenserian allegory has compelled me to make passing comparisons between the *Persiles* and *The Faerie Queene*, the two major allegories of the Renaissance.[21] In the context of allegorical agency, I contest assorted negative criticism of Cervantes's "exemplary fallacy," of his lack of "great character-creation," and of the "unflinching rectitude" of his heroes.[22]

In chapter 7 ("Thirteen Exemplary Novels"), I explore how the structure of the *Persiles*—with its breaks, shifts, and ellipses—constitutes a revolutionary form of writing, one that interweaves the idea of gender with the production of meaning. In a move neo-Aristotelians would judge harmful to suspense and *dispositio*, Cervantes ruptured his romance with over a dozen lively inset stories. I see these stories as framed "novelas ejemplares," *exemplary* both in the sense of providing templates for a reader's input and of serving as models for future fiction.[23] All of the interpolations bear on the relations between the sexes and on the idea of marriage as a cultural institution: "el verdadero eje [the true axis]" of the *Persiles*, as Emilio Carilla claims, is love.[24] Each tale, moreover, strategically destabilizes the conventional narrative progression toward marriage by representing one or another obstacle to intimacy: anger, lust, paranoia, masochism, greed, libidinal failure, the hypervaluation of honor (*honra*), alcohol abuse, psychopathic jealousy, blood vengeance, and misogyny.

[21] Although the model of Ariosto is common to both the *Persiles* and *The Faerie Queene*—and both texts invite comparison in their exaltation of marriage—these two Renaissance allegories, oddly enough, have never been brought into any significant relationship. Cervantes allegorized the romantic epic in order to fashion not "a gentleman," in the manner of his English and Protestant counterpart Spenser, but a new idea of marriage, one in which differences are created equal.

[22] William J. Entwistle, "Ocean of Story," in *Cervantes: A Collection of Critical Essays*, ed. Lowry Nelson, Jr. (Englewood Cliffs, N.J.: Prentice-Hall, 1969), 163; E. C. Riley, *Cervantes's Theory of the Novel* (Oxford: Oxford University Press, 1962), 54; William Byron, *Cervantes: A Biography* (New York: Doubleday, 1978), 514.

[23] Chapter 7 of this study shows its indebtedness to Harry Sieber's sense of the *exemplary* as the creation of model stories "dignas de ser imitadas [worthy of being imitated]" ("Preliminar," *Novelas ejemplares*, 2 vols. (Madrid: Cátedra, 1988), 1:14.

[24] Carilla, "Introduction," *Persiles*, 22.

In chapters 8, 9, and 10, I focus closely on three of these "exemplary" *novelas*, all portraying female protagonists from assorted European cultures, women represented as both desiring and speaking subjects: a self-exiled Irish translator, an unwed Spanish mother, an improvised Italian demoniac. Chapter 8 ("A Romance of Rape") deals with ritual defloration, both as a New World issue and as a literary topic during the Renaissance; chapter 9 ("Some Perversions of Pastoral"), with incest, specifically with Cervantes's subversive use of the Ovidian Myrrha legend within a hidden maternal discourse; and chapter 10 ("The Histrionics of Exorcism"), with institutionalized notions of demonic possession and exorcism in the Renaissance. Cervantes's last romance signifies not the unwelcome return of romance but its transformation into a product that looked to posterity for understanding. Cervantes's "last word" *on* romance is, indeed, the same as his last word *in* romance: "posteridad [posterity]" (475). Writerliness is "conservative," explains Barbara Johnson, "only in the sense that it is capable of inscribing and conserving messages the radicality of which may not yet have been explored."[25]

The epilogue to this study begins with an epigraph that is a postmodern postscript to Cervantes's pioneering labors. Carlos Fuentes lends it to me from *The Old Gringo*, in which a woman speaks the lines: "This would not be only a man's story from now on. A presence (my presence . . .) will alter the story."[26] Although written in the 1980s during the rich novelistic harvest of the Latin American baroque, this passage could have been conceived by Cervantes in the early seventeenth century. It is, in fact, an emblematization of the plot of the *Persiles*, in which the presence of woman "alters" the conventional love stories of men. Fuentes's lines also intersect with the prologue to the *Persiles* (in linear time, the epilogue). In that moving valediction, written four days before his death, Cervantes apologizes to his future readers for the "roto hilo [broken thread]" of his last romance. A time might come, perhaps, to tie it up again: "Diga lo que aquí me falta, y lo que me convenía [I would say what is missing here, and what would have been fitting]" (49). As the twentieth century draws to a close, innumerable texts such as Carlos Fuentes's are tying up broken strands similar to the one Cervantes left us. What is extraordinary for me about Cervantes's last work is that it articulates so many of the discourses of sexual and cultural difference that we are finally—and urgently—preparing ourselves to read.

[25] Barbara Johnson, *A World of Difference* (Baltimore: Johns Hopkins University Press, 1986), 31.

[26] Carlos Fuentes, *The Old Gringo*, trans. Margaret Sayers Peden and the author (New York: Farrar, Straus and Giroux, 1985), p. 112.

PART ONE

Context and Subtexts

Chapter One

KIDNAPPING ROMANCE

Ce que nous appelons monstres, ne le sont pas à Dieu.

[What we call monsters are not so to God.]

—Montaigne, *Essais*

ONE OF Borges's doomed protagonists reflects on how, down through history, generations of storytellers have always repeated two narratives: "la de un bajel perdido que busca por los mares mediterráneos una isla querida, y la de un dios que se hace crucificar en el Gólgota [that of a lost ship searching the Mediterranean seas for a loved island, and that of a god who has himself crucified on Golgotha]."[1] Although Cervantes exploits both narratives in the *Persiles*, he acknowledges only a Mediterranean quest story as his model: Heliodorus's *Aethiopica*, the most complex of the extant Greek romances.[2] Even more pertinently, Cervantes announces, in an official prepublication advertisement in the *Novelas ejemplares* (1613), that he dares to compete with his model: "libro que se atreve a competir con Heliodoro, si ya por atrevido no sale con las manos en la cabeza [a book that dares to compete with Heliodorus, if for all its daring it doesn't emerge with hands on its head]."[3] Cervantes's remark-

---

[1] Jorge Luis Borges, "El evangelio según Marcos," in *El informe de Brodie* (Buenos Aires: Emecé Editores, 1970), 133.

[2] The others are Chariton's *Chaereas and Callirhoe*, Longus's *Daphnis and Chloe*, and Achilles Tatius's *Leucippe and Clitophon*. Both Xenophon's *Ephesiaca* (also known as *Anthia and Habrocomes*) and Iamblichus's *Babyloniaca* are extant as epitomes. Thirty-four papyrus fragments (ten dubious) of ancient Greek novels have survived, all copied between the first and sixth centuries A.D. (Susan Stephens, " 'Popularity' of the Greek Novel" [Paper delivered at the Second International Conference on the Ancient Novel, Dartmouth College, 28 July 1989], 5). On the dating of the extant Greek romances, see Ben Edwin Perry's *The Ancient Romances: A Literary-Historical Account of Their Origins* (Berkeley: University of California Press, 1967), 350 n. 15. On the origins of the genre of Greek romance in the Hellenistic period (330–30 B.C.), see Tomas Hägg, *The Novel in Antiquity* (Berkeley: University of California Press, 1983), 87–90. The central book on the subject is Erwin Rohde's *Der griechische Roman und seine Vorlaufer* (Leipzig, 1914).

[3] Cervantes, "Prólogo al lector," *Novelas ejemplares*, in *Obras completas*, ed. A. Valbuena Prat, 18th ed. (Madrid: Aguilar, 1975), 2:10. The emergence of a book "con las manos en la cabeza" may be understood as a gesture of dismay. According to Covarrubias, the gesture signifies a person who is "descalabrado o maltratado [broken-headed or injured]" (*Tesoro de la lengua castellana o española según la impresión de 1611, con las*

ably explicit use of the verb *competir* here places him squarely in the class of imitation that has been called *eristic*, where "images of struggle, strife, and competition" abound, and where "a text may criticize and correct its model."[4] Indeed, the critical and personal implications of this announced intention to compete, with its oblique allusion to the cautionary Horatian monster lurking at the entrance to the *Ars poetica*, are manifold. For in his avowed competition with the Greek romancer Heliodorus, Cervantes did indeed produce a monster—at least in the sense of a being whose boundaries are unclear. The failure of traditional taxonomies to embrace Cervantes's monstrous progeny—the strange, hybridous, excrescent form of the *Persiles*—moves us here to explore the primal scene of its genesis. This chapter treats the relationship between Cervantes and Heliodorus in the light of both sixteenth-century imitation theory and contemporary genre theory. My aim is to enlighten at least one vexed question: why would Cervantes—so vocal and assiduous about toppling romance in *Don Quixote*—become engaged, toward the end of his life, in kidnapping it back again?

Cervantes's frank, funny, and slightly contentious prepublication announcement may evoke for readers the kind of imitation famously articulated in late antiquity by Longinus, who, in his treatise *On the Sublime* (chap. 13), described the process of Plato's imitation of Homer in terms of a "strife" or competition that was "good for mortals." In a masterly study on Renaissance uses of *imitatio* in Italy, France, and England (regrettably, not in Spain),[5] Thomas Greene distinguishes this type of competitive imitation, which he calls *dialectical*, from other, more reproductive, kinds. The whole process of Renaissance imitation is, for him, "a field of ambivalence, drawing together manifold, tangled, sometimes antithetical attitudes, hopes, pieties, and reluctances within a concrete locus." In a scattering of English and Continental quotations that gloss each nation's "hostility toward the pressure to imitate," Greene could have included Cervantes's prologue to *Don Quixote*, part 1, where "the pressure to imitate" is so flamboyantly ridiculed. "To imitate creatively,"

---

adiciones de Benito Remigio Noydens publicadas en . . . 1674, ed. Martín de Riquer [Barcelona: Horta, 1943], 786). In the passage leading up to Cervantes's announcement of the forthcoming *Persiles*, however, he speaks of the "engendering" and the "parturition" of his *Novelas ejemplares*: "Mi ingenio las engendró y las parió mi pluma" (10). His obstetrical discourse leads me to read the emergence of his *Persiles* in the teratological sense of a monstrous birth, with "hands on the head."

[4] G. W. Pigman III, "Versions of Imitation in the Renaissance," *Renaissance Quarterly* 23 (1980): 4.

[5] "In defense of the neglect of other literatures, most notably Hispanic, I can only say that my incompetence to deal with them has saved a long book from growing longer" (Thomas M. Greene, *The Light in Troy: Imitation and Discovery in Renaissance Poetry* [New Haven: Yale University Press, 1982], 2).

Greene stresses in a remark that sheds a useful light on Cervantes's experiment in the *Persiles*, "is to assume the historicity of one's particular place and moment and idiom."[6]

At the start, then, we must confront Cervantes's desire to transform—into the historicity of his own idiom—a Greek romance, a species of the genre that would represent for Nietzsche, to take one formidably modern example, the ultimate artful lie. To the young Nietzsche's need for superheroes as emblems of the unvarnished Dionysian "truth" of mortality, the Greek romances—conceived, as he claimed, by "Alexandrian man, who is at bottom a librarian and scholiast"—perpetrated only artful lies.[7] To the aging Cervantes writing the *Persiles* (as to the mature Shakespeare writing his own late romances), these same "lies" that made life desirable seemed worth imitating. "In every period of history," Northrop Frye notes, "certain ascendant values are accepted by society and are embodied in its serious literature. Usually this process includes some form of kidnapped romance, that is, romance formulas used to reflect certain ascendant religious or social ideas." Because Frye's approach to romance—as a *mythos* that translates into "the wish-fulfillment dream"—is less rooted in historical periods than his "kidnapping" metaphor would suggest, it offers no effective model for the generic transformation I wish to explore in the *Persiles*.[8] And because I am convinced that Cervantes saw all genres, and most especially romance, as more conventional than constitutive, theorists more alert to generic deviance—such as Rosalie Colie, Claudio Guillén, Alastair Fowler, Fredric Jameson, or Ralph Cohen—have seemed more useful to my argument.[9] Finally, because the *Persiles*

---

[6] Greene, *Light in Troy*, 47, 45.

[7] Lamenting the poisonous Alexandrian spirit that can spread over our existence "the blandishments of illusion," Nietzsche further complains that "our whole modern world is caught in the net of Alexandrian culture" (*The Birth of Tragedy*, trans. Francis Golffing [New York: Doubleday-Anchor, 1956], 109–10). Nietzsche's disdain for the Alexandrian "librarian" finds an echo in Charles Whibley's 1895 description of the *Aethiopica* as "the faded experiment of a studious pedant"; cited by Hägg, *The Novel in Antiquity*, 193.

[8] Northrop Frye, *The Secular Scripture: A Study of the Structure of Romance* (Cambridge, Mass.: Harvard University Press, 1976), 29–30. On Frye's theory of romance as "the Mythos of Summer," see *Anatomy of Criticism* (New York: Atheneum, 1966), 186–206. I agree with Arthur Heiserman's remark that Frye's definition of romance, as "a sequential or processional form" centering on a quest and an agon, "has little to do with the Greek romances" (*The Novel Before the Novel* [Chicago: University of Chicago Press, 1977], 226n).

[9] Genre theorists cited, seriatim, are Rosalie Colie, *The Resources of Kind: Genre-Theory in the Renaissance*, ed. B. K. Lewalski (Berkeley: University of California Press, 1973); Claudio Guillén, *Literature as System: Essays Toward the Theory of Literary History* (Princeton: Princeton University Press, 1971), especially essays 4 and 9; Alastair Fowler, *Kinds of Literature: An Introduction to the Theory of Genres and Modes* (Cambridge, Mass.: Harvard University Press, 1982); Fredric Jameson, "Magical Narratives: Romance as Genre," *New*

is a polygeneric work—an allegorical romance incorporating hymns, sonnets, masques, encomia, the epistolary genre of the fictional letter, the picaresque, the Italian novella, the mariological miracle narrative, and even a *florilegium* of epigrams—a theorist such as Bakhtin, who sees Greek romance as similarly having "fused together in its structure almost all genres of ancient literature," would offer a fitter guide to the later Cervantes.[10] But I wish here to imitate Frye's term for imitating romance, using in what follows a more historical and inductive approach to the kidnapped materials. The kidnapping itself evokes numerous questions at the outset. How was Cervantes engaged in the process of embodying his society's "ascendant" religious or social values in his last work? What was the nature of his competition with Heliodorus? Which romance formulas did he borrow in order to support, revise, or supplement the work of his acknowledged precursor?

Erōtika Pathēmata

In order to address these questions, we must first glance at some of the conventions of what we anachronistically call Greek romance, keeping in mind what Kevin and Marina Brownlee rightly see as "the constancy of generic transformation in the history of romance."[11] The Greeks themselves, for whom the genre names of romance and novel were not in currency, referred to these tales as *erōtika pathēmata*—that is, erotic sufferings or, in Harlequin romance parlance, erotic pangs. Frye's paratactic description may launch us on our quest for conventions: "In Greek romance the characters are Levantine, the setting is the Mediterranean world, and the normal means of transportation is by shipwreck."[12] A slightly more ample catalogue of romance codes, by Frank Kermode, fills in a few more blanks: "This is the world of lost princesses, great storms that sunder families, lifetimes spent in wandering or suffering, babies put to sea in little boats . . . and later recognized by a mole or jewel."[13] Greek romances, then, are tales of mysterious births and exposed infants; of foster parents; of star-crossed loves and ever-endangered chastity; of abductions, captivity, and prison; of hairbreadth escapes from beasts and

---

Literary History 7 (1975): 135–63; and Ralph Cohen, "Afterword: The Problems of Generic Transformation," in *Romance: Generic Transformations*, ed. Brownlee and Brownlee, 265–80.

[10] M. M. Bakhtin, *The Dialogic Imagination*, ed. Michael Holquist, trans. Caryl Emerson and Michael Holquist (Austin: University of Texas Press, 1981), 89.

[11] Kevin Brownlee and Marina Scordilis Brownlee, "Introduction," *Romance: Generic Transformations*, 11.

[12] Frye, *Secular Scripture*, 4.

[13] Frank Kermode, "Introduction," *Shakespeare: The Winter's Tale* (New York: Signet, 1963), xxv.

brigands; of pirates and prophetic oracles; and of near-deaths and resurrections and miraculous reunions where, to borrow Shakespeare's words,
"all losses are restored and sorrows end." Perhaps the most arresting catalogue of Greek romance codes, written in verse and by way of preface to
his own twelfth-century Byzantine romance, comes from Nicetas Eugenianus:

> Here read Drusilla's fate and Charicles'—
> Flight, wandering, captures, rescues, roaring seas,
> Robbers and prisons, pirates, hunger's grip;
> Dungeons so deep that never sun could dip
> His rays at noon-day to their dark recess,
> Chained hands and feet; and, greater heaviness,
> Pitiful partings. Last the story tells
> Marriage, though late, and ends with wedding bells.[14]

All of the above find their way into the *Aethiopica*, generally regarded
as the finest extant Greek romance. Anachronistically set in an ahistorical
time some five hundred years before Christ, its setting shifts from Athens
and Delphi to Memphis and finally to Meroe, the capital city of Ethiopia
(the northern part of modern Sudan), including en route many Mediterranean ports of call. As well as being a "world of lost princesses," the
Aethiopica is a world of pirates, organized piracy having reached terrorist
proportions during the Hellenistic period. But it is also a world of Egyptian prophets and satraps; of Delphic priestesses and Ethiopian gymnos-
ophists; of Athenian flute-girls, Thracian courtesans, and Phoenician
merchants; of phalanxes of Persian warriors; of Troglodytes and other
"cinnamon" peoples; of kings mounted on elephants whose subjects pelt
them with Nile lilies; and of professional thieves living along the marshes
of the Nile who roast their fish in the sun.

The author of this remote romance—and the object of Cervantes's daring competition—was a mid-third-century writer,[15] little known in our
postmodern, anti-epic age but lavishly praised during the Renaissance.
"What Schole-boy, what apprentice knows not Heliodorus?" asked the
satirist Joseph Hall in the early seventeenth century. What every apprentice knew, if we accept Hall's hyperbole, was not Heliodorus but his *Aethiopica*, the canonized classic among the Greek romances. Of the author
himself they knew nothing but what his "sign-off" to some nine thousand
lines of Greek prose revealed: "Heliodorus, son of Theodosius, a Phoe-

[14] Stephen Gaselee, "Appendix on the Greek Novel," in *Daphnis and Chloe* (Loeb Classical Library, 1916), 410–11.

[15] On the dating debate for Heliodorus—ascribing to him various dates between the early
second and the late fourth centuries—see Perry's page-long footnote in *The Ancient Romances*, 349n.

nician of Emesa, of the line of descendants of the Sun." Although born
into a pagan sun cult in the Syrio-Phoenician city of Emesa (modern
Homs), Heliodorus may or may not have finished his days in witch-ridden
Thessaly, where, as the Christian bishop of Tricca, he introduced a mod-
ified form of clerical celibacy.[16] Legend has it that when forced to choose
between keeping his bishopric and acknowledging that he had written a
romance, Heliodorus "made the only choice that any self-respecting author could make, and ceased to be a bishop."[17]

THE HUMANIST CRITIQUE OF ROMANCE

If the notion of a self-respecting author of romance seems amusingly dis-
sonant, it is perhaps because romance—whether Greek, chivalric, pastoral, gothic, family, or televised soap—has had to either fight *for* or alternately defend itself against the charge *of* respectability. Perhaps
because the genre has always attracted female readers, the humanist Luis
Vives was especially vehement in his wish, quite literally, to "blind"
women to the pleasures of romance: "Estas tales [las que leen de amores
ajenos], no sólo sería bien que nunca hubieran aprendido letras, pero
fuera mejor que hubieran perdido los ojos para no leer y los oídos para
no oír [It would have been good if such female readers (those who read
about other people's love affairs) had never learned their letters, but it
would have been better if they had lost their eyes in order not to read and
their ears in order not to hear]."[18] Vives may be regarded as an especially

---

[16] The early fifth century ecclesiastical historian Socrates reports the following popular
rumor about Heliodorus: "The first to institute this custom [clerical celibacy] in Thessaly
was Heliodorus who became bishop there, and who is said to have been the author of a love
story in several books which he composed when he was young and to which he gave the
title *Aethiopica*" (*Hist. Eccl.* 5, 22 [Migne, *Patri. Gr.* 67], col. 63). The prologue to the
1615 edition of the *Aethiopica*, published in Madrid, unwaveringly identifies its author as
a bishop and remarks, moreover, that it was Heliodorus who introduced into Thessaly the
rule that clerics who had contracted marriage while still secular could return to "cohabit"
with their women (*Historia etiópica de los amores de Teágenes y Cariclea*, ed. F. López
Estrada, trans. Fernando de Mena [Madrid: Aldus, 1954], lxxxiv).

[17] The legend, transmitted by Montaigne, originated in the fourteenth century with Ni-
cephorus Callistus (R. M. Rattenbury, "Heliodorus, the Bishop of Tricca," *Proceedings of
the Leeds Philosophical and Literary Association* [1927]: 168–78). Cited by Frye, *Secular
Scripture*, 91. Moses Hadas thinks it likely that the episcopal title was attached to Heliodorus's name in order to make his book "respectable reading for Byzantine monks, who
were exceedingly fond of novels and had many more to read than the few which have survived" ("Introduction," *Heliodorus: An Ethiopian Romance*, trans. Moses Hadas [Ann Arbor: University of Michigan Press, 1957], x).

[18] The *casus belli* of Vives's tract is the seduction of young women by the adulterous plots
of the Spanish and French romances. See *Instrucción de la mujer cristiana*, Colección Aus-
tral, 138 (Buenos Aires: Espasa Calpe, 1940), 34. The Latin version—*De institutione femi-*

austere representative of the moral abhorrence of many Spanish humanists for the great proliferation of Spanish "best-sellers" printed in the first half of the sixteenth century.[19]

The moralistic critiques of romance by these Renaissance guardians of the culture were crude and puritanical versions of similar indictments presented by Dante in the *Inferno*, where both the romance and its author are personified as intermediaries or panders for adultery: "Galeotto fu il libro e chi lo scrisse [A Galeotto was the book and he that wrote it]" (canto 5). Petrarch would further demean romance by troping the genre as the dream of "sick minds": "sogno d'infermi e fola di romanzi" (*Trionfo d'amore* 4.66), a phrase which echoed Horace's "velut aegri somnia" or "a sick man's dreams" (*Ars poetica* 1.7). For more than half of the sixteenth century, no end of speculation had focused on the craze of the Spanish public for the adventures of *Amadís de Gaula*, *Palmerín de Inglaterra*, *Don Belianís de Grecia*, and their many "sons" and sequels. It is well known that the soldiers accompanying Hernan Cortés compared their first sight of Moctezuma's Mexico with the enchantments they had read about in *Amadís*. Even a pair of revered saints—Ignatius Loyola and Teresa of Ávila—publicly confessed to having spent far too many youthful hours poring over chivalric romances. Allowing for a generic shift, such laments echo Saint Augustine's confession, of some twelve centuries earlier, that he had wasted time weeping for Dido's death.[20] In 1531, the Crown officially banned "idle and profane books such as *Amadís*" from its colonies in America.[21] As late as 1611, Covarrubias would still be inveighing against the chivalric romances in his *Tesoro*, where he depicts them as "ficciones gustosas y artificiosas de mucho entretenimiento y poco provecho [pleasure-filled, artful fictions of much entertainment and little profit]."[22]

Harry Sieber remarks that the "insatiable desire for romances" that

---

nae christianae, in *Opera, in duos tomos* (Basel: N. Episcopium, 1555)—enjoyed a wide humanist readership.

[19] According to Henry Thomas, between 1508 and 1550 the romances of chivalry were published in Spain and Portugal at the rate of almost one per year. See *Las novelas de caballerías españolas y portuguesas*, trans. Esteban Pujals (Madrid: CSIC, 1952), 113–14.

[20] The young Ignatius Loyola, before founding the Society of Jesus, was "muy dado a leer libros mundanos y falsos, que suelen llamar de caballerías [very given to reading those false and worldly books that are called chivalric]" (*Autobiografía*, ed. Cándido de Dalmases, s.i., in *Obras completas*, 4th ed. [Madrid: Católica, 1952], 92). Teresa of Ávila wrote in her *Vida* of her own obsession: "Que si no tenía libro nuevo, no me parece tenía contento [If I didn't have a new romance to read, I wasn't content]" (*Libro de la vida*, in *Obras completas*, ed. Efrén de la Madre de Dios and Otger Steggink [Madrid: Católica, 1962], 18). Saint Augustine's lament is from book 1 of the *Confessions*.

[21] See Henry Thomas, *Spanish and Portuguese Romances of Chivalry* (Cambridge: Cambridge University Press, 1920), 178.

[22] Covarrubias, *Tesoro*, 324.

characterized the first half of the century faded markedly on account of complex socioeconomic circumstances, including urban growth and demographic changes. These circumstances, Sieber suggests, created the "changing mentalité" of a new reading public demanding new kinds of fiction, an attitude that would lead to the displacement of the chivalric by the pastoral and the picaresque as Spain's dominant fictions.[23] Eisenberg, on the other hand, argues that the chivalric romances "retained considerable popularity at the beginning of the seventeenth century, to say nothing of the final years of the sixteenth, in which the idea of *Don Quixote* was probably born."[24] E. C. Riley, who sees the romances of chivalry as having "their ups as well as downs in the later sixteenth century," observes that when they hit their downs, romance in other Renaissance forms—Moorish, Greek, and pastoral—was flourishing.[25] Whatever the vicissitudes of the chivalric romances in the second half of the sixteenth century, the Renaissance intelligentsia, who had always scorned these books, managed to find a romance they could enshrine: the *Aethiopica*, courtesy of Heliodorus Redivivus. As the preface to its first French translation (1547) assured readers, in this Greek romance they would find all the verisimilitude lacking in the debased Spanish romances of chivalry.[26] If Greek romance was to have a more limited circulation than the romances of chivalry, that circulation would at least have the imprimatur of the humanists.

The long evolution in critical tastes toward the Italian *romanzi* and the Spanish *libros de caballerías*—from the puritanical indictments of the early humanists, through the more aesthetic critiques that emerged after the Pazzi translation of Aristotle's *Poetics* (1536), through Tasso's attempted reconciliations of epic and romance, to the neo-Aristotelian recognition of Heliodorus as the great aesthetic mediator—has been thoroughly traced across the Cinquecento by Alban Forcione. The attacks on both the Spanish and Italian romances of chivalry, as Forcione points out, focused relentlessly on the two cardinal principles of unity and verisimilitude that Cervantes subtly ridiculed.[27] The criteria for the developing concept of unity, it bears stressing, were being developed by Aristotelian,

---

[23] Harry Sieber, "The Romance of Chivalry in Spain," in *Romance: Generic Transformations*, ed. Brownlee and Brownlee, 203–19.

[24] Eisenberg, *Study of* Don Quixote, 35. Eisenberg documents the continuing popularity of the *libros de caballerías* and suggests that, with the accession to the throne of "pleasure-loving Felipe III," restrictions on their publication began to be removed (34–38).

[25] E. C. Riley, "Romance, the Picaresque and *Don Quixote I*," in *Studies in Honor of Bruce W. Wardropper*, ed. Dian Fox, Harry Sieber, and Robert ter Horst (Newark, Del.: Juan de la Cuesta Press, 1989), 238.

[26] The French preface of Amyot's translation was carried over into the Spanish version. See *Historia etiópica*, ed. López Estrada, lxxvii–lxxxiii.

[27] See Forcione, *Cervantes, Aristotle, and the* Persiles, 91–130.

not Platonic, theorists, who adopted for their arguments an increasingly rhetorical cast. It is difficult to discover in the writings of the period, as Bernard Weinberg reminds us, "any specifically Platonic principle that contributed to the developing concept of unity. Plato's suggestions were rarely applicable to structural matters, and the structure of plot was no exception."[28]

But Aristotelian principles, despite the intense ferment surrounding their solidification, were by no means the whole story. The Neoplatonic concept of proportion, as Forcione correctly points out in a footnote, could subordinate both unity and verisimilitude: "Here the *locus classicus* is neither Horace nor Aristotle, but rather the *Symposium* in the resurrected form which it took in the commentaries of such theorists as Ficino and Leon Hebreo."[29] Whereas Forcione's massively documented *Cervantes, Aristotle, and the* Persiles, as evidenced by its title, concerns itself largely with neo-Aristotelian poetics, my study is situated precisely within the climate of the *Symposium*. In the chapters that follow, I shall discuss a Neoplatonic concept—rooted in the theories of Leone Ebreo and related, if somewhat deviously, to both unity and proportion—that could also subordinate the neo-Aristotelian mania for unity and plausibility. I hope to show how Cervantes, through his competition with and transformation of Heliodorus, was constructing an as-yet-uncodified poetics of gender, a poetics which I more fully document in chapter 4. But first let us return to the genre of romance as the medium for these poetics.

THE DIFFERENCES WITHIN ROMANCE

Did Cervantes's imitation of Greek romance signal an unwelcome return of romance? Such a question invites us to confront some of the problematics of genre both in Cervantes's day and, as we rethink genre theory, in our own time. The neo-Aristotelians were deeply concerned about the differences *between* epic and romance, that staple binary of sixteenth-century criticism, but they did little to uncover the differences *within* the genre of romance itself, between its subgenres: chivalric romance differs conceptually from Greek romance. Cervantes himself acknowledged that no critical paradigm existed for chivalric romance—"de quien nunca se acordó Aristóteles [about which Aristotle never dreamed]" (*DQ* 1, Prologue). Nor had Aristotle ever pronounced on what we now call Greek romance. In this century, Gilbert Highet noted the "loose and inaccurate" use of the word *romance* for both the Greek romances and the twelfth-century stories of chivalrous adventure, but he excused the labeling on

---

[28] Bernard Weinberg, *A History of Literary Criticism in the Italian Renaissance*, 2 vols. (Chicago: University of Chicago Press, 1961), 2:803.

[29] Forcione, *Cervantes, Aristotle, and the* Persiles, 94n.

the odd grounds that all of this fiction is covered anyway under the "general contemporary use of the word *romantic*."[30] More recently, E. C. Riley has argued that the English term "romance" (which he rightly claims needs to be understood in quotation marks) subsumes a variety of species in Renaissance Spain: the books of chivalry, as well as pastoral, sentimental, and Byzantine "novels." Riley suspects that *romance* is a more lasting genre than the novel, and he even speculates about a renaissance of romance in contemporary film. But his insightful essay attempts no distinctions: "No he tratado de distinguir entre las diferentes clases del *romance* en tiempos de Cervantes [I have not tried to distinguish between the different classes of *romance* in Cervantes's age]."[31]

To distinguish between Greek and chivalric romance in an essay, or even a chapter, is a daunting exercise: one must omit some matters, and reduce others to schematic proportions. As is well known, the tradition of Greek romance was not lost during the rise of chivalric romance in the Middle Ages, but its diffusion was limited to two texts: the romance of Alexander in its multiple versions, and the highly popular *Apollonius of Tyre* (*Historia Apollonii Regis Tyri*). The latter, long considered a Latin version of a lost Greek novel, brought to the Middle Ages many of the stock themes of Greek romance: storms and shipwrecks, kidnapping by pirates, separations and recognitions, dreams and apparitions, remarkable constancy of affection, the topos of chastity, and finally the reunion of long-suffering lovers.[32] Greek romance, as Marina Beer argues, was "deeply felt" by Boccaccio, who exploited both its structure and themes in the *Filocolo* and in some *novelle* of the *Decameron*.[33] But whether Greek romance was deeply felt by chivalric romance is another question.[34] It is no simple matter to force the Greek romances (erōtika pathē-

[30] Gilbert Highet, *The Classical Tradition: Greek and Roman Influences on Western Literature* (New York: Oxford University Press, 1957), 612n.

[31] E. C. Riley, " 'Romance' y novela en Cervantes," in *Cervantes: Su obra y su mundo, Actas del I Congreso Internacional Sobre Cervantes*, ed. Manuel Criado de Val (Madrid: Edi-6, 1981), 5–13.

[32] The anonymous Latin prose romance *Historia Apollonii Regis Tyri*, the earliest surviving version of the Apollonius story, may or may not represent a lost original Greek story to which later Latin additions were made, probably around the fifth century. Ben Perry sees "no need at all" to suppose it a translation or imitation of a Greek romance (*The Ancient Romances*, 320). The Apollonius story became widely known through its inclusion (as chap. 153) in the *Gesta Romanorum*, the popular fourteenth-century collection of tales. Spanish readers knew the Apollonius story, as derived from the *Gesta Romanorum*, in the thirteenth-century *Libro de Apolonio*, and, by 1576, in Juan de Timoneda's *Patrañuelo*.

[33] Marina Beer, "Plot and *Fortuna*: Greek Romance in the Italian Renaissance" (Paper delivered at the Second International Conference on the Ancient Novel, Dartmouth College, 24 July 1989), 1.

[34] Carol Gesner mentions that *Apollonius* was retooled in the twelfth-century epic of

mata) and the pan-European romances of chivalry into the same generic mold. Spain's oldest romance of chivalry, *El Caballero Cifar* (1299–1305), shows elements of Greek romance, with signs of Arabic and Arthurian materials as well, but it seems to have had little discernible influence on the Spanish romances of chivalry that followed. Heliodorus, too, would appear to have little in common with the chivalric romances. Eisenberg, for one, claims that the *Aethiopica* would have seemed "to contemporary readers certainly the very antithesis of a romance of chivalry."[35] Let us confine ourselves for the moment to suggesting that Greek romance is different from, if not necessarily antithetical to, the chivalric. Both Greek and chivalric romances share many of the same devices, such as story motifs that may not even belong exclusively to the romance form. But, as I shall argue, real intertextuality or significance-creating relations do not operate smoothly between these two subgenres of romance, the Hellenic Greek texts and the books of chivalry that materialized in the medieval period.

The later chivalric romance form was generated by a merger between the cross and the stirrup, religion and chivalry, parallel traditions that gave rise, through an obscure and complicated process, to an identifiable genre in late twelfth century France. This subgenre, through many transformations, would itself evolve into Montalvo's primitive *Amadís* and the Castilian romances of chivalry that it spawned.[36] It was this species of romance which, by Cervantes's day and with his aid, was banalized and exhausted. To recapitulate the elements commonly found in a typical chivalric romance is instructive at this point, and is an exercise made easier by Eisenberg's composite summary of these works, which always pretend to be true histories or chronicles. First and foremost, the protagonist "is always male and invariably of royal blood"—a prince, often of illegitimate birth, who conforms to the image of the ideal medieval ruler he will in time become. He is not especially bookish but likes to travel instead. Given, or rather driven, to search for adventures, he generally travels by land, fulfilling the urge to "lanzarse a los caminos," as Don Quixote would parody this generic *Wanderlust*. But the chivalric hero's travel is selective and, tellingly, avoids the Mediterranean: "He may visit London, Paris, or Constantinople, cities already with some chivalric tradition, but

Jourdain de Blaie and linked to the Charlemagne cycle (*Shakespeare and the Greek Romance: A Study of Origins* [Lexington: University Press of Kentucky, 1970], 14).

[35] Daniel Eisenberg, *Romances of Chivalry in the Spanish Golden Age* (Newark, Del.: Juan de la Cuesta Press, 1982), 28. According to Eisenberg, the *Caballero Cifar* has "little in common with the Spanish romances as they were understood by Cervantes and other readers of the sixteenth century" (2).

[36] See Edwin Place, "Fictional Evolution: The Old French Romances and the Primitive *Amadís* Reworked by Montalvo," *PMLA* 71 (1956): 521–29.

never Rome, Jerusalem, nor a Spanish city such as Toledo or Santiago."
After being dubbed a knight, he will adopt a heraldic symbol from the
many medieval inventories of coats of arms. This hero seeks fame, reputation, and prestige, but never money: indeed, "money is so seldom mentioned . . . that it seems that the protagonists of the romances live in a
primitive era, outside the money economy altogether." Although court
life is not particularly to his taste, he is a good courtier with a well-devel-
oped ethical code. Apart from tournaments, which are de rigueur for the
chivalric hero, his favorite diversion is hunting, *caza de monte*, which
enables him to escape urban pressures: cities and civilized comforts make
him uneasy. In military action, he remains conscious of his princely
status, so much so that "he will not mix with the common soldiers." At
some point the knight will fall in love and eventually marry, but love is
always a pretext: "Women and love usually play a secondary role in the
Spanish romances of chivalry, serving more as background, or providing
motives for action, than taking part in the action themselves." Indeed,
"both literally and figuratively," Eisenberg summarizes, "women are the
spectators at the tournament."[37]

According to Martín de Riquer, the above catalogue of romance codes
may all be found in the thirteenth-century prose *Lancelot*, the chief model
for *Amadís* and therefore the father of the Spanish romances of chivalry.
What may also be found in the paternal text, however, is the motif of
adultery inherited from the Celtic sources. Edwin Williamson reminds us
that the adulterous passion in *Lancelot* was countered by *Erec et Enide*,
Cligès, and *Yvain*, romances that "commend marriage as the proper condition for lovers."[38] But these romances did not have the cultural impact
of *Lancelot*, whose name abounds in medieval Spanish annals. A glance
at Don Quixote's obsession—indeed, his identification—with "Lanza-
rote" enlightens this point. At the first inn on his first expedition, Don
Quixote addresses the inn prostitutes ("aquellas traídas y llevadas") with
his own adaptation of the old ballad about Lancelot beginning "Nunca
fuera caballero . . . [Never was there a knight . . .]," a ballad that Don
Quixote will cite again for Señor Vivaldo in 1.13, and yet again for Sancho and the Humanist Cousin in 2.23. Sancho will cite his master citing
the same ballad when he and Don Quixote arrive at the castle of the Duke

[37] Eisenberg, *Romances of Chivalry*, 55–74. There are, of course, exceptions to Eisenberg's paradigm. Marie Cort Daniels argues, for instance, that in Feliciano de Silva's *Amadís
de Grecia* (1530) and its successors, women are more central and knights are more femi-
nized. See "Feliciano de Silva: A Sixteenth-Century Reader-Writer of Romance," in *Creation and Re-creation: Experiments in Literary Form in Early Modern Spain. Studies in
Honor of Stephen Gilman*, ed. Ronald E. Surtz and Nora Weinerth (Newark, Del.: Juan de
la Cuesta Press, 1983), 77–88.

[38] Martín de Riquer, "Proemio," *Romances of Chivalry*, viii. See Edwin Williamson's ex-

and Duchess in 2.31. Although Don Quixote chooses to ignore the adulterous love context of the ballad, its repeated irruptions signal when the conflicts agitating him are attempting to emerge. Surfacing reiteratively throughout the text of *Don Quixote*—in the manner of Freud's "return of the repressed" (*SE* 7:60–61; *SE* 9:35)—are the aborted questions of the narrative, questions that the *Persiles* will try to address. The most nettlesome of these questions concerns the fraught relationship between love and marriage. The potent ideology of courtly love informing *Lancelot* had notoriously legislated, at least in its codification by Andreas Capellanus, that "love cannot exert its powers between two people who are married to each other." Even if we do not take Capellanus's *De amore* seriously, opting with more recent scholars for an ironic interpretation of this influential handbook,[39] it would still be difficult to argue that courtly love *promoted* the institution of marriage. One could say, however (without echoing the hysterical phillipics of a Luis Vives), that the courtly ideology in chivalric romance countenanced, and in the case of *Lancelot* even valorized, adulterous love. As Douglas Kelly sees it, love in chivalric romance, at least in the principal models for the later Castilian books of chivalry, is "first and foremost, sexual gratification for privileged people."[40]

By contrast, love in Greek romance is, first and foremost, marital fidelity for ordinary people. Most of the adventures in Greek romance are organized as trials of the protagonists' unflinching *mutual* fidelity, despite innumerable temptations, to a love whose goal is marriage, either attained or, as in the *Ephesiaca* (Habrocomes and Anthia) or *Chaereas and Callirrhoe*, restored. Marriage in Greek romance is relentlessly exalted, even when a husband is abusive, as in Chariton's romance, in which Chaereas kicks his bride Callirrhoe in the stomach. (Like Shakespeare's Leontes, another avatar from Greek romance, he will have to earn back the wife he abused.) Even in the comic *Leucippe and Clitophon*, which has been categorized as a parody of Greek romance, the "merry widow" Melitte wildly caricatures the standard goal of "to wed and to bed." The idea or, more correctly, the difficult *process* of monogamous love is, in

cellent *The Half-way House of Fiction: Don Quixote and Arthurian Romance* (Oxford: Clarendon Press, 1984), 26.

[39] Andreas Capellanus, *Art of Courtly Love*, trans. John J. Parry (New York: F. Ungar Publishing Co., 1941), 106. On the presence of irony in *De amore*, see Don A. Monson, "Andreas Capellanus and the Problem of Irony," *Speculum* 63 (1988): 539–72. On Chrétien himself as an ironist, see Eduardo Urbina, "Chrétien de Troyes y Cervantes: más allá de los libros de caballerías," *Anales cervantinos* 24 (1988): 1–11.

[40] Douglas Kelly, "Romance and the Vanity of Chrétien de Troyes," in *Romance: Generic Transformations*, ed. Brownlee and Brownlee, 79. Eduardo Urbina, however, sees *Cligés*, in the wake of *Erec*, as constituting a conscious effort to oppose the antisocial force of adultery in the Tristan legend ("Chrétien de Troyes y Cervantes," 143).

short, the chief focus of Greek romance. Such a focus is not to every man's taste, as shown by Samuel Lee Wolff's exasperation with the "sentimentality" of Greek romance, "analyzed to death by means of a shallow and distorted 'psychology.' "[41] In its glorification of marriage, family, and domestic life, however, Greek romance offered the Renaissance an implicit critique of the chivalric system of values. Greek romance formulas were useful for reflecting the ascendant idea that love could, after all, exert its powers between married people.

But the exaltation of marriage in Greek romance by no means exhausts its differences from the chivalric romance patterns. The split between these two subgenres of romance may provide, in addition, a functional ideology of class, and even race, distinction. As the medieval cultural expression of a feudal nobility, of a dominant ruling class, chivalric romance idealized an essentially aristocratic tradition, one concerned with the behavior of knights and vassals, proper conduct in love affairs, and the duties of rulers. The value systems of chivalric romance, with its demand for "elevated" characters, were trumpeted for the genre, virtually upon arrival, in Chrétien's *Yvain*: "Better a courtier, dead, / Than a vulgar peasant, alive."[42] Although Frye speaks of the "curiously proletarian status" of romance as a form, the content, value systems, and elevated characters of chivalric romance were scarcely proletarian. Indeed, Frye's own notion of romance, as Heiserman observes, "reflects the ideals of the ruling social or intellectual class." Frye's model, in other words, "does not fit the 'world,' and the rather plain style, of the Greek romances."[43] The ideals of the ruling class behind the chivalric enterprise center on issues of honor in and around the court, and valor in the defense of one's king and kingdom, a valor exhibited—as the term *chivalric* itself implies—by cavalry not infantry. But the chivalric was also an enterprise whose class solidarity, by the mid–sixteenth century, was rapidly being undermined by nascent capitalism, by a value system in which the erotics of money and property had begun to displace the erotics of courtly love and holy war. This failure of an aristocratic ideology to describe a reality increasingly pervaded by early forms of capitalism, as David Quint cogently argues, doomed the epic, with its rigid classical structures, leaving the more flexible genre of romance to adapt quickly to the new commercial world of money and materiality.[44] One way the genre could adapt

[41] Samuel Lee Wolff, *The Greek Romances in Elizabethan Prose Fiction* (New York: Burt Franklin, 1912), 6.

[42] See Burton Raffel's excellent translation of Chrétien de Troyes's *Yvain: The Knight of the Lion* (New Haven: Yale University Press, 1987), 4.

[43] Frye, *Secular Scripture*, 23; *Anatomy of Criticism*, 383, cited by Heiserman, *The Novel Before the Novel*, 222n.

[44] David Quint, "The Boat of Romance and Renaissance Epic," in *Romance: Generic Transformations*, ed. Brownlee and Brownlee, 178–202.

was by looking backward to Greek romance. Cervantes was already doing this in his novella *El amante liberal* (1612), a reworking of "the byzantine form and mode," according to Karl-Ludwig Selig, and a work
distinguished by its "frequent and insistent mention of money, ransoms,
trade, goods, commerce, and monetary exchanges."[45] In *La española inglesa*, too—which has been called a Byzantine romance in miniature—
Carroll B. Johnson sees an "almost obsessive reference to the prosaic details of international commerce and banking." This text, for Johnson,
subverts all the official rhetoric that "maintained the superiority of feu-
dalism over mercantile capitalism."[46] Exactly when Cervantes began
reading the Greek romances is unknown, but traces of them have been
documented in some of the more idealistic *Novelas ejemplares*, those assigned to the post-1606 period.[47] The move to Greek romance, in short,
offered Cervantes a way of criticizing—or at least of refusing to rational-
ize and perpetuate—aristocratic class interests.

Yet another divergence between Greek and chivalric romance turns on
the ancillary concept of honor, so crucial to the collective aristocratic sentiments of chivalric romance, so visibly earned through the public displays of quests and jousts and tourneys. When the hero of *Primaleón*
and his opponent Don Duardos are violently thrown from their horses
during a tourney, both men instantly leap up from the ground because
of the shame—the explicit "vergüenza"—of having fallen. In Greek romance, by contrast, honor is a more private affair: readers are often made
privy to dishonors known only to the sufferer, unknown to the other
characters in the narrative. When, in the *Ephesiaca*, Anthia is exposed to
customers in the brothel, she does not worry about her public humilia-
tion, her loss of honor, as much as about the shame of being forced to
transgress her marital vows. Private issues of shame (Gk. *aidos*) in Greek
romance seem to take precedence over public notions of what is and is
not honorable.

Issues of survival may also distinguish the forms of Greek romance,
which were developed by marginalized races concerned, indeed, about
their collective survival: by the descendants of peoples living on the pe-
ripheries of the Greek world, people who had been reduced to serfdom
by Alexander the Great's conquests. In order to promote "at least the
cultural survival of their people," Moses Hadas explains, "Assyrians,

---

[45] Karl-Ludwig Selig, "Some Observations on Cervantes' *El amante liberal*," *Revista hispánica moderna* 40 (1978–1979): 68.

[46] Carroll B. Johnson, "*La española inglesa* and the Practice of Literary Production," *Via-
tor* 19 (1988): 398, 411. The view of the *Persiles* as a miniature "Byzantine romance" belongs to Rafael Lapesa, "En torno a *La española inglesa* y el *Persiles*," in his *De la edad
media a nuestros días* (Madrid: Gredos, 1967), 242–63.

[47] See Ruth El Saffar, *Novel to Romance* (Baltimore: Johns Hopkins University Press,
1974), xiii–xvi.

Egyptians, Phrygians, Babylonians, and Jews wrote fanciful tales involving their legendary heroes and usually including a love story."[48] One of these marginalized writers—Chariton, a lawyer's clerk from Aphrodisia—was even called, by the second-century Sophist Philostratus, a "nobody" whose work was sure to perish.[49] Linkages between Greek romance and marginalized races or authors may, indeed, reinforce Constance Hubbard Rose's theory that sixteenth-century *conversos* were responsible for the rediscovery of and vogue for the Greek novel. Seeking new modes of expression by which to relate their historical predicament—the enforced exile, endless wanderings, and assorted travails connected with the Second Diaspora—Spanish and Portuguese conversos remotivated the genre of Greek romance. In Rose's challenging reading, the Golden Age Byzantine revival may be read as a diagnosis of the sickness of the age.[50]

Something about cultural survival, the sickness of the times notwithstanding, may invite the critical labeling of *bourgeois*, an anachronistic term used with astonishing frequency in connection with the Greek romances. R. M. Rattenbury notes how Achilles Tatius, for instance, "degrades romance from the realm of princes to the level of the bourgeoisie." Gerald Sandy claims that Greek romances, in their move away from the "classical canons," began "dealing with the private lives of bourgeois individuals." B. P. Reardon reiterates the adjective in his interpretation of *Chaereas and Callirrhoe*, whose ambience he regards as "sentimental, bourgeois, and rather similar in tone to the ladies' magazines of today." Brian Vickers speaks of Greek romance as "an idealization of the bourgeois marriage." And Arthur Heiserman—joking about "bourgeois kids" as characters in, and "bourgeois families" as readers of, Greek romance—sees married love as "the underside of [this] so-called bourgeois exuberance": the implicit message of Greek romance, he concludes, is that "the bourgeois values of marriage and home can conquer the world."[51]

Along similar but more originary lines, Bakhtin has noted that Greek

---

[48] By the postclassical period, during which the extant Greek romances all flowered, the "erotic element" had displaced the heroic or "historical" element ("Introduction," *Heliodorus: An Ethiopian Romance*, viii).

[49] Philostratus, Letter No. 66, cited by Heiserman, *The Novel Before the Novel*, 227n.

[50] Constance Hubbard Rose, *Alonso Núñez de Reinoso: The Lament of a Sixteenth-Century Exile* (Rutherford, N.J.: Farleigh Dickinson University Press, 1971).

[51] R.M. Rattenbury, *New Chapters in the History of Greek Literature*, Third Series (Oxford, 1933), 219–23; Gerald Sandy, *Heliodorus* (Boston: Twayne Publishers, 1982), 5–6; B. P. Reardon cited in Erich Segal's "Heavy Breathing in Arcadia," *The New York Times Book Review*, 29 September, 1985, 48; Brian Vickers, "The Ingredients of a Romance," Review in *TLS*, 20 April, 1984, 427; Heiserman, *The Novel Before the Novel*, 114, 96, 116, 68.

romance "reveals it strong ties with a *folklore that predates class distinctions.*"[52] Unlike folklore, however, Greek romance itself does not predate class distinctions. As many of the main characters in Greek romance are well born—and some, like Heliodorus's heroine, are even lost princesses—Greek romance can hardly be said to project a utopian world of classless values. In Longus's *Daphnis and Chloe*, for instance, which turns on the device of the kidnapped child or foundling brought up among goatherd and shepherd families, the discovery of lofty origins at closure would offer Jameson, for one, little or no "class relief."[53] Yet no less an egalitarian reader than Citizen Rousseau aligned himself with *Daphnis and Chloe*, its values even moving him to begin the composition of a pastoral opera based on Longus's text.

Greek romance, then, offered Cervantes a cultural expression different from the bankrupt libros de caballerías, a species of romance historically aligned with the aristocratic values he had so fatally ironized in the Cave of Montesinos episode (*DQ* 2.25). Casalduero sees the Cervantes of the *Persiles* conceiving "el nuevo heroismo burgués, el de la virtud [the new bourgeois heroism, that of virtue]."[54] Whatever Casalduero means here by that slippery word *virtud*, it is certain that Cervantes, for his last romance protagonist, repudiated the profile of a chivalric hero that Eisenberg sketches: the kind of man who enjoyed hunting over reading, preferred his women either absent or in the role of spectators, would never mention money, and could never visit Rome. The value system in these romances of chivalry, Eisenberg stresses, is "that of the Spanish nobility at the end of the Middle Ages and beginning of the Renaissance," and the characters firmly endorse the system: "For this reason it was a reassuring world, one free of the moral and political confusion characteristic of early modern Spain."[55] While the Canon of Toledo and his neoclassical real-life colleagues were worrying about the unreal issues of unity and verisimilitude in this "reassuring world" of chivalric romance, Cervantes was looking for a world elsewhere. As they were tortuously trying to purify the dialect of the court, Cervantes was remotivating the protobourgeois genre of Greek romance, using its formulas to reflect new ideas about love and marriage. If in *La española inglesa* Cervantes hoped to concretize, as Carroll Johnson argues, "the triumphant emergence of a new class, the urban bourgeoisie, to replace the aristocracy as the protagonist of history," in the *Persiles*—although that utopian vision is tempered—Cer-

---

[52] Bakhtin, *The Dialogic Imagination*, 105.

[53] Jameson writes that at the denouement of Eichendorff's transgressive novella *Taugenichts*, "we find, to our class relief, that the girl in question, far from being a noblewoman, is none other than the porter's niece!" ("Magical Narratives," 157).

[54] Casalduero, "Introduction," *Sentido y forma de las* Novelas ejemplares, 54.

[55] Eisenberg, *Romances of Chivalry*, 74.

vantes's quarrel remains directed at both the official rhetoric of the aristocracy and its self-serving feudal fictions.[56]

HELIODORUS REDIVIVUS

Long before Cervantes elected to compete with Heliodorus, however, he would have known how favorably sixteenth-century readers regarded the *Aethiopica*. Itself in the romance convention of the "discovered manuscript topos," Heliodorus's romance was found by a soldier who, while the Turks were sacking Buda in 1526, may have himself been sacking the library of the King of Hungary, Matthias Corvinus. By 1534 the manuscript was in the hands of Vincentius Obsopoeus, who published it in Basel in the original Greek. It was not until the appearance of Jacques Amyot's French version in 1547, and the translations that followed it— Latin (1551), Spanish (1554), and Italian (1556)[57]—that the *Aethiopica* began to enjoy considerable prestige in Continental literary circles. Cervantes may have been familiar with the 1554 Spanish version of Heliodorus (an anonymous Spanish translation of Amyot's French version), but his source was probably Fernando de Mena's popular 1587 translation, the *Historia etiópica de los amores de Teágenes y Cariclea*.[58] Thomas Underdowne's lively English translation (c. 1569) of the "no lesse wittie than pleasaunt" Greek romance converted it into an Elizabethan best-seller.[59] For well over fifty years, then, as Riley notes, Heliodorus was considered "the darling of the humanists."[60]

[56] Carroll Johnson rightly celebrates Cervantes's fiction for bringing to the surface the socioeconomic realities suppressed by the official rhetoric of Golden Age Spain—a rhetoric that depicted "a feudo-agrarian economy controlled by the aristocracy and stout Old Christian peasants, and suppressed all positive references to mercantile capitalism on the grounds that *tratos y mercancías* had historically been the province of Jews." See "La Española Inglesa and the Practice of Literary Production," 408–16.

[57] The editorial fortunes of the *Historia delle cose ethiopiche*, trans. L. Ghini (Venice: Giolito di Ferrari Press, 1556) show that the Italian reading public enjoyed eleven editions of the *Etiopiche* between 1556 and 1636.

[58] On the particulars of de Mena's 1587 Spanish translation, see Francisco López Estrada's excellent 1954 edition of *Historia etiópica*, with some eighty-five pages of prefatory materials. Because Cervantes himself worked from Francisco de Mena's translation, all citations from Heliodorus in my text are taken from López Estrada's edition of de Mena's version, and all bracketed English translations are my own.

[59] The *Aethiopica*'s English career began with Underdowne's translation, based on Warschewicski's Latin version (1552) and entitled (in the 1587 second edition) *An Aethiopian Historie written in Greeke by Heliodorus, no lesse wittie than pleasaunt*. That Shakespeare knew the *Aethiopica* in Underdowne's translation is shown by an allusion in *Twelfth Night* (5.1.115–18).

[60] Riley, *Theory of the Novel*, 53. For contemporaneous allusions to Heliodorus, see Rabelais's *Pantagruel* 4.63; Guarini's *Pastor Fido* 5; Tasso's *Gerusalemme liberata* 12; Mon-

The sociohistorical circumstances of Heliodorus's rising popularity in the second half of the sixteenth century among the Spanish Erasmians—a large number of whom were conversos, and all of whom had fallen from grace—have provoked surprisingly little critical interest. The anonymous translator of the first Spanish version of the *Aethiopica* (Antwerp, 1554) was an Erasmian, evidently living in exile. Rose speculates that "perhaps the early Spanish translators of Heliodorus's *Aethiopica* were drawn to the work for the resemblance it bore to the social situation they shared with a certain portion of potential readers."[61] Peninsular Jews and conversos, she argues, could "identify" with the heroes of Byzantine romance, whose literary lives of wandering and travail adumbrated their own very real *trabajos* during the Second Diaspora. Rose's study focuses on one of these *déracinés*, the sixteenth-century exile Alonso Núñez de Reinoso, who translated the final four books of Achilles Tatius's romance, *Clitophon and Leucippe*. According to Rose, Núñez de Reinoso also chronicled his own sufferings in *Clareo y Florisea*, a text that, in Menéndez y Pelayo's opinion, Cervantes was certain to have read. Cervantes may have even borrowed the names of his protagonists from the *Amores de Clareo*, whose cast of characters includes a "Periandro," a "Periandra," and an "Aurismunda." Could the first two have been conflated into Cervantes's "Periandro," and the latter partitioned into his "Auristela-Sigismunda"?[62]

Whatever the degree of converso influence behind the rise of Heliodorus in Spain, Continental critics assured his dissemination among the *docti*. Julius Caesar Scaliger began canonizing the *Aethiopica* in 1561, when his vast and influential *Poetices libri septem* praised the romance as a "librum epico Poetae censeo accuratissime legendum, ac quasi pro optimo exemplari sibi proponendum [a book that I believe should be read most attentively by the epic poet, and that should be proposed to him as

---

taigne's "De l'affection des peres aux enfants," in *Essais* 2.8; and Shakespeare's *Twelfth Night* 5.1.

[61] Rose, *Lament of a Sixteenth-Century Exile*, 159. On the popularity of the *Aethiopica* among the Spanish Erasmians, see Bataillon, *Erasmo y España: Estudios sobre la historia espiritual del siglo XVI*, 2d ed., trans. Antonio Alatorre (Mexico: Fondo de Cultura Económica, 1966), 622.

[62] Menéndez y Pelayo cited by Rose, *Lament of a Sixteenth-Century Exile*, 98. The title of Núñez de Reinoso's novel—*La historia de los amores de Clareo y Florisea y de los trabajos de la sin ventura Isea*—as well as its binary structure and its gender reversals lead us to pose the question of influence once again. See Robert Palomo's "Una fuente española del *Persiles*," *Hispanic Review* 6 (1938): 57–68. On the coinciding names, see Rodolfo Schevill and Adolfo Bonilla, "Introduction," *Persiles y Sigismunda*, 2 vols. (Madrid: Imprenta de Bernardo Rodríguez, 1914), 1:xix. Further scholarly work needs to be done on Núñez de Reinoso's possible impact on the *Persiles*.

the best possible model]."⁶³ A generation later, Tasso, too, exalted the *Aethiopica* in his *Art of Poetry* (1587), calling for inclusion into the epic canon of "gli amori di . . . Teagene e di Cariclea [the loves of . . . Theagenes and Chariclea]."⁶⁴ And nearly a decade after Tasso, El Pinciano, Spain's principal Renaissance literary theorist and author of the influential *Philosophía antigua poética* (1596), was placing those same loves on an equal footing with Homer and Virgil: "Los amores de Theágenes y Cariclea, de Heliodoro . . . son tan épica [*sic*] como la *Ilíada* y la *Eneyda* [The loves of Theagenes and Chariclea, by Heliodorus . . . are as epic as the *Iliad* and the *Aeneid*]." Not only did El Pinciano lavishly praise the Greek romancer's execution of the Horatian *in medias res* technique, which he claimed was observed even more rigorously than in Homer or Virgil, but the Spanish theorist even canonized Heliodorus, in an ecstatic pun, as a "don del sol [gift of the sun]."⁶⁵

Even before El Pinciano's hyperboles were published, however, fiction writers had begun to use Heliodorus as a model. His influence is visible in Montemayor's *Diana* and, according to a remark of Jerónimo de Arbolanche in 1566, indirectly on Gil Polo's continuation, the *Diana enamorada*.⁶⁶ What neither Cervantes nor his Canon of Toledo could have appreciated, however, because they could not follow the fortunes of Greek romance into English, was the complex serial influence from the "sweet and subtle" Heliodorus to Montemayor to the patently Heliodoran structure of the *New Arcadia* (1590), refashioned from an older version by that celebrated "Heliodore d'Angleterre," Sir Philip Sidney.⁶⁷ But Cervantes would doubtless have caught the unmistakable traces of the *Aethiopica* in the story of "Ozmín and Daraja," interpolated into Mateo Alemán's *Guzmán de Alfarache* (1599).⁶⁸ He would have known, too,

⁶³ See facsimile of the 1561 edition of Lyon by August Buck (Stuttgart: F. Frommann Verlag, 1964), 6.

⁶⁴ Torquato Tasso, *Discorsi dell'arte poetica e del poema eroico*, ed. Luigi Poma (Bari: G. Laterza, 1964), 13.

⁶⁵ Alonso López Pinciano, *Philosophía antigua poética*, ed. A. Carballo Picazo, 3 vols. (Madrid: Biblioteca de Antiguos Libros Hispánicos, 1953), 3:165, 3:207, and 2:86, respectively.

⁶⁶ See M. Schlauch, *Antecedents of the English Novel 1400–1600* (Warsaw: PWN—Polish Scientific Publishers, 1963), 176–77.

⁶⁷ Sidney, called the "Heliodorus of England" by Marechal in the sixteenth century, not only put Theagenes on a par with Cyrus and Aeneas, but also exalted the *Aethiopica* as a heroic "poem" in spite of its prose, arguing in his *Defence of Poesy* (in an Aristotelian move that Cervantes would have found gratifying) that "it is not rhyming and versing that maketh a poet." Sidney's point is made in the somewhat cloying context of the "sweet and subtle" Heliodorus and of "his sugared invention of that picture of love in Theagenes and Chariclea," in *A Defence of Poetry*, ed. Jan Van Dorsten (Oxford: Oxford University Press, 1966), 27.

⁶⁸ See D. McGrady, "Heliodorus' Influence on Mateo Alemán," *Hispanic Review* 34 (1966): 49–53.

of Lope de Vega's allusions to "Eliodoro." Lope referred twice to Heliodorus in his *Novelas a Marcia Leonarda*, used him as a model for *El peregrino en su patria*, and devoted an entire scene of *La dama boba* (1.5) to
a critical discussion of the "griego poeta divino [divine Greek poet]." In
this *comedia* (with a manuscript date of 28 April 1613, roughly the period when Cervantes was also preoccupied with Heliodorus), a learned
lady modishly catalogues the *Aethiopica*'s attractions: its delayed prologue, since there was no understanding the work "hasta el quinto libro
[until the fifth book]"; its "mil exornaciones / y retóricas figuras [thou-
sand embellishments and figures of speech]"; and its obscure poetics—
"escura aun a ingenios raros [dark even for exceptional wits]."[69]

Although modern readers would scarcely endorse these Renaissance
plaudits for Heliodorus, William Byron's easy dismissal of the *Aethiopica*
as "a cyclonic bore" is both condescending and untrue. "What we piti-
lessly tend to call boring," Ortega y Gasset reminds us, "is a whole literary genre, although one that has failed. The boredom consists in the narration of something which does not interest us. The narrative must be
justified by its subject matter, and the more superficial it is, the less it
comes between the events and ourselves, the better it will be."[70] Although
Greek romance, with its terrible perils and multiple swoonings, is an acquired taste, I agree with E. C. Riley's guarded judgment, litotes and all,
that the humanists' praises for the *Aethiopica* were "not unfounded."[71]
But our modern boredom is hardly the issue here, because we are addressing Cervantes's and not our transaction with a genre, his and not our
conception of an ideal romance. Cervantes was "probably the world's
most attentive reader of Heliodorus," as Margaret Anne Doody puts it,[72]
and it is time to attend to his reading.

[69] See Marina Scordilis Brownlee, *The Poetics of Literary Theory: Lope de Vega's Novelas a Marcia Leonarda and their Cervantine Context* (Madrid: José Porrúa Turanzas, 1981),
esp. 51–60; Lope de Vega, *La dama boba*, in *Lope de Vega: Fuente Ovejuna and La dama
boba*, ed. Everett W. Hesse (New York: Dell Publishing Co., 1964), 134–36. The Spanish
translation of Amyot's preface had earlier promised readers of Heliodorus that they would
remain mystified until the close of book 5: "Que no entienden lo que han leído en el comienzo del primer libro, hasta que veen el fin del quinto" (López Estrada, "Introduction,"
Historia etiópica, lxxx–lxxxi).

[70] Byron, *Cervantes: A Biography*, 512; Ortega, *Meditations*, 131. Although Ortega's
reflections are about the books of chivalry, his lament here is equally applicable to Greek
romance.

[71] Riley, *Theory of the Novel*, 54.

[72] Margaret Anne Doody, "Heliodorus Rewritten: Samuel Richardson's *Clarissa* and
Frances Burney's *The Wanderer*" (Paper delivered at the Second International Conference
on the Ancient Novel, Dartmouth College, 24 July 1989), 8.

Chapter Two

CANONIZING ROMANCE

AT THE CLOSE of the opening chapter of her celebrated study on genre, *The Resources of Kind*, Rosalie Colie notes that for Don Quixote—"as for his master"—the notion of literary kind was "essential" to the imagination. For Don Quixote, who saw the world screened through the books of chivalry, the genre of romance was, as Colie puts it, "his fix on the world." The parallel claim that romance was essential to "his master," Cervantes, requires a breadth of discussion not given it by Colie. If she means that Cervantes used a genre, with all the decorum it supplied to Renaissance artists, in order to counter it (as did Marino, whose subversion of the genre-system Colie does discuss), or to transform it (as did Cervantes himself in the *Persiles*), then I would agree with her equation of Don Quixote, who played into romance, with his creator, who generally played with or against it.[1] Cervantes was no doubt well aware of the bitter genre battles that raged thoughout the sixteenth century—fueled by the 1536 Pazzi translation of Aristotle's *Poetics*—over the canonicity of Dante's *Commedia* as epic and of Speroni's *Canace e Macareo* as tragedy, and over the "mixed styles" in Guarini's *Il pastor fido*. But during the years Cervantes was generating his pastoral romance *La Galatea* (1585), he would have been especially alert to the polemic, following the publication of *Gerusalemme liberata* in 1581, over the nonclassical *romanzi* produced by Ariosto and Tasso. Although strict Aristotelian constructionists repeatedly deprecated Ariosto's digressive *Orlando Furioso* (1516–1532) as a monstrous aberration from the epic norm, the highly successful *Furioso*'s ironic subversion of all the hierarchies, and many of the pieties, was a crucial event for Renaissance letters. That Cervantes chose the subversive *Furioso* as a model—even as what Marina Brownlee calls the "programmatic subtext" for *Don Quixote*—caused a further crisis in the codification of romance.[2] How would Cervantes—about to entertain the "fola di romanzi" as a generic possibility once again for the

---

[1] Colie, *The Resources of Kind*, 31, 26–27. Colie sees a genre-system as offering an interpretive set of "frames" or "fixes" on the world, but she also sees Renaissance genre-theory as revealing an enormous degree of confusion, and even some craziness, about these "fixes" (8).

[2] This critical furor is discussed in Weinberg's *Italian Renaissance* 2:954ff., 2:812. Marina Brownlee, "Cervantes as Reader of Ariosto," in *Romance: Generic Transformations*, ed. Brownlee and Brownlee, 220–37.

Persiles—respond to the same neo-Aristotelian standards he had earlier ironized?

THE CANON'S BLUEPRINT

The literary dialogue between the deranged Quixote and the Canon of Toledo (*DQ* 1.47–49)—in which the whole issue of canonicity is aired and, indeed, personified—includes the neo-Aristotelian program or recipe for the ideal romance. We recall that the Canon, who accompanies the encaged and "enchanted" Don Quixote for some leagues of his journey home, spends a fair amount of the trip downgrading the romances of chivalry, first on moral and then on aesthetic grounds, these latter based on the predictable precepts of unity and verisimilitude. But although Cervantes's Canon is generally regarded as a spokesman for the Aristotelians, he is quite ready (unlike Luis Vives) to admit to reading and even (unlike Nietzsche) to finding pleasure in romances, having first repressed their mendacity: "De mí sé decir que cuando los leo, en tanto que no pongo la imaginación en pensar que son todos mentira y liviandad, me dan algún contento [For my part, I can say that when I read them, as long as I refrain from recalling that they are all lies and trivia, they give me a certain pleasure]" (1.49). In a humorous exchange that anticipates Coleridge's theory of dramatic illusion—based on the audience's "willing suspension of disbelief"—Don Quixote turns angrily on the Canon for his *un*willing suspension of disbelief, for not choosing to be deceived. Don Quixote would have also turned angrily on Gilbert Highet for a similarly canonical twentieth-century judgment of the Greek romances: "They are immensely long and, unless the reader decides to believe them, immensely tedious; but if given belief they are delightful."[3]

The Canon had qualified himself even earlier in the argument, when he came out in favor of romances of chivalry, although only of romances purged of their implausibilities. He could not approve, for instance, "un libro o fábula donde un mozo de diez y seis años da una cuchillada a un gigante como una torre, y le divide en dos mitades, como si fuera de alfeñique [a book or story in which a sixteen-year-old lad deals one sword-blow to a giant as tall as a tower and cuts him into two halves, as if he

---

[3] Setting himself up against a later generation of rigid Aristotelians, the French classical critics who were aiming for "perfect delusion" in stagecraft, Coleridge was to counter them with "that willing suspension of disbelief for the moment which constitutes poetic faith." Earlier he glosses the suspension as when, "in an interesting play, read or represented, we are brought up to this point [the suspension of will and the comparative power], as far as it is requisite or desirable, gradually, by the art of the poet and the actors; and with the consent and positive aidance of our own will. We *choose* to be deceived" (*Coleridge's Shakespearean Criticism*, 2d ed., ed. T. M. Raysor [London: Dent, 1960], 2, 116). Gilbert Highet's remark is from *The Classical Tradition*, 164.

were made of marzipan]."[4] Later in the exchange, Cervantes's strategically inconsistent Canon is even ready to qualify his qualification: "Con todo cuanto mal que había dicho de tales libros, hallaba en ellos una cosa buena: que era el sujeto que ofrecían para que un buen entendimiento pudiese mostrarse en ellos [For all the bad things that he had earlier said about such books, he found in them one good thing: the fact that they offered a good intellect the chance to display itself]" (*DQ* 1.47). In what amounts to an ecstatic manifesto, the Canon then describes the kind of "long and spacious" writerly field that the romance genre still offers, through which the pen could run without the slightest embarrassment ("sin empacho alguno"), inscribing shipwrecks, storms, encounters, and battles; brave, prudent, and eloquent captains; beautiful, chaste, intelligent ladies; Christian knights; barbarous braggarts; and courteous princes with their loyal vassals. In the romance field, the Canon concludes, a writer could display his talents as an astronomer, a cosmographer, a musician, a statesman, or even, should the occasion arise, a necromancer.[5] This is by no means an original catalogue of epic events and characters; variants of the Canon's description appear in numerous Italian theoretical treatises.[6] But Cervantes turns the Canon's "long and spacious" writerly field into a "field of ambivalence" when he closes with the churchman's defensive fantasy of himself as a necromancer. The Canon's avocation nearly rivals, in its mordant irony, that of the Bishop irreverently cited by Cervantes as a reliable literary "authority" on prostitutes (*DQ* 1, Prologue).

[4] Luis Vives had earlier denounced a similar literary scenario: "Hic . . . sexcentis vulneribus confossus, ac pro mortuo iam derelictus, surgit protinus, et postridie sanitati viribusque ridditus, singulari certamine duos gigantes prosternit [A man is riddled with six hundred wounds, and having already been left for dead, gets up right away and on the very next day, restored to health and strength, cuts down two giants in single combat]" (*De institutione feminae christianae*, in *Opera* 2:658).

[5] The Canon's manifesto reads as follows in the original: "Los libros de caballerías . . . daban largo y espacioso campo por donde sin empacho alguno pudiese correr la pluma, describiendo naufragios, tormentas, rencuentros y batallas, pintando un capitán valeroso con todas las partes que para ser tal se requieren, mostrándose prudente previniendo las astucias de sus enemigos, y elocuente orador persuadiendo o disuadiendo a sus soldados, maduro en el consejo, preso en lo determinado, tan valiente en el esperar como en el acometer; pintando ora un lamentable y trágico suceso, ahora un alegre y no pensado acontecimiento; allí una hermosísima dama, honesta, discreta y recatada; aquí un caballero cristiano, valiente y comedido; acullá un desaforado bárbaro fanfarrón; acá un príncipe cortés, valeroso y bien mirado, representando bondad y lealtad de vasallos, grandezas y mercedes de señores. Ya puede mostrarse astrólogo, ya cosmógrafo excelente, ya músico, ya inteligente en las materias de estado, y tal vez le vendrá ocasión de mostrarse nigromante, si quisiere" (*DQ* 1.47).

[6] See, for instance, Tasso's catalogue, closing his *Discorso secondo* in *Discorsi del poema eroico*, in *Opere* (n.p.: Classici UTET, 1955), 675.

In the following chapter, the Canon confesses to having himself already written more than a hundred pages of a romance, a text that critics have generally read as Cervantes's blueprint for the *Persiles*. "Here we have, in a nutshell, the plan that Cervantes was to follow in the *Persiles*," writes Manuel Durán, following in the critical wake of Schevill and Bonilla, who claimed to see the Canon's blueprint writ large in Cervantes's last romance: "De todo esto hay ejemplo en el *Persiles* [There's an example of all of this in the *Persiles*]."[7] But Cervantes's formula for the *Persiles*— evident in the romance codes of its first hundred pages—does not correspond that closely to the Canon of Toledo's blueprint. Unlike the contents of the Canon's prospectus, there are no exemplary "Christian knights"— not even anachronic and demented ones—nor "loyal vassals" in the *Persiles*, which is a Renaissance romance set in and around the identifiable 1560s. Because no military battles occur in this text, there is no call for that "eloquent orator" in the Canon's formula—for the captain seen as valiant when "persuading or dissuading his soldiers" or as bold when "making an attack" (*DQ* 1.47). The only attacks in the *Persiles* are made by pirates or bandits, never by cavalry. The only notable horse in the text belongs to King Cratilo of Poland, and it materializes only to be tamed by Periandro, just as Heliodorus's hero had tamed a sacrificial bull. Chivalric romances were famous for their war interest: their documenting of endless battles, or of tournaments and single combats with sword and lance, with mace and battle-axe. So little combat transpires in the *Persiles*, however, that the narrator is moved to comment on its absence during an interrupted skirmish with some armed highwaymen: "Hasta aquí, desta batalla pocos golpes de espada hemos oído, pocos instrumentos bélicos han sonado [Until now, we have heard few swordblows in this battle, few warlike instruments have sounded]" (375). The chivalric surfaces once or twice in the *Persiles* as parody, such as in the interpolation of Eusebia and Renato, a tale that examines courtly love in exile and advancing age, and that Schevill and Bonilla regard as "genuinamente caballeresco [genuinely chivalric]," if a trifle "extraño [strange]."[8] Although Alban Forcione speaks of Cervantes's "submission to the theories of the canon in the general plan of the *Persiles*," theories that amount to the "purification" of chivalric romance,[9] that "purification" process seemed to usher Cervantes directly into the world of Greek romance: "robbers and prisons, pi-

---

[7] Manuel Durán, "Cervantes's Swan Song," 89–90. Schevill and Bonilla, "Introduction," *Persiles*, vii. Alban Forcione thinks "it is clear that the Canon of Toledo's plan for the ideal book of chivalry was Cervantes' general formula for the *Persiles*, and it is tempting to believe that the hundred pages which the canon claims to have written and abandoned are Cervantes' first sketch of his final work" (*Cervantes, Aristotle, and the* Persiles, 169).

[8] Schevill and Bonilla, "Introduction," *Persiles* 1:xxxi, ftn.

[9] *Cervantes, Aristotle, and the* Persiles, 126, 91.

rates, hunger's grip," scenes of sacrifice, and even the presence of translators and transvestites—all subjects peculiarly associated with Greek romance—abound in the *Persiles*. The hundred pages that the Canon claims to have written and then abandoned may have been Cervantes's earlier draft of a chivalric romance—perhaps of "el famoso *Bernardo*," the work mentioned in the dedication to the *Persiles* and regarded by Eisenberg as the best candidate to fill the position of Cervantes's libro de caballerías.[10] We should try to account for the gap, in other words, between the Canon's projection of the chivalric for his nascent romance and Cervantes's rejection of the chivalric, at least as the avowed model for his own last romance.

There is remarkable critical divergence regarding Cervantes's attitudes toward chivalric romance, from the suggestion that he did not reject it "out of hand" to the claim that he gave it its "death knell."[11] Ruth El Saffar thinks it a mistake to imagine that Cervantes's aim was to dispense with a genre that gave him so much pleasure: "His problem was to find a literary form that would preserve that pleasure in the face of an active critical intelligence." Along the same lines, E. C. Riley declares that Cervantes never rejected romance: "Pese a toda la crítica que hace Cervantes de los *romances* caballerescos en el *Quijote* y la burla que hace de ellos, nunca llegó a rechazar el *romance* [Despite all the criticism of chivalric *romances* that Cervantes gives in *Don Quixote*, not to mention the ridicule, he never came to reject *romance*]." And John J. Allen, in turn, wisely asks us to see *Don Quixote* "as involving a parody of the excesses of a literary form, a historical genre [the books of chivalry], but not a criticism of the fictional mode of romance."[12]

If the *Persiles* is any index, we can speak of a death knell for the subgenre of the books of chivalry but not for the pleasure-yielding genre of romance. What Cervantes does not—what he cannot—reject from the books of chivalry out of hand are some of the semantic codes they share with Greek romance. Erotic sufferings, for instance, are the props of both

[10] See Eisenberg's chap. 2—"The Ideal *Libro de caballerías*: The *Bernardo*"—in *Study of Don Quixote*, 45ff.

[11] Ciriaco Morón-Arroyo claims that "Cervantes does not . . . reject the books of chivalry out of hand. He recognizes that they provide structure for a new content which their authors have not introduced so far in those structures" ("Cooperative Mimesis: Don Quixote and Sancho Panza," *Diacritics* 8 [Spring, 1978]: 77). Maria Corti argues that Cervantes "deliberately set side by side, without annihilating them, the typical traits of the various genres in a subversive mixture of codes—a death knell for the chivalric genre" (cited in *Romance: Generic Transformations*, ed. Brownlee and Brownlee, 137).

[12] Ruth El Saffar, "The Truth of the Matter," in *Romance: Generic Transformations*, ed. Brownlee and Brownlee, 240–41; Riley, " 'Romance' y novela en Cervantes," 13; and John J. Allen, "*Don Quixote* and the Origins of the Novel," in *Cervantes and the Renaissance*, ed. Michael McGaha (Easton, Pa.: Juan de la Cuesta Press, 1980), 129.

Greek and chivalric romance, even though the sources and outcomes of these sufferings may radically differ. The ordeal as an organizing device in Greek romance may also be found in chivalric romance, for instance, in *Amadís de Gaula* (fourteenth century) and *Palmerín de Inglaterra* (1547). Greek and chivalric romance also share the motifs of presumed death and recognition. Both, moreover, include denouements in which the true identities of the protagonists are disclosed. It would seem, then, that the Canon's critique of romance *in* the novel *Don Quixote*, as well as Cervantes's more critically intelligent critique of romance *through* that novel, attacks some of the codes peculiar only to chivalric romance. That Cervantes felt the same about these codes at the end of his life, when he was writing the *Persiles*, is evidenced by the detectable note of affectionate malice that emerges in his parody, toward the end of the *Coloquio de los perros*, of a diseased poet's unborn chivalric romance. Projected as a supplement to the *Historia de la demanda del Santo Brial*—a deformation of the *Demanda del Santo Grial* (a text that includes versions of *Lancelot*)—the chivalric Grail legend is literally "travestied" as a quest for the "Holy Skirt."[13]

Whether or not he "smiled away the chivalry of Spain," as Byron put it, Cervantes did not, in the end, recant and return to the chivalric, as Marthe Robert claims: "After symbolically burning the chivalric romances he struggled to renounce, Cervantes began again and died writing a last chivalric work."[14] After his symbolic burning of the books of chivalry, Cervantes turned to Greek romance as his "invitation to form."[15] What specific romance elements does Cervantes "kidnap" from Greek romance? Where does he criticize and correct his model? How does he modulate and transform it? The ritualistic repetition of Heliodoran themes and events in the *Persiles*, perhaps the simplest kind of humanist imitation, was outlined by Rudolph Schevill as early as 1907. Schevill's useful catalogue included such Greek romance staples as the defense of the ideal of chastity; the pretense of the protagonists to be siblings; the use of the "saving lie" for trying circumstances; the signs by which parents may recognize a lost child; the frequent allusions to the disease of love; the world of magic, curses, prognostications, and dreams; the inter-

[13] Cervantes, *Novelas ejemplares*, ed. Rodriguez Marín, 2 vols. (Madrid: Espasa-Calpe, 1975), 2:331. A copy of the *Demanda del Santo Grial* was included in Queen Isabela's library (Diego Clemencín, "Ilustraciones sobre varios asuntos del reinado de Doña Isabel la Católica, que pueden servir de pruebas a su Elogio," *Memorias de la Real Academia de la Historia* 6 [1821]: 459).

[14] Marthe Robert, *The Old and the New: From Don Quixote to Kafka*, trans. Carol Cosman (Berkeley: University of California Press, 1977), 3. The Byron reference is from *Don Juan* 13.11.1.

[15] "A genre is an invitation to form," notes Claudio Guillén in *Literature as System*, 109.

est in explaining and unraveling knots in the plot; and the fact that the characters exchange the stories of their lives, and find consolation in the telling.[16] My own readings have turned up a cluster of other specific traces of Heliodorus in the *Persiles*.[17]

That substantial differences exist between Cervantes and his model has been recognized, if scarcely accounted for, by Louisa D. Stanley, the nine-teenth-century English translator of the *Persiles*: "Though the *plan* of *Persiles and Sigismunda* is taken from Heliodorus, I do not think they have *any* resemblance in style."[18] To this overemphatic judgment I would add that the *Persiles* bears little resemblance to its predecessor in formal structure, mood, and occasion. But it still resembles Heliodorus, whom it modulates and transforms, far more than it does any chivalric romance. The point of Cervantes's additions, deletions, and contrasts is to show how one set of fundamental values about romantic love—values incompatible with the earlier chivalric romance models—could be transformed into another. The *Persiles* is a generic transformation of Heliodorus, then, a modification of Greek romance that supplements but does not supplant its basic value system, founded on the romance of marriage. The relationships of generic change to social change enhance our understanding of Cervantes's achievement. He manipulated his model fairly vigorously—expanding its generic limits, transforming the antecedent story into a new kind of structure with new meanings for the early seventeenth century—

---

[16] For Schevill's complete summary of the intertextuality, see López Estrada, "Introduction," *Historia etiópica*, xxviii–ix.

[17] The swamp fire in the *Aethiopica* may lie behind the consuming blaze on the Island of Barbarians (1.4–6); the character of the barbarized Greek Cnemon, behind the barbarized Spaniard Antonio (1.5–6); Thisbe's last rites, behind the burial service given Auristela's nanny (1.6); Calasiris's self-exile as punishment for lust, behind Rutilio's similar self-exile (1.8–9); the recognition scene between Calasiris and his daughter, behind the surprise meeting between Mauricio and his daughter (1.12); the opening *tableau vivant* of carnage on the Nile, behind Cervantes's episode of Sulpicia, the piratelady (2.14); Calasiris's dream of Ulysses, behind Periandro's dream of Sensuality (2.15); Theagenes' horse-taming exploits, behind Periandro's antics with Cratilo's wild horse in Lithuania (2.20); the felucca bearing good tidings of an enemy's death, behind the Christian galley in Renato's episode (2.21); the Delphic dance of the Thessalian maidens, behind the rustic dance of the *villanas* of Toledo (3.8); Arsace's lust for Theagenes, behind Hipolita's passion for Periandro (4.7–10); and the prophecy of near-fratricide for Calasiris's two sons, behind the enmity between Persiles and his brother (4.14). Heliodorus's lovelorn Arsace may be the model for Cervantes's smitten Policarpa (2.3–17), both of them shades of the Virgilian Dido; and the "nets of lust" in the satrap Oroondates' residence, the model for all the palace intrigues on Policarpo's island (bk. 2). Charicleia's many clever dodges and subterfuges may have evoked Auristela's gratuitous lies to the wretched Policarpa (2.3ff.); her momentary twinge of jealousy, Auristela's long siege of it (most of bk. 3); and her early hatred of love and marriage, Auristela's marked pudicity (4.10–11, to cite one sustained example).

[18] Louisa Dorothea Stanley, "Preface," *The Wanderings of Persiles and Sigismunda; A Northern Story* (London: Joseph Cundall, 1854), x.

but he did not overturn it. The ascendant ideas of early modern Europe, with its emergent bourgeois reality principle and its new conception of married love, surface in the *Persiles* in three areas, to be addressed in what remains of this chapter: Cervantes's skeptical response to the neo-Aristotelian category of verisimilitude; his "novel" response to the neo-Aristotelian category of unity; and his revolutionary response to certain Aristotelian categories of difference—to those structures of thought inherited from Aristotle that provide the most ancient semantic codes of romance.

TRUTH OR CONSEQUENCES

The posing of "questions of truth," which Michael McKeon chronicles in the origins of the English novel, is internalized and even anatomized in the *Persiles*.[19] Cervantes's response to the vexed and vexing questions of verisimilitude reveals, moreover, his distance from Heliodorus, his constitutive subtext. The legitimizing of believability for the *Aethiopica* during the Renaissance appears today as itself unbelievable. Heliodorus's romance, from start to finish, embraces the magical, or at least what modern readers would regard as an abundance of incredible elements. In the *Aethiopica*, herbs magically close wounds (in the style of Don Quixote's "bálsamo de Fierebrás"); gems serve as antidotes for drunkenness and even for a burning at the stake; an infallible brazier tests the chastity of all suspects forced to tread on it; a mother compels the dead body of her son to rise and speak; characters seem to be wafted by a *deus ex machina* from the middle of Greece to remotest Egypt; a white daughter is born to black parents, the infant's race generated by the mother's glimpsing, during the act of conception, a white woman's portrait (a detail Tasso borrowed for the genesis of his own Clorinda).[20] Somehow none of these events distressed the preceptarians, because the remote setting was enough to justify absurd or bizarre happenings and make them worthy of credence: they could be legislated as "credible" rather than "incredible" marvels. Because Heliodorus set his fictions in faraway Ethiopia—where nobody could say that there had *not* been a king Hydaspes or a Queen Persina—he managed to receive the imprimatur of El Pinciano for having fulfilled the demands of verisimilitude. Today, after the Romantic period and the breakdown of the neoclassical code, we smile in amazement at the very notion of what E. C. Riley calls the "latitudes of

[19] See the whole of pt. 1, entitled "Questions of Truth" (25–128), as well as the excellent chapter on Cervantes, subtitled "Cervantes and the Disenchantment of the World" (273–94) in McKeon, *Origins of the English Novel*.

[20] On Clorinda, see Tasso's *Gerusalemme liberata* 12.23–37.

the poetically probable."[21] What now seems most improbable are the extremes of tortuous rationalizing on the part of Renaissance men to legitimize probability, to codify the precept that an implausible event could be swallowed if only it were distanced to some remote clime, to a place where its truth could never be documented.

In his transformation of Heliodorus, Cervantes chose to internalize the whole problem of verisimilitude, to shake its absolute status by calling attention to the circumstances of interpretation—to how the implausible should or should not be taken. Although no resurrections or magic braziers appear in the *Persiles*, a great many strange things happen. When, for instance, some characters in the narrative seem to be miraculously delivered from a capsized vessel that drifts ashore on an Irish island, Cervantes has a spectator dryly observe that if these "twice-born people" survive, "no se ha de tener a milagro sino a misterio [it should not be taken for a miracle, but rather for a mystery]." This same spectator then explains to the ever-anxious crowd that miracles always occur outside the order of nature, whereas mysteries are simply events so rare that they pass for miracles (163–64). When a psychotic husband pitches his wife from a high tower in Provence, and this "mujer voladora [flying woman]" descends safely to the ground on her bell-shaped skirts, the narrator quickly glosses her fortunate fall: "cosa posible sin ser milagro [a possible event without being a miracle]" (373). This overt rationalizing—a process whereby supernatural "miracles" are supplanted by natural "mysteries"—occurs with stubborn frequency throughout the *Persiles*: just as the reader begins to marvel at a strange event, some skeptic in the text can be counted upon to demythologize the dominant mode of reception, to naturalize the supernatural.[22] As the sage Soldino conveys the pilgrims into a dark cave where they discover a sunny meadow, he is quick to disenchant the spectacle: "Señores, esto no es encantamiento [Sirs, this is not magic]" (395). Moving toward a rationalism that admits and even admires the supernormal, Cervantes's vision in this text is future-related, anticipating both the Enlightenment and the reaction it would generate in the Romantic period, with the naturalizing of the supernatural.

Despite Cervantes's built-in demystifiers, several traditional critics—resisting his attempt to loosen the grip of verisimilitude on Renaissance

[21] In El Pinciano's words, "cumplió con la verosimilitud el poeta, porque nadie podría dezir que en Ethiopia no huvo rey Hydaspes, ni reyna Persina" (*Philosophía antigua poética* 2:332). See also 3:195, where Fadrique adds that "fue prudentíssimo Heliodoro que puso reyes de tierra incógnita, y de quienes se puede mal averiguar la verdad o falsedad . . . de su argumento." I am indebted in this section to E. C. Riley's excellent discussion of the "latitudes of the poetically probable," in his chapter on "Verisimilitude and the Marvelous," *Theory of the Novel*, 179–99.

[22] On this remarkable rationalizing tendency, see Riley, *Theory of the Novel*, 188.

readers—have continued, like the Canon, to pose "questions of truth" about his last work. Ortega y Gasset, for instance, maintained that "el *Persiles* nos garantiza que Cervantes quiso la inverosimilitud como tal inverosimilitud [the *Persiles* testifies that Cervantes loved the incredible *as* incredible]"; Américo Castro, too, regarded the *Persiles* as "conscientemente inverosímil de la cruz a la fecha [consciously incredible from beginning to end]." Lamenting that Cervantes "overdid his use of the marvelous and then betrayed too many doubts about it," E. C. Riley sees this ambivalence as one of "the great faults" of the *Persiles*, as well as one of the reasons why Cervantes failed where Heliodorus succeeded.[23] I believe that Cervantes saw "questions of truth" as entirely impertinent to the artistic process. What is clear to us now, or at least what the Romantic movement has made clearer, is that Cervantes regarded some of the rigid neoclassical criteria for credulity as themselves incredible. It is evident everywhere across his writings that he saw verisimilitude as a tyrannical but slippery precept, as a metaconvention that dictated readerly expectations about fiction and therefore about writerly success. Indeed, Cervantes appears to have recognized that the same elements that made romances aesthetically credible would, in their turn, serve to make novels incredible. He seems, indeed, to have intuited that what defines verisimilitude is what Gerard Genette would call "the formal principle of respect for the norm" and, further, that a precondition of plausibility is the stamp of public approval: "Real or assumed, this 'opinion' is quite close to what today would be called an ideology, that is, a body of maxims and prejudices which constitute both a vision of the world and a system of values."[24]

Countering this system of values, of course, would result in unpleasant consequences. Out of an understandable concern to have his *Persiles* published and read, Cervantes evidently perfected several techniques of "respect for the norm," of placating watchful neo-Aristotelians even while risking extravagance, that is, exclusion from the canon.[25] He uses the standard epic device of remoteness, situating events in the little-known Northern regions of Friesland, Hibernia, and Norway—in latitudes of the "poetically probable"—until he can comfortably localize them in Lisbon,

[23] Riley, *Theory of the Novel*, 195, 54; Ortega and Castro are cited by Riley, 179–99.

[24] Gerard Genette, "Vraisemblance et motivation," in *Figures II* (Paris. Seuil, 1969), 174, 73; cited and trans. by Nancy K. Miller in "Emphasis Added: Plots and Plausibilities in Women's Fiction," *PMLA* 96 (1981): 36. Miller prefers to translate *vraisemblance* as "plausibility," a term she sees as having "a richer semantic field of connotations than 'verisimilitude' " (47n).

[25] In French, at least, the first definition of "extravagant" was used to refer "to texts not included in the canon": "S'est dit de textes non incorporés dans les recueils canoniques" (*Le Petit Robert* [Paris: Société du Nouveau Littré, 1967], 668).

or Lucca, or Rome, where readers could readily entertain closer-to-home "mysteries." Or he narrates events that would be in accord with popular, if not with learned, beliefs: astrology, witchcraft, teratology (which focused on assorted monsters), lycanthropy (which worried the question of werewolves), and the Christian marvelous all fit under this scheme. Or— and this trick he saves for a few outrageously fantastic events—he trusts the narration to one of his characters, as when the Tuscan Rutilio relates a story of a flying carpet that conveys him and his werewolf-mistress from Rome to Norway in four hours (90). Narration by a convenient third party, after all, had won the approval of as eminent an Aristotelian as Francesco Robortelli, who regarded the technique as handy for representing the supernatural.[26] Bernardo de Balbuena reinforced this third-party strategy by noting, in the prologue to *El Bernardo*, that it was perfectly plausible that men would tell implausible stories: that "Gravinia should be changed into a tree or Estordián into a silkworm" was not plausible, he allowed, but that such stories should be in circulation was both plausible and possible.[27] Although plausibility should not depend on all these rationalizing and suspect constraints of likeliness, as Cervantes's theory of the emergent novel suggests, his practice shows that he entertained and even internalized them. In order to subvert the Canon's stance—the canonical stance—on the primacy of plausibility, Cervantes both acknowledges and resists it throughout the *Persiles*.

THE BODY QUIXOTIC

Unity of plot, so often metaphorized by sixteenth-century poeticians as body language, constitutes the second phase of Cervantes's competition with Heliodorus. One of the Canon of Toledo's most vivid laments about the romances of chivalry was that they lacked "un cuerpo de fábula entero [an integrated body of fiction]," being instead composed of so many members that they seem intended to form "una quimera o un monstruo que a hacer una figura proporcionada [a chimera or monster rather than a well-proportioned figure]" (1.47). These "many members" recall the famous octopus simile in *El coloquio de los perros*, where Cipión insists that Berganza stick to his story "sin que la hagas que parezca pulpo, según la vas añadiendo colas [without making it look like an octopus, what with all those appendages you keep tacking on]."[28] But the Canon's com-

[26] Francesco Robortelli, *In librum Aristotelis de Arte Poetica explicationes* (Florence: L. Torrentinus, 1548), 87.

[27] In Balbuena's words, "si no lo es [verosimil] que Gravinia se convirtiese en árbol, y Estordián en gusano de seda, eslo, y muy posible, que aquellos cuentos anduviesen en las bocas de los hombres de aquel mundo"; cited by Riley, *Theory of the Novel*, 192–93.

[28] Cervantes, *Novelas ejemplares*, ed. Marín, 2:251.

plaint also evokes that ubiquitous presence in Renaissance treatises—
Horace's monster in the *Ars poetica*. The specter of this monster had
made a fleeting appearance in Cervantes's announcement, in the mock
dread of his assumed competition with Heliodorus, that the *Persiles*
might emerge "with hands on its head." Horatian body language also
reached Cervantes's age in the depreciation, by Francisco Cascales, of all
topsy-turvy plots: "Como sueños de enfermos se describen / Sin que con-
forme el pie con la cabeza [They may be described like sick men's dreams
/ With the foot in no relation to the head]."[29] The body of Heliodorus's
text, however, was most wholesomely proportioned: its formal unity of
plot was, to the delight of all Aristotelians, impeccably maintained. With
its rigorously observed delayed prologue and its complicated pattern of
interlaced retrospective narratives, Heliodorus's work was held in great
esteem as a technical model for *dispositio* in epics: "Il lasciar l'auditor
sospeso, procedendo dal confuso al distinto, da l'universale a'partico-
lare e una de le cagioni che fa piacer tanto Eliodoro [Keeping the listener
in suspense while proceeding from the confused to the clear, from the
universal to the particular is one of the reasons why Heliodorus gives so
much pleasure]."[30] This feature of suspense, so highly prized by Renaissance readers of Heliodorus, is artfully maintained by the *Aethiopica*'s
logically constructed plot, whose development and conclusion are ar-
rested by nothing irrelevant. When Cnemon and Calasiris narrate their
life stories, these narrations function as the delayed prologue of the main
narrative, strategically deferred by an in medias res opener. They are not
appendages but flashbacks, narratives whose deletion would distort the
main plot. The *Aethiopica*, in short, is distinguished by a tightness and
coherence which guarantee suspense: the most rigid Aristotelian could
not fault its unity of plot. Heliodorus was not one to confound his head
with his hands or his feet.

Unlike his model, however, Cervantes seems not to have been greatly
concerned about creating suspense. Losing the main thread of the narrative was, for him, an opportunity rather than a disaster, even though it
resulted in what Riley has deprecated as "an excess of incident" not
found in Heliodorus: "The ancient author never loses the main thread of
his narrative, the fortunes of his hero and heroine, who incidentally are a

[29] Francisco Cascales, *Tablas poéticas* (Madrid, 1779), 39. Giambattista Giraldi Cintio,
in his *Discorsi intorno al comporre de i romanzi* (Venice, 1554), had compared a well-
wrought poem to a body, with its subject as the skeleton and its episodes as the members
(16–18); Cascales and Giraldi cited by Forcione, *Cervantes' Christian Romance*, 14.

[30] *Le lettere di Torquato Tasso*, ed. Cesare Guasti, 5 vols. (Florence: Le Monnier, 1854),
1:77–78. Amyot, too, had earlier noted the satisfactions Heliodorus afforded readers by
keeping them constantly in suspense (López Estrada, "Introduction," *Historia etiópica*,
lxxx–lxxxi).

much more appealing couple than Persiles and Sigismunda."[31] Whose couple is more appealing is debatable, although which narrative "never loses the main thread" is not: Cervantes did not write a suspenseful book, largely because he chose to delay and even arrest its plot by some dozen subplots. The technique of fragmentary clarification is scarcely enhanced by repeated interruptions of whatever needs to be clarified. Unity of plot, moreover, at least for the more rigid neo-Aristotelians, meant a single plot with a single hero. Into Cervantes's plot (of not one but two heroes) are interpolated thirteen autonomous or semiautonomous stories with one or two heroes apiece. This rupture of narrative by a multiplicity of micro-narratives radically distinguishes the *Persiles* from its model: unlike the personal stories in Heliodorus, Cervantes's stories are not integral to the plot. The practice of inserting tales detached from the main diegesis was transplanted from Apuleius to the Carolingian chivalric fictions, and from there to Ariosto, who upgraded the technique, increasing the number of *novelle* from ten to thirteen between the first (1516) and the third revised edition of the *Furioso* (1532). These interpolated novelle allowed the insertion of bourgeois themes into the body of epic narrative.[32] As will be more fully discussed in chapter 7, the *Persiles* is a romance undergoing "novelization," that is, penetration by the nascent Renaissance novel that Cervantes was helping to create. These novelistic subplots both modulate the allegory of the main romance plot and tend to deflect readerly interest away from it. The late antiquity scholar Tomas Hägg notes, in his brief look at the *Persiles*, that "the parts triumph over the whole as in a piece of Baroque art."[33] The triumph of the interpolations over the main narrative was described even more succinctly by William J. Entwistle: "It is . . . the inset stories that make the *Persiles*."[34] But it is also the inset stories that made the *Persiles* a monster, one that still awaits our validation.

A preview of Cervantes's attitudes to digressiveness may be found in *Don Quixote*, part 2, where Cide Hamete, from the perspective of constrained "author," had grumbled about having to write a plot without daring to spread himself out into "otras digresiones y episodios más graves y más entretenidos [other more serious and entertaining digressions and episodes]." The Arab historian saw this exercise in restraint as "un trabajo incomportable, cuyo fruto no redundaba en el de su autor [an unbearable labor, whose fruits could in no way redound on their author]" (*DQ* 2.44). In Cervantes's imitation of Greek romance, however, this unbearable labor would be lightened: the narrator of the *Persiles*

[31] Riley, *Theory of the Novel*, 195.
[32] Beer, "Plot and *Fortuna*," 7.
[33] Hägg, *The Novel in Antiquity*, 202.
[34] William J. Entwistle, "Ocean of Story," 166.

would dare to spread himself out into some dozen autonomous tales such as Heliodorus had never written and Cide Hamete had felt obliged to repress.

But first, however, a sop for Heliodorus. Miming his model with a semblance of the cherished Aristotelian devices for unity, Cervantes gave the *Persiles* a beginning, middle, and end; a classically correct delayed exposition by use of the in medias res technique; and a variety of strategically placed summarizing devices to recall former events.[35] But the *Persiles* cannot finally be measured by Aristotelian criteria alone, because their ideas of unity were based on plot, whereas Cervantes's ideas of unity, expressed through a countercanonical figural mechanism, were more recondite. Cervantes offends not against unity but against neo-Aristotelian notions of unity. The *Persiles*, as chapter 4 of this book argues, both thematizes and structurally reiterates a different notion of unity, one borrowed from the "unique compound" of the renascent Platonic androgyne. If genre transformation can indeed be traced through structural elements, as Ralph Cohen claims,[36] then Cervantes's concepts are embodied in his daring transformation of Heliodorus's seamless plot.

THE CATEGORIES OF DIFFERENCE

The third bout in the competition with Heliodorus takes place in an arena scarcely mentioned by Renaissance poeticians: in the categories of difference, a structure of thought inherited from Aristotle as a two-term system for organizing discourse. Renaissance scholars were familiar with Aristotle's ten pairs of contraries, which he attributed to the Pythagoreans in his *Metaphysics*: "(i.) Limit and the Unlimited; (ii.) Odd and Even; (iii.) Unity and Plurality; (iv.) Right and Left; (v.) Male and Female; (vi.) Rest and Motion; (vii.) Straight and Crooked; (viii.) Light and Darkness; (ix.) Good and Evil; (x.) Square and Oblong" (986a). The Renaissance found an even more sophisticated presentation of modes of opposition in Aristotle's *Categories* (11b), where oppositions were handily divided into correlatives (" 'double' and 'half' "), contraries (" 'good' and 'bad' "), privatives and positives (" 'blindness' and 'sight' "), and affirmatives and negatives (" 'he is sitting' and 'he is not sitting' "). Centuries before the Renaissance, in the *Romance of the Rose*, Jean de Meun had tried to describe the production of meaning through contraries: "Thus things go by

---

[35] For instance, the canvas in bk. 3, which rehearses all the main events of bks. 1 and 2; the narrator's recapitulation in 3.19 of former alfresco dinners and of earlier prophecies; and Arnaldo's long *plática* in 4.8, recounting the recent fortunes of the population of sub-characters met during the Northern adventures of bks. 1 and 2.

[36] Ralph Cohen, "Afterword," *Romance: Generic Transformations*, ed. Brownlee and Brownlee, 278.

contraries; one is the gloss of the other. If one wants to define one of the pair, he must remember the other, or he will never, by any intention, assign a definition to it; he who has no understanding of the two will never understand the difference between them, and without this difference no definition that one may make can come to anything."[37] Renaissance thinkers, however, seemed peculiarly resistant toward these exhortations to "remember the other." The humanists perceived such speculations on abstract categories as mechanically arid, as the intellectual apparatus, if not the detested baggage, of a scholasticism that Luis Vives, for one, denounced as a "pestilencia"—a "gangrene" that had infected the minds of men for over five centuries. Even Sir Philip Sidney, who lived and died within Cervantes's lifetime, would continue to dismiss the medieval schoolmen, with their "thorny arguments" of "*genus* and difference," as "men casting largess as they go, of definitions, divisions, and distinctions." This kind of hostility to arguments of difference suggests that "concepts of difference, division, definition and opposition" were more than "problematic," to use Ian Maclean's term, to Renaissance thinkers. Maclean justly views the concept of *female* difference, however, a concept intimately involved with this Aristotelian area of speculation, as reflecting well "the hesitancies and incoherences inherent in Renaissance modes of thought."[38] The concept continues to reflect hesitancies and, even in modern modes of thought regarding romance, more blindness than insight.

Modern critics who have focused on Otherness as an archaic character of romance tend to privilege moral oppositions as the genre's organizational categories. Frye, for instance, writes that "every typical character in romance tends to have his moral opposite confronting him, like black and white pieces in a chess game." Elsewhere Frye speaks of "the curious polarized characterization of romance, its tendency to split into heroes and villains," its wish to avoid "the ambiguities of ordinary life, where everything is a mixture of good and bad."[39] Fredric Jameson, although bent on modifying Frye's transhistorical notions of romance, similarly stresses the semantic code of moral opposites as primary to romance. Indeed, Jameson would suggest "that the most important of those organi-

---

[37] This is Kevin Brownlee's translation of vv. 21573–82 of Jean's *Rose* in "Jean de Meun and the Limits of Romance: Genius as Rewriter of Guillaume de Lorris," in *Romance: Generic Transformations*, ed. Brownlee and Brownlee, 129.

[38] Juan Luis Vives, *Adversus pseudodialecticos*, in *Juan Luis Vives: Obras completas*, ed. and trans. Lorenzo Riber, 2 vols. (Madrid: M. Aguilar, 1947–1948), 2:310. Sir Philip Sidney, *A Defense of Poesy*, ed. Jan Van Dorsten (Oxford: Oxford University Press, 1966), 29. Ian Maclean, *The Renaissance Notion of Woman: A Study in the Fortunes of Scholasticism and Medical Science in European Intellectual Life* (Cambridge: Cambridge University Press, 1980), 2–4.

[39] Northrop Frye, *Anatomy of Criticism* (Princeton: Princeton University Press, 1957), 195, and *Secular Scripture*, 50.

zational categories is the conceptual opposition between good and evil, under which all the other types of attributes and images (light and darkness, high and low, etc.) are clearly subsumed." Stressing that belief in good and evil "is a very old form of thought," Jameson adds that "it is by no means without an intimate link to the social structure, in which such a belief fulfills a crucial function." Linking this form of thought with the Marxist notion of man's prehistory up to socialism, Jameson then goes on to conflate evil with Otherness: "In the shrinking world of today," he laments, "with its gradual leveling of class and national and racial differences, it is becoming increasingly clear that the concept of evil is at one with the category of Otherness itself: evil characterizes whatever is radically different from me."[40]

But James never mentions, in his study of romance, the one difference that has not been leveled, and that can never be leveled no matter how much our world shrinks—sexual difference. Aristotle, who notes in the *Categories* that "whatsoever is better, more honourable, is said to be naturally prior" (14b), actually gives the organizational category of male/female priority over the good/evil opposition in his *Metaphysics* (986a). Although I would scarcely wish to rest my case on Aristotle ("the founder of the law of gender as well as of the law of genre," as Barbara Johnson dryly reminds us),[41] I question Jameson's need to enshrine the opposition of good and evil as the most important organizational category in romance. This unapologetic privileging of good or evil behavior tends to eclipse the agents of such behavior, and agency, as we are beginning to register, usually comes in two genders. "When you meet a human being," Freud writes, "the first distinction you make is 'male or female?' "[42] Hélène Cixous and Luce Irigaray are not alone in speculating that all "hierarchized oppositions" ultimately derive from gender difference, that most ancient and fundamental of distinctions. For Cixous, the man/woman ratio is the basis for many other oppositions, such as sun/moon, day/night, head/heart, activity/passivity, culture/nature, father/mother—a thread of invidious binarism that runs down through centuries of representation, through literature and criticism, philosophy and reflection.[43] Jameson's privileged opposition of good and evil, in any case, is pointedly destabi-

[40] Jameson, "Magical Narratives," 40.

[41] Johnson, *A World of Difference*, 33. One code of that Aristotelian "law of gender" represents the deliberative capacity of women as *akuron*, that is, as "lacking in authority" or as "easily overruled" (*Politics* 1260al).

[42] Freud, *SE* 22:113.

[43] See section entitled "Any Theory of the 'Subject' Has Always Been Appropriated by the 'Masculine,' " in Irigaray's *Speculum of the Other Woman*, trans. Gillian C. Gill (Ithaca: Cornell University Press, 1985). Passages from Cixous cited in *New French Feminisms: An Anthology*, ed. Elaine Marks and Isabelle de Courtivron (Amherst: University of Massachusetts Press, 1980), 90–91.

lized in Cervantes's late romance, by a narrator who refuses to keep his poles apart: "Parece que el bien y el mal distan tan poco el uno del otro, que son como dos líneas concurrentes, que aunque parten de apartados y diferentes principios, acaban en un punto [It seems as if good and evil are distanced so little from each other that they are like two concurrent lines that, although departing from different principles, end up in one place]" (4.12).

This Cervantine estrangement of the good and evil polarity constitutes a definitive break from the conventional chivalric romance models. "Black is black and white is white in the romances of chivalry," Eisenberg notes, adding that their "heroes and villains are clearly distinguished."[44] Instead of the hero/villain organizational category, however, I believe that the *Persiles* invites focus on the male/female dualism, of increasing complexity in Renaissance romance, where it is sometimes but not always an opposite of privation. Jameson notes that any analysis of romance as a mode should come to terms with the relationship between the form and what he calls "the deep-rooted ideology of good and evil."[45] Coming to terms with the relationship between the *Persiles* and Jameson's cherished ideology of good and evil, however, means coming to an impasse. If, instead, we recast the problem, we begin to observe how issues of good and evil in Cervantes's last romance (as in most of Shakespeare's late romances) tend to be generated by sexual difference, an ideology whose roots are as deep and as ancient. Indeed, coming to terms with sexual difference sheds a useful light on Cervantes's remotivation of Greek romance, on his avowed intention to compete with Heliodorus. That he was not attracted to Heliodorus for his epic perfections—for his admired unity of plot or for his exemplary use of verisimilitude—the *Persiles* as an agonistic imitation makes clear: suspense and plausibility were not, for Cervantes, the call to emulation. Other motives, however, all clustered around gender difference, seem more likely candidates for his choice of Greek romance. One reason may have been tropological: Cervantes's understanding that the master trope of Greek romance, a rhetorical figure that would seem to dominate over others, was *syllepsis*. This complicated and uncommon scheme, which engenders such topoi as transvestism, provides readers with a double logic: suspended between "two divergent codes," as Daniel L. Selden explains, the Greek romance text becomes "a delirious seam edging incompatible systems of order which will never

---

[44] Eisenberg, *Romances of Chivalry*, 74. Manuel Durán notes that the *Aethiopica* also "makes a clear distinction between good and bad characters, with the good ones always winning out at the end" ("Cervantes's Swan Song," 84).

[45] Jameson, "Magical Narratives," 140.

manage to address each other face to face."[46] Something very like this scheme operates in the *Persiles*—the figure of *syneciosis* discussed in chapter 4 of the present book, a scheme of joined contraries that motivates the formal, thematic, and intertextual features of Cervantes's romance. Another reason for Cervantes's return to Greek romance may have been the bourgeois elements that, with or without a converso cast, made it more absorbable into the ascendant ideology of love and marriage. Yet another reason may have been the fact that Greek romance addresses "feminine" concerns, and Cervantes's lifelong trajectory, as Ruth El Saffar has movingly argued in *Beyond Fiction*, was toward "a recovery of the feminine." Most likely all of these motives—tropological, ideological, and sexual—were tangled in the process of Cervantine imitation. That they converge on issues of gender difference, as we shall see in the chapters that follow, is a speculation borne out by textual *loci* where Cervantes expands the limits of romance to embrace what chivalric romance seemed so stubbornly to resist: the notion of sexual Otherness as both different *and* equal.

It is a prosaic fact, but one that enhances our understanding of Cervantes's imitation, that he kidnapped from Heliodorus a Greek romance, what the Hellenist Thomas Hägg characterizes as "the first great literary form to have had its main support among women." Because Hägg sees the heroic epic and the classical theater as "typically masculine" forms, he speculates that the Greek romances would have appealed especially to women. He even wonders whether some writers of Greek romance of the Second Sophistic may have been women.[47] This last speculation remains an unproven hypothesis, but the gynocentricity of the Greek romances is in any event not our concern here. What does interest us, rather, is the projection of gendered alterity in some forms of romance, whatever the sex of the projector. The development of a literary heroine as a resourceful, albeit suffering, woman may be the most significant legacy of Greek romance to later fiction—and not only to Cervantes's. The women of Greek romance are both resourceful and visible, worthy of an appearance on title pages. Woman is given positional significance in this literature by being ritually advertised (along with her man) on the title page. Her "en-

---

[46] Daniel L. Selden, "Genre of Genre: Theorizing Ancient Fiction" (Paper delivered at the Second International Conference on the Ancient Novel, Dartmouth College, 24 July 1989), 9–10.

[47] Hägg ultimately resists his own speculation on the grounds that the image of Woman idealized in these romances may have been "a typically male product" (*The Novel in Antiquity*, 96). Susan A. Stephens, professor of classics at Stanford University, thinks the readership question to be a complicated one with respect to women, because even literate women would have been denied the rhetorical education in which the Greek romances were steeped. She finds it interesting, however, that "all women, even slaves, read in the novels themselves" (Letter to author, 1 September 1989).

titlement" occurs in virtually all of the surviving Greek romances and, again, in the twelfth-century Greek romances of the Byzantine revival (*novelas bizantinas* such as *Hysmine and Hysminias*), with their obsessively heterosexual titles. Even in the fourteenth century, during the interplay of Byzantine and Western institutions, we meet a postscript of Greek romances whose titles are similarly dual-gendered: *Callimachus and Chrysorrhoe, Libystrus and Rhodamne, Phlorius and Platzia Phlore*, and so forth.[48] In imitation of Heliodorus's *Aethiopica*, whose official title is *The Loves of Theagenes and Chariclea*, the copulative conjunction of Persiles *and* Sigismunda on Cervantes's title page links together a man and a woman as co-owners of an unspecified sum of travails.

The significance of this sex-coded detail is made evident only by the clamour of its absence in the Spanish chivalric romances—generally named after heroic males such as Amadís, Belianís, Clarián, Lisuarte, Primaleón, Esplandián, Olivante, Cristalián, Felixmarte, Florisel, Florismarte, Palmerín, Tirante, the Caballero del Febo, and others—and even in the Italian romance epics, where only the male hero is entitled to be *maggiore* or *innamorato* or *furioso*. Indeed, of the many romances scrutinized in Don Quixote's library (the reading that "dried up" his brain), only one little-known work is heterosexual in its conjunction: the pastoral *Nimphas y pastores de Henares* (*Nymphs and Shepherds of Henares*), by Bernardo Gonzáles de Bovadilla (1587).[49] Apart from *Paris e Viana* (c. 1494), included by Henry Thomas in his antecedents (pre-1500) to the Spanish romances of chivalry, and *Curial y Guelpha*, part of Catalonian chivalric matter, no libros de caballerías entitled after two lovers seem to exist. Although Cervantes swerves from the chivalric—even from those "good" books of chivalry saved from the inquisitorial bonfire of Don Quixote's library—to choose a model with a more egalitarian title, his imitation of Heliodorus, as we have noted repeatedly, is never parasitic. Generic transformation is inscribed directly into Cervantes's title where he employs the word *trabajos* (trials, labors, ordeals) as a substitute for Heliodorus's use of *amores* (loves).[50] Love in the late Renais-

---

[48] Three verse imitations of Heliodorus are among the four twelfth-century novels written in learned literary Greek: *Hysmine and Hysminias* (by Eustathius Macrembolitis); *Rhodanthe and Dosicles* (by Theodore Prodomus); *Aristandros and Callithea* (by Constantine Manasses); and *Drosilla and Charicles* (by Nicetas Eugenianus). On the fourteenth-century Byzantine romances, with their newly westernized folk-tale motifs, see Hägg, *The Novel in Antiquity*, 80.

[49] The sixteenth-century Spanish pastoral romances were distinguished by such monogendered female titles as *La Diana, La Galatea*, and so on. On the enormous popularity and subsequent erasure of *La Diana*, the prototype of these pastoral works, see Elizabeth Rhodes, "Skirting the Men: Gender Roles in Sixteenth-Century Pastoral Books," *Journal of Hispanic Philology* 11 (1987): 131–49.

[50] *Historia etiópica de los amores de Teágenes y Cariclea* is the full title of the Spanish translation Cervantes was imitating.

sance, as the *Persiles* makes clear, is becoming harder work for men and women alike.

But titles are only the most superficial symptom of what Greek romance offered Cervantes toward a poetics of sexual difference. Hägg finds "room for a closer analysis" of Greek romance "from the point of view of sex roles," an enterprise not within the organizing interest of this chapter. We should bear in mind, however, his claim that the Greek romances are remarkable for eschewing a double standard: indeed, they generally "set the same high moral requirements for the hero as for the heroine." John J. Winkler has recently argued, for instance, that "what is truly remarkable about *Daphnis and Chloe* is the sensitive portrayal of the lovers' equality." This equality is in stark contrast to most of the literature of Cervantes's age, which both reflected and perpetrated the kind of double standard described by Cardinal Bibbiena (Bernardo Dovizi) in *Il cortegiano*: "We ourselves, as men, have made it a rule that a dissolute way of life is not to be thought evil or blameworthy or disgraceful, whereas in women it leads to such complete opprobrium and shame that once a woman has been spoken ill of, whether the accusation be true or false, she is utterly disgraced for ever."[51] The atypical single standard for both sexes found in Greek romance was not lost on Cervantes. As a retrospective construct, the *Persiles* not only competes with Heliodorus on this issue, but outdoes him in its self-conscious acknowledgment of sexual Otherness, by literally "embodying" a "two-in-one" sexual program in its text, a strategy to be elaborated in chapter 4 of the present book. Cervantes had sketched out a rough draft of this gendered structure in *La Galatea*, his first romance. Ruth El Saffar points out the remarkable "division of the whole work into masculine and feminine halves," adding that "what is probably central to any deep analysis of the work, is that the shepherds are kept quite distinct from the shepherdesses almost throughout the entire novel."[52] Sexual difference is also central to any deep analysis of Cervantes's last romance, the *Persiles*. In response to the ascendant roles of bourgeois love and marriage that were just emerging in early modern Europe, the Cervantes of the *Persiles* newly posits gender as socially constructed through cultural fiats, through laws or maxims never dreamed of in the poetics of El Pinciano. Always an active disrupter of the signifier, Cervantes was revolutionary in his use of sexual oppositions as a category for a poetics of the Other. Such a text would predictably have seemed strange to many Renaissance readers, locked as they

[51] Hägg, *The Novel in Antiquity*, 95–96. Baldesar Castiglione, *The Book of the Courtier*, trans. George Bull (New York: Penguin, 1967), 195. John J. Winkler, *The Constraints of Desire* (London: Routledge, 1990), 114–15.

[52] "The whole work pivots around four major interpolated tales, two told to men by men, and two told to women by women" (Ruth El Saffar, "*La Galatea*: The Integrity of the Unintegrated Text," *Dispositio* 3 [1979]: 340).

were in the rigid embrace of neo-Aristotelian notions of genre, of cautions that would ironically be catalogued, centuries later, in the postmodern era: "As soon as genre announces itself," Derrida writes, "one must respect a norm, one must not cross a line of demarcation, one must not risk impurity, anomaly, or monstrosity."[53] In competing with Heliodorus, Cervantes did indeed risk monstrosity. When the *Persiles* came into the world "with hands on its head," as Cervantes suspected it would, the reading public was fascinated.[54] But later critics, upon whose fosterage he depended, were more apprehensive. Suspecting that Cervantes had crossed a line of demarcation, they felt compelled to abandon the infant.

[53] Jacques Derrida, "The Law of Genre," in *Glyph 7: Johns Hopkins Textual Studies* (Baltimore: Johns Hopkins University Press, 1980), 203–4.

[54] Cervantes's contemporaries must have liked the *Persiles*, judging from the ten Spanish editions that followed the 1617 edition, the two French versions of 1618, the English translation of 1619, the Italian translation of 1626, and the remarks of various writers of the period (see Schevill and Bonilla, "Introduction," *Persiles*, xliii).

Chapter Three

SOME VERSIONS OF ALLEGORY

Non simplex natura hominis.

[Human nature is not simple.]

—Prudentius, *Psychomachia*

EL PINCIANO concluded his long eulogy to Heliodorus with the observation, one surely not lost on Cervantes, that readers could extract an allegory ("exprimir alegoría") from the *Aethiopica*, and not a bad one ("no mala") at that. A modern critic of Greek romance assures us, however, that "Heliodorus is not writing allegory but romance."[1] The relations between romance and allegory, intimate ones for centuries, continue to put theorists asunder. Unlike El Pinciano's Ugo—who could comfortably claim to have no "doctrina de Aristóteles" on allegory[2]—modern readers must confront far too many doctrines on allegory and its relations to other genres and modes. Where one critic writes that suggestions of allegory are constantly "creeping in" around the fringes of romance, another sees allegory as having, in the manner of a vital blood transfusion, already penetrated the genre: allegory, so Angus Fletcher rectifies Northrop Frye, "does more than creep in around the edges of romance; it is the very lifeblood of the type." Or, climbing outside his inside metaphor, Fletcher continues, "romance is the natural, popular medium for allegorical expression."[3]

Whether allegory creeps in around the fringes of romance or infuses it with lifeblood depends on the sometimes tenuous, often hasty, and seldom uncontested marriage between the ambivalent tradition of allegory and the embattled genre of romance. Allegory is, however, conducive to a variety of genres apart from romance: "It can use almost any external structure or 'outside' allegorically, making it the husk or *sens* of an inner

---

[1] López Pinciano, *Philosophía antigua poética* 3:167; Heiserman, *The Novel Before the Novel*, 193.

[2] López Pinciano, *Philosophía antigua poética* 3:174.

[3] Angus Fletcher, *Allegory: The Theory of a Symbolic Mode* (Ithaca: Cornell University Press, 1964), 221n. Fletcher is responding to Frye's more cautious view of allegory, which he sees as ultimately "deriving from medieval statements about polysemous meaning" (221).

matière—and modifying it generically in the process."[4] This chapter seeks to examine the ubiquitous notion of allegory, looking at both its depreciated critical status in Cervantes's age and its emptily modish one in the postmodern period. After exploring some of the theories of allegory available to Cervantes as he began writing, we shall consider what Cervantes's characters have to say about the matter. We will then examine the uses of personification in the *Persiles*, focusing on the third and last allegorical pageant in the text, perhaps the last in the Cervantine canon. This allegory occurs within the hero's manifest dream and, as such, leads us to pose the question of whether Freud's own "allegories" of love follow upon or explain Cervantes's.[5]

If we begin with the seemingly simple inquiry "What is allegory?"—as does one critic in a chapter headed by that very question and another in a pioneering genetic study of allegory—we seem to get nowhere. "In so complex a matter," this latter writer cautions, "a definition or a series of definitions will not even hint at its manifold uses and adaptations."[6] A catalogue of its historical definitions, indeed, makes the concept of allegory seem especially forbidding.[7] Allegory is "protean," as Fletcher re-

---

[4] Fowler, *Kinds of Literature*, 192.

[5] For a challenging discussion of psychoanalytic interpretation as following upon rather than explaining Renaissance texts, see Stephen Greenblatt, "Psychoanalysis and Renaissance Culture," in *Literary Theory/Renaissance Texts*, ed. Patricia Parker and David Quint (Baltimore: Johns Hopkins University Press, 1986), 210–24.

[6] Stephen A. Barney, *Allegories of History, Allegories of Love* (Hamden, Conn.: Arcon Books, 1979), 49; and Edwin Honig, *Dark Conceit: The Making of Allegory* (Evanston: Northwestern University Press, 1959), 8. Barney aims to be "properly responsive to allegory, if not definitive of it": "*Allegory*, in its referential aspect, *pretends to name, not things, but whatever lies under things*—substances, relations, intentions, faculties, categories, powers, ideas" (*Allegories of History*, 16–23).

[7] *Allegoria*—"*lit.* speaking otherwise than one seems to speak" (OED)—comes from the Greek prefix *allos*, meaning "other," inverting through its suggestions of private language its second and public component part, the verb *agoreuein*, meaning "to speak in the assembly" or *agora*. The first appearance of the word may be in the treatise *De elocutione*, arguably in 270 B.C. by one "Demetrius." Cleanthes of Assos (third century B.C.) has been nominated for earliest critical use of the adverb (*allēgorikōs*). Allegoria is first treated as an ordinary trope (*tropos*) in a Greek rhetorical treatise by Philodemus (c. 60 B.C.), having been earlier translated into Latin as "permutatio" in the *Rhetorica ad Herennium* (by an *auctor incertus*, although attributed to Cicero until 1491; ed. and trans. Harry Caplan [Loeb Classical Library, 1954], 4.34.46). Cicero first used the Greek term *allēgoria*, in his Latin treatise *De oratore* (trans. E. W. Sutton and H. Rackham, 2 vols. [Loeb Classical Library, 1942], 3.41.166), in the sense of "continua *metaphora*," to be canonized by Quintilian's *Institutio oratoria* (trans. H. E. Butler, 4 vols. [Loeb Classical Library, 1921–1922], 9.2.46). In the exegetical tradition of allegory, the term *hyponoia* (under-meaning) was used until Strabo (turn of the first century A.D.) used *allēgoria* to refer to interpretation of Homer. Although Heraclitus and Philo both use both the terms *hyponoia* and *allēgoria* to describe exegeses of Homer and the Bible, respectively, it was Plutarch who, in *De audiendis poetis* (4.19), tracked the change in terminology: what "long ago" used to be called *hyponoiai*, he writes,

minds us, a device "omnipresent in Western literature from the earliest times to the modern era."[8] Between what Plutarch termed *allēgoria*, choosing to detour its older Greek equivalent *hyponoia* (undermeaning), and what the late Paul de Man called "the allegory of unreadability" have passed some nineteen hundred years and perhaps as many critical attempts to define allegory. Allegories are interesting, as de Man himself often argued, because they are haunted by meanings that have come before, a "haunting" that invites exegesis. My own exegesis of the *Persiles* operates from a rhetorical but not unhistorical nor undecidable perspective. Even when I "personify" the text, I shall not liberate it from the burden of meaning. Nor shall I feel obliged to renounce "the nostalgia and the desire to coincide."[9]

On the contrary, my aim in this and the following chapter is to contextualize, necessarily to historicize, Cervantes's widespread use of a rhetorical figure that provides a locus of meaning for precisely this nostalgia and this desire. I hope to show that the complicated allegorical machinery of the *Persiles*—which Avalle-Arce views as having been conceived by a mind "magnetized" ("imantada") by hierarchy, by the metaphysical assumption of "the great chain of being"[10]—derives from a trope of nostal-

---

are "now" called *allēgoriai*; Plutarch cited by Jean Pépin, *Mythe et allégorie* (Paris: Editions Montaigne, 1958), 87–88.

[8] Fletcher, *Allegory*, 1. Aiming to provide a model of allegory by arriving at the essence of a "symbolic" mode, Fletcher moves from isolated figures (schemes and tropes) into modal concepts of allegory. His theory of allegory predictably takes Coleridge as its starting point, locating him "at the center of the disputation which has so obscured the problem." For a useful discussion of the rupture between symbol and allegory that Coleridge initiated, see 15–23. Honig also sees Coleridge as responsible "for instigating numerous pedantic distinctions between symbolism and allegory" (*Dark Conceit*, 44–50).

[9] De Man sees any narration as being primarily an allegory of its own rhetorical reading, a process that he variously describes as "a disruptive intertwining of trope and persuasion" and as an "allegory of unreadability." De Man's view of allegory bears rehearsing for its predictable opposition to Coleridge's depreciation of it. De Man, in contrast, downgrades symbolism in favor of an allegory that holds sign and meaning to be discontinuous, thereby canceling the unity of experience promised by the symbol: "Whereas the symbol postulates the possibility of an identity or identification, allegory designates primarily a distance in relation to its own origin, and, renouncing the nostalgia and the desire to coincide, it establishes its language in the void of this temporal distance." His own reading of Rousseau's *Julie*—an example of "allegories of reading" *allegories*—shows the difficulties of escaping the circularity involved in describing abstractions in a language of abstraction (*Allegories of Reading: Figural Language in Rousseau, Nietzsche, Rilke, and Proust* (New Haven: Yale University Press, 1979), ix, 206. Elsewhere, de Man writes that it is the personified text that tells "the allegory of its misunderstanding," a telling he attempts to disclose through a complex process of disengaging the narrative from history and authority, emptying it of meaning, and proceeding to dismantle its more stubborn tropes (Paul de Man, *Blindness and Insight: Essays in the Rhetoric of Contemporary Criticism* [Minneapolis: University of Minnesota Press, 1983], 136).

[10] Avalle-Arce views the *Persiles* as resting on a metaphysical assumption operative in

gic desire first articulated in the *Symposium*, a trope that displaces such notions of hierarchy. Appearing as a sustained series in the *Persiles*, this trope accounts for the androgynous figuration of, and throughout, Cervantes's last romance. Grounding my argument on Quintilian's remark that "a continuous metaphor makes an allegory" ("*allēgorian* facit continua *metaphora*") (*Institutio oratoria* 9.2.46), I shall constitute the main plot of the *Persiles* as a formal allegory of sexual difference.

Apart from their programmatic undecidability, their personification of texts, and their relentless focus on tropes, poststructuralist "allegories of reading" had been foreshadowed in the 1950s by Frye's remark that "all commentary is allegorical interpretation," that as soon as we make a critical comment about a work, we begin "to allegorize."[11] Centuries before Frye, however, within the Renaissance exegetical tradition of allegory, we encounter the notion that all literature is susceptible to the exegetical readings commonly given to Scripture, or as Bernard Weinberg puts it, the assumption that "all poetry—even the comedies of Terence—is essentially allegorical in character."[12] This assumption may create some confusion: all writings are "allegorical in character" insofar as they invite interpretation. But formal allegories would seem to invite it more coaxingly, even more urgently. In trying to account for the internal operations that organize allegorical works, it is useful to pry apart the two strains or traditions of allegory whose strategies, even before the Renaissance, had gradually come to interact: the compositional method that personifies abstractions, and the exegetical technique that interprets those, but not only those, abstractions. The one is a technique of fiction-writing, the other a method of interpreting literature. The first tradition—of narratives peopled by personifications and other similarly frozen agents moving about in a resonant world of language—we may call *allegory*. The second—the tradition of discursive interpretation or textual commentary—I prefer to call *allegoresis*, the term used by Maureen Quilligan, recognizing that it is only this tradition of allegory that has become so fashionable under

Western literature from Plato's *Timaeus* down to the eighteenth century—what Alexander Pope, in the century after Cervantes, was to label "the vast chain of being." According to Avalle-Arce, "sin este archi-tradicional presupuesto metafísico de la cadena y escala ontológicas, el *Persiles* no podría ser como es [without this archtraditional metaphysical assumption of the ontological ladder and chain, the *Persiles* could not be what it is]." What the *Persiles* "is"—and whether it is well served by a spatial analogy like "the great chain of being"—are, of course, arguable points ("Introduction," *Persiles*, 20–21).

[11] Such an exegetical exercise, however, Frye distinguishes from "actual allegory," which he defines as a "contrapuntal technique" (*Anatomy of Criticism*, 89–90). Elsewhere Frye adds that allegorical commentary not supplemented with archetypal criticism is an exercise in futility (342).

[12] Weinberg, *Italian Renaissance* 1:294.

structuralist and poststructuralist "allegories of reading."[13] With virtually all interpretation construed "as an essentially allegorical act"—as
what Fredric Jameson calls "rewriting a given text in terms of a particular
interpretive master code"[14]—to write about the *Persiles* is necessarily "to
allegorize" about allegory.

Although allegory eludes definition, readers have no problem calling
this or that macrosyntactical structure "an allegory"—seeing allegory, in
other words, as a form genetic to whole narratives. One thinks of the
world's canonical allegories, such as the *Romance of the Rose*, the *Commedia*, *The Faerie Queene*, *Pilgrim's Progress*, or, to leap over a few centuries and climb down a few rungs on that "great chain of being," *Animal
Farm*. A number of critics have even suggested, some without mounting
any considerable argument for it, that *Don Quixote* is an allegory.[15] The
issue of whether such whole narratives are in the mode of allegory—a
mode understood as fundamentally a process of encoding speech—seems
less useful at this point than a close analysis of how Cervantes uses allegory in his last romance.[16]

Let us begin by measuring the *Persiles* against Frye's standards for de-
tecting allegory: "We have actual allegory when a poet explicitly indicates
the relationship of his images to examples and precepts, and so tries to
indicate how a commentary on him should proceed." The allegorical
poet, Frye suggests, must be outspokenly secretive: "A writer is being allegorical whenever it is clear that he is saying 'by this I *also* (*allos*) mean
that.' " If he seems to be doing this "continuously, we may say, cau-
tiously, that what he is writing 'is' an allegory."[17] Frye's strict standards

[13] On "the allegorical problem," see Jon Whitman, *Allegory: The Dynamics of an Ancient
and Medieval Technique* (Cambridge, Mass.: Harvard University Press, 1987), 1–13. See
also Whitman's useful Appendices on the histories of the terms *allegory* and *personification*,
263–272. Maureen Quilligan's distinctions between allegory and allegoresis are in *The Language of Allegory: Defining the Genre* (Ithaca: Cornell University Press, 1979), 21, 26, 29–
32, 224–25.

[14] Fredric Jameson, *The Political Unconscious* (Ithaca: Cornell University Press, 1981),
10.

[15] Honig, *Dark Conceit*, 14, 16, 33, 46, 94, 131, 171; Fletcher, *Allegory*, 37. In an excellent study of the confrontation between the autobiography of Ginés de Pasamonte and the
novel of *Don Quixote* that includes it—a confrontation "effected in terms of representative
human figures"—E. C. Riley writes that "one almost catches a whiff of allegory" ("Romance, the Picaresque and *Don Quixote I*," in *Studies in Honor of Bruce W. Wardropper*
[Newark, Del.: Juan de la Cuesta Press, 1989], 245).

[16] On the term *mode* as "the stumbling block of allegorical theory," see Barney, *Allegories
of History*, 29. Michael McKeon, although not concerned with allegory, views the idea of
"literary mode" as a convenient way of acknowledging the persistence of literary forms
without having to account for their historicity (*Origins of the English Novel*, 15). Alastair
Fowler calls allegory a "generic modulation," that is, "a modal abstraction with a token
repertoire" (*Kinds of Literature*, 191).

[17] Frye, *Anatomy of Criticism*, 90. Frye divides allegories into continuous allegory (as

might prevent us from calling the *Persiles* a "continuous allegory," if only because the allegorical reference seems to be dropped during the interpolated stories. The main narrative, however, does indeed meet his standards: it systematically refers to traditional examples—to the Bible, Virgil, Ovid, Heliodorus—as well as to a large constellation of moral precepts. Cervantes's text has, in fact, provoked at least one critic to regard it as a Renaissance manual of moralities—"como repertorio de moralidades [as a repertoire of moralities]," to cite the unseductive title of an essay on the *Persiles*.[18]

Frye's recipe for "actual allegory" may be enriched by adding a few ingredients from Alastair Fowler's "token allegorical repertoire": "personification, abstraction, metaphorically doubled chains of discourse and of narrative, generated subcharacters, deletion of nonsignificant description, and several topics (journey, battle, monster, disease)." Every one of these features is found in the *Persiles*, together with the "discontinuity of form" that Barney includes in his own checklist.[19] The *Persiles* abounds in formal discontinuities that may dismay traditional readers. Mimetic episodes repeatedly disrupt its main plot, making the allegory intermittent. But the allegorical main plot is reinforced by three different *tableaux* of personification, to be elaborated at the close of this chapter. To all these intimations of allegory in Cervantes's last work may be added de Man's linguistic qualifications for calling a mode allegorical: "The copresence of thematic, exhortative discourse with critical analytical language points to an inherent characteristic of all allegorical modes."[20] An acute preoccupation with critical analytical language informs the whole of the *Persiles*, peaking in Periandro's long recitation in book 2, where the text examines the various neoclassical theories that dictate audience response. As for the presence of "exhortative discourse," Cervantes's work abounds in *sententiae* that codify behavior: the narrative even includes its own little anthology of hortatory maxims, a text ostentatiously collected by a thinly disguised authorial stand-in (4.1).

Much ink has been spilled over the allegorical potential of romance, but in the light of all of the above clues from divergent critical sources, I think we may safely conclude that the *Persiles* is a formal allegory, albeit

---

used by Dante, Spenser, Tasso, and Bunyan); *freistimmige* or freestyle allegory (as used by Ariosto, Goethe, Ibsen, and Hawthorne); and naive allegory ("schoolroom moralities, devotional exempla, local pageants, and the like").

[18] A. Sánchez, "El *Persiles* como repertorio de moralidades," *Anales cervantinos* 4 (1954): 199–223.

[19] Fowler, *Kinds of Literature*, 192; Barney, *Allegories of History*, 20. See also Honig's catalogue of allegorical features: "elemental symbols, tables of basic contrarieties, concepts of dualism, tradic and tetradic categories, and all the philosophical metaphors used to demonstrate identification, motion, unity, and immutability" (*Dark Conceit*, 30).

[20] De Man, *Allegories of Reading*, 209.

a discontinuous one, in that Cervantes repeatedly deallegorizes his narrative. "If allegory may be said to have a standard form," Barney suggests, "it would be the comic form of the Bible set in terms of the individual narrative, a Bildungs-roman: an unbalanced man quests for salvation, endures adventures, and sees the city."[21] By giving that "unbalanced man" his rightful "other," we can have the *Persiles* tally perfectly with the above standard form of allegory: an unbalanced couple quests for salvation, endures adventures, and—in the climactic vision of Rome in book 4—"sees the city." Allegory, or the "allegorical quality," in sum, gestures to us in literature from a special kind of text: "a twice-told tale written in rhetorical, or figurative, language and expressing a vital belief."[22] The *Persiles*, a twice-told tale in its imitation of Heliodorus, is written in the figurative language of love that Cervantes was to discover in Platonism, a relatively new force in Renaissance literary criticism.

To see the *Persiles* as an allegory, then, is neither "mistaken allegoresis" (to cite a widespread critical *caveat*) nor even an original reading. In accounting for his hatred of the *Persiles*—which he sees as entirely lacking in the "raw philosophical problems" of pragmatism and existentialism posited by *Don Quixote*—Mack Singleton unwittingly describes precisely the kind of *tableaux vivant* that signal allegory: "Its world is a 'seen' world—a hysterical procession of violent images. The exterior world of appearance is *pictured* as absolutely final; there is no room for speculation about it. The only psychological problems grow out of the erotic."[23] Singleton's complaint about the erotic foundation of the work is quite accurate; but his pointed dismissal of any room for speculation about it seems overdetermined, especially since other allegorical readings have programmatically shunned those more "hysterical" aspects of the *Persiles*. Casalduero's allegorical exegesis of the *Persiles*, for instance, using orthodox Catholicism as its point of departure, proffers a reductive series of Baroque "this-for-that" allegories in a reading that multiplies, it

[21] Barney, *Allegories of History*, 33–34. This "standard form" of allegory suggestively parallels what Leland H. Chambers describes as "the Neo-Platonic concept of the soul's departure from Oneness, its 'adventures,' and its return to the One." Chambers sees Cervantes as employing this pattern in *Don Quixote*, "which begins with the onset of Alonso Quijano's madness, carries him through his three sallies, and returns him to his previous balanced state of mind once more." Chambers persuasively argues that "Cervantes' prior and most enduring esthetic commitment in the novel" was founded "on a group of Neo-Platonic concepts, the most important of which is *discordia concors*." See " '*Harmonia est Discordia Concors*': The Coincidence of Opposites and Unity in Diversity in the *Quijote*," in *Cervantes: Su obra y su mundo. Actas del Primer Congreso Internacional Sobre Cervantes*, ed. Manuel Criado de Val (Madrid: Edi-6, 1981), 608–15.

[22] Honig, *Dark Conceit*, 12.

[23] Mack Singleton, "The *Persiles* Mystery," in *Cervantes Across the Centuries*, ed. Ángel Flores and M. J. Benardete (New York: Dryden Press, 1947), 230.

would seem, precisely the kind of allegory that Cervantes was prone to ridicule. Identifying the group of pilgrims huddled in Antonio's cave as the church of the Counter-Reformation is tantamount to revealing the true identity of this fountain or that sewer, as the pedantic guide to the Cave of Montesinos does with his *alegorías* in the *Quixote* (2.22). Casalduero's Spanish equations of Sinforosa with (bad) Protestantism and Auristela with (good) Catholicism would seem to be in the same league as Miss Winstanley's English equations, for Shakespeare's *Tempest*, of Sycorax with (bad) Catherine de Medici or Caliban with (bad) Jesuitism.[24] The binary thinking of these two critics—amazingly, both twentieth-century interpreters of allegorical romance—continues in the tradition of the Renaissance holy wars. Forcione's is another allegorical exegesis of the *Persiles*, a thematically much more focused and structurally far more complex reading than Casalduero's, and one that usefully probes at the modern idea of allegorical meaning as "an organized thought system which generates and is embedded in the very structure of the work." Forcione's archetypalism, however, motivates him to address the *Persiles* as a quest romance animated by "the spirit of orthodox Christianity."[25] What neither of these allegorical readings confronts, however, is what Singleton correctly identified as "the only psychological problems" in the *Persiles*, namely, those that "grow out of the erotic."

Where did Cervantes find the allegorical repertoire he used to explore these erotic problems? How do his own characters understand the notion of allegory? What does he tell us in his works about the extant traditions of allegory? To pose these questions is to see Cervantes, traditionally regarded as the founder of realism in fiction, in a strange new light, in what many readers would consider an artificial one. Cervantes clearly regarded himself as a pioneer in personification, that staple device of allegory, when, in the prologue to his *Ocho comedias*, he claimed to have been "el primero que representase las imaginaciones y los pensamientos escondidos del alma, sacando figuras morales a teatro [the first to represent the imaginings and hidden thoughts of the soul, bringing moral figures to the stage]."[26] However we may judge the accuracy of this boast, a far cry from the false modesty topoi that abound in Renaissance texts, we must reflect on Cervantes's avowed intention to figure not virtues or vices or universal concepts but "hidden thoughts." That Cervantes regarded such

---

[24] Casalduero's *Sentido y forma de* Los trabajos de Persiles y Sigismunda (1947) uses the kind of historical allegorizing that A. D. Nuttall, who cites Miss Winstanley's correspondence with Robert Graves (c. 1925), calls "a blameless occupation," apart from "a mysterious inner principle of self-multiplication and extension." See *Two Concepts of Allegory* (New York: Barnes and Noble, 1967), 6.

[25] Forcione, *Cervantes' Christian Romance*, 54, 60.

[26] *Obras completas*, ed. A. Valbuena Prat (Madrid: Aguilar, 1956), 180.

thoughts as unconscious, rather than as deliberately concealed, will be made apparent in the closing discussion of this chapter, whose focus is an erotic dream. But first we must survey the disparate notions of allegory held by the literary theorists of Cervantes's day.

RENAISSANCE NOTIONS OF ALLEGORY

To understand the critical context in which Cervantes was writing, we must confront at least three characteristics of the age: its governing traditions of allegory; its stubborn view of allegory as inextricably associated with the incredible, the impossible, or the false; and its increasingly vocal distrust of the exegetical powers of the masses, the so-called *ignoranti*. The rhetorical or tropological tradition inherited from Quintilian, the one that defines *allegoria* as a figure of speech, was the only notion of allegory countenanced by Renaissance neo-Aristotelians. The second tradition of allegory extant was the hermeneutic tradition of interpreting texts reaching back to Hellenic and biblical allegoresis. What hampers our quest for allegory in Cervantes is the lack of any articulate tradition in the Renaissance for the poetic process of crafting a *total* symbolic fiction, that is, for the process whose products are those macrosymbolic structures we now call "actual allegories." To appreciate Cervantes's project, then, we must envision the Renaissance leap from trope to mode, from sporadic usage to continuous technique. Such a leap is noted implicitly in Charles Sears Baldwin's remark that "allegory, hardly more than a figure of speech with Tasso, is announced by Spenser as his plan."[27] What Spenser, in the "Letter" to Sir Walter Raleigh appended to his 1590 edition of *The Faerie Queene*, announced as his "whole intention" was to write "a continued Allegory, or darke conceit," a work to be "clowdily enwrapped in Allegorical devises." Unlike Spenser, Cervantes never mentioned the word *allegory* in connection with his last romance. It would appear, nonetheless, that, like Spenser, he too was writing an allegory—a work whose structures reveal a systematic, not ornamental, system of thought. Both Cervantes and Spenser were writing during an age when thinkers were beginning to probe at how the allegorical sense works, how it functions to further a poet's meaning. The very structure of the *Persiles* reveals the thought that generated it: it shows that Cervantes must have been thinking the way that allegorical poets write. Many clues in Cervantes's text disclose the thought system embedded in its pages: by pointing out the relationships of his images to antecedent examples and pre-

[27] Charles Sears Baldwin, *Renaissance Literary Theory and Practice* (New York: Columbia University Press, 1939), 123.

cepts, Cervantes tries to indicate how a commentary on him should proceed.

In pursuit of Cervantes's thinking about allegory, it may help to scan a few Renaissance treatises, ones representative not only of Aristotelian, but also of Platonic and Horatian ideas. When these three classical systems find their way into Renaissance poetics, they carry with them the term *allegoria* in various critical senses, all of which Cervantes appears to have engaged. The assorted views of these systems will afford at least a skeletal idea of the changing state of allegory in Cervantes's day. They also qualify E. C. Riley's vision of the dominant Aristotelian strain in Cervantes's theory of the novel, a view dismissive of the imprint of Platonic ideas: "From Aristotle's *Poetics* or treatises based on it derive many of his most important principles and the greatest single issue, the nature of truth in poetic fiction."[28] Although the eclectic sixteenth-century poetics of allegory tends to be dominated by the neo-Aristotelian view of it as either a trope or a fable—with many theorists recoiling because it intimated for them falsity, multiplicity, or both—other, larger views of allegory were nonetheless in the air. Robert L. Montgomery claims, misleadingly, that by the end of the Renaissance it is almost impossible to find any "critic who does not consider allegory as a special kind of literature"—that is, as a false or incredible fable—rather than as "a quality inherent in all imaginative works which attempt to be meaningful."[29] In the vast and diversified welter of documents that appears toward the end of the Cinquecento, it is possible to detect a small but vocal group of critics who are groping—albeit tentatively and in a language often suffused with value judgments—for precisely this quality inherent in meaningful imaginative works: a new sense of secular allegory that is not divorced from the ordinary objects of imitation, that is not conjured up to justify the fabulous or the monstrous, and that is not affected by the post-Ramist fear of figurative language.

Neo-Aristotelian poetics in the Renaissance tend either to invoke their master's silence on the subject of allegory or to rank it as an ornamental trope: most of these critics give short theoretical shrift to allegory. The neo-Aristotelians generally recapitulate the same traditional rhetoric set forth by the Roman rhetoricians, in which allegory was regarded as accidental, extrinsic, unessential: as an ornament usually confined to a single sentence and generally connected to the idea of metaphor. When Minturno defines allegory, for instance, he reaches back to the Latin rhetoricians for support, giving allegory its old Ciceronian status as a trope, as

[28] Riley, *Theory of the Novel*, 7.
[29] Robert L. Montgomery, "Allegory and the Incredible Fable," *PMLA* 81 (1966): 46.

one of those "figure de parole" to be classified along with metaphors.[30] As Exhibit A of the fact that Cervantes knew about allegory as a figure of speech, we need only summon up the "infanta Antonomasia," that poor fallen damsel named after a trope (*DQ* 2.39). Riley's list of Cervantes's boyhood reading fortifies our speculations of how much rhetoric he was exposed to: "No doubt some standard works like Quintilian's *Institutio oratoria*, Cicero on oratory, and perhaps the *Rhetorica ad Herennium* and Horace's *Ars poetica*, figured as part of his formal education."[31] Had the schoolboy Cervantes read, as Riley believes, Quintilian's handbook on rhetoric, he might even have pondered the inclusion of irony—"where the meaning is contrary to that suggested by the words"—as a subcategory of allegory, which Quintilian saw as largely connected with metaphor, either alone or in a series.[32] Had Cervantes read the *Rhetorica ad Herennium*, he would have noted only the ornamental quality of allegory (*permutatio*, in its status as one of ten verbal embellishments, *exornationes verborum*). One of the *Rhetorica*'s seven lively examples of allegory seems closer to what we could call irony, even though classical rhetoric considered irony as a subcategory of allegory: "ut si quem impium qui patrem verberarit Aeneam vocemus, intemperantem et adulterum Hippolytum nominemus [if we should call some undutiful man who has beaten his father 'Aeneas,' or an intemperate and adulterous man 'Hippolytus']."[33] Although allegory and irony share the same characteristic of obliquity, the relations between them remain, as Fletcher puts it, "not very clear."[34] What is clear is that *ironia*—a subcategory of allegory—was

[30] Antonio Sebastiano Minturno, *L'arte poetica* (Venice: Gio. Andrea Valuassori, 1563), 137–38. For Cicero's stance, see *De oratore* 3.41.165.

[31] Riley, *Theory of the Novel*, 7.

[32] "Allegoria, quam inversionem interpretantur, aut aliud verbis aliud sensu ostendit aut etiam interim contrarium [Allegory, which is translated (in Latin) as *inversio*, either presents one thing in words and another in meaning, or even something contrary to the meaning of the words]." Quintilian's last definition of allegory nudges his own definition of irony, where words and meaning are contraries: "Quo contraria ostendentur, ironia est" (*Institutio oratoria* 8.6.44–59).

[33] "Permutatio est oratio aliud verbis aliud sententia demonstrans [Allegory is a manner of speech denoting one thing by the letter of the words, but another by their meaning]" ([Cicero], *Rhetorica ad Herennium* 4.34.46).

[34] Fletcher, who sees irony as "the extreme degree of ambivalence," calls ironies either "collapsed" or "condensed allegories" on the grounds that irony "still involves an otherness of meaning, however tenuous and shifty may be our means of decoding that other (*allos*) meaning" (*Allegory*, 229–30); Wayne Booth, who sees irony as "the mother of confusions," maintains a rhetorical focus in seeing the trope as "used" or "achieved" within "every conceivable kind of literature," *including* allegory (*A Rhetoric of Irony* [Chicago: University of Chicago Press, 1974], ix, xiii–xiv); John Freccero concludes that "irony is the destructive counterpart of allegory" ("The Text on the Gates of Hell in Dante's *Inferno*" [Paper delivered to the Dante Society at the annual meeting of the Modern Language Association, San Francisco, 29 December 1979]); and Paul de Man sees irony as "the undoing of the decon-

to become the most privileged trope in Cervantes, in practice if not in name.[35]

On the basis of his study of the relations between the *Persiles* and sixteenth-century neo-Aristotelian poetics, Forcione rightly concludes that "little theoretical energy" was wasted upon allegory by these critics, who tended to see the exercise as incompatible with their cherished notions of verisimilitude. He also dismisses what he regards as Cervantes's occasional ridicule of the term *alegoría* as typical of the view of his epoch, stressing that such an attitude should be "understood in the context of contemporary literary theorizing, with its limited comprehension of the symbolical workings of literature."[36] Granted that the neo-Aristotelians displayed a "limited comprehension" of what we now call "symbolical workings," but even from within that resistant tradition, Jacopo Mazzoni could presciently view the ways in which impossible and marvelous subjects "may be made credible through allegorical treatment."[37]

A second tradition of allegory accessible to Cervantes would have been that of the Renaissance Neoplatonists, a tradition considerably weakened in his day by the increasing authority of Aristotle's *Poetics*. The "language of mysteries" that had been their special province was familiar to Cervantes, however, who steeped his *Galatea* (1585) in Neoplatonism. Because it would have seemed frivolous to discuss mysteries in plain, everyday language, Pico della Mirandola had actually suggested, in *De hominis dignitate*, that official mystagogues should speak in words "editos esse et non editos [to be published and yet not published]," that is, in allegory—in words for the marketplace (*agora*) and yet for other (*allos*) ears.[38] In the introduction to his *Heptaplus*, Pico had exalted the allegorical sense as springing out of the analogical nature of the whole universe.[39] But the mysterious language that distinguished these Renaissance

---

structive allegory of all tropological cognitions, the systematic undoing, in other words, of understanding" (*Allegories of Reading*, 301).

[35] Edwin Williamson—who laments the absence of any study of the history of the term *ironía* in Spanish—sees Cervantes's declaration of ironic intent as expressed by the proverb, in the prologue to pt. 1 of *Don Quixote*, "debajo de mi manto, al rey mato" (*The Half-Way House of Fiction*, 82–83).

[36] Forcione, *Cervantes' Christian Romance*, 54–6.

[37] Mazzoni claimed that none of his arguments were inconsistent with Aristotle's theory (see esp. chaps. 38–42 of *Della difesa della Comedia di Dante*; cited by Weinberg, *Italian Renaissance* 2:879).

[38] Giovanni Pico della Mirandola, *De hominis dignitate, Heptaplus, De ente et uno, e scritti vari*, ed. Eugenio Garin (Florence: Vallecchi, 1942), 156.

[39] "Ab hoc principio (si quis fortasse hoc nondum advertit) totius sensus allegorici disciplina manavit. Nec potuerunt antiqui patres aliis alia figuris decenter repraesentare, nisi occultas, ut ita dixerim, totius naturae et amicitias et affinitates edocti" (*De hominis dignitate*, 192).

adaptations of the Neoplatonists strategically detoured literary analysis: its basis was relentlessly metaphysical. Edgar Wind, who attempts to trace "the mysteries of the ancients" from their introduction by Plato, acknowledges that much of the Neoplatonic tradition has been colored by the eccentricity of its more fervent disciples.[40] It is not their eccentricities, however, but their aversion to "literariness" that makes the Neoplatonists unrewarding for students of literary allegory. Since these Renaissance mystagogues were concerned mostly with ethical or religious criteria, their invocation of these figurative mysteries did little to advance the poetics of allegory. We cannot look to the Renaissance Neoplatonists for any real articulation of the symbolic workings of fiction because fiction was not their province. Pico, indeed, was violently abusive of the art of poetics, even given to inveighing against poetry (which he had loved in his childhood) and to seeing most poems as "made foul by filthiness and obscenities" or as encouraging men "to impure and lewd loves and to lives of drunkenness."[41] Regardless of this antipoetic bias, however, the Neoplatonic sense of literary mysteries aligns itself with the Platonic sense of veiled truths, which, in turn, adumbrates the idea of allegory as a symbolic mode. Mindful that the very origins of allegory were religious rather than literary, we might regard our quest for Cervantes's quest for an allegorical poetics as an interdisciplinary one. When Cervantes invokes his own "figurative mysteries" in the *Persiles*, however, unlike Pico, he writes in defense of poetry.

Whereas the Neoplatonic humanists had based their thinking on Plotinus and his disciples, the Platonic critics of the Cinquecento looked back to Plato, or at least they manifested a critical stance in relation to the key problems of Platonism in literature. But if the Neoplatonist's addiction to esoteric studies may have kept him, at least where poetics was concerned, critically unforthcoming, the Platonists were hampered by a different problem: "The Platonic critic," according to Weinberg, "was essentially a man without a text."[42] Because he was unable to derive his theoretical doctrine from any central text, the Platonic critic was obliged to base his Platonism upon dicta, scattered across various dialogues, on, say, the divine furor, the process of imitation, or the ban on poets. Cervantes shows his familiarity with this last, for example, when he represents the countess Trifaldi as stoutly endorsing the ban, presumably well known to her and

---

[40] Wind surveys these mysteries from their introduction by Plato through their systematization by Plotinus, and from their "betrayal" into magic by Plotinus's followers to their nearly unanimous endorsement by Renaissance Neoplatonists like Landino, Ficino, and Pico, who saw them through the eyes of Plutarch, Porphyry, and Proclus. See *Pagan Mysteries in the Renaissance*, rev. ed. (New York: W. W. Norton, 1968), 1–16.

[41] Weinberg, *Italian Renaissance* 1:256.

[42] Ibid., 250.

her age from book 3 of the *Republic*: "He considerado que de las buenas y concertadas repúblicas se habían de desterrar los poetas, como aconsejaba Platón [I have considered that the poets should be banned from all good, sound republics, as Plato recommended]" (*DQ* 2.38). Platonic critics, in short, looked back to Plato through assumptions, presuppositions, and general attitudes; they did not have the benefit of a body of precepts, such as the *Poetics* gave to the neo-Aristotelians. Regarding notions of allegory, however, the Renaissance Platonists shared with the Neoplatonists the basic assumption that truths come veiled—a point of contact that has critical implications for the kind of allegory we find in the *Persiles*. Such an assumption had its precedent in what Curtius sees as one of the fundamental characteristics of Greek religious thought: "the belief that the gods express themselves in cryptic form—in oracles, in mysteries."[43]

Authors of Cinquecento Platonic treatises seem exceedingly articulate about this doctrine of veiled truth: although they scarcely ever mention the rhetorical uses of allegory, they wax on and on about allegory's underlying meanings and the powers of readers to arrive at them. Both Lodovico Ricchieri in his *Lectionum* (1516) and Bernardino Tomitano in his *Ragionamenti della lingua toscana* (1545), for example, speak of truth as being represented in the "garb" of myths or fictional narratives.[44] This strain of Platonism is virtually indistinguishable from the Horatian view of allegory as a fictional wrapping for beneficial truths. Within the Horatian tradition, allegorical readings could be made to serve the *prodesse* end of Horace's "aut prodesse volunt, aut delectare poetae" (*Ars poetica* 1.333). Cervantes taps this Horatian tradition of "utile dulci" for the prologue to his *Novelas ejemplares*, when he speaks of the "sabroso y honesto fruto que se podría sacar [the delicious and honest fruit that could be extracted]" from all the novelas. The idea of allegory as a fictional wrapping for delicious *fruto* is, of course, as ancient as the earliest allegorical interpretation of Greek myths: before Plato, we find it in Homer and Aeschylus; and after Plato, it flourishes in the practice of the Stoics and Neoplatonists and becomes a poetic resource for Virgil and Ovid. When, in the Renaissance, the interpretation of that fictional "garb" sat-

[43] E. R. Curtius, *European Literature and the Latin Middle Ages*, trans. Willard Trask (New York: Pantheon, 1953), 205.

[44] Cited by Weinberg, *Italian Renaissance* 1:259, 266. Commentators like Cristoforo Landino (1482), Lilio Gregorio Giraldi (1545), and Francesco Lovisini (1554) express this pragmatic view of allegory: meaning purposely hidden under wraps in order to morally improve us. The practical criticism inspired by the *Ars poetica* includes Pietro Pagano's sanctimonious chastisement of Petrarch, who could have been a more profitable poet, "quando si volesse allegoricamente dichiarare, et christianamente [if he had cared to express himself allegorically and in a Christian manner]" (see Weinberg, *Italian Renaissance* 1:189).

isfies the need for prodesse—when what is hidden behind the "veil" prudently teaches the reader what is best in this life ("quid optimum in vita sit," in Lovisini's words)—then we may safely call this reading a Horatian allegory. When, however, we read that only rare intellects can perceive the meaning hidden within the poetry ("l'intention nascosa nella poesia," in Leonardi's words), or when a treatise points to the masses of people who cannot penetrate to the allegorical meaning of the poets, then we have shifted over to more Platonic terrain.[45] This notion of the difficulty of penetrating through to hidden core meanings recalls Pico's earlier self-congratulatory remarks on a philosophical study: "If I am not mistaken, it will be intelligible only to a few, for it is filled with many mysteries from the secret philosophy of the ancients."[46]

By the late 1500s, however, about the time Cervantes is engendering his "stepchild" *Don Quixote* in a prison, a strong reaction appears to arise against the idea of veiled and unintelligible truths, of ineffable revelations and catalogues of arcana. Theorists begin to worry loudly about the opacity of exegetical allegory for ordinary minds, and a high premium is placed on clarity in writing. Even Don Quixote's anxieties that the published book of his exploits—*Don Quixote*, part 1—would require a commentary to be understood ("tendrá necesidad de comento para entenderla") reveals the age's increasing aversion to unintelligibility (2.3). One contemporary poetician concedes that poets may tell the truth "in the guise of allegory," but insists that such truth is simply too inaccesible for pedagogical purposes. And so he concludes in praise of Aristotle, whose poetic theories he regards as both more reasonable and more appropriate for Christian readers and spectators.[47] When concern over the appetites of this audience becomes paramount in critical thinking, the prescription of Aristotelian catharsis is welcomed as a purge for any potential corruption. Toward the close of the sixteenth century, almost all the theoretical schools are joined in what Weinberg calls "a common point of departure, their contempt for the public to which they assumed that poetry was addressed."[48] This contempt, as hindsight tells us, would be tempered by history, specifically by the advent of the pre-Romantics who held that true poetry was incompatible with literary culture, indeed, in Curtius's words, that "it flowered only among barbarians and savages."[49]

[45] Francesco Lovisini, *Commentarius* (1554); Giovanni Giacomo Leonardi's *Discorso qual sia piu utile al mondo ò l'historia ò la poesia* (c. 1550–1560) and *Il dedalione overto del poeta dialogo* (1560). Cited by Weinberg, *Italian Renaissance* 1:134, 271, 278.

[46] Cited by Wind, *Pagan Mysteries*, 10.

[47] Girolama Frachetta, *Dialogo del furore poetico* (1581); cited by Weinberg, *Italian Renaissance* 1:312.

[48] Weinberg, *Italian Renaissance* 1:346–47.

[49] Curtius, *European Literature*, 393–94.

Although detailed analysis of figurative form is a rarity in the Cinquecento, the views of two Renaissance thinkers on the workings of allegory, in texts well known to Cervantes, offer a notable theoretical departure from the notions rehearsed above: Tasso and El Pinciano. Tasso's understanding of allegory, splendidly conflicted, sheds some light on Cervantes's own unexpressed poetics of allegory. Seeing Tasso as having devoted "little theoretical attention to allegory," Forcione finds in the *Discorsi del poema heroico* (1594) that Tasso "presents allegory as one of the rhetorical figures, very similar to enigma in its effect of mystery." According to Forcione, Tasso "asserts" that allegory "is an accidental rather than an essential quality of poetry, and [he] shows little sympathy for a poet's sacrificing verisimilitude in his use of the figure." Theoretically, then, the mature Tasso appears to align himself with the neo-Aristotelian mainstream, although Forcione does allow that, at various points in his career, Tasso "resorts to allegorical readings to justify implausibilities and offenses against strict morality in poetry."[50] This kind of face-saving, retrospective allegorical practice has been variously called "justification allegory," "afterthought allegory," or, in Croce's colorful phrase, "*post festum* allegory."[51] But another kind of allegory appears in Tasso, what Weinberg sees as the "hidden Platonism" in his theorizing: "the extent to which he sees behind every poem or every part of a poem an Idea which the poet seeks to imitate through the happy combination of matter and form."[52] Whether we choose to regard Tasso's earlier *Apologia in difesa della sua Gerusalemme* (1581) as a sop for post-Tridentine religious censors, it is worth noting that its arguments there move well beyond the idea of allegory as either justification or as an "accidental" trope. In this *Difesa*, Tasso sees heroic poetry as composed of both imitation and allegory, "quasi Animale, in cui due Nature si coniungano [like an animal in which two natures are conjoined]." As the contrary of imitation, he declares that allegory concerns "passions and opinions and customs" in what he calls "their intrinsic being": allegory "signifies them more obscurely, with what one might call mysterious notes, and which

[50] Forcione, *Cervantes' Christian Romance*, 56.

[51] "Given the *Gerusalemme Liberata*, the allegory was imagined afterwards; given the *Adone* of Marino, the poet of the lascivious insinuated afterwards that it was written to show how 'immoderate indulgence ends in pain'; given a statue of a beautiful woman, the sculptor can write on a card that the statue represents *Clemency* or *Goodness*." Croce judges this kind of allegory as "harmless," since it does not change the original work of art (*Aesthetic as Science of Expression and General Linguistic*, 2d ed., trans. Douglas Ainslie [London: Vision Press, 1922], 56).

[52] Weinberg, *Italian Renaissance* 1:341. Unlike Forcione, Weinberg sees "the Aristotelian framework" in the *Discorsi* as "well-nigh destroyed by Tasso's attempt to force incompatible materials into it" (2:687).

can be fully understood only by those who know the nature of things."[53] Tasso's notion of "passions and opinions and customs" as being signified "nel lor essere *intrinseco*," anticipating the Wordsworthian coalescence of personification with the passions, suggests a notable divergence from the Aristotelian view of allegory as *ex*trinsic to a literary work, as something of a tropological accessory. Citing part of this very passage to argue that Tasso, unlike his contemporaries, is able to "force the allegorical and the verisimilar" into the same kind of fiction, Montgomery is obliged to invoke the "Platonic connection": "Tasso arbitrarily assumes a comprehensive, essentially Platonic connection between the experience of the senses and the inner life of man, which allows him to read his own work as the endeavor of the soul toward civil and spiritual felicity."[54] This "essentially Platonic connection" in Tasso's *Difesa* will be remotivated by Cervantes in the *Persiles*, a work that internalizes in its pilgrimage narrative, through a remarkable eulogy, "Torcuato Tasso" and his *Jerusalén libertada* (4.6).

Because critics have generally regarded the *Philosophía antigua poética* (1596) as the most influential of all treatises for Cervantes's literary theories, El Pinciano's notions of allegory are especially pertinent. Riley, for one, thinks that El Pinciano might have made Cervantes "cautious" about the use of allegory in the novel.[55] It bears noting, however, that as a single document the *Philosophía* appears to reveal some eclectic if not contradictory attitudes about allegory. El Pinciano uses a seeding metaphor—"sembrar alegorías [to sow allegories]"—to describe the poet's technique, and the corresponding "sacar alegorías [to extract allegories]" to describe the process of interpretation, allegoresis. He claims to forgive Homer and the rest ("Homero y los demás") for occasionally sacrificing imitation to allegory only because they knew no better—they did so as philosophers and not as poets. And he refers to the kind of allegory used by Aesop and others in their moral fables ("apólogos") as "disparates y frívolas [frivolous nonsense]." Allegory, then, either as an unessential trope that writers "sow" and readers "reap," or as the continuous metaphor of a moral fable, would seem a silly and mechanical device to El Pinciano's Aristotelian soul. But that is by no means the whole story of allegory in El Pinciano. In the context of trying to pin down the essence

---

[53] "[L]e passioni, & le opinioni, & i costumi, non solo inquanto essi apparino; ma principalmente nel lor essere intrinseco, & piu oscuramente le significa con note (per cosi dire) misteriose, & che solo da i conoscitori della Natura delle cose possono essere a pieno comprese" (cited by Weinberg, *Italian Renaissance* 1:206–7).

[54] Montgomery, "Allegory and the Incredible Fable," 54–55.

[55] Riley, *Theory of the Novel*, 9. Riley views Cervantes's literary indebtedness in the following "order of priority": "El Pinciano, Tasso, Carvallo, Piccolomini, Huarte, Giraldi Cinthio, Gracián Dantisco, Vives, and possibly Castelvetro" (10).

of the epic, his discourse betrays a Platonic coloring that is unmistakable: the plot or "argumento" of the epic, he claims, "queda hecho cuerpo y materia debaxo de quie[n] se encierra y esconde la otra ánima más perfecta y essencial, dicha alegoría [becomes the body and matter under which is locked and hidden that other more perfect and essential soul, called allegory]."[56] In this Platonic reading, El Pinciano envisions allegory as the soul that animates the body of the epic, a figure as vital for his age as Fletcher's, at the opening of this chapter, is to the modern: allegory as the "lifeblood" of the body of romance.

CERVANTES'S CHARACTERS ON ALLEGORY

The Spanish term *alegoría* is either employed or alluded to by a cluster of Cervantes's more critically minded characters. Readers of *Don Quixote* remember the Humanist Cousin, that self-congratulatory young scholar who accompanies the hero to the Cave of Montesinos, cataloguing en route the works that he ritually dedicates to princes. There is, for one, his *Ovidio español*, where he has revealed the true identity of a Salamanca church-tower angel, of several prominent fountains, and of a certain sewer in Córdoba—a research enterprise he is quick to celebrate for its "alegorías, metáforas y translaciones [allegories, metaphors, and translations]." In his *Supplement to Polydore Virgil*, taking up where the Italian humanist left off in *De inventoribus rerum*, Cervantes's young pedant has exhaustively researched such fields of conjecture as "quién fue el primero que tuvo catarro en el mundo [who was the first man in the world to catch a head cold]" (*DQ* 2.22). The Humanist Cousin, in short, appears to fall into the same fatiguing tradition as Bernardus Sylvestris, the leading allegorical poet of the School of Chartres, who depicts a book of records that reveals, for all time, "why lions are fierce, and why some plants have their virtue in the root, others in the seed."[57] A kind of mechanical inanity invades the scholarship that scrutinizes such origins. Through the Humanist Cousin's inert scraps of erudition and his "this-for-that" *alegorías*, Cervantes shows a mature awareness of the risible excesses committed under the venerable influence of exegetical allegory.

But in two other episodes in the *Quixote*, which cite the practice of allegory if not the term, the sense of ridicule veers notably away from its practitioners. Although the *primo*'s "alegorías" conjure up useless and

[56] López Pinciano, *Philosophía antigua poética* 3:167–76, 2:95, 3:249–50, 3:174–75. From yet another self-styled contemporary Aristotelian, Alessandro Sardi (1586), we are informed that it was Plutarch who made allegory the principal, the essential, part of the poem—as well as its *ánima* (cited by Weinberg, *Italian Renaissance* 2:871–73). El Pinciano, then, may be indebted to Plutarch for his allegorical notions here.

[57] Cited by Lewis, *Allegory of Love*, 93–94.

pedantic exercises, Cervantes appears to view the idea of a poetic fiction locking within itself moral secrets—a fiction that most contemporaneous Platonists were quite ready to call an "allegory"—more favorably. When the curious Anselmo is impertinently about to test his wife's fidelity in *El curioso impertinente*, his best friend and self-fulfilling rival Lothario asks him to be mindful of Ariosto's story of the magic cup: "Puesto que aquello sea ficción poética, tiene en sí encerrados secretos morales dignos de ser advertidos y entendidos e imitados [Granting that it be a poetic fiction, hidden within it are moral secrets worthy of being heeded and understood and imitated]" (*DQ* 1.34). As it turns out, being a poor exegete costs Anselmo his marriage, his health, and his life: because he cannot or does not wish to penetrate the secrets locked within the legendary drinking-glass test, he will never understand the real nature of the disease that he himself allegorizes as an eating disorder.[58]

In yet another episode dealing with allegorical reading, the ridicule of allegoresis is itself ridiculed. When Don Diego de Miranda, "El Caballero del Verde Gabán [the Man in Green]," complains that his son, a student of Latin and Greek at Salamanca, can waste whole days fretting over "si se han de entender de una manera o otra tales y tales versos de Virgilio [if such and such Virgilian lines are to be understood this or that way]" (*DQ* 2.16), we understand his exasperation. But we are also moved, along with Don Quixote, to resist the father's derision. The Man in Green's disgust over his son's love of multiple readings recalls the Cartesian project to purge language of its duplicity. Don Diego's want of literary sensibility is revealed by his insensitive depreciation of poetry to other more lucrative disciplines. Wishing his son to study law or any other *ciencia*, Don Diego incites Don Quixote into one of his most lucid discourses: if the boy does not have to study a discipline "*pane lucrando* [for earning his daily bread]," argues Don Quixote, then the father should stop his careerist grumblings. The Man in Green's scornful attitude toward the unremunerative discipline of poetry will be rectified, once again, by the hero of the *Persiles*, to whom Cervantes gives a long paean to poetry, including the economic observation that "tanto vale cuanto se estima [it is worth as much as it is valued]" (3.2). Seen from this curiously modern perspective, critical interpretation gains in stature even as its extravagances are acknowledged: Virgilian exegetical allegory is both critiqued for its excesses and celebrated for its vital possibilities. This little pedagogical altercation on the pros and cons of allegory may be fruitfully situated within the climate of the Virgilian cult of late paganism, which Ernst Robert Curtius sees as absent during the Renaissance: having gleamed "like a

---

[58] See my treatment of this episode in " 'Passing the Love of Women': The Intertextuality of *El curioso impertinente*," *Cervantes* 7 (Fall 1987): 9–28.

mystic lamp in the evening of the aging world," it was then extinguished, "for almost a millennium and a half," until the Romantic period. Curtius's assessment of the contributions of the Virgilian cult—that it "first expressed the idea of the poet as creator, if only gropingly"—is most suggestive in the light of Cervantes's own pre-Romantic gropings toward a similar poetics.[59]

Perhaps the most enigmatic treatment of that "sentido que he oído decir se llama alegórico [meaning which I've heard say is called 'allegorical']" appears in the *Coloquio de los perros* (1613), an exemplary novel whose very title suggests one of the more déclassé kinds of Renaissance allegory—the so-called "false or incredible" beast fable. Within this story, the dog Cipión cites and proceeds to interpret literally an oracle whose exegesis is to be his liberation from bestiality. In a kind of canine cognition of *de te fabula narratur*, Cipión directs the oracle's prophecy at himself and his brother Berganza. But then he peremptorily rejects "el sentido alegórico [the allegorical sense]" in favor of "el literal [the literal]." The oracle itself, as conveyed by the witch Cañizares, promises the dogs' transformation into their true form when they witness an inversion of worldly power, namely, the fall of the high and mighty, and the rise of the downtrodden ("Derribar los soberbios levantados / Y alzar a los humildes abatidos"). Cipión's "literal" reading refuses to embrace, however, the import of the two venerable texts subtending this elusive prophecy: Mary's Magnificat and Anchises' prophecy in Virgil's *Aeneid* ("parcere subiectis et debellare superbos") (6.853). Incorporated within the oracle, these texts produce a violent intertextuality that, as Forcione notes, degrades and even disfigures them.[60]

For all their venerable values, however, there are elements in these supercanonical texts that—like Cervantes's deceitful soldier narrating the dog's colloquy, who has "asked for" a disfiguring case of syphilis—invite disfigurement. Let us remember that both the *Aeneid* and the Magnificat are myths of origin that erase female sexuality: either consigning it, in the name of *pietas*, to a bodiless underworld; or reconstituting it, in the name of patriarchy, as immaculate. Fernando de Vera y Mendoza's contention, in 1627, that the Virgin Mary composed verses "tan sentenciosos como

[59] For the excesses of Virgilian allegoresis, see the *Continentia Vergiliana* of Fulgentius (c. 480–550), which interpreted the whole of the *Aeneid* as an allegory of man's life, and which even the hospitable Boccaccio considered as "too fanciful, recondite, and unreliable" (Charles G. Osgood, *Boccaccio on Poetry* [Princeton: Princeton University Press, 1930], xvii). For the positive side of the Virgilian cult of late paganism, however, see Curtius, *European Literature*, 400–401.

[60] Alban Forcione sees the oracle's intertextuality with the Magnificat and the *Aeneid* as "a travesty of the sacred," a "disfigurement of two venerable texts" capable of "infuriating its readers" (*Cervantes and the Mystery of Lawlessness: A Study of* El casamiento engañoso y El coloquio de los perros [Princeton: Princeton University Press, 1984], 47).

los lyricos de su Magnificat [as pithy as the lyrics of her Magnificat]" is rightly understood, in Elizabeth Rhodes's words, as "a double-edged sword designed to inspire women's creative impulses, while leading them into the repressive circle of Virgin-imitation."[61] In a gesture that comments upon the Virgin's exclusion from human sexuality, Cervantes tries to create a bridge, a playful and alliterative link, between the divine birth of Christ and the shameful birth of the dogs: "Este perruno parto de otra parte viene, y algún misterio contiene [This doggish birth comes from another source, and it contains some mystery]." But the dog Cipión shows a stubborn aversion to confronting this "mystery": his rejection of allegory in favor of literality is followed in the text, strategically, by his rejection of his own base origins, specifically of his mother Montiela. Cipión cannot bear to think of himself as a son-of-a-witch: "Que yo no la quiero tener por madre [I don't want to have her for a mother]." As readers of the oracle along with Cervantes's wonderfully loquacious dogs, however, we are discouraged from opting for Cipión's "literal" reading of the text of his "delivery": his method of reading is here equated with a refusal of the mystery and the shame of origins, with a denial of the mother. Indeed, the "other" (allos) texts incorporated into the parodic oracle encourage us to read it as a critique of those symbolic orders where, as Cervantes's talking dog documents the event, the first word uttered by nursing infants is the curse of "puta [whore!]" flung at their mothers.

The allegorical oracle at the core of Cervantes's canine colloquy inverts, in addition, the celebrated orders of aggression of its two prestigious subtexts. Long before the Virgilian prophecy found its way into Cervantes's colloquy, it was roundly critiqued by Saint Augustine: "To be merciful to the conquered and beat the haughty down" was a phrase that emblematized, for Augustine in A.D. 413, the arrogant self-praise "of that city which lusts to dominate the world."[62] Mary's Magnificat, too, has been exposed, if along less aggressive lines, as both "bellicose and triumphalist."[63] As a parody of its precursors, then, Cervantes's oracle ironizes empire, suggesting in its inversion a truly Erasmian critique of the ideology of conquest. When, in addition, the schoolboys in the Colo-

---

[61] Rhodes, "Skirting the Men," 136. In an altogether different context, Geoffrey Hartman reflects on how the Annunciation "magnifies" a woman—how it "issues in a Magnificat" because it removes from her the "curse" of "impure, because infertile, menstruation: A potential denunciation becomes an annunciation" ("Psychoanalysis: The French Connection," in Literature and Psychoanalysis, ed. Edith Kurzweil and William Phillips [New York: Columbia University Press, 1983], 354).

[62] Saint Augustine, City of God, trans. Gerald G. Walsh, s.j., Demetrius B. Zema, s.j., Grace Monahan, o.s.u., and Daniel J. Honan (New York: Image Books, 1958), bk. 1, 40.

[63] Marina Warner, Alone of All Her Sex: The Myth and the Cult of the Virgin Mary (New York: Vintage, 1983), 13.

quio sell their grammar books (their "Antonios") in order to feed their beloved dog, the ideology famously inscribed in Antonio Nebrija's prologue to his 1492 *Gramática castellana*—hailing Language as the "compañera del Imperio [handmaiden of Empire]"—is tacitly debunked. Through the *Coloquio's* exceedingly complex case of double citation allegory, then, Cervantes signals a desire to move beyond the Western narrative epic tradition of quest and conquest.

PERSONIFICATION IN THE *PERSILES*

Having examined how Cervantes's characters—whether fathers or lovers, pedants or dogs—envision allegory, it is time to sample what Cervantes himself does with it in the *Persiles*. The remainder of this chapter will discuss the text's three blatant scenes of personification, for all critics a staple of allegory and the most trustworthy evidence of its presence. As it turns out, Cervantes engendered a surprising population of personified abstractions throughout his career, beginning with those "moral figures" he brought to the stage who were designed to reveal "hidden thoughts": allegorical figures such as "Comedia" and "Curiosidad" in *El rufián dichoso* (act 2), or the clutch of patriotic personifications—Fame, Spain, the River Duero, Disease, Hunger, and War—in the *Numancia*. *Don Quixote* features various flamboyant personifications in the "Carreta de las Cortes de la Muerte" episode (2.2), as well as in the speaking masque within the "Bodas de Camacho" episode, starring a serene little company of concepts such as "Amor" and "Interés," who lead two trains of dancing personifications (2.20). The semicomatose Durandarte, languishing in his crystal palace within the Cave of Montesinos, may be, in addition, an unwitting personification of Roland's sword (2.23). And Cide Hamete's pen ("péñola") is personified in situ, when the Arab historian instructs her to shout "¡Tate, tate, folloncicos! [Beware, beware, you rogues!]" in order to deflect any future historians who might try to "profane" her (2.74). When we move from *Don Quixote* to the *Persiles*, however, we find a denser population of personifications, Cervantes's last work being an allegorical text where even "Silence" speaks (1.10).

The rhetorical technique of personifying objects (such as pens) and ideas (such as silence), of giving them a semblance of personhood, is also known as *prosopopeia*, a Latin transliteration of the Greek composite term.[64] This "figure of thought" applied to the practice of fashioning a presence for an absence—what Cervantes called representing "the hidden

---

[64] The original Greek composite term, which Quintilian first transliterated, corresponds to "personification" (from the Latin *persona* + *facere* = to make a mask/person). The *Rhetorica ad Herennium* expresses the trope as *conformatio* and groups it among "figures of thought" (4.53).

thoughts of the soul"—emerged into prominence centuries earlier, with the advent of Prudentius's *Psychomachia* (c. A.D. 405), the first full-scale personification allegory. This work, and by tradition any succeeding psychomachia, featured a clutch of theatrical personified abstractions, agents of Virtue and Vice engaged in a full-pitched battle. Prudentius is significant for our study of Cervantine allegory because, among his cast of personified puppets, he included one "Libido," a Latin precursor of Cervantes's "SENSUALIDAD," whose capitalized personhood will be addressed in what follows. Cervantes seems to acknowledge the *Psychomachia* as a subtext when the narrator of the *Persiles* recalls the island where the dreaming hero saw "los dos escuadrones de virtudes y vicios [the two squadrons of virtues and vices]" (3.1). That Prudentius was also responsible for the technical shift, or expansion, into continuous allegory of what had formerly been "isolated allegories" fortifies his intertextuality with Cervantes.[65]

Nothing will repel a modern reader more rapidly than the approach of a squadron of virtues and vices, but here we must pause to wonder why a writer who could create a Sancho Panza or a Maritornes would reach for such *invisibilia*. Why would Cervantes resort to naive allegory? What are the stakes in his resurrecting a psychomachia? Personifications of all stamps have had a bad press in the past few centuries. We recall how neatly Dr. Johnson castrated the trope for the English tradition: "Thus Fame tells a tale and Victory hovers over a general or perches on a standard; but Fame and Victory can do no more."[66] Coleridge's later hostility to what he called the "rage for personification" might have been tempered, however, had he recognized the same rage dwelling in what he called "the perfectly sane mind of Cervantes."[67] Wordsworth, another reader of Cervantes, abjured the figure of personification because he wished, oddly, "to keep the reader in the company of flesh and blood" and within earshot of "the very language of men," although Barbara Johnson wonders, with some justice, whether he did not, instead, transfer "the abuse from personifications to persons."[68] In any event, because Wordsworth did allow that personifications are "often prompted by passion," readers of Cervantes may wonder what passion prompted him in

[65] For an excellent discussion of the consolidation of the *Psychomachia* as an allegorical poem, see Whitman, *Allegory*, 83–91.

[66] Samuel Johnson, "The Life of Milton," in *Works*, ed. Arthur Murphy (New York: A. V. Blake, 1843), 2:241–55.

[67] In Coleridge's citation of Cervantes, "the general truth may be unconsciously in the writer's mind during the construction of the symbol; and it proves itself by being produced out of his own mind—as *Don Quixote* out of the perfectly sane mind of Cervantes" (*Miscellaneous Criticism*, ed. T. M. Raysor [London, 1936], 29).

[68] Barbara Johnson bases her arresting speculation on the indisputable fact that women in the Wordsworth canon tend to be "abused, mad, or dead" (*A World of Difference*, 97).

the *Prelude* to personify that "Arab phantom" of his reverie into a "living man."[69] This chapter is scarcely the place, however, to rehearse the slow loss of purchase of the trope of personification from Cervantes to the present. It is perhaps sufficient for our purposes to note that Cervantes's tropes formed part of a goodly company of Renaissance personifications that included such vivid figures as Spenser's Despair, Shakepeare's Time, and Milton's Laughter.

Cervantes's personifications in the *Persiles*, three pageants of them, all deal with erotic problems, the first two in an inert, even naive, way. At the celebratory boat races that follow the scene of the fishermen's double wedding in book 2, the rowers race under the insignias of four allegorical entities: Cupid, Diligence, Good Fortune, and Self-Interest. Although some mordancy lurks in the idea that Cupid is incapacitated by Self-Interest in this nautical competition, in the thought that Diligence is as unrewarding a virtue as Self-Interest is a vice, or in the notion that Good Fortune is all that is needed to win love, these abstractions seem thin and dull and exhibit, as it were, all their devices. They provide a good working example of the twilight of the personifications, to wrench a line from C. S. Lewis, who notes in the context of Statius that "the twilight of the gods is the mid-morning of the personifications."[70]

Later in book 1, Cervantes weaves into the main narrative a second tapestry of allegorical figures, Clodio and Rosamunda, a middle-aged couple from England, the one by career a satirist and *maldiciente*, the other, a woman of "torpes apetitos [base appetites]." Enchained to each other in a highly emblematic pose, the two figure forth, respectively, the intertwined agencies of Satire and Lust (1.12, 1.14). The *significatio* of Rosamunda as a personification newly minted by Satire is revealing: it is the satirist Clodio who labels her, through a *munda/inmunda* Latin wordplay, as an "unclean" woman: "O Rosamunda, o por mejor decir, rosa inmunda [O Rosamond, or to put it better, O Unclean Rose]" (1.14). After an attempted but unsuccessful seduction of an "inesperto mozo [inexperienced youth]," Rosamunda-Lust repents and dies of natural causes.[71] Clodio-Satire, however, who confesses that the sins of his

---

[69] "Full often, taking from the world of sleep / This Arab phantom which I thus beheld, / This semi-Quixote, *I to him have given / A substance, fancied him a living man*" (*The Prelude* 1799, 1805, 1850, ed. Jonathan Wordsworth, M. H. Abrams, and Stephen Gill [New York: W. W. Norton, 1979], 159; emphasis added). See Wordsworth's "Preface to Lyrical Ballads" for his rejection of personifications (*Literary Criticism of William Wordsworth*, ed. Paul M. Zall [Lincoln: University of Nebraska Press, 1966], 44–45).

[70] Lewis, *Allegory of Love*, 52.

[71] How Rosamond Clifford, the mistress of England's Henry II (1133–1189), found her way into a Spanish narrative that purports to be set in the mid–sixteenth century is as curious as how her reputation for wantonness, which seems to have been strictly Continental, was disseminated. In the "Complaint of Rosamond," for instance, the sixteenth-century

tongue have been legion, is killed in book 2 by an arrow through the tongue (2.8), a death that reiterates the homicidal practices on the Barbaric Isle (1.4).

The last pageant of personification in the *Persiles* merits our closest look, because it reveals Cervantes's allegorical techniques *in ovo*. In this episode (2.15), the erotic comes alive posthumously, as it were, personified for the first time in Cervantes's career with the publication of the *Persiles* the year after his death (1617). Gendered as a "she," the erotic materializes here as "SENSUALIDAD." She appears to Cervantes's hero in a dream, and she walks and talks. It is instructive to address the "personhood" of SENSUALIDAD, not only because she sheds some retrospective logic on Don Quixote's dream in the Cave of Montesinos (*DQ* 2.23), but also because she remains the *Persiles*'s Exhibit A of the technique of personification.

The dream plot, which will be presented in more detail in what follows, has a familiar allegorical ring.[72] The dreamer arrives at an island paradise; he witnesses two parades of ladies ("los dos escuadrones de virtudes y vicios"); he cites a garbled version of Garcilaso's Sonnet 10 and abruptly awakens. On the day before the dream, his ship had encountered some vast sea-beasts that rained water out of holes ("ventanas") beneath their eyes. The neck of one of these—"como de serpiente terrible [like a terrible serpent]"—had slithered onto the ship's deck and gobbled up a mariner. Cervantes chooses to call these marine serpents "náufragos" [shipwrecks]," denaturalizing them through a cause-and-effect metonymy.[73] Although the hero and his mariners escape these sea-beasts as if fleeing from a huge enemy "armada" ("como si huyéramos de alguna gruesa armada de enemigos"), the serpents return that night in his dream of an island paradise irrigated by streams of liquified diamonds that resemble "sierpes de cristal [crystal serpents]" (240–41). An elementary Freudian reading would regard these metaphoric dream serpents as the day's residue from that "real" armada of sea-beasts, and perhaps go on to invoke childhood animal phobias, arguing that wild animals in dreams

---

English poet Samuel Daniel unambiguously pictures Henry II as her first and only lover (see *Poems and a Defense of Ryme*, ed. Arthur Colby Sprague [Cambridge, Mass.: Harvard University Press, 1930], 39–63).

[72] In "The Method of Interpreting Dreams," Freud writes that "what we must take as the object of our attention is not the dream as a whole ["en masse"] but the separate portions of its content" ["en detail"] (*SE* 4:136).

[73] This sea-beast is described by Olaf Magnusson (*History*, bk. 21) and Torquemada (*Jardín de flores curiosas*, bk. 6) under the name of *physeter* (*fisiter*). See Schevill and Bonilla's useful note on the *náufrago*, explaining that Cervantes took the name from the "naufragi grandissimi" on the captions of Italian engravings of physeters in action, and including several reproductions of these *láminas* or engravings (*Persiles*, 346–48).

represent sexual fears.[74] This twentieth-century allegory is precisely borne out by the rest of Cervantes's dream, which is a pageant of terrifying sexuality.

The dream island the hero visits is startling for its abundant lapidary iconography, its most insistent image being stones, precious stones to begin with, metaphorizing the dream landscape: gold and pearls for the coastline; emeralds for the meadows; rubies, topazes, and amber for its forests of fruit trees. Even the obligatory serpent in this garden is troped as "crystal." This entirely mineralized landscape dimly recalls the garden of God in Ezekiel's Eden, where there were precious stones instead of fruit trees (Ezek. 28:13). A parallel from Cervantes's own day may be found in Marinell's "rich strond," that seashore in Spenser's *Fairie Queene* composed of "pretious stones" that Britomart despises (3.4.18–20). Yet another Spenserian analogue, one with more sexual resonances, may be found near the entrance to the Bower of Bliss, in the Porch made of rubies, emeralds, and jacinths, under whose jeweled grapevines the figure of Excesse squeezes wine into her golden bowl (2.12.54). Perhaps the most generative subtext for Cervantes's dreamscape of petrified fruits lies within the *Persiles* itself, however, in the chapter just preceding the dream vision, where the "trees" of a ship's rigging "produce the fruit" of forty hanged men (237). The hero's dream vision may be responding more to the waking nightmare of Sulpicia's ship, covered with the blood and severed limbs of her would-be rapists, than to that slithering sea-serpent, which functions as a kind of manifest screen. The episode of this avenging pirate woman, to be taken up in more detail in chapter 7, reveals a striking narrative connection with the hero's dream vision: both tales dramatize the cost of male libido, constrained and unconstrained. Cervantes's Sulpicia—wearing a helmet shaped like a coiled serpent ("enroscada sierpe") and adorned with an infinite number of variously colored stones ("piedras de colores variados")—serves as a kind of fierce guide into the hero's libidinal dreamworld of serpents and stones.

Although his dream landscape is described as a place wholly undisturbed by the seasons ("las *diferencias* del año"; 241)—undisturbed, in fact, by any *difference*—the disturbance begins with the advent of SENSUALIDAD. The imagery of precious stones gives way to that of solid rock as she emerges, literally, from the heart of a rock ("del corazón de una peña") and, Medusa-like, petrifies all the men: "Estábamos atónitos, como si fuéramos estatuas sin voz, de dura piedra formados [We were struck dumb, like statues without voice, all formed of hard rock]." We marvel at how uncannily Cervantes dramatizes "the latent thread" that, for de Man, inhabits prosopopeia, a trope whose symmetrical structure

---

[74] See Freud, *SE* 5.410, 394.

implies that, by making a "dead" personification speak, by the same token, "the living are struck dumb" ("estábamos atónitos"; 243).[75] The
sign of all this petrification is SENSUALIDAD, perhaps Cervantes's most
arresting personification, who rides into the dream, trumpets blaring, in
a carriage shaped like a broken-down ship, pulled by twelve powerful and
lascivious apes ("doce poderosísimos jimios [simios], animales lascivos";
242). This simian imagery, although wanting in classical solemnity, is frequent in Renaissance iconography.[76] The Platonic metaphor, from the
Phaedrus, of steeds for the baser passions is yielding, across the Renaissance, to images like Othello's "goats and monkeys." The twelve apes of
Periandro's dream pull the leading lady into the scene, a very handsome
woman ("hermosísima dama") dressed in a parti-colored outfit and
crowned with bitter yellow oleanders. Near her "person" is a black rod
on which an escutcheon identifies her, in eleven uppercase letters, as
"SENSUALIDAD." If one capital letter increases the potential for personification, as Coleridge averred, readers of Cervantes must wonder what
eleven will do.[77] In any case, this overendowed personification is a caricature of herself, or, in psychoanalytic parlance, "overdetermined."
When she speaks to the hero, it is a revealing one-liner: "Costarte ha,
generoso mancebo, el ser mi enemigo, si no la vida, a lo menos el gusto
[Being my enemy, young man, shall cost you, if not your life, at least your
pleasure]." The dream message here, a long way from Prudentius, would
seem to be about the wages not of sin but of virtue.

But another leading lady, Auristela-Sigismunda, enters this allegorical
dream, and she comes to the rescue flanked by two decorous personifications, who introduce themselves as Continence and Shame ("la Continen-
cia" and "la Pudicia"). What is striking about this episode is that Cervantes takes advantage of the personification process, in which an idea or
concept is given personhood, to turn his own heroine into a personified

---

[75] Paul de Man, "Autobiography as Defacement," *MLN* 94 (1979): 928.

[76] Cervantes's simian imagery may be a chaste echo of a contemporaneous "Gorillas-in-
the-Mist" story reported in Torquemada's *Jardín de flores curiosas*, a text cited during the
scrutiny of Don Quixote's library (1.6). The "Tratado Primero" of Torquemada's work
includes the report of a woman who, for some crime she had committed, was abandoned
on an island populated by "muy gran cantidad de ximios [a great quantity of apes]," one of
which "vino a aprovecharse de ella [took advantage of her]" ([Madrid: Editorial Tradicio-
nalista, 1943], 74–76; cited by Stanislav Zimic, "El *Persiles* como crítica de la novela bizantina," *Acta Neophilologica* 3 [1970]: 55n).

[77] In a discussion of Gray's "YOUTH at the prow and PLEASURE at the helm" (*The Bard*, l.
74), Coleridge notes that whether "mere abstracts" would turn into a personification
seemed to depend on a typographical distinction: namely, on whether or not they were
printed with capitals. See *Biographia literaria*, vol. 1 of *The Collected Works of Samuel
Taylor Coleridge*, ed. James Engell and W. Jackson Bate (Princeton: Princeton University
Press, 1983), 20.

puppet. Her two handmaidens explain to the dreaming hero that Auristela is not really herself, that the figure of Chastity has today chosen to "disguise herself as" his beloved Auristela ("Castidad . . . que en figura de tu querida . . . Auristela hoy ha querido disfrazarse"). Whereas Spenser in *The Faerie Queene* turns a character into an abstraction—Malbecco into Jealousy ("Gealosie") (3.10)—Cervantes here turns an abstraction into a character: Chastity "becomes" Auristela, but a false Auristela. Her literary production, indeed, seems to resemble that of Spenser's "false Florimell," into whom a "Spright" is installed "to rule the carkasse dead" (3.8). Considering Auristela's overpudicity—her obsessive concern, throughout the novel, with her *pudor*—Cervantes's inversion is distinctly ironic.

The response of the dreamer to the appearance of his beloved, to this abstraction masquerading as a woman, is to convert her, by a hysterical trope, into precious stones. Already an abstract quality or idea, she is apostrophized, courtesy of the garbled sonnet from Garcilaso, as "Oh ricas prendas por mi bien halladas [Oh precious stones, discovered for my own good]."[78] As the supposed creator of these personified concepts, Cervantes's dreaming hero constitutes himself as both endangered and reactive. Having been petrified by SENSUALIDAD, he now proceeds to petrify his own chaste lady. The cultural recipe for crystallizing, for "fixing," sexual otherness here could not be more complete. Sexuality, in this fictional Golden Age dream, would seem to be somewhere between a rock and a hard place.

With his apostrophe to Chastity, a figure of speech to a figure of speech, the dreamer abruptly awakens. The uses of personification in this dream illustrate the sensual and continent parts of the hero's nature in a pictorial and condensed manner. The complex imagery of the pageant—the emerald meadows, the musical rocks, the nautical chariot, the squadrons of chaste and sensual ladies, and even those mighty monkeys—provides an amazing mapa mentis of the Golden Age male confronting female Oth-

---

[78] The dreamer's two-line poem—"Oh ricas prendas por mi bien halladas, dulces y alegres en este y en otro cualquier tiempo!"—parodies and distorts Garcilaso's famous Sonnet 10, beginning "Oh dulces prendas por mi mal halladas. . . ." Later in the *Persiles* we read that Garcilaso's works had just been published, an event that occurred in 1543; that they were popular among Northern (i.e., Icelandic) circles of courtiers; and that Periandro had read and admired them some time back (3.8). Garcilaso's Sonnet 10 is often cited for its adulterous and postmortem context, the dramatic situation of the poem being the discovery of some trinkets that had belonged to his now dead mistress, who was another man's wife. For an account of Garcilaso's courtship of Doña Isabela Freire, see Elías Rivers' edition of the *Poesías completas* (Madrid: Castalia, 1969), 11. Casting doubts on this courtship is Frank Goodwyn's essay, "New Light on the Historical Setting of Garcilaso's Poetry," *Hispanic Review* 46 (1978): 1–22. Cervantes also cited Garcilaso de la Vega in *Don Quixote* 2.18 and in *La guarda cuidadosa*.

erness. But Cervantes's strategies of personification also inscribe change: his hero configures both the Renaissance fictions of love and the ways in which such fictions were beginning to collapse. No longer could the courtly verses of Garcilaso be cited properly, not even in a dream.

The fact that this dream rewrites an entirely asexual dream in Heliodorus's *Aethiopica*—the aged Calasiris's dream encounter with Odysseus—reveals that Cervantes has explicitly eroticized his avowed model: Odysseus had threatened that Calasiris would have to "pay" merely for not having saluted him as he sailed by Ithaca.[79] The dream in Heliodorus glosses the ancient belief that, as Honig recalls it, "dreams speak the symbolic language of a super-intelligence communicating commands and cautions which the reason is unwise to dismiss." That belief is transformed into the modern notion, the one fictionalized by Cervantes's dream of personifications, that "the irrationality of dreams has a meaning which the reason fears to admit."[80] Whereas Heliodorus's Odysseus is a "super-intelligence," the fantastic and abstract personification of Cervantes's SENSUALIDAD is closer to what we moderns would call a subconscious intelligence. Although both dreamers, ancient and modern, have failed to render homage to a major power, only Cervantes's dreamer has personified the binary nature of his erotic desire. As he participates in the pageant of his own sexual ambivalence, his dream reveals a world of concentrated psychic stress. Insofar as it depicts the self-embattled psyche of an "impersonating" male adult—the crystalline world he visits, the agreeableness of the dream landscape, the undecidability of the dream in its manifest presentation, and the "love and cash" nexus at its core—Periandro's allegorical dream furnishes useful retrospective logic for Don Quixote's earlier dream in the Cave of Montesinos. Aligning Cervantes's two dreaming heroes, in a kind of "coloquio de los sueños" [colloquy of the dreams]," is a revealing critical exercise.[81] If Don Quixote's venting sub-

[79] As an Egyptian gymnosophist and chief narrator of the calamities of Theagenes and Chariclea, Calasiris is a revered elderly figure whose dreams have cautionary aspects remotivated by Cervantes. In the dream in question, a limping and desiccated but astute-looking old man accuses the dreamer Calasiris of ignoring his dwelling place, of not saluting his memory, when he sailed by the island of Cephalonia (south of Ithaca). For this oversight, the unnamed Odysseus prophesies that Calasiris must imitate his own wandering life, suffering similar calamities on land and sea. The key phrase in Odysseus's threatening prophecy may have provided Cervantes the germ for SENSUALIDAD's warning about the "cost" of being her enemy: "Mas no pasará mucho que lo paguéis [But before long you will pay for it]" (*Historia etiópica*, 202–3).

[80] Honig, *Dark Conceit*, 69.

[81] Don Quixote's dream had featured a "cristalino palacio," with interiors of "alabastro [alabaster]" and "mármol [marble]"; he too had carried a false name and identity throughout his novel; he too had reinforced the incertitude of dreaming ("vi que no dormía, sino que realmente estaba despierto"); he too had exalted his dream (as "la más sabrosa y agradable vida y vista que ningún humano ha visto ni pasado"); he too had confronted two

conscious released material that subverted his system, what is rising from
Periandro's subconscious? His dream, indeed, would seem to be a less
displaced version of Don Quixote's dream of unaffordable sexuality—of
the excessive cost, for a man with only *cuatro reales*, of redeeming Dulcinea's petticoat. SENSUALIDAD comes "in person" to the dreamer in the
Persiles, not "in a camouflaged form," as Freud would have it,[82] but as
herself in all of her bold-faced literality. Unlike the psychoanalytic symbols that veil repression—and unlike her more covert role in Don Quixote's dream vision—Cervantes's SENSUALIDAD does not need decipher-
ing. It is the Golden Age figure of Chastity who arrives, perversely, in a
layer of disguise.

ANTICIPATING FREUD'S ALLEGORIES

What Freud was to uncover—the startling picture of human beings un-
avoidably riven by unconscious sexual needs and desires, urges and guilts,
fears and aggressions—is the historical consequence of the representations of poets and philosophers who, long before the advent of psychoanalysis, had known about an unconscious mental region that dreamers
could access. Cervantes's dream in the *Persiles* singles him out as one of
these pioneers. He chose to set his sexual allegory in a dream because, in
advance of Freud but following, as did Freud, a tradition of dream interpretation reaching back to the ancients, Cervantes saw dreams as an expression long understood to be allegorical, that is, as having "other"
meanings that call for interpretation. Harold Bloom notes, with some justice, that "our map or general theory of the mind may be Freud's," but
Bloom is too myopic in claiming that Freud, "like all the rest of us, inherits the representation of mind, at its most subtle and excellent, from

---

squadrons of ladies ("dos hileras de hermosísimas damas"); and he too had created, in his
dream, an abstraction who metaphorized love as money (2.22–23). On the "love and cash"
nexus, see Javier Herrero's admirable reading of Cervantes's parody, in "Emerging Realism:
Love and Cash in *La ilustre fregona*," in *From Dante to García Márquez: Studies in Romance Literatures and Linguistics*, ed. Gene H. Bell-Villada, Antonio Giménez, and George
Pistorius (Williamstown, Mass.: Williams College, 1987), 47–59.

[82] See Freud, *SE* 5.396; also *SE* 9.123–38. Freud's interpretation of dreams is being radically challenged by the new neurophysiological model of "the dreaming brain" as developed at Harvard University by Allan Hobson and colleagues. This brain-based theory may
provide the model for some as yet undreamed of neurophilosophies. Unlike the Freudian
model of dream activity, the Hobson-McCarley model holds that the significant content of
dreams *is* the manifest content, redolent with meanings that the dreamer can read directly
and literally, without any decoding. In dreams, according to Hobson, a cigar *is* a cigar—
and not only, as Freud put it, "sometimes." See J. Allan Hobson, *The Dreaming Brain* (New
York: Basic Books, 1988).

Shakespeare."[83] Freud inherited the representation of mind from multiple predecessors, including Cervantes, whose eminent candidacy for this visionary company must now be acknowledged. Although Freud refers to Cervantes some half-dozen times in the *Standard Edition*,[84] it is not generally known that, as a young man, Freud appropriated the secret name of Cipión—"Ich, Scipion"—in private conversations and correspondence with a boyhood friend called Silberstein. In an instructive reading of this identification, S. B. Vranich shows how Cipión's analytic role in the novel anticipates Freud's lifetime professional career: the talking dog Cipión "puts things into perspective, separates reality from fantasy, and evaluates and interprets the events that have molded his interlocutor's [Berganza's] personality."[85]

Further affinities may be traced between Cervantes and the mature Freud, who would himself use—if guardedly—the adjective "allegorical" in connection with dreams: dream-work needing to represent "highly abstract thoughts from waking life," he allowed, will sometimes reach for *other (allos)* intellectual material—"somewhat loosely related (*often in a manner which might be described as 'allegorical'*)."[86] Could Freud have coaxed Cervantes's hero to his couch, he would very likely have interpreted Periandro's personified dream as a "castration scenario," decoding the cleft "peña" from which SENSUALIDAD emerges as the Medusa-like petrifying female genitalia, the broken-down ship that conveys her as the uterus, and the black "bastón" with her escutcheon (an "ebony rod" in the 1741 English translation) as the phallus. The lure of Freudian interpretation, perhaps the master discourse of our time, tempts us to forget that Freud based his self-described "scientific project" on figurative writing, that he gave us essentially a new rhetoric of tropes, of versions of the mind that were themselves to become new figures. Stephen Greenblatt has written, in the context of the French trial of Martin Guerre, of how the Renaissance fashioned a "historical mode of selfhood that psychoanalysis has tried to universalize into the very form of the human condition." In Greenblatt's terms, and not only his terms, Cervantes's dream would pro-

---

[83] Harold Bloom, *Ruin the Sacred Truths: Poetry and Belief from the Bible to the Present* (Cambridge, Mass.: Harvard University Press, 1989), 58.

[84] See Freud, *SE* 6:181n; 8:71, 141, 231n; 13:51; 19:289.

[85] S. B. Vranich, "Sigmund Freud and 'The Case History of Berganza': Freud's Psychoanalytic Beginnings," *The Psychoanalytic Review* 63 (1976): 80.

[86] Freud, *SE* 5.524; emphasis added. In the John Huston film called *Freud* (1962), Anna O. is cured when she understands the "allegorical" manner—when Dr. Freud tells her, "This makes your dream an allegory." For an excellent essay on this film, see Diane Waldman and Janet Walker, "John Huston's *Freud* and Textual Repression: A Psychoanalytic Feminist Reading," in *Close Viewings*, ed. Peter Lehman (Tallahassee: Florida State University Press, 1990).

vide "the classic materials" of what we now recognize as Freudian speculation.[87]

I have found it fruitful here to probe at Cervantes's historical modes of selfhood, to situate his hero's dream within the context of personification rather than castration, within a literary rather than a psychoanalytic discourse. The role of personification within Renaissance dreams remains largely unexplored: its forms and meanings and presuppositions; its role as a figure "prompted by passion"; and its signification, in turn, of the passion that motivated it. We might usefully measure Cervantes's minting of SENSUALIDAD against the notion that the trope of personification is rooted in causality, that the device is prompted by a writer's attempt to track down the causes of things. Or we could align it against Huizinga's less anxious account of the roots of the personifying impulse, a theory of origins that is notable for its curious personification of allegory itself: "allegory is born," he writes, because the mind, having attributed "a real existence" to an idea, "wants to see this idea alive, and can only effect this by personifying it."[88] We might consider, further, what it means for a dreamer to call SENSUALIDAD into being, to will her into a speaking subject who constitutes the dreamer himself as endangered.

Cervantes's allegorical dream, in sum, moves us to reconsider the deep and mysterious correspondence between figures of speech as formal techniques and the processes of the unconscious that Freud would map. This dream invites us to inquire about the obscure linkages between prosopopoeia and projection. Fletcher has remarked on "our psychological and linguistic uncertainty as to what is going on when language is used figuratively," stressing that "figurative language is not understood at the present time in any final way."[89] Similarly, Freud himself allowed that the projection of inner perceptions of emotional or ideational processes is "a primitive mechanism" that operates "under conditions that have not been sufficiently determined." What literature has for millennia recognized as the technique of personification is clinically depicted by Melanie Klein as an infantile process of anxiety: "What we discover in the analysis of every child [is] *that things represent human beings*, and therefore are things of anxiety." By the same token, Jung has asserted that whatever adults wish to repress or conceal will typically become personified in their dreams as the "shadow" figure. Freud, and psychologies other than Freud's, have translated projection "back into psychology," to cite Freud's own motivated rhetoric, without consulting the literary personifier, the maker of prosopopoeia who, like Cervantes, also turns signs—especially signs of

[87] Greenblatt, "Psychoanalysis and Renaissance Culture," 216.

[88] Johan Huizinga, *The Waning of the Middle Ages*, trans. F. Hopman (New York: St. Martin's Press, 1967), 205.

[89] Fletcher, *Allegory*, 11.

sexual anxiety—into agents.[90] Why primitive men, anxious children, allegorical heroes, and "real-world" dreamers are all driven to project or
generate secondary personalities—to refract their very selves into alter
egos or personifications bears further inquiry. Why, for example, would
Cervantes be driven to fragment the hero of his last romance into sexually
loaded abstractions? Reading the hero's projections as a symptom of *Cervantes*'s sexual pathology—the author taken here as the locus of psychoanalytic interest—privileges the Freudian implications at the cost of Cervantine literary artistry. This kind of curiosity is, I believe, impertinent.[91]
Cervantes chose to write an allegory, a "dark conceite" he was still trying
to finish on his deathbed—"casi entre los aprietos de la muerte [almost in
the very grips of death]," as the censor's "Approval" of the *Persiles* sen-
sationally put it (41). His experiment—which discloses many of the strategies that psychoanalysis later sought to universalize—shows that the aging Cervantes was still trying to "figure out" sexuality, in both senses of
that phrase.

[90] Freud, *SE* 13.857; Melanie Klein, *The Selected Melanie Klein*, ed. Juliet Mitchell (Har-
mondsworth, Middlesex, Eng.: Penguin [Peregrine] Books, 1986), 89; on projection, see
Fletcher, *Allegory*, 197-98. Jack Spector reminds us that "neither Freud nor his followers
. . . have ever shown concretely how specific formal techniques correspond to the processes
of the unconscious" (cited by Peter Brooks, "The Idea of a Psychoanalytic Literary Criticism," *Critical Inquiry* 13 [Winter 1987]: 337).

[91] See Rosa Rossi, *Escuchar a Cervantes: Un ensayo biográfico* (Valladolid: Ámbito Ediciones, 1988), a biographical study which proposes to examine the interaction between Cervantes's "diversidad sexual [sexual diversity]"—the homosexual fantasies that entered his
life—and his writings. See also Louis Combet, *Cervantès ou les incertitudes du désir* (Lyon:
Presses Universitaires de Lyon, 1980), a psychostructural approach to Cervantes. Ruth El
Saffar castigates Combet's book in a judicious review essay in *MLN* 97 (1982): 422–27.
Peter Brooks regards the posing of the author as *object* of analysis in literary studies as a
critical approach that is "the most discredited, though also perhaps the most difficult to
extirpate" ("The Idea of Psychoanalytic Literary Criticism," 334).

Chapter Four

___

CERVANTES AND THE ANDROGYNE

Ma onde viene questa diversitá . . . ?

[But whence comes this difference?]

—Leone Ebreo, *Dialoghi d'amore*

FOR DEALING WITH the subject of love in literature—the lively and clever "amigo" advises Cervantes himself in the prologue to *Don Quixote*, part 1—there is really only one literary reference to consult: "Con dos onzas que sepáis de la lengua toscana, toparéis con León Hebreo, que os hincha las medidas [With a smattering of Tuscan you can apply to Leon the Hebrew, who will supply you to your heart's content]." Although Cervantes undoubtedly had those "two ounces" of Italian, he did not need them to understand Leone Ebreo, since a splendid Spanish translation was available to him as early as 1590: Garcilaso Inca de la Vega's rendering of the *Diálogos de amor*, one of the most significant subtexts of the *Persiles*. In the previous chapter, I mentioned Cervantes's experimentation with Neoplatonic doctrines in his works, most notably in *La Galatea*. Leone Ebreo's Neoplatonic doctrines of love had weighed heavily in Cervantes's first romance, a work whose sequel Cervantes repeatedly promised, and one that contains a thirty-five-line passage lifted intact from Leone's *Dialoghi*.[1] For the treatment of love in the *Persiles*, Cervantes turned, once again, to the Hebrew Neoplatonist. As I suggest in what follows, Leone

___

[1] Book 4 of *La Galatea* contains a discussion about the nature of love that Marcelino Menéndez y Pelayo described as "derivado de León Hebreo, hasta en las palabras [derived from Leone Ebreo, even in his own words]." In a later study of *La Galatea*, Francisco López Estrada printed parallel passages from Leone Ebreo alongside quotations from Cervantes. The above claims of influence are cited and contested by Geoffrey Stagg, who—aiming to diminish Cervantes's alleged direct debt to Leone Ebreo—argues that Cervantes "is mocking, rather than praising, the *Dialoghi*" for the purpose of "making sport of Montemayor." According to Stagg, since Cervantes "may have shared common knowledge" of Montemayor's plagiarism, "the chance to laugh up his sleeve would be irresistible to the master ironist" ("Plagiarism in *La Galatea*," *Filologia romanza* 6 [1959]: 255–76). My own study of Leone Ebreo's influence in this chapter takes issue with Stagg's vision of what "may" or "would" have been probable at the scene of Cervantes's writing. Detection of "the master ironist" at work in a passage is always arguable. I take Cervantes's reference to Leone in the prologue to *Don Quixote*, pt. 1, as an unironic confession of indebtedness and admiration.

supplied Cervantes with the organizing metaphor for his last romance: the androgyne, a figure that subtends the entire verbal body of the text of the *Persiles* and even divides it into two problematic halves. Cervantes's text, which is structured like a giant dualism, is organized around a scheme that classical rhetoricians called *syneciosis*, a figure in which, as Susenbrotus explained it to the Renaissance, a contrary is joined to its opposite or two different things are conjoined closely.[2] This figure operates in the *Persiles* as a formula or configuration that resembles an architect's model: from its lineaments and dimensions, in other words, we may deduce the proportion of the whole work. The present chapter focuses on the lineaments of the androgyne in the *Persiles*, its place in the discourse of the Renaissance, and its subtle reinscription for the age by Leone Ebreo.

In order to hypothesize a kind of mutual, or nondominant, sexual difference that would displace hierarchy, Cervantes exploits the androgyne, a figure of ancient if classically debased pedigree, regarded by many Renaissance thinkers as a "category of monster."[3] As is well known, the androgyne has its Western literary inaugural as a primordial myth in Plato's *Symposium,* where Aristophanes explains how the original nature of mankind embraced not two but three sexes: man, woman, and androgyne (man/woman), all circular beings with eight hands and feet, four ears, and two privy members apiece. Zeus punished the insolence of these octopods by cutting them all in half, "like a sorb apple which is halved for pickling, or as you might divide an egg with a hair"—amusing kitchen similes that betray the Platonic denial of all difference between the two halves of the heterosexual androgyne. This disarmingly ludicrous account of the genesis of two yearning, incomplete sexes is aptly articulated by Aristophanes, represented in Plato's dialogue as a buffoon given to prolonged seizures of the hiccups. His account of the degeneration of the happy androgynes, nonetheless, includes a passage of considerable resonance in Western culture. Its language of division and reunion, with its well-known metaphysics of nostalgia, will find its way, centuries later, into the *Persiles*: "After the division the two parts of man, *each desiring his other half*, came together . . . longing to grow into one . . . : so ancient is the desire of one another which is implanted in us, reuniting our original nature, *making one of two*, and healing the state of man. *Each of us when separated . . . is always looking for his other half*." Cervantes's imitation of this scene of splitting and fusion, however, although overpacked with redundant

---

[2] *Syneciosis* is also known as *contrapositum, conjunctio,* or *commistio.* See Joannes Susenbrotus, *Epitome troporum ac schematum et grammaticorum et rhetorum* (Antwerp, 1566), 82; cited by Lee A. Sonnino, *A Handbook to Sixteenth-Century Rhetoric* (London: Routledge and Kegan Paul, 1968), 61.

[3] See Maclean, *Renaissance Notion*, 39.

echoes of mathematical language, cannot be regarded as simply another "footnote to Plato." In the Platonic text, it bears recalling, the androgynous sex is roundly disdained: the term *androgynous* there signifies "adulterous" men and women and is preserved, as Aristophanes is careful to explain, only as "a term of reproach." The deprecation of heterosexual coupling is reinforced by his teasing endorsement, albeit within an ironic discourse, of the "manly" sex, the sex represented by "the best of boys and youth."[4] Elaine Pagels reminds us that, in the *Symposium*, Plato showed "a group of men fighting hangovers from the night before by praising the glories of erotic—and especially homoerotic—love."[5] In a study of the vicissitudes of Eros in Western culture, Suzanne Lilar laments that "it is to the love of boys that we owe the one and only great Western philosophy of love."[6] The androgyne that informs the *Persiles*, however, as what follows will elaborate, is a syncretic Renaissance creation that corrects and criticizes its Platonic model. By way of formal endorsement of the sexuality it proposes, Cervantes's text is itself metaphorically "an" androgyne—a fiction structured in the shape and by the conjunction of two different halves. This metaphor suggests no irenic escape into some utopian realm where all differences are left behind: rather, it investigates the laborious journey into a new discursive space that can incorporate them all.

Before we focus on Cervantes's rhetorical uses of the figure of the androgyne, it will be revealing to take a fresh look at the traditional criticism lamenting the *Persiles* as a "split" text, with part 1 set in the Arctic zones, and part 2 along the Mediterranean. Forcione has rightly observed that "the view of the *Persiles* as a 'split' work survives in its most recent commentators, even in the one study [Casalduero's] which argues for its thematic unity."[7] Indeed, excepting Forcione himself, the majority of serious commentators since Friedrich Bouterwek (1804) have shared a view of the *Persiles* as a work split into two parts, or, as Rafael Osuna puts it, as "escendida [cut, divided, separated]." Osuna, in fact, speaks of this "escisión [scission]" as "sin duda de lo más misterioso del *Persiles* [without a doubt the most mysterious thing about the *Persiles*]."[8] Avalle-Arce

4 Plato, *Symposium*, trans. Benjamin Jowett (New York: Bobbs-Merrill, 1956), 30–32; emphasis added.

5 Elaine Pagels, *Adam, Eve, and the Serpent* (New York: Random House, 1988), 85.

6 Suzanne Lilar, *Aspects of Love in Western Society*, trans. Jonathan Griffin (New York: McGraw-Hill, 1965), 68.

7 Forcione, *Cervantes' Christian Romance*, 11. Forcione argues that "far too much emphasis" has been placed on the differences between the two halves of the novel: "The traditional distinction between a symbolical and a realistic half of the *Persiles* . . . ignores the fact that the second half of the work continues to reactualize the Christian mythology and employs the symbolic methods of the first half to do so" (46–47n).

8 Osuna, "El olvido del *Persiles*," 61.

writes of that "diferencia tan tajante entre las dos mitades del *Persiles* [cutting difference (lit.) between the two halves of the *Persiles*]," and he sandwiches the writing of *Don Quixote* in between them.[9] Casalduero likens the two halves to the "dos mundos que encontramos constantemente en el Barroco, de cuya tensa oposición surge la unidad [two worlds found constantly in the Baroque, from whose tense opposition arises a unity]."[10] In a similar vein, Alberto Navarro González distinguishes between the "idealistic" and "realistic" halves of the *Persiles*.[11] The traditional distinction between the two halves of the work is pointedly addressed by William Atkinson, who writes of the "obvious concern with symmetry in the architecture of the novel, which, as it balances the action between North and South, unknown and known, symbolical and material, introduces too in the first half one significant national of each of the four known countries to be traversed." Atkinson both acknowledges and resists being seduced by all this symmetry. And so his insightful study, confessedly entitled "The Enigma of the *Persiles*," breaks off abruptly, with the odd conclusion that "mere realism was not and could not be Cervantes's concern." The enigmatic notion of a text divided against itself has even led scholars to promote one half of the text over the other, producing a striking critical clash. Atkinson, for instance, sees only the first half of the *Persiles* as the "vital" half, where "everything is relevant."[12] Menéndez y Pelayo, at the other pole, claims that the *Persiles* "contiene en su segunda mitad algunas de las mejores páginas que escribió su autor [contains in its second half some of the best pages ever written by its author]."[13] Noting that the lack of unity in the novel is a problem yet to be studied, Osuna concludes his useful agenda for *Persiles* scholarship with the question: "Si las dos partes son tan diferentes, ¿qué es lo que las agrupa en un todo? [If the two parts are so different, what is it that joins them together?]"[14]

This chapter addresses that crucial critical question. If the "enigma" of the *Persiles* demands to be articulated on the level of theory, such a theory might well begin with the signifying capacity of a pair, an ensemble, of

[9] "Introduction," *Los trabajos*, 20. Avalle-Arce dates pt. 1 of the *Persiles* to between 1599 and 1605, and pt. 2 to between 1612 and 1616, with *Don Quixote* interpolated between the two parts (18–20).

[10] Joaquín Casalduero, *Sentido y forma de* Los trabajos de Persiles y Sigismunda (Madrid: Editorial Gredos, 1975), 14.

[11] Alberto Navarro González, *Cervantes entre el* Persiles *y el* Quijote (Salamanca: Universidad de Salamanca, 1981), 56.

[12] William C. Atkinson, *Bulletin of Spanish Studies* (Liverpool), 24 (1947): 248.

[13] Marcelino Menéndez y Pelayo, "Cultura literaria de Miguel de Cervantes y elaboración del 'Quijote,' " in *Discursos*, ed. J. M. Cossío (Madrid, 1956); cited by Emilio Carilla in "Introduction," *Persiles*, 14.

[14] Osuna, "El olvido del *Persiles*," 67.

two split halves. It is the enigma of the "split," in short, that asks us to organize the text in relation to splitting, scission, or division as forces of signification. A split need not be a flaw if it can be shown to be a structuring and a strategy. As I construe it, the *Persiles* is a strategically split discourse, a cunning analogue of the ancient split between the sexes it aims to explore. The overarching figure of the androgyne is made visible for us through rhetorical, emblematic, onomastic, genealogical, and metafictional devices throughout Cervantes's text.

THE ANDROGYNOUS *PERSILES*

The rhetoric in the *Persiles* perhaps most blatantly figures the androgyne by iterating variants of the formula of splitting followed by imaginative, blissful fusion. Cervantes makes use not only of the scheme of syneciosis, the composition of contraries discussed above, but also of figures such as *anagogy*, in which two entities are inscribed as one. His striking use of anagogic or copular metaphor—a mystical mathematics of two-in-one that transcends all syntax and logic—bears rehearsing.[15] In response to Auristela's long disease of jealousy, for example, Periandro invokes the androgyne when he speaks, in alchemical terms, of producing a compound out of their conjoined souls: "un compuesto tan uno y tan solo . . . que tendrá mucho que hacer la muerte en dividirle [a compound so singular and so unique . . . that death will have much to do in dividing it]" (185). This same anagogic metaphor is even ironized in the *Persiles* when, during one of the lovers' most divisive exchanges, they each insist loudly on their unity: "He dicho mal en partir estas dos almas, que no son más que una [I have spoken ill to divide our two souls, since they are no more than one]," the heroine protests; and the hero, in turn, replies that no contentment can equal the experience of "dos almas que son una [two souls who are one]" (414–15). These mathematical dynamics of yearning are echoed throughout the text by an ostentatious partitive construction that focuses rhetorically on the concept of halves. The hero's first address to the heroine, whispered during their transvestite embrace, underlines the primacy of this iterated structural formula: "¡O querida mitad de mi alma! [O dear half of my soul!]"(67).[16] Allowing that this remote formula

---

[15] See Patricia Parker's enlightening discussion of the "twain-made-one" in four English texts ("Anagogic Metaphor: Breaking Down the Wall of Partition," in *Centre and Labyrinth: Essays in Honour of Northrop Frye*, ed. Eleanor Cook, Chaviva Hosek, Jay Macpherson, Patricia Parker, and Julian Patrick [Toronto: University of Toronto Press, 1983], 38–58).

[16] To cite some other instances of this formula: "Auristela, *mitad de su alma* sin la cual no puede vivir" (57); "donde iba *la mitad de su alma*, o la mejor parte della" (251); "*no la mitad, sino toda su alma* que se le ausentaba" (252); "¿Qué mudanza es ésta, *mitad de mi alma?*" (364); and "*la mitad que le falta*, que es la del marido" (399).

"abunda [abounds]" in the Cervantine canon, Avalle-Arce traces its origins back to Horace's use of *pars animae meae* (*Ode* 3.8) to address his friend Virgil, thereby editorially consigning it to a long literary tradition of male friendship (57n). As a classical topos, this critical phrase does indeed appear not only in Horace's ode but also in Ovid's *Metamorphoses* (8.406), Augustine's *Confessions* (4.6), and Petrarch's *Epistola metrica* (1.1)—to note only a sample of Latin writers who employ variants of the vocative *pars* (or *dimidium*) *animae meae* to address their male friends. Cervantes himself used this figure of speech homoerotically at the start of his career: in the pastoral *Galatea* (1585), Timbrio laments that both his female love and his male rival for this love are the "dos verdaderas y mejores mitades de su alma [two true and better halves of his soul]."[17] The transgressive logic of precisely this kind of metaphor may have moved Aristotle to remark, centuries earlier, that the idea of Aristophanes' androgyne appears to be somewhat diluted when it embraces more than two persons (*Politics* 1262bl). Cervantes must have outgrown such triangulated figurations, however, since they never occur in the *Persiles*, where the "other half" is always and only the other gender. As such, the phrase gestures back to origins even more remote than Horace and to notions of Otherness less in complicity with all-male interests. It is the myth of the two *different* sexual halves (andro/gyne) that funds both the thematics and the structures of the *Persiles*.

Figures like anagogy or syneciosis, among Cervantes's principal rhetorical resources, engender the topos of transvestism in his last romance. Emblematic representations of the androgyne surface through Cervantes's frequent use of cross-dress, a traditionally androgynous hallmark, in different episodes of the *Persiles*. The cross-dressed emblem of the androgyne, indeed, is programmatically installed at the threshold of his narrative. When the protagonists of the *Persiles* first come together in the text, the heroine Auristela, in male clothing, is being readied for sacrifice on the Barbaric Isle. In order to rescue her, the hero has pressed another character into cross-dressing him so lavishly that he resembles, as the narrator explains, "la más gallarda y hermosa mujer [the most elegant and handsome woman]" (60). This duplex "metamorfosis" saves the protagonists' lives, for their androgynous embrace triggers the holocaust on the Barbaric Isle that allows them to escape to freedom. At the end of the *Persiles*, the narrator sums up its beginning episodes in one memorably androgynous image: "la Isla Bárbara, cuando se vieron [Auristela] y Periandro en los trocados trajes, ella en el de varón, y él en el de hembra: metamorfosis bien estraño [the Barbaric Isle, when (Auristela)

---

[17] *La Galatea*, ed. Juan Bautista Avalle-Arce, 2 vols. (Madrid: Espasa-Calpe, 1968), 1:158; subsequent citations are to this edition and will be parenthetically documented.

and Periandro found themselves in traded garments, she in the male, and he in the female ones: a very strange metamorphosis]" (341). Cross-dressing is a signal event in allegory, where clothing sharply defines agency and roles. Cervantes's use of cross-dress in his allegorical romance may be a recuperative technique. The double transvestism of the *Persiles*'s introductory scenes gestures back to the ancient Greek practices of "initiatory androgyny," wedding customs recounted by Plutarch in which exchanges of clothing took place between men and women.[18]

The strange "metamorphosis" mentioned by the narrator (the word is used twice) also serves to rectify the sexual asymmetry of Renaissance literary cross-dress, whose most demonstrable function was to allow female characters to escape from a repressive home environment and then to keep them safe while on the road. The *Persiles* includes one of these conventional transvestites, Ambrosia Agustina, who serves as a drummer boy in Philip II's army while chasing after her new husband (361–66). Her character does not stray very far from a literary inquiry into the social pressures that kept most Renaissance women at home while their men went off to the wilderness or the wars. But some of the subcharacters in the *Persiles* appear in extreme variants of cross-dress, their own "metamorphoses" augmenting the gender reversal of Cervantes's protagonists in their opening embrace. The young Lithuanian widow Sulpicia, for example, becomes an avenging pirate after hanging some forty would-be rapists from the tackle and yards of her ship. This character is represented as literally "dressed to kill," with a stiff white corselet and a high-crested helmet, brandishing a javelin before a squadron of pirate women whom she—as their *capitana*—is expertly drilling. Sulpicia is clearly one of the more militant of the "lovely lethal female piratemen" Cervantes has depicted.[19] For all its sanguinity, however, this sexual boundary shift is less striking than the bizarre transvestism of Tozuelo, from an episode (3.8) that Schevill and Bonilla regard, presumably for its earthiness, as an index of "el verdadero Cervantes [the real Cervantes]," as opposed to the author who produced the idealized population of the *Persiles*, those personages "que no pertenecen a este mundo [who do not belong to this world]."[20] Tozuelo is a rustic who impersonates his pregnant girlfriend in order to spare her a possible miscarriage during some country dances in Toledo: "Ella está encinta, y no está para danzar ni bailar [she is expecting, and is in no condition to dance and sing]" (329). Although Tozuelo's gender disguise signifies, in fact, a rare literary act of male nurturing, it

[18] See Mircea Eliade, *The Two in the One*, trans. from *Mephistopheles et l'Androgyne* by J. M. Cohen (Chicago: University of Chicago Press, 1962), 112–13.

[19] See Arthur Efron's "Bearded Waiting Women, Lovely Lethal Female Piratemen: Sexual Boundary Shifts in *Don Quixote*, Part 2," *Cervantes* 2 (1983): 155–64.

[20] Schevill and Bonilla, "Introduction," *Persiles*, xlv.

may strike some readers as a kind of "viscerally unbearable" androgynous scenario.[21] The text itself acknowledges its potential for repellency when the mayor of Toledo berates Tozuelo for the "delinquimiento [delinquency]" of his cross-dressing, an act that the mayor demeans as "mucous-like" ("es mocosa la culpa"). Although Tozuelo is accused of having "profaned" the country dances, Toledo's famous *villanas de la Sagra* ("¿Bailes son éstos para ser profanados?"), ultimately it is the civic and paternal authorities in the text who are asked to give up their wrangling and marry the couple, on the spot, with the groom still in female garb. As an ad hoc "pregnant male," Cervantes's Tozuelo would seem one of the truly liminal figures of the carnivalesque world.[22] This kind of liminality is justly celebrated for its daring in Rosa Rossi's *Escuchar a Cervantes*, a study that chillingly reminds us how transvestism was used, in Cervantes's Spain, as part of the death sentence for homosexuality. The suspect who confessed under torture to such practices, and was sentenced to burn for them, could expect to approach his death disguised as a woman: in his last walk to the stake, the condemned man would be exhibited "trasvestido y rizado [in cross-dress and with his hair curled]."[23]

Despite these rebarbative associations of male transvestism—which has canonically represented emasculation and, in the context above, even death—the *Persiles* asks its readers to respond to its blurring of sexual categories with a suspension of the old aversions: androgyny is represented as an enterprise vital to its practitioners, vexing to its critics, and fatal to its opponents. Its representation gestures toward a different ordering of sexual relations, toward an economy founded on an ethical exchange of gendered subjectivities. Such an exploration does not *require* transvestism. There are characters in the *Persiles* who experience the reality of the other gender without cross-dressing: the polyglot Transila, based upon the model of the Italian "virago," is celebrated for her "varonil *brío* [manly *brío*]" (69); the putative "adúltero [adulterer]" Rosanio is dubbed "el caballero de la criatura [the Knight of the Infant]" because he inherits the care of his son when the infant's unwed mother must flee for her life (290); and Isabela Castrucha, perhaps the most protean figure in the text, is addressed as "malino" and a "viejo"—as an obscene old man—while she successfully feigns demonic possession (409).

An onomastic strategy that signals Cervantes's alertness to sexual fusion bears exploring at this point. Persiles, the male protagonist of this work, travels across the text under a pseudonym that begs for interpre-

---

[21] Carolyn G. Heilbrun uses this phrase in *Toward a Recognition of Androgyny* (1964; rpt. New York: W. W. Norton, 1982), x.

[22] See Elemire Zolla for a discussion of "Carnival, When Men Get Pregnant," in *The Androgyne: Reconciliation of Male and Female* (New York: Crossroad, 1981), 90–91.

[23] Rossi, *Escuchar a Cervantes*, 7; see also her instructive footnote on this page.

tation. When we recall how Cervantes's earlier hero, Alonso Quijano, agonized about choosing a name that was "sonoro y significativo [resonant and significant]" for himself, his lady, and his horse (*DQ* 1.1), we are tempted to examine the compound pseudonym of Periandro for its own resonant signification. From the Greek prefix *peri*-(meaning round, around, about) and the noun *andros* (man), we infer a gender yoked to its own qualifier: *Periandro*, a region or place lying around the fixed gender of masculinity, much as the region about the heart is called the *pericardium*. Cervantes may, in fact, have borrowed the name of Periandro from Greek romance, from characters oddly called Periandro and/or Periandra in Achilles Tatius's *Leucippe and Clitophon*.[24] As will be discussed in some detail in chapter 6, Cervantes's hero, in response to repeated criticism of his narrative techniques, likens himself to some anagogic region containing all time and space, a narrative container where "all things fit" (227). Speaking from a peripheral reality, Cervantes's ex-centric protagonist insists on incorporating—both into himself and his narratives—all differences, sexual and otherwise. This refusal to limit or confine either gender or speech is characteristic not only of Periandro but also of the narrative that contains him, the *Persiles* itself.

The genealogical transactions in the *Persiles* also show Cervantes using gender metaphorically, again as a way of figuring the androgyne. Two queen mothers, heads of Thule and Friesland, engineer a union designed to remove the threat of sterility from their respective all-male and all-female royal lines, isolated within their separate Northern kingdoms. Since one of the notable distinctions of Spanish Golden Age texts is the virtual absence of the figure of the mother,[25] the spectacle here of the absent father (so to speak) is an unorthodox touch. As if to compound this early subversion of the father, the text also chooses to ridicule the institution of primogeniture: Thule's queen, it appears, regards her eldest son Magsimino, perennially away at wars, as "aborrecible [detestable]," in a countercultural reversal of priorities of first and second-born sons that recalls, for one, the biblical case of Jacob and Esau. Since Magsimino has been officially engaged to the prepubescent heroine Sigismunda, his younger brother's growing passion for the visiting princess threatens a domestic triangle. In order to foil her elder son, who is off fighting some war, Queen Eustoquia packs the lovers off to Rome under a pretext that is revealed as the pre-text only in the book's final chapters. Her plan

---

[24] The debt of the *Persiles* to *Leucippe and Clitophon* may be an indirect one, via the Castilian version of Núñez de Reinoso, the *Historia de los amores de Clareo y Florisea* (1552). See Menéndez y Pelayo, *Orígenes de la novela* 1:cccxliiiff. See also Palomo, "Una fuente española del *Persiles*."

[25] On the increasing presence of the figure of the mother across the Cervantine canon, see Ruth El Saffar's *Beyond Fiction*.

works when, two years and many shipwrecks later, the marriage of the protagonists, blessed by the dying Magsimino, effects a merger between the gender-specific royal lines. The main genealogical exchange in the *Persiles*, then, empowered exclusively by mothers, reverses the economy of the text's opening scenes on the Barbaric Isle: traffic *by* women ultimately replaces traffic *in* women. The success of their endeavors once again validates the androgyne, the figure disseminated throughout the text that radically calls into question both patriarchal and hierarchical mechanisms of sexual control.

Finally, as we would expect from an author for whom the book, for better or worse, is a paramount cultural entity, the *Persiles* incorporates into its fourth and final book the metafiction of a gendered book (415–18). Like the divided androgyne, male and female are represented in this microtext as two split halves: male aphorisms, conveying general truths, stand in binary opposition to female maxims, offering sexual advice. This is a text that fictionalizes division and inserts it into the "reality" of a metaphoric pilgrimage. It is also a text that inscribes the authorial intrusion of Cervantes himself—or at least a character whose capsule autobiography evokes the historical Cervantes—in its plot. As if the *Persiles* were formally aware of the difficulties of its own future readings, its author steps in to help us with a "commentary." In what amounts to a radical textual strategy, he ruptures the narrative with a personal appearance, perhaps the last in his canon. Once again he comes to posit the problem of the book, this time a book inscribed by his own characters. Thinly disguised as a Spanish man of letters, writing tools and portfolio in hand, he abruptly enters the dining room of an inn outside Rome where the protagonists and their party are lodged. Although he identifies himself only generically, as "a curious man," he follows this greeting with a thumbnail *vida* that could pass for Cervantes's own self-portrait:

> Yo, señores, soy un hombre curioso. Sobre la mitad de mi alma predomina Marte, y sobre la otra mitad Mercurio y Apolo. Algunos años me he dado al ejercicio de la guerra, y algunos otros, y los más maduros, en el de las letras. En los de la guerra he alcanzado algún buen nombre, y por los de las letras he sido algún tanto estimado. Algunos libros he impreso, de los ignorantes no condenados por malos, ni de los discretos han dejado de ser tenidos por buenos. (415–16)

> [I, sirs, am a curious man. Mars presides over half of my soul, and Mercury and Apollo over the other half. I have given over some years to the profession of war, and some others, the more mature ones, to the practice of literature. I have published some books, neither condemned as bad ones by ignorant readers, nor not appreciated by men of discretion.]

The bookish temperament of this pilgrim extends to a design on the other pilgrims, whom he wishes to enlist in a curious literary project. He asks them all to contribute to an anthology that he is editing, a text entitled *Flor de aforismos peregrinos* (*Posy of Peregrine Aphorisms*), essentially a parody of Renaissance *florilegia* of edifying classical maxims. The *Flor* recalls such popular texts as Joaquín Setanti's *Centellas de varios conceptos*, a collection of 500 aphorisms making the rounds in 1614, when Cervantes was writing the *Persiles*. The multivalent pun in the adjective of Cervantes's title for his pilgrim's anthology—*peregrino* is an errant word in Spanish, meaning not only pilgrim or palmer, but also foreign, strange, wonderful—establishes a network of formal correspondences among the peregrine aphorisms, the pilgrims-errant, the pilgrim-editor, his "peregrine idea" for the collective production of the *Flor*, and the *Persiles* itself—a text with a pilgrimage frame. The linguistic errancy of the aphorisms themselves—their tendency to "peregrinate," as it were—advertises their inherent arbitrariness. And the dramatic situation of their in situ inscription further indicates how categories of behavior are all-too-human constructions. The pilgrim-editor's collection, which he claims to number over 300 entries already, lifts our attention from the *Persiles* to the process of its own writing. This device of a character in search of his "authors" serves, through its self-reflexivity, to destabilize the narrative, to move us abruptly into a scriptive realm. We watch an author asking his culture to set down the maxims it lives by. And we watch him materialize within his text to show us the degree to which authority *is* a fiction—to warn us, once again, of the dangers of viewing life in terms of literature. The distracting image of this text within a text forces an encounter between two discourses: the *Flor* that explains the *Persiles* that contains it. How do the two texts bespeak each other?

Unlike the much-heralded arrival of the *Persiles* discussed in my opening chapter, a text anticipated as a possible monster but at no time disowned, the *Flor* is produced through studiously celibate means. The pilgrim-editor announces his intention to produce a book "a costa ajena [at the cost of others]," a book that will not appear under his own name ("no en nombre mío"). In a narrative stance of disavowal, he eschews all literary paternity for the *Flor*, yet this orphaned text exposes both the structures and the strategies of the *Persiles*. The overwhelming first impression of this collection of maxims is its gendered arena of production, male divided from female. None of the entries especially fits the character of its contributor, only of his or her gender. Even the obsessively chaste Auristela's entry—"La mejor dote que puede llevar la mujer principal, es la honestidad [The best dowry an illustrious woman can bring to marriage is her chastity]"—has already been cited by a not-very-chaste tavern wench in an earlier episode, who recalls as *her* source of the maxim "la madre que me parió [the mother who bore me]" (322). Under the masculine entries, inscribed first, desire is exultantly displaced onto the battlefield, for example, "Más hermoso parece el soldado muerto en la batalla, que sano en la huida [The soldier appears more attractive dead in battle than alive and well in flight from it]." In the women's maxims, desire hovers anxiously around the bedroom, for instance, "La mujer ha de ser como el armiño, dejándose antes prender que enlodarse [A woman must be like the ermine, better trapped than sullied]."[26] The male aphorisms in this collection inscribe agency and achievement, the female maxims, anxiety and admonition. In the masculine ledger we find postures of aggression, desires for honor, fame, and death; in the feminine column, passivity, dispensability, and a mania for spotlessness. Cervantes's solicited book of maxims projects, *in nuce*, a world of violence and complicity—a world where men only desire to seem (that is, be seen as) heroic, and where women, having fully internalized the gender-codes of their Golden Age culture, only desire "not to displease."[27]

As an ensemble, these aggressive/servile discourses, two mutually uninfluencing currents, represent in boldface the sexual norms of Renaissance fiction. But they also adumbrate, with uncanny accuracy, Freud's theory of sexual difference, especially his heroic/erotic antinomy, in which he maintains that the unsatisfied dreams and desires of women are mostly erotic, whereas those of men are ambitious as well as erotic.[28] More to our purposes, the maxims stand out as a textbook demonstration of how the sexes are imprisoned in their separate languages, within their own maxims of desire. The positive/privative opposition between the sexes fictionalized in the *Flor*, however, also stands out as a manifest fiction—as a book produced at the "cost" of the author's culture and destined to become, in turn, a producer of that culture. An author here commissions the text he would subvert. It will be a species of canonized literature, one that the Renaissance invested with power and honorific status: the encoding of their collective wisdom as universal truths of human experience. It would seem that Cervantes is saying here, along with George Eliot, that "the mysterious complexity of our life is not to be embraced by maxims." Certainly this pivotal opening chapter of the closing book of the *Persiles* plays out the insight, close to our fragmented postmodern sensibility, that all the maxims passing for the truth of human experience, as well as their encoding in literature, are often cultural or-

---

[26] This ermine maxim was earlier invoked, in a fit of hysterical moralizing, by Lotario, the sullier-to-be of his best friend's wife in *El curioso impertinente* (*DQ* 1.33).

[27] Barbara Johnson, "Teaching Ignorance: *L'Ecole des Femmes*," *Yale French Studies* 63 (1982): 179.

[28] Freud, "The Relation of the Poet to Daydreaming," in *On Creativity and the Unconscious*, trans. I. F. Grant Duff (New York: Harper, 1958), 47–48.

ganizations, and even sometimes fantasies.[29] By inviting his own characters to enter their favorite maxims within a chapter of his own work,
Cervantes is showing readers the dynamics of propagation of gender-
coded cultural "fantasies" which, as both editor of the *Flor* and author
of the *Persiles*, he then repudiates.

Cervantes's stance of dissociation from his collection of maxims—an
exposé that will be published anonymously—is made explicit at the end
of this key chapter, when he recites to the company the one maxim ("sólo
uno") that he claims to know by heart: "No desees, y serás el más rico
hombre del mundo [Do not desire, and you shall be the richest man in the
world]." This maxim comes with its own signature: "Diego de Ratos,
corcovado, zapatero de viejo en Tordesillas, lugar en Castilla la Vieja,
junto a Valladolid [Diego de Ratos, hunchback, longtime shoemaker in
Tordesillas, a place in Old Castile, close to Valladolid]." Editorial tradition has long considered this maxim as an allusion to Avellaneda, the
false author of the second part of the *Quixote*, because his spurious novel
appeared in Tordesillas, the shoemaker's hometown.[30] This demographic
coincidence, however, scarcely sheds light on the maxim itself, or on its
privileged status as the most memorable, as well as the most subversive,
of all the maxims to which it provides closure. An obvious reference to
Plato's *Symposium* (for Cervantes, the *Banquete*), the shoemaker's
maxim also communicates its derivation from Leone Ebreo's *Dialoghi*,
whose opening argument, addressing the Platonic theme of desire as lack,
includes the analogous maxim that "el verdadero rico es el que se con-
tenta con lo que posee [the truly rich man is he who is content with what
he has]."[31] The shoemaker's abrupt call for renunciation is pointedly
ironic in its context—a clutch of aphorisms telling people what they
should desire—and radically calls into question that context. Desire, this
closing maxim suggests, need not be organized through a logic of polar
oppositions, which habitually divides the masculine desire from the feminine. The "fiction" of the *Flor* is that it is a fictional version of these
binary habits of thought. Although indirectly conveyed, the pilgrim-editor's patent disaffection for the structures of desire inscribed in his mis-
cellany could not be clearer. The gendered microtext that he commissions
resembles, in its unhappily split structures, the divided androgyne.

---

[29] See Miller, "Emphasis Added," 46; George Eliot's dictum cited by Miller.

[30] On this 1614 Tordesillas event, and on the nature of Avellaneda's spurious continuation of *Don Quixote*, see Edward T. Aylward, *Towards a Revaluation of Avellaneda's False
Quixote* (Newark, Del.: Juan de la Cuesta Press, 1989). For the notion of the maxim's
allusion, see Avalle-Arce, *Los trabajos*, 418n.

[31] León Hebreo, *Diálogos de amor*, trans. Garcilaso Inca de la Vega, ed. P. Carmelo-Sáenz
de Santa María, s.i., Biblioteca de Autores Españoles edition, 4 vols. (Madrid: Ediciones
Atlas, 1965), 1:21.

THE ANDROGYNE IN THE RENAISSANCE

Where in the world—or at least in his own Renaissance signifying world, the *mundus significans* available to his culture[32] could Cervantes have found the organizing metaphor for his last romance? The androgynous tableau of his transvestite protagonists, which exhibits the intentional axis of the narrative from its beginnings, may have been suggested to him by an emblem. Countless emblems, many of them linked to alchemical processes, helped to fund the European mania engendered by Andrea Alciati's first collection of *Emblemata*, published in 1531. One manuscript illustration of alchemical androgynization, for instance, depicts a dead king and queen who share one crown, one body, and one soul—this last seen flying from them heavenward.[33]

Cervantes may have read about an androgynous fusion in Ovid's *Metamorphoses* (4.285–388), where the gods, granting Salmacis's prayer, fuse her and Hermaphroditus into one creature. This Ovidian text is behind Spenser's representation of the hermaphroditic union of Amoret and Scudamour in his 1590 edition of *The Faerie Queene*—"Had ye them seene, ye would have surely thought, / That they had beene that faire Hermaphrodite" (3.12.45–46). Although it is unlikely that Cervantes knew about Spenser, let alone about an androgynous passage that was repressed for the 1596 edition, it is certain that he knew Spenser's Ovidian subtext.

It is likely, too, that Cervantes was familiar with Pliny's famous review in his *Natural History* of certain foreign peoples with "prodigious and incredible" characteristics, among whom were included the androgynous people of Nasamona, who were said, during intercourse, to assume alternate sexes (book 7). Covarrubias had devoted over a page of his *Tesoro* (1611) to the "Andrógeno," citing Pliny (7.3) prominently as an authority.[34] It is also likely that Cervantes was familiar with the androgyne in the "resurrected" form it took within the multiple free translations, reconstitutions, and adaptations of Plato's *Symposium* that came forward in the Cinquecento.

But the androgynous figuration subtending the *Persiles* is critically different from all of the above renderings, most notably from the androgyne invoked within the humanist hermeneutics associated with learned Latin,

[32] I use *mundus significans* here in Thomas Greene's specialized sense of "a unique semiotic matrix," that is, "a rhetorical and symbolic vocabulary, a storehouse of signifying capacities potentially available to each member of a given culture" (*Light in Troy*, 20).

[33] See Arnold of Villanova's *Rosarium philosophorum*, MS 394a, sixteenth century, Stadbibliothek Vadiana, Saint Gallen.

[34] "Gignuntur et utriusque sexus, quos Hermaphroditos vocamus, olim Androgynos vocatos et in prodigiis habitos, nunc vero in deliciis" (Covarrubias, *Tesoro*, 118–19).

a tradition whose "puberty-rite mentality" has been well documented.[35] Cervantes does not share the ascetic strain found in certain Neoplatonic thinkers, for example, in Mario Equicola's declared aversion to "the filth of coitus"; in the speculations within Castiglione's *Il cortegiano* that sensual lovers feel only those pleasures "which unreasoning animals feel"; or in Marsilio Ficino's seminal invocation of the androgyne within his Latin Commentary of the *Symposium* (1469). In this last work, essentially a Christian celebration of chaste male bonding, the androgyne is represented as an anemic personification of Justice ("aliae secundum *iustitiam*").[36] Unlike the gynophobic Ficino, Cervantes does not unsex his androgyne. Although Ficino's system of Neoplatonic love was regarded as revolutionary, his writings show that he was not above citing Aquinas to refer to women's imperfect nature, nor declaring that wives should be subservient to their husbands, nor advising men to beware of the dangers of effeminacy.[37] It was Ficino's phrase, we recall, that Don Quixote borrowed to describe his Platonic love—his "amores tan platónicos"—for Dulcinea (*DQ* 2.3).[38] But all traces of the militant asceticism that characterized both Ficino and Don Quixote are absent from the *Persiles*.

From its pastoral romance beginnings to its Greek romance endings, Cervantes's literary project focused on one recurrent question: how does one articulate the concept of desire? The chivalric romances seemed to talk of little else, but their language of desire turned relentlessly on the same courtly love topoi that maddened and ultimately destroyed Don Quixote. His quest for his ideal lady, with its ascetic and triangulated dynamics, was a literalizing of that "dead-end street" ("una callejuela sin salida") on which Sancho speculates Dulcinea lives (*DQ* 2.9). The *Persiles* tries both to rectify this failure of Eros in *Don Quixote* and, by way of unfinished business, to finish the *Galatea* (1585), a work that was self-evaluated, during the scrutiny of Don Quixote's library, as inconclusive ("propone algo, y no concluye nada") (*DQ* 1.6). In order to propose "something" about sexual difference for an imperfect, sublunary world— and for an age in which women remained notionally inferior—Cervantes

[35] See Walter J. Ong, "Latin Language Study as a Renaissance Puberty Rite," in *Rhetoric, Romance, and Technology* (Ithaca: Cornell University Press, 1971), 113–41.

[36] Equicola's attitude is discussed by John Charles Nelson in *Renaissance Theory of Love: The Context of Giordano Bruno's Eroici furori* (New York: Columbia University Press, 1958), 70. Castiglione's *The Book of the Courtier*, trans. Charles S. Singleton (Garden City, NY: Anchor Books, 1959), 339. Ficino's Latin Commentary of the *Symposium*, ed. Sears Reynolds Jayne, vol. 19, University of Missouri Studies, 1 (Columbia: University of Missouri Press, 1944), 58.

[37] See *In Plotinum*, "De providentia primum," 2, in *Opera omnia* (Paris, 1641), 2.645; and *Epistolae*, in *Opera omnia* 1:721, 722; cited by Maclean, *Renaissance Notion*, 25.

[38] On the circumstances of Ficino's coinage of "Platonic Love," see Nelson, *Renaissance Theory of Love*, 69n.

needed a literary formula that would make a concord of discords, that would account for the "labors" of romance outside Arcadia. A model for this kind of synthesis—mutual sexual love and spiritual integration—was already part of the authentic philosophical discourse of the Renaissance, courtesy of Leone Ebreo, the esteemed author recommended to Cervantes by his know-it-all "friend."

LEONE EBREO AND THE PLATONIC ANDROGYNE

Born Jehuda Abravanel in the century before Cervantes (c. 1460), Leone Ebreo (León Hebreo), the son of the distinguished rabbinical authority Isaac Abravanel, belonged to an ancient and illustrious family of Spanish Jewry and was personal physician to Ferdinand and Isabella of Castile. During the expulsion of the Jews from Spain in 1492—a shameful act of racism periodically remotivated in Cervantine criticism[39]—Leone marched with his family at the head of the exiles. After the expulsion he eventually settled down in Naples, where he was recognized as both physician and philosopher. Legend had it that he converted to Christianity before he died, but it is highly unlikely that he ever apostasized, as he is extravagantly praised in the Hebrew literature of the period.[40] According to Cecil Roth, Leone studied with members of Ficino's Platonic Academy during his exile.[41] Intellectual historians remember him for his radical syncretistic tendencies, for having conjoined the Platonic, and especially the intellectualistic Plotinian, tradition with both Jewish and Christian theology.[42] His *Dialoghi d'amore* (1535), in which are combined ele-

---

[39] In a deservedly neglected passage, for instance, Ernesto Giménez Caballero tries to dismantle Américo Castro's thesis regarding Cervantes's converso origins as follows: "Físicamente, aparte de las notas semíticas señaladas en nariz y rostro . . . , el tipo de Cervantes fue el de un hombre occidental, ario. . . . Esa su alegría tan antisemítica y antioriental, típicamente aria, le duraría hasta la vejez [Physically, apart from the semitic notes signaled by his nose and face . . . , Cervantes was a type of occidental man, Aryan. . . . That gaiety of his, so antisemitic and antioriental, typically Aryan, would last him until old age]." See "La sangre de Cervantes," in *La estafeta literaria* (1976), n. 372; cited by Rosa Rossi, *Escuchar a Cervantes*, 52n.

[40] The second and third Aldine editions of the *Dialoghi d'amore* (Venice, 1541, 1545) emended the authorial information of the first edition (Rome, 1535): "Leone medico hebreo" was escalated to "*Dialoghi de Amore composti per Leone Medico, di Natione Hebreo, et di poi fatto Christiano.*" This emendation, however was deleted in the fourth and fifth editions of the *Dialoghi* (xiii). See the informative introduction by Cecil Roth in *The Philosophy of Love*, trans. F. Friedeberg-Seeley and Jean H. Barnes (London: Soncino Press, 1937). See also the section on Leone Ebreo in Nelson, *Renaissance Theory of Love*, 85–102.

[41] Cecil Roth, *The Jews in the Renaissance* (Philadelphia: Jewish Publication Society of America, 1959), 128–36.

[42] See Suzanne Damiens, *Amour et intellect chez Léon l'Hébreu* (Toulouse: Privat, 1971).

ments from Plato, Plotinus, Proclus, and the Pseudo-Dionysius, greatly popularized Neoplatonism for the Italian Renaissance, and was especially influential in Spain.[43] Within Leone's *Dialoghi*, two allegorical protagonists, Filone and Sofia (Filo/Sofia), enter into a complex dialogical exchange on the nature of love and desire. We are indebted to the third of these dialogues for the most resonant rehabilitation of the myth of the androgyne within the Platonic tradition. Leone's androgyne, I propose, contains the meaning of the "enigma" of the *Persiles*.

Although ideas, for Leone, had the nature of Plato's Forms or archetypes, his generative retailoring of the Platonic androgyne both critiques and rectifies its model. In what amounts to a major literary breakthrough for the cultural model of heterosexuality, Leone's text rescues the androgyne from both Plato's misogyny and Ficino's chastity. Rescripting Aristophanes' jocular discourse of male camaraderie in the *Banquete* (*Symposium*), Leone isolates what he regards as specific distortions of Plato's text and provides various correctives. The androgyne appears in the closing book of Leone's vast treatise, a work structured as a male/female dialogue and distinguished throughout for its metaphoric use of gender. The philosophy found in this treatise shows traces of the Kabbalah, an influence which Catherine Swietlicki usefully documents for us in Leone's "Cabalistic references to the secret oral tradition of Adam, Moses, and their successors and to the Judaic Jubilee as signifying 50,000."[44] The Kabbalah may also be the subtext of what T. Anthony Perry calls Leone's "radical polarization of the entire universe in terms of male and female symbols." These polarities, Perry argues in his excellent study of the erotic tradition of Continental literature originating from the *Dialoghi*, are integrated by Leone's nondualist stance.

The Platonism of the *Persiles*, to my mind, fits smoothly within Leone's tradition of integrative eroticism, a celebration of nonascetic conjugal relations that entirely bypasses the masters of Italian Neoplatonism. Perry would include within this tradition three French Platonists—Maurice Scève, Pernette du Guillet, and Antoine Héroët—who used Leone's *Philosophy* as their "breviary"; Jorge de Montemayor, the father of Spanish pastoral and a noted apologist of marriage; and John Donne, whom Perry regards (perhaps too generously, considering some of the early poems) as an "apostle of mutual love and sane sexual relations." Perry's study,

[43] For Leone's influence on Montemayor, Cervantes, Lope, Tirso, Quevedo, and others, see Otis H. Green, *Spain and the Western Tradition*, 4 vols. (Madison: University of Wisconsin Press, 1963–1966), 1:323.

[44] Catherine Swietlicki, *Spanish Christian Cabala: The Works of Luis de León, Santa Teresa de Jesús, and San Juan de la Cruz* (Columbia: University of Missouri Press, 1986), 38. This study includes an excellent overview of Christian Cabala and its diffusion in the Renaissance (1–41).

which he claims is "the first to examine in an extensive way the implications of Leone Ebreo's erotic philosophy for literature," has, I believe, a missing chapter: Cervantes's *Persiles* not only belongs squarely in this neglected tradition, but might also serve as its most powerful narrative prose statement.[45] In any case, the integrative, carnal, and Kabbalistic tendencies underlined in Perry's study all feed into Leone's interpretation of "la fábula del Andrógeno de Platón [the fable of Plato's Androgyne]"—as Inca Garcilaso de la Vega rendered Leone's syncretic androgyne for Golden Age readers.[46]

Corresponding to the modes of thought I have earlier situated in the *Persiles*, Leone's double-voiced discourse chooses to explore the androgynous aspects of Creation itself. It is this feature of Leone's Judeo-Platonism—his attempt to yoke the Platonic myth of the Androgyne with the Mosaic tradition of Genesis—that is fictionally reflected in the "split" structures of Cervantes's romance journey, in its two-in-one merger of Greek erotic odyssey with Exodus typology pilgrimage. Leone's hitherto incompatible traditions would have appealed greatly to Cervantes's certifiably iconoclastic leanings. The androgyne had never been welcomed into orthodox Christian circles: it had, in fact, been roundly rejected by the Western church, perhaps because it threatened their image of a patriarchal God. The theory of an androgynous Adam, as will be elaborated below, had been explicitly refuted by both Augustine (*De Genesi ad litteram* 3.22, *PL* 34.294) and Aquinas (*Summa theologica* Ia, 92, 4). Such a theory would have necessarily implied that God, in whose image Adam was created, was also androgynous. This gnostic idea of an androgynized God, which may be found in Paracelsus, was consigned to marginalized theology.[47]

Leone Ebreo's syncretistic mind recuperated this idea, however, for the dialogical imagination beginning to surface in the literature of the Renaissance. His solution was to splice together the Platonic myth of the androgyne with the Mosaic tradition of Genesis. Leone argues that Plato's fable was actually "translated" from Holy Scripture, from the Mosaic creation story of Adam and Eve. In his theory of this Greek imitation, Leone suggests that Plato vigorously manipulated the Genesis story, amplifying and adorning it in order to make it conform to Greek rhetoric.

[45] T. Anthony Perry, *Erotic Spirituality: The Integrative Tradition from Leone Ebreo to John Donne* (University: University of Alabama Press, 1980), 1–2, 37.

[46] León Hebreo, *Diálogos de amor*, ed. Eduardo Juliá Martínez, trans. Garcilaso Inca de la Vega, 2 vols. (Madrid: Ediciones Villaiz, 1949). All subsequent citations are taken from this edition, in which Leone's Androgyne commentary is found in 2:211–43.

[47] See, for instance, the Hermetic treatise *Asclepius*, which argues for a God containing both sexes (*Corpus hermeticum*, ed. A. D. Nock, trans. A.-J. Festugiere [Paris: 1945], 2:321f.).

The result was the Aristophanic myth of the androgyne, essentially "una mezcla desordenada de las cosas hebreas [a disordered mixture of Hebrew ideas]" (214). What was poor Plato to do, however, considering that he had to work with that maddening Mosaic "contradición [*sic*]" (216n), namely, the two creation stories in the book of Genesis? These contradictory stories are now known, as they were not in Leone's day, as the "P" or "Priestly" and the "J" or "Yahwist" accounts.[48] The first creation story ("P") represents the simultaneous creation of both sexes and may be found in Genesis 1.27: "So God created man [*ha-'adam*] in his own image, in the image of God created he him: male and female created he them." The second creation story ("J"), which depicts the secondary creation of Eve, is the authoritative account in Genesis 2:

> 21. And the Lord God caused a deep sleep to fall upon Adam, and he slept; and he took one of his ribs, and closed up the flesh instead thereof;

> 22. And the rib, which the Lord God had taken from the man [*hā-'ādām*], made he a woman ['*iššâ*], and brought her unto the man [*hā-'ādām*].

> 23. And Adam [*hā-'ādām*] said, This is now bone of my bones, and flesh of my flesh; she shall be called Woman [*iššâ*], because she was taken out of Man ['*îš*].

In order to appreciate what Leone does with these two contradictory accounts of creation, it will be useful to digress here, to glance at a number of exegetical attempts—both before and during Leone's day—to reconcile their differences.

Informed commentaries on these two Mosaic creation stories had been circulating ever since the hellenized Philo Judaeus, the most influential figure of Alexandrian Judaism, maintained that Plato knew Mosaic theology.[49] A curious reversal of influence may be found in Genesis Rabba 1.1, a gnostic gospel whose own creation account appears to be imitating Plato's myth of the androgyne.[50] Augustine had famously attempted to

---

[48] Ever since the late nineteenth century, "P" and "J" have been regarded as two separate texts. According to Elaine Pagels, the account now placed second—Gen. 2:4f—is regarded as the older of the two accounts (1000–900 B.C.), whereas the account now placed first—Gen. 1:1–2:3—dates to postexilic theologians (c. 400 B.C.) (*Adam, Eve, and the Serpent*, xxii).

[49] Philo's Platonic schema for relating the two texts is starkly misogynistic: the first or androgynized account in Gen. 1:27 he reads as "an ideal or type or seal, an object of thought (only), incorporeal, neither male nor female, by nature incorruptible"; the second account in Genesis 2, however, he reads as the corporeal, with Eve's secondary creation as divisive and thus identified with evil. See "On the Account of the World's Creation Given by Moses," secs. 46 and 53, in *Philo*, trans. F. H. Colson and G. H. Whitaker, 10 vols. (Loeb Classical Library, 1929), 1:107, 119–21.

[50] Elaine Pagels, "The Gnostic Vision," *Parabola* 3 (1978): 7.

combine the two Mosaic creation stories into some kind of congruent account in *De Genesi ad litteram*. His conclusion, resolutely adopted by the Western church, was that woman had been made in the image of God insofar as image is understood to mean "an intelligent nature"; but insofar as she was created both *out* of man and *for* man—"ex viro propter virum"—she is not in God's image. This observation iterated the Pauline passage in 1 Cor. 11:9: "Neither was the man created for the woman, but the woman for the man." (Or as Milton, that paradigmatic patriarch of English letters, would be echoing it over a millennium after Augustine, "He for God only, she for God in him.") In Augustine's vision, woman is in God's image only by grace, "for it is grace which accords an intelligent nature to every human being." Nature, then, yielding to grace, inscribes woman's secondariness in the Augustinian tradition. In *De civitate Dei* (14.11), Augustine would roundly declare that the formation of woman from Adam's rib established her as the "weaker part of the human couple."[51]

Aquinas, in turn, had resolved the two contradictory creation stories in Genesis by handily synthesizing them with Aristotle's notions (in *De generatione animalium*) of woman as an imperfect or botched male: "[Quasi]mas laesus" or "animal occasionatum" was the Latin rendering for this sorry state. Aquinas's reflections on woman's creation went for centuries scarcely challenged: "It seems that woman ought not to have been produced in the original production of things. For Aristotle says that the female is an incomplete version of the male. But nothing incomplete or defective should have been produced in the first establishment of things; so woman ought not to have been produced then." But since woman *was* produced and, moreover, was needed, as Aquinas himself acknowledged, for "the work of procreation," he concluded that she was defective "only as regards nature in the individual," and not "with reference to nature in the species as a whole."[52] Nature in the Thomist tradition, then, at least partly rescues woman from her original defectiveness.

When these theories of the creation pour into the Renaissance, commentators begin to "fatigue themselves," as Leone Ebreo would put it, trying to make sense of the contradictory Genesis stories. One commentator whose account seems especially overdetermined is Thomas de Vio, Cardinal Cajetan (1469–1534), whose Latin commentary on the five Mosaic books was published in Paris in 1539, in the decade before the birth of Cervantes. This Dominican cardinal's ingenious interpretation of the Mosaic production(s) of woman is worth an uninterrupted citation:

[51] Saint Augustine, *De Genesi ad litteram* 12.42, *PL* 34.452; cited by Maclean, *Renaissance Notion*, 13. The translation from *De civitate Dei* is by Philip Levine; cited by Pagels, *Adam, Eve, and the Serpent*, 114.

[52] Saint Thomas Aquinas, *Summa theologica* Ia, 92, 1.

What philosophers have said about the production of woman [that she is a botched male] is recounted metaphorically by Moses. There is a great difference between the point of view of philosophers and that of Moses; for the former considered the production of woman only in relation to sex, whereas Moses considered the production of woman not only as it concerns sex but also with regard to moral behaviour as a whole [*universam vitam moralem*]. Therefore he used a complex metaphor . . . as the sleep of Adam should be understood metaphorically, Adam is described asleep, not being woken up or keeping vigil. A deep sleep is sent by God into the man from whom woman is to be produced, and this defect of male power bears a likeness from which woman is naturally produced. For a sleeping man is only half a man; similarly, the principle creating woman is only semi-virile. It is for this reason that woman is called an imperfect version of the male by philosophers.[53]

The significance granted to Adam's priority in creation is maintained in this Renaissance commentary, even though a bout of sleep temporarily unmans Adam (or rather, *half*-mans him) for his own sleepy creation work, the production of woman, the "imperfect" man.

Such Thomist notions of woman seem to have been scarcely improved by the advent of Protestantism. The Reformation commentary of Martin Luther, ex-Augustinian monk, on the first Genesis story (1:27) bears recalling as part of an instructive sampling of Renaissance interpreters who tried to neutralize the discrepancies of the Mosaic Genesis stories:

Lest woman should seem to be excluded from all glory of future life, Moses mentions both sexes [in Gen. 1:26–27]; it is evident therefore that woman is a different animal to man, not only having different members, but also being far weaker in intellect [*ingenium*]. But although Eve was a most noble creation, like Adam, as regards the image of God, that is, in justice, wisdom and salvation, she was none the less a woman. For as the sun is more splendid than the moon (although the moon is also a most splendid body), so also woman, although the most beautiful handiwork of God, does not equal the dignity and glory of the male.[54]

---

[53] Thomas de Vio, *Commentarii in quinque Mosaicos libros* (Paris, 1539), 25; cited by Maclean (98 n. 12), who adds that the passage was quoted without comment by Jean de la Haye (1593–1661), *Arbor vitae concionatorum cuius radix liber Geneseos* (Paris, 1633), 245, and refuted by Benedictus Pererus, *Commentarii et disputationes in Genesim* (Cologne, 1601), 212–14.

[54] Martin Luther, *Werke. Kritische Gesamtausgabe* (Weimar, 1883), 42.51–52; cited by Maclean, *Renaissance Notion*, 9–10. "Luther also refers playfully in his *Tischreden* to the scholastic belief that the different shape of men and women is accountable to the latters' imperfect formation, claiming that it is not because of insufficient generative heat and body temperature that women have wide hips and narrow shoulders, but rather a sign that they have little wisdom and should stay in the home" (10).

Luther stresses woman's difference, a difference he regards not as mutual but as privative—as manifested by her weakness of intellect. Calvin fortifies this complacently masculinist Protestant scheme by commenting on the creation of the woman as "nothing else but the addition and furniture of the man [*quae nihil aliud est quam viri accessio*]. It cannot be denied, but the woman also was created after the image of God, though in the seconde degree."[55]

About the same time as the European imagination was hatching these new Reformed methods of reconciling the two Mosaic creation stories, the first edition of Leone's *Dialoghi d'amore* (1535) was published in Rome. Leone's theory about these Mosaic contradictions, the tension between the two Genesis accounts, rests on the critical notion of intentionality: Moses contradicted himself so manifestly, Leone argues, that he must have meant us to read his intention at an allegorical level. Leone claims to be able to interpret the allegorical significance of this primal incoherence ("lo que sinifica [*sic*] alegóricamente la fábula platónica") (240). In Leone's allegorical reading of what he has adduced as a Mosaic strategy, the first human being (that is, the generic *hā-'ādām*) contained in him/herself male and female without division. Leone glosses this two-in-one "Adam" with "comentarios hebreos en lengua caldea [Hebrew commentaries in Chaldean]" (219) that claim that Adam was created out of two persons, out of one part male and the other female. This reading squares with the *first* creation story in Genesis, of which the *second* story, for Leone, is simply a continuation: God's decision that "it was not good for man to be alone" has nothing to do here with the male's coming *temporally* first. Rather, it is interpreted by Leone as God's disaffection with the inconveniently lonesome structure of the original Adam's body: "Adam macho y hembra en un cuerpo solo, coligado por las espaldas, a contra visso [Adam, male and female in one single body, their backs attached, countervisioned]" (219). God was unhappy, in other words, with the fact that his creature resembled a dual-gendered, back-attached Siamese twin, with poor prospects for intimacy. Leone's depiction of God's earth-creature Adam would seem to be a monstrous version of the Chinese ideograph for *bei* (to compare), which figures opposition or incompatiblity by showing two people with their backs to each other.[56] In Leone's text, God puts this compound being "Adam" to sleep (not yet to dream, a feature that awaited Milton's intervention) in order to remove one of its sides

[55] Jean Calvin, *A Commentarie of John Calvine, upon the first booke of Moses called Genesis*, trans. Thomas Tymme (London: Imprinted for I. Harison and G. Bishop, 1578), 47.

[56] Wang Jun, a former graduate student in my English Renaissance Poetry course at the University of Denver (Spring 1989), called my attention to this ideograph in a paper he wrote comparing Western metaphor with Chinese *Bi*.

("sus lados"), a word which in Hebrew, Leone insists, is ambivalent ("equívoco") and can mean "either side [*lado*] or rib [*costilla*]" (220).

By disturbing the signifier *costilla*—which "aquí y en otras partes [here and in other places]" also means *lado*—Leone works to erode the notion of a created, originary Hebrew meaning for Adam's "rib." One of those "other places" where that erosion was operative was in the eleventh-century commentary on the Pentateuch written by Rashi or Rabbi Solomon Izhaqui (1040–1105), for Jews the most beloved and most reprinted of all commentaries on the Mosaic books. Rashi's commentary, written in the century befopre Maimonides was to amalgamate Aristotelianism with Mosaism, not only observed that "God created man at first with two faces," but also noted the linguistic equivalence of "rib" and "side." Both Rashi and Leone appear to be writing counter to the stubborn Renaissance belief, recalled by Thomas Greene, "that Hebrew was a 'natural language' whose names for things corresponded to their true nature."[57] The errancy of one Hebrew word, in short, empowers Leone to replace Adam's "rib"—a trope of male primacy—with the androgyne's "other half"—a trope of sexual parity. Thanks to linguistic drift, Eve can become what Moses always "intended": that is, "el lado o la persona femenina que estaba detrás a las espaldas de Adam [the side or feminine person who was behind Adam's back]" (220). Moses, we note, is here construed as a brilliant allegorist who prefigured the Platonic androgyne. Plato is pictured as having misread Moses by creating, in the *Symposium*, an androgyne with "adulterous" qualities, with suggestions of reproach. And Leone's spokesman Philo, with his newly retailored androgyne, is credited with having theorized away the contradictions between the two Genesis accounts and unveiled "la persona feminina" always already present at Creation. Postmodern feminist analyses now trying to find in Gen. 1:27 "the absent or repressed maternal body, which has been unveiled by modern critical methods but still assigned a place apart from the sacred text itself" might profit from Leone's early sixteenth century critical method.[58] Drawing upon the instability of the Hebrew language for his reading of Plato's reading of Genesis, Leone's cool allegoricity separates him, as he himself claims, from those "comentadores ordinarios

[57] In Rashi's Commentary on Genesis, he acknowledges the seeming contradiction between the two Mosaic creation accounts, adding that "a Midrash provides the folklore that God created Adam with two faces (bisexual), and that later God divided him." Rashi concludes that "the plain meaning of the text" is that "male and female were both created on the sixth day without explaining how." I am indebted to T. Anthony Perry for his insights on Rashi's *Commentaries on the Pentateuch*, trans. Chaim Pearl (New York: W. W. Norton, 1970), 33. Thomas Greene's remarks on the Hebrew language are from *Light in Troy*, 6.

[58] See Mary Nyquist's excellent "Gynesis, Genesis, Exegesis, and the Formation of Milton's Eve," in *Cannibals, Witches, and Divorce: Estranging the Renaissance*, ed. Marjorie Garber (Baltimore: Johns Hopkins University Press, 1987), 151.

[quienes] se fatigan en concordar literalmente este texto [ordinary commentators (who) fatigue themselves in making this text agree literally]" (218). Whom this allusion to fatigued literalists is meant to embrace is not clear. But it bears recalling that Augustine, in *De Genesi ad litteram* (12.42), had attempted—with what degree of fatigue we can only infer from his *Confessions*[59]—to struggle with the question of sexual otherness.

By the turn of the sixteenth century, Adam's rib has wandered into the opening pages of Covarrubias's influential *Tesoro* (1611), where, in his address to the reader of his dictionary ("Al Letor"), he finds it necessary to rehearse the whole account from Genesis 2 of God's creation of "our first father." Having placed Adam in a rich and endowed Paradise, God then has second thoughts: "*Non est bonum hominem esse solum, faciamus et adiutorium simili sibi*; y embiando en Adán un sueño, sacóle una costilla del costado, y formó della a Eva [It is not good for man to be alone; let us make a help meet for him; and God put Adam to sleep, removed a rib from his side, and from it formed Eve]." The privileged place Covarrubias gives to this "Yahwist" version of the Genesis story in the dedication of his text is undercut in the text itself in his entry on "ADÁN," which, citing the authority of Genesis 5, features only the androgynized (the "Priestly") Adam: "En la lengua santa todo hombre se llama Adán, y comprehende ambos sexos [In the holy language, every man is called Adam and comprehends both sexes]." How were Golden Age readers to reconcile the contradiction internalized in this dictionary? Covarrubias, not an exegete, only asked that all the "errors" in his *Tesoro* be charitably forgiven him ("que todo aquello que yo errare, se me enmiende con caridad").[60]

The perceived contradiction between the two Genesis stories has had wide-reaching implications, well beyond Covarrubias, for Western culture. Patricia Parker forcefully argues that it is the second creation story, the Adam's dream story, that "has for centuries authorized woman's place as second place."[61] It was the version of Genesis underwriting the oppressive social practices that were for centuries justified by 1 Tim. 2:11–14: "Let the woman learn in silence with all subjection. But I suffer not a woman to teach, nor to usurp authority over the man, but to be in

[59] "Recalling in the *Confessions* his own experience, Augustine instinctively identifies the question of self-government with rational control over sexual impulses"—with "his struggle to be chaste." He then "takes his own experience as paradigmatic for all human experience" (Pagels, *Adam, Eve, and the Serpent*, 105–6).

[60] Covarrubias, *Tesoro*, 19, 41, 21.

[61] For various insights in this present chapter, I am indebted to Patricia Parker's illuminating study, "Coming Second: Woman's Place," in *Literary Fat Ladies: Rhetoric, Gender, Property* (London and New York: Methuen, 1987), 178–233.

silence. *For Adam was first formed, then Eve.*"[62] As late as the 1860s, a *californio* called Ignacio Coronel, speaking for men of Mexican heritage across America's Southwest, would be citing biblical sources to justify women's secondariness: "Man born before woman is thus more noble than she."[63] Chronological priority here—the assumption that "first is best" or most noble—is the kind of thinking that privileges first causes, first principles, or firstborn sons.[64] It is possible, of course, to use an alternative valorization—such as the paradigm of "progress" with its presupposition that "later is better"—to promote Eve at the expense of Adam. Phyllis Trible's work on "depatriarchalizing" biblical interpretation rests on this paradigm: "But the last may be first, as both the biblical theologian and the literary critic know. Thus the Yahwist account moves to its climax, not its decline, in the creation of woman. She is not an afterthought; she is the culmination."[65] This argument adopts what Derrida calls the logic of supplementarity, in which a temporally later term is superior to and perfects an earlier term. In addition, Trible's remark reminds us that, along with the theologian and the critic, the talking dogs in Cervantes's *El coloquio de los perros* also know, courtesy of the oracle that holds the key to their deliverance from animality, that "the last may be first."

In sum, then, although the Genesis 2 account of Adam's rib was to have a powerful and pervasive influence in literature down to Milton—who sublimely remotivated for English poetry the wifely role, the lure of derivative power—Leone Ebreo provides us an arresting sixteenth-century glimpse of its reversal. In Leone's counterdiscourse, the Genesis sequence is androgynized, emptied of all hierarchical value: the sexes are imagined in relations of parity, mutuality, sexuality, generativity, and—what was novel to the Renaissance—nondominant sexual difference: symmetry *without* hierarchy. This kind of thinking, which ran counter to Leone's age, found its parallels in various Neoplatonic and gnostic ideas. Paracelsus (1494–1541), for example, a near contemporary of Leone's, postulated woman as part of the Godhead, and connected her with mystical forces systematized in alchemical writings.[66] It has become a common-

[62] Mieke Bal's essay, "Sexuality, Sin, and Sorrow: The Emergence of the Female Character (A Reading of Genesis 1–3)," *Poetics Today* [Special Issue: *The Female Body in Western Culture: Semiotic Perspectives*, ed. Susan Rubin Suleiman] 6 (1985): 21–42, opens with this quotation from 1 Tim. 2:11–14 and critiques the misogynist reading of the creation account in Genesis 2.

[63] Richard Griswold del Castillo, *La Familia: Chicano Families in the Urban Southwest, 1848 to the Present* (Notre Dame, Ind.: University of Notre Dame Press, 1984), 29.

[64] On this kind of privileging, see Nyquist, "Gynesis," 158.

[65] Phyllis Trible, "Depatriarchalizing in Biblical Interpretation," *Journal of the American Academy of Religion* 16 (1973): 35–36.

[66] See W. Pagel, *Das medizinische Weltbild des Paracelsus* (Wiesbaden, 1962), 62–70; cited by Maclean, *Renaissance Notion*, 22.

place to say that women in the Renaissance were exalted by Neoplatonic theories, which systematically distanced themselves from the Aristotelian systems of thought borrowed to fortify the Adam's rib creation story. Maclean provides a useful overview of these Neoplatonic ideas:

> Love is the *vinculum mundi*, binding the whole of the creation together; earthly love is a step on the ladder of love leading eventually to ecstatic re-union with the Godhead. When a woman is loved, her lover is loving not only her, but God and himself as well. The perfection of love is in reciprocity; but its origin lies in beauty, which women possess in greater store than men. Physical beauty reflects mental goodness; thus women are better than men. Furthermore, the being least weighed down with earthly matter is the most spiritual, and its soul is more free to escape from the fetters of physical existence; women therefore are able more easily to transcend the limitations of this world.[67]

It is not always easy to translate all this ecstatic discourse—the mystical prerogatives that Renaissance Neoplatonism supposedly gave to women—into any cognitive advances in the writings of the period. But Leone Ebreo's Neoplatonism posed, as the above commentaries on the creation should make clear, an unorthodox challenge to the dominant scholastic infrastructures that informed most Renaissance notions of women. In recognizing androgynous implications that would blur the preemptive category of maleness in the Yahwist version of Genesis, Leone cleared a new conceptual space. Leone's Neoplatonism—which reconstituted the androgyne as a dialogical relation between the sexes—gave Cervantes, and not only Cervantes, a new understanding of carnal love and creativity.

When Cervantes sat down to one of his final tasks of literary creation, taking a page out of Leone, he created a countertext to "Adam's Dream." At the close of the *Persiles*—and the close of his life—Cervantes represents some penitents in Rome declaring to his heroine the mysteries of the Catholic faith: "Discurrieron por la verdad de la creación del hombre [They discoursed over the truth of the creation of man]" (435). What kind of discourses they had over "the truth" of the contradictory creation stories rehearsed in this chapter is entirely glossed over by Cervantes's narrator, who gives a dismissive nod to what he calls the "principales y más convenientes misterios [the principle and most useful mysteries]" (435). But some seven pages later this same narrator closes a chapter with a remark that unexpectedly returns to these undisclosed mysteries. He suddenly feels compelled to inform us, in a mini-genesis story, that "la naturaleza [nature]" had created Cervantes's protagonists as equals on issues of sexuality: "hecho iguales y formado en una misma turquesa [cre-

[67] Maclean, *Renaissance Notion*, 24.

ated as equals, out of the same bullet-mold]" (442). Sexual parity is established here through the curiously aggressive metaphor of a *turquesa*, a mold in which clay bullets ("bodoques") were formed to shoot from crossbows ("ballestas").[68]

Cervantes's Nature, no longer yielding to grace as she did in Augustine, is semi-personified here as a kind of munitions worker, creating from clay an androgynized Adam, privileging the "equal rights" or "P" version of the Genesis story. She is essentially dramatizing a statement made by Mauricio, the sage in the opening book of the *Persiles*: "Las almas todas son iguales y de una misma masa en sus principios, criadas y formadas por su Hacedor [All souls are equal, in the beginnings created and formed by their Maker out of the same material]" (133). The nature of Cervantes's Nature would be fortified, some two decades after the publication of the *Persiles*, by María de Zayas, an attentive reader of Cervantes, in an address to the reader of her *Novelas amorosas y ejemplares* (1637):

> Porque si esta materia de que nos componemos los hombres y las mujeres, ya sea una trabazón de fuego y barro, o ya una masa de espíritus y terrones, no tiene más nobleza en ellos que en nosotras, si es una misma la sangre, los sentidos, las potencias y los órganos por donde se obran sus efetos son unos mismos, la misma alma que ellos, porque las almas ni son hombres ni mujeres.

> [Whether this matter that we men and women are made of is a bonding of clay and fire, or a dough of earth and spirit, whatever, it has no more nobility in men than in women, for our blood is the same; our senses, our powers, and the organs which perform their functions are all the same; our souls the same, for souls are neither male nor female.][69]

Cervantes's filiation to Leone Ebreo, in sum, is both thematic and structural. The figure of the androgyne in the *Persiles* destabilizes not only that most ancient of hierachized oppositions, male/female, but also every other "split" in the text: novel/romance, pagan/Christian, allegory/mimesis, main plot/interpolations, first half/second half, North/South, land/sea, Madonna/whore, and many more seemingly irreconcilable differ-

---

[68] In addition to a mold, Covarrubias also defines *turquesa* as a turquoise: "piedra de alguna estima de color azul [a blue stone of some worth]" (*Tesoro*, 983–84). *Autoridades* cites this very passage from the *Persiles* as an example of usage. "*Turquesa*: el molde donde se hacen los bodoques [pelotillas de barro] para tirar con la ballesta y por extensión se dice de otras cosas." "*Bodoque*: una pelota . . . tamaño de la ciruela pequeña, munición de la ballesta."

[69] María de Zayas y Sotomayor, *Novelas amorosas y ejemplares*, ed. Agustín g. de Amezúa (Madrid: Aldus, 1948), 21. The English version cited here is from H. Patsy Boyer's excellent and long-awaited translation of María de Zayas, entitled *The Enchantments of Love: Amorous and Exemplary Novels* (Berkeley: University of California Press, 1990).

ences are juxtaposed and then mixed or merged, their differences forever blurred. In the *Galatea*, his earliest romance, Cervantes first began to conceive of the possibility of a narrative designed by "formando de contrarios igual tela [weaving one fabric out of contraries]" (2.102). In the *Persiles*, his last romance, taking up the unfinished business of that earlier project, he wove an entire text in the figure of the androgyne, that ancient pattern of contraries yearning to be whole once again.

PART TWO

The Text

Chapter Five

CERVANTES ON CANNIBALS

Je ne sçay . . . quels barbares sont ceux-ci.

[I do not know what barbarians these are.]

—Montaigne, "On Cannibals"

ALTHOUGH the fictive time of Cervantes's Barbaric Isle narrative,[1] the opening text of the *Persiles*, coincides with Montaigne's celebrated interview, in 1562, of a Brazilian cannibal in Rouen, Montaigne's essay—perhaps the *locus classicus* for Renaissance notions of New World cannibalism—is often cited and widely anthologized, whereas Cervantes's reflections on cannibals remain unremarked. Montaigne's famous adage on barbarism arose out of his speculations on the above encounter: "We call barbarous anything that is contrary to our own habits." The prelapsarian savages he would famously fictionalize could be called "barbarous," he cautioned, only "by reference to the laws of reason, but not in comparison to ourselves, who surpass them in every kind of barbarity." In one kind of barbarity, however, "we" predatory Europeans did not surpass them: the habit of polygamy, extolled by Montaigne as a "beautiful thing" about barbaric marriages and, indeed, as a "proper marital virtue." The impropriety of the "proper" here may have struck certain Renaissance women readers, whose incredulity Montaigne himself predicted.[2] Readers of both sexes today, however, are as amused by Montaigne's pious depiction of polygamy among the cannibals as by, say, the Spanish historian López de Gómara's contemporaneous put-down of the habit and, indeed, by his handy displacement of it onto female Amerindians: "Poco confianza y castidad debe haber en las mujeres, pues esto dicen y hacen [There must be little confidence and chastity in the women,

---

[1] For internal evidence of the fictive time of the *Persiles*, see my chap. 6, n. 1.

[2] Montaigne's projection of masculine desire here curiously qualifies his own watchword of *restraint* ("Je m'abstiens"). He sees the wives of the barbarians of "Antarctic France" (Villegaignon's term for Brazil) as "anxious to procure [the friendship and kindliness of other women] for their husbands," and as being "more concerned for the honour of their men than for anything else." Such conjugal concern is not, for Montaigne, "a miracle"—as he anticipates Renaissance wives will exclaim—but rather one "of the highest virtues" ("On Cannibals," in *Essays*, trans. J. M. Cohen [Middlesex, Eng.: Penguin Books, 1958], 117–18).

since they practice such a thing]."[3] Whether extolled as Edenic or vilified
as unchaste, however, the documented polygamy of the American natives
usefully foregrounds the opening chapters of Cervantes's *Persiles*. Both
sides of this sixteenth-century debate—blindly insisting on the Otherness
of what was in fact their own essence—would find their way into Cervantes's fertile and leveling imagination, where so many of history's fictions are exposed. Situating his own literary fiction on an Old World island in the Arctic North Sea around the 1560s, Cervantes retools various
New World topoi of cannibalism and polygamy. For the beginnings of his
last romance, but with its entire trajectory in mind, Cervantes cannibalizes sixteenth-century notions of cannibalism.[4]

As soon as we begin to reflect on the difference between cannibal and
cannibal, we discover that Cervantes's barbarians are not instructive exceptions to High Renaissance culture, as Montaigne depicts his Brazil-
ians. Rousseau's "bon sauvage" is not implicit in Cervantes's narrative
because his barbarians are neither noble nor happy. They are not even
honorably polygamous, in the mode of Montaigne's utopian model, because polygamy implies an oversupply of women. How, then, do we
know what barbarians these are? Their representation in the *Persiles* is
distinctly New World: they dress both themselves and their tents in animal hides; they eat and drink, from vessels made out of tree bark, a "natural" diet of dried fruits and nuts, unleavened bread, and water; they sail
about in ad hoc wooden rafts; and they fight with bows and arrows. The
main concern of this chapter is the status and meaning of these barbarians
in and for Cervantes's last work. I would argue that they are grotesque
and manic representations of some of early modern Europe's most cherished orthodoxies; that they express in extreme and unmediated form the
disguised motives of Renaissance patriarchy; and that they are the invention of an experimental writer out to disrupt what he inscribes as the "Ley
Bárbara," a Barbaric Law that dimly foreshadows the Lacanian "Law of
the Father," the law of symbolic language. I suggest, finally, that the Barbaric Isle narrative functions as the germinal staging for a revolutionary

---

[3] On the customs of the natives of "la isla Española," see Franciso López de Gómara,
Hispania victrix. Primera y segunda parte de la historia general de las Indias, 2 vols. in 1,
*Biblioteca de autores españoles, desde la formación del lenguage hasta nuestros días: His-
toriadores primitivos de Indias* (Madrid: M. Rivadeneyra, 1877), 1:173.

[4] As is well known from Columbus's diaries, the Spanish term *caníbal* is a deformation of
"Caribe." See Cristóbal Colón, *Los cuatro viajes del Almirante y su Testamento*, ed. Ignacio
B. Anzoátegui (Buenos Aires: Espasa-Calpe Argentina, 1946) for entries written on 23 November 1492 (67), 5 December 1492 (80), and 17 December 1492 (94), in which the people
"de los Caniba" or "los Caníbales" and their habit of eating people "a bocados" is noted;
26 December 1492 (113), in which "los de Caniba" are identified as those whom the natives
call "caribes"; and 13 January 1493 (131), in which the natives called "Caniba" or "Carib"
are said to eat people ("comen la gente").

poetics of gender—a poetics unwritten in Cervantes's day, just beginning to be codified in ours. For a Cervantine text that explores the induction of gender, that enriches our literary explorations of sexual difference, and that queries the hegemonic or dominant discourses of the Renaissance, it is to the *Persiles*, far more than to *Don Quixote*, that we must turn.

THE BARBARIC ISLE NARRATIVE

The text of the *Persiles* begins with a barbarian's voice, its desired emphasis secured through *transgressio*, that strategic disruption of normal word order: "VOCES daba el bárbaro [The barbarian shouted]." In the beginning of Cervantes's last writing is not the Word but rather "un terrible y espantoso estruendo [a terrible and frightful shout]" (51). We are moved, from the start, to reflect on the difference between voice as speech and voice as sound: the barbaric voice is not constituted by the words it utters but by a shout for more sacrificial victims. Instantly focusing its grim concerns, the text ushers its readers, in medias res, into an emblematic scene of male sacrifice—not, as scholars have tirelessly universalized it, of "human sacrifice," a critical difference I shall return to later. The rebarbative nature of Cervantes's Barbaric Isle narrative has moved at least one of the text's modern editors, perhaps as a call to readerly patience, to apologize for its "largo comienzo repelente [long repellent beginning]."[5] As locative and evasive as his earlier "lugar de la Mancha,"[6] Cervantes's Barbaric Isle is a "place" of messianic male sacrifice situated somewhere in the icy wastes of the North Sea.

The isle sustains a community of agitated males whose "Law" or ritual idolatry dictates a continual circulation of women, robbed or purchased with precisely those "heavy metals" that Montaigne's happy natives never saw—"en pedazos de oro sin cuño y en preciosísimas perlas [with chunks of gold ore and extremely precious pearls]" (57). This male traffic in women, the text is careful to note, has not brutalized the barbarians: the women who are imported into the island as commodities, and who are circulated like currency between pirates and barbarians, are well treated by the islanders, "que sólo en esto muestran no ser bárbaros [who only in this show themselves not to be barbarians]" (57). As the hero later explains it, "en esta isla no hay muerte para las mujeres [on this island

---

[5] See the Espasa-Calpe edition (Buenos Aires, 1952) of *Los trabajos de Persiles y Sigismunda* for this anonymous editorial caveat.

[6] George Haley used these haunting adjectives to describe the opening phrase of *Don Quixote* in "The Implied Author in *Don Quixote*" (Paper delivered at the Newberry Library, Chicago, 1 July 1982). See Haley's elegant essay on "The Narrator in *Don Quixote*: Maese Pedro's Puppet Show," *Modern Language Notes* 80 (1965): 145–65; rpt. in *Critical Essays on Cervantes*, ed. Ruth El Saffar (Boston: G. K. Hall, 1986), 94–110.

there's no death for women]" (67), a condition that may evoke for readers the one woman deprived of death by Western Christianity, the Virgin Mary, who closes her earthly career either in an Assumption or, in the Eastern church, by a Dormition.[7] Fetishized as incubators for the tribe's forthcoming messiah, the women on Cervantes's Barbaric Isle would appear to suffer only one notable deprivation: speech. That these costly and venerated women have no rights of articulation, that they are silenced or "infantilized" by their owners, that they are consigned to the role of the silent Other in a merchandising culture is explained, both to the European characters and to the reader, by the Isle's captive female interpreter: "Que estos mis amos no gustan que en otras pláticas me dilate, sino en aquellas que hacen al caso para su negocio [These my masters do not wish me to dilate my speech in anything but what is pertinent to their business]" (62).

Their "business" is cannibalism, though with a Cervantine twist that distinguishes it not only from Montaigne's Brazilian variety but also (as I explain later) from every single one of the *Persiles*'s proposed models. For the cannibalism on this male fantasy island implicates women within a symbolic economy of reproduction based on an imperialistic paternal law. As disclosed by one of the potential female slaves,

> esta ínsula, donde dicen que estamos, la cual es habitada de unos bárbaros, gente indómita y cruel, los cuales tienen entre sí por cosa inviolable y cierta, persuadidos, o ya del demonio, o ya de un antiguo hechicero a quien ellos tienen por sapientísimo varón, que de entre ellos ha de salir un rey que conquiste y gane gran parte del mundo. . . . (57)

> [this island, where they say we are, is inhabited by certain barbarians, a cruel and indomitable people, who hold as a certain and inviolable truth, having been persuaded either by the devil or by an ancient sorcerer whom they regard as the wisest of men, that from among them a king will come forth who will conquer and win a great part of the world. . . .]

Oscillating between prophecy and legislation, the word among the barbarians is a fixity, a "cosa . . . cierta." Cervantes—who elsewhere left us the ironic assurance that he would sacrifice "un dedo / por saber la verdad segura, y presto [a finger / to know the truth for certain, and quickly]"[8]— here links what his barbarians hold as "truth" to a form of patrilineal imperialism. By representing the source of this truth as the prophecy of

---

[7] On this and other maternal issues related to my argument, see Julia Kristeva's "Stabat Mater," in *Histoires d'amour* (Paris: Denoel, 1983) (*Tales of Love*, trans. Leon S. Roudiez [New York: Columbia University Press, 1987], 242–43).

[8] "Diera un dedo / por saber la verdad segura, y presto." The lines are from *Viaje del Parnaso*, chap. 6. On the issue of Cervantes's quest for truth, see Juan Bautista Avalle-Arce's compelling first chapter, "Conocimiento y vida en Cervantes," in *Nuevos deslindes cervantinos* (Barcelona: Editorial Ariel, 1975), 15–72.

an ambiguous devil/sorcerer, Cervantes may be advertising his familiarity with the Andean historian Pedro Cieza de León (1553), whose depiction of the devil would seem to be a model for Cervantes's "sapientísimo varón."[9]

Animated by the "impertinente profecía [impertinent prophecy]" that one of them will father a world conqueror on an imported woman, Cervantes's barbarians have determined that such a paternal honor will be signed by the lack of "any sign" of repugnance in a ritual drinking test. The chief ingredient for the drink in question, according to the prophecy's fixed and immutable recipe, derives from a crop of sacrificed males:

> Este rey que esperan no saben quién ha de ser, y para saberlo aquel hechicero les dió esta orden: que sacrificasen todos los hombres que a su ínsula llegasen, de cuyos corazones . . . hiciesen polvos, y los diesen a beber a los bárbaros más principales de la ínsula, con expresa orden que, el que los pasase sin torcer el rostro ni dar muestra de que le sabía mal, le alzasen por su rey; pero no ha de ser este el que conquiste el mundo, sino un hijo suyo. (57)

> [It is not known who this king they await will be, and in order to know his identity, that sorcerer gave them this order: that they sacrifice all the men who arrive at their island, pulverize their hearts, and give them to the chief barbarians of the isle to drink, with the express order that whoever could swallow them without wincing, or without giving any sign that they tasted bad, would be raised as their king; *he* would not be the one to conquer the world, however, but his son.]

Confining ourselves to European subtexts for this strange passage, we might invoke, if only to dismiss, the legend of the eaten heart, encountered regularly in the medieval literature of Western Europe, irregularly and belatedly in Castilian literature. In most of these narratives—traditionally traced back to troubadour biography, to the *Vita nuova*, or to the *Decameron*—a woman, more often than not a faithless wife, eats her lover's heart, either forcibly or unwittingly.[10] But the patriarchal taste test

---

[9] On Pedro Cieza de León as a possible source for the *Persiles*, indirectly via Inca Garcilaso, see Schevill and Bonilla, "Introduction," *Persiles* 1:xxvii, ftn.

[10] I am indebted to Ciriaco Morón-Arroyo for calling to my attention Hispanic criticism of the *corazón comido* legend. Hearts are devoured by female lovers in the biography of the Provençal poet Guilhem de Cabestaing, in chap. 3 of Dante's *Vita nuova*, and in the ninth novella of the fourth day of Boccaccio's *Decameron*. The two Castilian accounts that Cervantes may have known are in Antonio de Torquemada's *Coloquios satíricos* (1553) and in Juan Bautista de Loyola's *Viaje y naufragios del Macedonio* (1587) (see John D. Williams, "Notes on the Legend of the Eaten Heart in Spain," *Hispanic Review* 26 [April 1958]: 91–98). Let me add to this grisly catalogue Marguerite de Navarre's *Heptameron* (1558), which includes, in story 51, an interesting variant on the eaten heart: a Ghibelline captain tears a dead Guelph's heart out of his chest, roasts it over a charcoal fire, and eats it, swearing "that

in Cervantes—in its exclusive focus on the male gender and on issues of generation and succession—would seem to owe nothing at all to the European legend of *el corazón comido.*

The test itself reveals, on the other hand, an important if critically unacknowledged trace of the *Comentarios reales* (1609), where Inca Garcilaso cites the tattered papers of Padre Blas Valera's report on certain barbaric Mesoamericans who would eat their live victims piecemeal, in slivers and protuberances: "Si al tiempo que atormentaban al triste hizo *alguna señal de sentimiento con el rostro* [If while they tortured the poor man he showed any signs of response in his face]," the victim's corpse would then be dumped unceremoniously into a river.[11] Cervantes may have adapted this scenario for his own fictional needs: a facial grimace as a way of thinning out the barbarian candidate pool for messianic fatherhood. *Not* signing facially, among his barbarian horde, is expected to identify the father of their Messiah—to trigger the visibility of paternity. Although Cervantes may have borrowed Garcilaso's "if-clause" to exclude facial gesturers from honored paternity, his cannibals must be distinguished from Garcilaso's cited cannibals, whose *victims* alone do the signing.[12] By the style of their homophagy—by their affectless ingestion of the charred and pulverized hearts of other men—Cervantes's cannibals would appear to be challenging the notion that fatherhood is always uncertain. Freud called an "old legal tag" ("*pater semper incertus est*") what Castiglione had dramatized for Cervantes's day through the character of Ottaviano Fregoso in *Il cortegiano*: "For since women are very imperfect creatures, and of little or no dignity compared with men, they are incapable in themselves of performing any virtuous act, and so it was necessary, through shame and fear of disgrace, to place on them a restraint which might foster some good qualities. And it appeared that more necessary than anything else was chastity, *so that we could be certain of our own children.*"[13] A parodic version of Fregoso's restraining males, Cer-

he had never tasted a more delicious or enjoyable morsel" (trans. P. A. Chilton [Middlesex, Eng.: Penguin Books, 1984], 431–32).

[11] Inca Garcilaso strategically distances these cannibals—who live in the "Antis," having emerged from the Mexican region ("la región mejicana") to settle in the regions of Darien/Panama—from his own Inca nation, which he regards as one of the cradles of civilization. See *Comentarios reales de los Incas*, vol. 133 of the Biblioteca de Autores Españoles, ed. P. Carmelo-Sáenz de Santa María, s.i. (Madrid: Ediciones Atlas, 1960), 20–21; emphasis added. Schevill and Bonilla think that Cervantes "leyó con detenimiento [carefully read]" Inca Garcilaso's commentaries, and that he began the *Persiles* after their publication (Lisbon, 1609) ("Introduction," *Persiles*, ix).

[12] Cervantes's cannibals are also an inventive departure from Columbus's inaugural *caníbales*, whose very appearance supposedly defines their occupation: "La deformidad de su gesto lo dice [The deformity of their faces reveals it]." See *Cuatro viajes*, 199.

[13] For the incitude of the father (while the mother is "certissima"), see "Family Ro-

vantes's cannibals eat hearts so that they can be certain of their own children. A far cry from the practices of any of the Conquest narratives I am familiar with, the cannibalism in the *Persiles* would seem to be a way of stomaching, as it were, the invisibility of paternity. By ridiculing this hunger for certainty, Cervantes's text demystifies the symbolic amplification of the invisible that Freud, nearly four centuries later, was to privilege as paternity.

In an abrasive passage that nonetheless sheds light on Cervantes's Barbaric Isle, Dorothy Dinnerstein observes that it is the very *un*certainty of paternity that drives men to engage in "various initiation rites through which they symbolically and passionately affirm that it is they who have themselves created human beings, as compared with the mere flesh spawned by woman."[14] Seen in the light of Dinnerstein's caustic view of masculine creativity, the antics on Cervantes's Barbaric Isle would appear to invoke the latent ideal of male parthenogenesis. The classic spokesman for this ideal is, of course, Euripides' Hippolytus, who wishes that males could have simply "bought the seed of progeny": that a man might have dedicated to Zeus images of gold, silver, or bronze and been given, in turn, "his worth in sons according to the assessments / of his gift's value." Cervantes's barbarians buy their vessels if not their seeds of progeny: but they represent a masculine yearning not too remote from Hippolytus's desire to live "in houses free of the taint of women's presence."[15]

The rites of Cervantes's cannibals invite comparison not only with Freud's promotion of paternity but also with his (not unrelated) Oedipal cannibalism of "the primal horde," with which they share at least a tyrannical father-complex. Cervantes's narrative begins with a dream of imperial propagation, with a barbarian horde trying to identify the father of its future despot, a man predicted to enslave the whole world. The narrative ends, four chapters later, with all of the barbarians having killed each other in a blazing orgy of parricide. Freud's so-called vision or hypothesis, however (which he allows has "a monstrous air"), opens with

mance" in Freud, *SE* 9:239. Freud elsewhere promotes paternity over maternity precisely because of its incertitude: "This turning from the mother to the father points in addition to a victory of intellectuality over sensuality—that is, an advance in civilization, since maternity is proved by the evidence of the senses while paternity is a hypothesis, based on an inference and a premiss" (*Moses and Monotheism: Three Essays, SE* 23:114). Baldesar Castiglione, *The Book of the Courtier*, trans. George Bull (New York: Penguin, 1967), 195.

[14] *The Mermaid and the Minotaur: Sexual Arrangements and the Human Malaise* (New York: Harper and Row, 1976), 80.

[15] "Women! This coin which men find counterfeit! / Why, why Lord Zeus, did you put them in the world, / in the light of the sun? If you were so determined / to breed the race of man, the source of it / should not have been women" (*Hippolytus*, in *Euripides*, trans. David Grene, vol. 3 of *The Complete Greek Tragedies*, ed. David Grene and Richmond Lattimore, 4 vols. [Chicago: University of Chicago Press, 1959], 189).

his "unlimited despot" already on the scene—an identifiable "primal father" who has killed or driven away his sons and seized all the available women for himself. The surviving sons unite to kill and devour their father, thus replacing "the patriarchal horde" with "the fraternal clan." This band of brothers, collectively deciding to forego the possession of the women for whom they have killed their father, are now driven to find strange women—to the exogamy which, for Freud, is so intimately tied to totemism and the taboo of incest. Their totem feast, so Freud's speculation ends, is the commemoration of this cannibalism, a deed that marked the beginning "of social organization, of moral restrictions and of religion."[16] If Cervantes's barbarians seem also driven to exogamy, it is not because of their guilt over patricide, a guilt they will not live to regret. Cervantes, it would seem, is hypothesizing a horde sometime *prior* to its eugenic reproduction of a tyrannical father, a global conqueror, a despot who is always already in the wings: but the text is also erasing that father *before* conception. Instead of a primal father, Cervantes's barbarians cannibalize alien males, a technique for incorporating them into the Barbaric Law. Social and cultural institutions cannot originate from Cervantes's cannibals, however, because he kills them off before they can destroy his protagonists. It is not the guilt of any "totemic brother-clan," but the guilt of sexual difference that Cervantes then explores. The cannibalism envisioned in the *Persiles*, in short, is far more polemic than totemic.

At the heart of the Barbaric Isle's social contract, however, both guaranteeing its continuity and sustaining its "vanidad [vanity]" (58), is a version of that drive to find "strange women." The barbaric initiation rite requires imported women, whose only function is to ensure procreation, vendible women, who are circulated like currency between man and man. As the character Taurisa elaborates on this traffic in potential mothers, "cosarios andan por todos estos mares, ínsulas y riberas, robando o comprando las más hermosas doncellas que hallan, para traerlas por granjería a vender a esta ínsula [pirates roam all these seas, islands, and coasts, stealing or purchasing the most beautiful women they can find, in order to bring them to sell for a profit on the Barbaric Isle]" (57). The first mention of Cervantes's female protagonist is that "se vio vendida, y comprada [she found herself sold, and then bought]" (56). It is a fate that aligns her with those obligatory shepherdesses that Sansón Carrasco wants to buy for the projected pastoral sabbatical of Don Quixote and his friends: "Que pues las venden en las plazas, bien las podemos comprar

---

[16] I have used Freud's account of the "primal horde" from *Totem and Taboo*, SE 13:82, 141–55; from *Moses and Monotheism*, SE 23:81–90, 131; and from Freud's *An Autobiographical Study*, trans. James Strachey (New York: W. W. Norton, 1963), 128–30. On cannibalism and incest as earliest instinctual wishes, see SE 21:10–11.

nosotros y tenerlas por nuestras [For as they sell them in the market-places, we can easily buy them and keep them for our own]" (*DQ* 2.73).[17]

The text of the *Persiles* explains, with similar mordant irony, that the barbaric men buy *only* women: "Si son otras mercancías las vuestras, no las hemos menester [If your cargo is anything else, we don't need it]," the resident interpreter shouts at the arriving Europeans, explaining that the barbarians have "todo lo necesario para la vida humana, sin tener nece-sidad de salir a otra parte a buscarlo [everything necessary for human life, without having to go elsewhere to look for it]" (62). How do we interpret an economy that arrogantly possesses all things "necessary for human life" except for the maternal function, which it must appropriate? An economy that must detour through a purchased woman in order to prop-agate and conquer? An economy that requires all its women to be ex-cluded from its signifying ventures? Although the status accorded to the exchange of power and goods on the Barbaric Isle has provoked scarce exegetical interest, it can be lost on few readers today that Cervantes's Barbaric Isle is a culture mediated by chunks of gold, a tiny Renaissance patriarchy in which the commercial is confounded with the genealogical transaction.

The French psychoanalyst Luce Irigaray, among others, has labeled women as the "goods" through which patriarchal power passes. In an-other and more uterine context, Irigaray laments that the womb, under patriarchal law, remains simply a passive receptacle with no claims on the "product" of sexual union—the womb "itself possessed as a means of (re)production."[18] Cervantes's barbarians explicitly possess wombs "as a means of (re)production," as commodities. Whatever patriarchal power passes through the "goods" in his text, it does not pass randomly, nor even, for that matter, pleasurably. It must be ingested and tested, courtesy of sacrificed male outsiders, for its biosymbolic clout. The institutional-ized cannibalism in the *Persiles*, in other words, turns on the issues, the ideologies, and the tensions of sexual difference. It is a strictly gendered ritual, expressing a variety of powerful psychosexual dispositions. It en-ables Cervantes's barbaric society to establish relationships of similitude and difference, of equality and domination that resolve crucial issues of

[17] These images recall Cervantes's well-known metaphor for poetry in *Don Quixote* as an "under no circumstances vendible" young woman: "no ha de ser vendible en ninguna manera" (2.16).

[18] Luce Irigaray, "Des marchandises entre elles" ("When the Goods Get Together"), trans. Claudia Reeder, in *New French Feminisms: An Anthology*, ed. Elaine Marks and Isabelle de Courtivron (Amherst: University of Massachusetts Press, 1980), 107–10. *Spec-ulum de l'autre femme* (Paris: Editions de Minuit, 1974), 16. Irigaray links Marx's analysis of the commodity as the basic form of capitalist wealth to the status of women in patriarchal societies.

order and identity. It endorses and expands the Aristotelian notion of woman as an incubator, man as an imparter of life.[19] It automatically eliminates wincing males from potential paternity. And it flamboyantly seeks out women in their maternal, virginal, and queenly representations.

Pertinent to this Cervantine fiction may be one of Julia Kristeva's most astute psychoanalytic inquiries: "What is there, in the portrayal of the Maternal in general and particularly in its Christian, virginal, one, that reduces social anguish and gratifies a male being?"[20] Put another way, what kind of compensatory fictions has this male being created to reduce his social anguish? The question Kristeva poses now, in our "post-virginal" age when the discourse of motherhood is distant or even lacking, Cervantes seems to have asked implicitly in the early 1600s, when the powerful imaginary construct of the Virgin Mother was still among the master discourses of the Renaissance. It is a construct that still funds traditional readings of the *Persiles*, and may be detected, for instance, in Casalduero's twentieth-century claim that, within the Baroque world Cervantes was representing, every woman had to elevate her "ojos llenos de lágrimas [tear-filled eyes]" toward the Virgin Mary as a paradigm of virtue.[21] Such baroque speculations apply more to the Baroque Age than to Cervantes's text, in which the figure of the Virgin Mother, as chapter 9 of the present book shows, is represented as salvific, as deeply caring of women, even of "fallen women," but not as a paradigm for female sexuality.[22] In our current urgency to reformulate what are felt to be coercive representations of Western femininity and motherhood, Cervantes's early dissidence appears especially striking.

Into this fantasy world, then, of men compulsively driven to a sanctimonious violence that both appropriates and organizes the maternal libido, Cervantes's hero is twice, and in both senses of the word, *delivered*. In the opening scene of the text, he is represented as being hoisted out of "la estrecha boca de una profunda mazmorra [the narrow mouth of a deep dungeon]" into "la luz del claro cielo que nos cubre [the light of the clear sky which covers us]" (51). This literalization of the Spanish idiom

[19] Aristotelian accounts of sex determination *in utero*, chiefly from *De generatione animalium*, were being heavily refuted by Galenists and others during the late sixteenth century, the fictive time of the *Persiles*.

[20] Kristeva, "Stabat Mater," 236.

[21] Casalduero, *Sentido y forma de* Los trabajos, 17.

[22] "Far from being the glory of her sex, she is *not of her sex* in its malediction, tribulation and imperfection," argues Marina Warner, whose historical research into the cult of the Virgin Mary has led to her disenchanted assessment of Mary's enshrined virginity. See *Alone of All Her Sex*, an avowed subtext of Kristeva's "Stabat Mater" essay. Ian Maclean similarly argues that the figure of the Virgin Mary, despite her redemptive role in medieval and Counter-Reformation literature, presents a "questionable advantage to womankind" (*Renaissance Notion*, 23).

for giving birth—*dar a luz*—links Cervantes, in a violent variant of the famously funny prologue to part 1 of *Don Quixote*, to a hermeneutic tradition of "birthing" ideas, characters, or texts that stretches back to Plato.[23] All readers of *Don Quixote* will also recall a similar hoisting out of a cave in the Cave of Montesinos episode—a place, according to Sancho, "que debe de ser peor que mazmorra [which must be worse than a dungeon]." Before the descent, Sancho invokes God to guide his master safely "a la luz desta vida [into the light of this world]," and after it he mockingly inquires whether Don Quixote has remained in the cave "para casta" (2.22). One could argue that Don Quixote *did* "found a family" in that generative cave, one whose lineage would include the hero of the *Persiles*, that storytelling self "born" on the opening page who will begin narrating his pre-textual adventures, the text's deferred prologue, to a chorus of gender-coded responses in book 2.[24]

Having narrowly escaped, thanks to a providential tempest, the fate of sacrificial victim after his emergence into the barbaric order, the hero returns to the Barbaric Isle to rescue the heroine. For this enterprise, he assumes gender disguise, appearing in woman's dress among the barbarians, an avatar of Don Gaspar Gregorio in *Don Quixote* who was forced to live, also in cross dress, "entre aquellos bárbaros turcos [among those barbarous Turks]" (2.63). When Persiles meets up with Sigismunda, who is being readied for sacrifice, the couple has undergone a "metamorfosis bien estraño [very strange metamorphosis]," as book 3 of the text recalls it: they are wearing "trocados trajes, ella en el de varón, y él en de hembra [cross-dress, she in male and he in female clothing]" (341). Their tearful embrace, each in gender disguise, inspires a fatal desire in the barbarian warrior Bradamiro for the man he thinks is a woman.[25] Bradamiro's articulation of his specular desire is one of the few examples we are given of direct discourse among the barbarians: "Esta doncella es mía, porque yo la quiero [This woman is mine because I want her]" (67). Even this brief expression of extravagant desire—this encounter of a male with what he perceives, if mistakenly, to be sexual difference—constitutes a deviancy from the barbaric code (and their language *is* a code). For his transgression, Bradamiro is instantly punished by the Isle's governor with

[23] See, for example, Plato, *Symposium* 209a, b, c.

[24] Ruth El Saffar notes, under the rubric of "The Symbology of Rebirth and Union," that the *Persiles* "begins with a scene rich in the imagery of rebirth" (*Beyond Fiction*, 131).

[25] The suggestive resemblances between Bradamiro, *bramar*, and *miro* may be worth mentioning. Cervantes's barbarian doubtless inspired Francisco de Rojas Zorilla's representation, in a deservedly little-known melodrama first performed in 1633 of a barbarian called Bradamiro who leads an army of woman warriors. See Raymond R. MacCurdy, *Francisco de Rojas Zorilla* (New York: Twayne Publishers, 1968), 101–3.

a deadly arrow into the mouth, "quitándole el movimiento de la lengua [stopping the movement of his tongue]" (68).

Now death by lingual penetration would generate a surplus of meaning even in the least fantastic of narratives. What is striking about the received readings of this passage, however, is that its metaphors of penetration have been consensually elucidated by acts of sodomy. Alban Forcione, for instance, writes of the barbarian Bradamiro's "sodomitic passion." Eduardo González—who wisely sees Cervantes's barbarians as "monosexual" rather than "homosexual"—still reads the ingestion of those pulverized hearts as metaphorizing "el autóctono ajetreo sodomita del grupo [the aboriginal sodomite agitation of the group]." Even Joaquín Casalduero, who interprets the *Persiles* through a sternly Christian this-for-that allegory, allows that he gets "una impresión de sodomía [an impression of sodomy]" from his reading of this episode.[26] The impressions of the above critics would seem to continue in the tradition of some of the Conquest chronicles suggested as possible sources for Cervantes, where the barbaric and the sodomitic are often interchangeable: one thinks, for example, of the overheated description of the natives of "la isla Española" as "grandísimos sodométicos, holgazanes, mentirosos, ingratos, mudables, y ruines [tremendous sodomites, idlers, liars, ungrateful, fickle, and despicable]."[27] At pains to gloss his reading of that "sodomite agitation" among the barbarians, González interprets its function there as a kind of pre-Oedipal polymorphous perversity, as a touchstone for "un deseo primordial activador de los primeros tropismos de la cría humana. Dicho deseo no tiene, por supuesto, que referirnos necesariamente a la sodomía [a primordial desire that activates the first tropisms of the human infant. Such a desire need not, of course, necessarily refer to sodomy]."[28] Such a desire, as González himself admits, is explicitly represented by Cervantes as the collective tropism of a monosexual community, specifically of a legislated phallic community that cannot, will not, accept sexual difference. That this phallic representation squares with the nature of what González calls "la cría humana" is, of course, arguable. Psychoanalysis comes up against its limits when faced with the

[26] Forcione, *Cervantes' Christian Romance*, 40; Eduardo González, *La persona y el relato: Proyecto de lectura psicoanalítica* (Madrid: José Porrúa Turanzas, 1985), 127; Casalduero, *Sentido y forma de* Los trabajos, 28.

[27] De Gómara, *Hispania victrix*, 173. On the "maldito oficio de sodomitas," see also Bernal Díaz del Castillo, *Historia de la Conquista de Nueva España* (Mexico: Editorial Porrúa, 1986), 86–87, 89.

[28] González, *La persona y el relato*, 127. González's chapter—inspired by two Lacanian essays and suggestively entitled "Érase una vez una isla obstinada"—is a brilliant psychoanalytic inquiry into the obstinacy of the masculinist consciousness.

first tropisms of the *female* infant, whose pre-Oedipal agitations may not lend themselves to such penetrating readings.[29] Freud's claim that "psycho-analysis does not try to describe what a woman is . . . but sets about enquiring how she comes into being" may be recast as Jacqueline Rose's Lacanian account of the "peculiar nature" of femininity: "Psychoanalysis does not produce that definition. It gives an account of how that definition is produced."[30] In any case, the issue here is not whether Cervantes's barbarians are practicing sodomites but—more crucially, I think— whether they can recognize a gendered subjectivity different from their own. The whole narrative shows us that the masculinity of these barbarians depends on an illusion of unequivocal gender identity. A female reading of Cervantes's scene of lingual murder might be less displaced: instead of sodomy, for example, I get the impression of an arrow through the tongue, of a reactive violence on the part of the barbarians, who—in keeping with their aversion to "dilated" speech—must stop the tongues of all dissidents. As Freud himself reminded us, sometimes a cigar is just a cigar.

In any event, the arrow that dispatches Bradamiro invites the predictable revenge scenario: one arrow leads to another and then to wholesale patri/fratricide in the tiny all-male kingdom, "sin respetar el hijo al padre, ni el hermano al hermano [son not respecting father, nor brother, brother]" (68). After one faction sets the island on fire, the inhabitants of the Barbaric Isle are turned, in a flagrantly Dantean *contrapasso*, into the very "ashes" they ritually consumed: "La isla se abrasa, casi todos los moradores de ella quedan hechos ceniza [The isle is aflame, and almost all of its inhabitants turned into ashes]" (70). Cervantes himself acknowledges the regrettable hardiness of such a culture, however, when in book 4 a minor character revisits the island, some two years after the holocaust, and reports on its resettlement: "Se tornaba a poblar la isla Bárbara, confirmándose sus moradores en la creencia de su falsa profecía [The Barbaric Isle was being repopulated, its inhabitants confirming their belief in its false prophecy]" (451).

Cervantes's invention of the Barbaric Isle, of a violent and sacrificial *mapa mentis* for the beginnings of his narrative, is neither a patriotic project nor a culturally self-congratulatory device: there is no attempt to exalt

---

[29] What Freud called "the prehistory of women" is at present engendering intense debate. See, e.g., pt. 2 of Sarah Kofman's *The Enigma of Woman: Women in Freud's Writings*, trans. Catherine Porter (Ithaca: Cornell University Press, 1985), 101–225, for a reading that takes issue with Luce Irigaray's extended reading of Freud's "On Femininity" in *Speculum de l'autre femme*, 13–129.

[30] *SE* 22:116; *Feminine Sexuality: Jacques Lacan and the ecole freudienne*, ed. Juliet Mitchell and Jaqueline Rose (New York: W. W. Norton, 1983), 57.

the value of the civilization the protagonists ultimately arrive at in Spain and, later, Italy. I cannot agree with the traditional criticism of Cervantes's barbary as a kind of Arctic hell opposed to Rome's heaven: to take a few examples, "la distancia que separa la isla bárbara de Roma [es] la que existe entre la violencia y Cristo [the distance that separates the Barbaric Isle from Rome (is) that which exists between violence and Christ]"; or "de las mazmorras de la Isla Bárbara al 'cielo de la tierra' [from the dungeons of the Barbaric Isle to 'heaven on earth']."[31] These readings overlook the fact that Rome itself in the *Persiles* turns out to be a nightmare world of some very subcelestial violence. Barbarism and civilization do not seem to me to function as binary oppositions in the *Persiles*, as various critics would have it, because the "civilization" represented in the second half of Cervantes's work is a radically contested concept.[32] The closing two books contain one elaboration after another of the buying and selling of sexuality—of the confounding of sexual and commercial signifiers—that earlier constituted the Barbaric Isle. Cervantes himself implicitly comments on the civilization/barbarism polarity when, in the prologue to the *Novelas ejemplares*, he declares that writings in praise of famous men are not always truthful, "por no tener punto preciso ni determinado las alabanzas ni los vituperios [because there is nothing either precise or calibrated about either praise or censure]." In like manner, there is nothing precise or calibrated about either barbarism or civilization in the *Persiles*. Both entities, although widely divergent at their starting points, appear to end up "en un punto [in one place]," as the discursive narrator muses about good and bad fortune in a chapter near the end of the book (464). Subverting various ancient dichotomies familiar to Western metaphysics, frozen like the genders within the Aristotelian foundations of our thinking, Cervantes's writing reaches for another "place"—for other logics, other poetics—from which to articulate desire. If civilization and barbarism end up in any one place in the *Per-*

---

[31] Cesáreo Bandera, *Mimesis conflictiva* (Madrid: Gredos, 1975), 131. Avalle-Arce, "Introduction," *Los trabajos*, 26.

[32] If anything, the concept of civilization in the *Persiles* resembles, perhaps even adumbrates, what the American novel has so obsessively represented as "the confrontation of a man and a woman which leads to the fall, to sex, marriage, and responsibility." Leslie Fiedler's description of "the typical male protagonist" of American fiction may be applied, even more generatively, to Don Quixote: "a man on the run, harried into the forest and out to sea, down the river and into combat—anywhere to avoid 'civilization,' which is to say, the confrontation of a man and a woman" (*Love and Death in the American Novel* [New York: Stein and Day, 1975], 26). For the psychology of Don Quixote's midlife sally as an avoidance technique, see Carroll B. Johnson's *Madness and Lust: A Psychoanalytical Approach to Don Quixote* (Berkeley: University of California Press, 1983).

siles, that place is Cervantes's narrating self, in all its marginal and eccentric hospitality.

AMERICAN SUBTEXTS

Numerous subtexts have been proffered as models for Cervantes's Barbaric Isle narrative, from Aristotle to various sixteenth-century chronicles
of the New World. Avalle-Arce, for instance, proposes that Cervantes
used Aristotle's "caso de Ifigenia [case of Iphigenia]" as his source, working from El Pinciano's rendering of the *Poetics*.[33] If so, it bears pondering
why Cervantes chose to alter the genders of his sacrificial victims: Iphigenia would not have been up for sacrifice on the Barbaric Isle because
"there is no death for women" there.

Various other critics have claimed, along with William Entwistle, that
Cervantes's barbarians "practise the rites and wear the clothing of Garcilaso de la Vega el Inca's American aborigines," as depicted in his *Comentarios reales* (1609), a text that Schevill and Bonilla think Cervantes
"leyó con detenimiento [attentively read]."[34] Although I, too, regard the
Comentarios as a powerful subtext of the *Persiles*, I believe that Cervantes's compositional principles require further scrutiny. This is no simple revivalist or ornamental initiative on Cervantes's part, as Entwistle's
remark suggests. Cervantes is engaged here in a creative imitation of a
cultural Other—using a heuristic imitative strategy—in which he assumes
the historicity, and indeed all the vulnerabilities, of his own particular
culture. Inca Garcilaso's was a subtext drawn from an alien culture, written in Spain while Cervantes himself was writing, but evoking a mundus
significans entirely remote in place if not in time. The Barbaric Isle narrative advertises its partial derivation from the *Comentarios reales*, but
then abruptly distances itself from its model.[35] Cervantes's allusiveness to
Inca Garcilaso's text is highly sophisticated in that the *Persiles* blatantly
sex-codes the aboriginal sacrifices represented in the *Commentaries*. Un-

---

[33] Avalle-Arce, *Los trabajos*, 51n.

[34] See Entwistle, "Ocean of Story," 164. Schevill and Bonilla had earlier noted in their
1914 edition of the *Persiles*, however, that Garcilaso himself had copied "bastante" from
various New World historians without ever specifying his source: Francisco López de Gómara, Pedro Cieza de León, Agustín de Zárate, and José de Acosta (ix, xxvii, ftn.). Mack
Singleton's thesis of the *Persiles* as an "amateurish" early work does not allow the later
influence of Inca Garcilaso ("The Persiles Mystery," in *Cervantes Across the Centuries*, ed.
Ángel Flores and M. J. Benardete [New York: Dryden, 1947], 227–38).

[35] "Heuristic" is one of Thomas M. Greene's four terms for types of strategies of humanist
imitation of remote texts—"reproductive," "eclectic," "heuristic," "dialectical." I am aware
that Cervantes's text, contemporaneous with Inca Garcilaso's, does not fully engage the
problem of anachronism assumed by Greene's study. See *Light in Troy*, esp. 37–48.

like Cervantes's barbarians, the pre-Incas were much more egalitarian in their cannibalistic rites: "Sacrificaban hombres y mujeres de todas edades [They sacrificed men and women of all ages]," Garcilaso informs us, noting in horrific detail the manner of this sacrifice. Cervantes's cannibals may "practise the rites" of Garcilaso's cannibals, but the heterosexual pool of victims has changed. Only the hearts of men are consigned, in the *Persiles*, to further the barbaric institution of a cannibalizing patrimonial world. Describing certain Indians on the outposts of the Inca empire as "bárbaros en la lengua como los castellanos [barbaric in their speech as the Castilians]," Inca Garcilaso succeeded in constituting the Spaniards as models of "barbarismo" in relation to language. Cervantes, in turn, manages to suggest that they are models of barbarism in relation to sexuality.[36]

In a recent historicist study of Garcilaso's *Commentaries*—chronicling how a "patrimonial bureaucratic state" affected both the writing of American history and the origins of the novel—Roberto González-Echevarría sees the picaresque novel as emerging "to lay bare the conventionality" of an individual's "process of legitimization, to uncover its status as an arbitrary imposition from the outside." González-Echevarría's reading of the picaresque as "an allegory of legitimization" could be usefully extended to the Barbaric Isle narrative, where Cervantes exposes, even mocks, the regulated codes of an imperial authority in all their arbitrary hypostatization. The absent patrimonial authority addressed in the picaresque narrative comes forward, as it were, in Cervantes's Barbaric Isle narrative: the "core of the picaresque" may have become the preface to the *Persiles*.[37]

A double subtext for the Barbaric Isle has been suggested by Forcione, who sees Cervantes's cannibalizing barbarians as linked "not only with the American Indians but also with the powers of Hell." This moralized merger, in the interpretive tradition of various sixteenth-century "natural and moral" histories of the Indies, reinforces Forcione's reading of the "barbarians' grotesque marriage . . . and its prophetic offspring" as "demonic counterweights of the various Christian marriages which the work

---

[36] *Comentarios reales de los Incas*, 20–21, 202. Note also that Hernán Cortés, writing to Carlos V in 1519 under cover of "la audiencia" de Vera Cruz, speaks of the abominable sacrifices of *both* sexes. See *Cartas de relación* (Mexico City: Editorial Porrúa, 1985), 214. On Cortés and cannibalism, see also 64–65, 88, 141, and 148.

[37] Considering the rich tangle of relationships between the New World and the novel, it is significant that González-Echevarría links Garcilaso to Cervantes at the start of this insightful essay: "Only Cervantes, Garcilaso's contemporary, with whom he shared a crepuscular humanism, was a better prose writer in Spanish at the end of the sixteenth and the beginning of the seventeeth centuries." See "The Law of the Letter: Garcilaso's *Commentaries* and the Origins of the Latin American Narrative," *The Yale Journal of Criticism* 1 (Fall 1987): 107–31.

celebrates and of the true Messiah." Forcione's conflation of hell with the American Indians may be part of a worthy indictment of "human sacrifice" as a morally abhorrent phenomenon.[38] Beyond its power to invoke moral horror or rhetorical *admiratio*, however, the cannibalism in Cervantes explicitly functions to streamline a patriarchal institution of sexual circulation: charred hearts are the indispensable ingredients for validating a world—indeed, an aspiring empire—of fathers and sons. It is the institution itself, and not Iphigenia or the American Indians or the powers of hell, that requires another look. Moral or rhetorical readings tend to screen out the *gendered* nature of a peculiar scapegoating mechanism that is Cervantes's insightful contribution to Renaissance literature on cannibals. For the institution that fabricates the sacrificial process in his narrative can no longer, by any critical sleight of mind or lapse of pen, be globalized as "human society": it is conspicuously emblematized, in the first six chapters of the *Persiles*, as an all-male society desperately and defensively questing, courtesy of an interstitial woman, for patriarchal permanence. The self-evident universality implicit in the repeated critical enunciations of "human sacrifice" is misleading: males sacrifice only each other in Cervantes's text. The only self-representation on the Barbaric Isle is (in) the name of the father.

A promising if remote subtext for the Barbaric Isle narrative is gingerly nudged by Eduardo González in a footnote that begins by oddly eliminating the possibilities it would recall: "Elimínese, recordándola, la posibilidad de una vida perpetua de varones aislados [Let us eliminate, after recalling, the possibility of a perpetual life of isolated males]." The second example González recalls in order to reject is that of Pliny's documented all-male community, living alone on the shores of the Dead Sea, "sine ulla femina" (*Natural History* 5.17). Rather than eliminate the deep fantasies invoked by this inviting subtext, let us instead try to imagine Cervantes reading about Pliny's monosexual community and *not* wanting to write parody! We know that Cervantes knew his Pliny because one of his characters noisily cites a similarly outlandish passage from the *Natural History* (8.22) within the *Persiles* itself (134). In an early essay on the "post-tragic" generic status of the *Persiles*, González tried to articulate (parenthetically, as if to whisper so unsavory a revelation) the paradigm supporting the barbaric "Institution": "(Hubo hombre antes que mujer) [Man was here before woman]." The time has come to bring this paradigm out of its closeting parentheses. González himself prepares us for

[38] See Forcione, *Cervantes' Christian Romance*, 38n. Forcione's perspective is already present in Heliodorus, whom Cervantes was rewriting for the Renaissance. In Heliodorus's romance, the gymnosophist community decides to give up human sacrifice for good: "Y dejemos agora y para siempre las humanas víctimas [And let us give up, once and for all, human victims]" (*Historia etiópica*, 424).

such a task when, in a revised and enlarged version of his essay, he justly
allows that the Barbaric Isle episode is narrating "la exclusión de un sexo
por otro [the exclusion of one sex by another]."[39] If indeed "barbaric"
institutions are supported by (un)consciously held cultural beliefs in male
primacy, then by the turn of the seventeenth century these beliefs were
already coming into question, if only on the margins of discourse, where
Cervantes was working. The seventy-five chapters that follow his Barbaric Isle narrative, in turn, may be read as a linguistic experiment to
refocus a Western symbolic economy that fetishizes its women and cannibalizes its men.

The initial display of "barbaric" power is restaged in the *Persiles* in
some dozen interpolations or embedded micronarratives, the focus of the
second half of this book. Courtesy of these internal commentaries, the
emblematic traffic in women is repeated, in variations of increasingly sophisticated barbarism, throughout the text. If iteration indicates intent in
a text, then the fetishistic and eroticized aggression of Cervantes's barbarians reveals a structural purposiveness that is striking. Later in book
1, the captive "interpreter" for the barbarians, Transila Fitzmaurice, will
relate her former escape from the *ius primae noctis* or "costumbre bárbara [barbarous custom]" (112) of her own country, an Irish culture that
legislates the rape of all brides by their new kinsmen. Early in book 3,
Spain is found to have its own "barbarians" who traffic in women while
violently "giving forth voices": Feliciana de la Voz's raging kinsmen,
"que parecían más verdugos que hermano y padre [more like executioners than father and brother]" (307), attempt to kill this new mother for
the infamy of a premarital pregnancy that skews their own marriage plans
for her. Even in civilized Italy, toward the close of book 3, Alejandro
Castrucho will try to force his niece Isabela into a cross-cousin marriage
in order that "la hacienda se quedase en casa [the wealth would remain
in the family]" (406). The marriage market in Renaissance Italy, as Cervantes knew from his travels and as the historian Gene Brucker has recently reminded us, "was not unlike a modern stock exchange; indeed
marriageable girls were sometimes characterized as 'merchandise' (*mer-
catanzia*)."[40] There would appear to be little difference, in short, between
the male traffic on the Barbaric Isle and the attempted traffic in women,
always foiled, in Cervantes's interpolations.

One notable difference is the barbarians' language, a semiotic practice

---

[39] "Del *Persiles* y la Isla Bárbara: Fábulas y Reconocimientos," *MLN* 94 (1979): 222–57.
González is the only scholar I know to have wondered (if, again, in a footnote) about the
destiny of the women imported into Cervantes's fictional isle and there "barbarized"
(255n). These issues are further refined in chap. 3 of González's *La persona y el relato*, 108.

[40] Gene Brucker, *Giovanni and Lusanna: Love and Marriage in Renaissance Florence*
(Berkeley: University of California Press, 1986), 107.

that merits a few remarks. What first strikes the reader of the Barbaric Isle narrative is that a highly, even baroquely, verbal text is straining to represent a language requiring translation. No doubt again under the spell of the New World chroniclers, who regularly described the American Indians as speaking "por señas [by signs],"[41] Cervantes depicts here, ironically, a hegemonic culture of imperial subjects—of aspiring conquerors—who communicate in terrorizing "signs": a barbarous archer, "dando señales [giving signs]" that he wishes to impale the hero with an arrow, will later assure him "por señas, como mejor pudo [by signs, as best he could]" of his nonviolent intentions (53); succession to kingship is determined by drinking powdered hearts "sin . . . dar muestras [without showing signs]" of repugnance (57); the barbarians wave strips of cloth in the air "en señal [as a sign]" that they will receive a dinghy in peace (61); the hero, disguised as a potential bride, is carried on the horde's shoulders "con muestras de infinita alegría [with signs of infinite joy]" (65). After such signal saturation, readers of Cervantes come to feel that they are in the presence of some "notorias muestras [notorious signs]," to borrow a phrase from Grisóstomo's posthumous suicidal verse (*DQ* 1.14).

What happens to the language and psyche of a dominant core of sixteenth-century adult males? we are moved to ask. How is it that these bonded men prefer to speak "en pocas razones [in few words]"? (63) Why is their royal succession determined not by a sign but by the sign of its absence? If language is the "compañera del Imperio [handmaiden of Empire]," as Antonio Nebrija exclaimed in the dedication of his *Gramática* to Fernando and Isabela in 1492, why is the language of these proto-imperialists so pared down? Why did Cervantes name the handmaiden of their language—the captive translator who mediates between their nascent empire and the outside world—"Trans-ila"? What unconscious discourse is this strangely subversive narrative enacting?

Although Cervantes's barbarians appear to be locked into childhood and filled with infantile rage, theirs is not a pre-linguistic world: the barbarians are not mute, although they are capable of making others so. The Italian dancing master Rutilio, for instance, survives for three years on the Barbaric Isle only by pretending to be a deaf-mute (94–95). The first thundering imperative of the first barbarian who speaks in the *Persiles* is immediately qualified as meaningless: "De nadie eran entendidas articuladamente las razones que pronunciaba [The sentences he pronounced

---

[41] See, for example, Columbus's journal entry of 5 December 1492 in *Cuatro viajes*: "Otras cosas le contaban los dichos indios, por señas, muy maravillosas" (80). See also the following letters from *Cuatro viajes*: 11, 13, and 14 October 1492; and 6 and 12 November 1492. In his entry of 2 November 1492, Columbus mentions the use of a translator who knew "hebraico," "caldeo," and "aun algo arábigo" (53).

were understood articulately by nobody]" (51). That "nobody" is even further qualified when we learn that only two women—the young interpreter and an old nurse (51, 62)—seem to understand the barbarian tongue. The various European languages spoken by the multinational pilgrims are, in turn, Greek to the barbarians, including the Norwegian spoken by the hero that the text renders in Spanish: "Ninguna destas razones fue entendida de los bárbaros [None of these words meant anything to the barbarians]" (52). Our psycholinguistic interpretive labors are courteously anticipated by the discursive narrator of the *Persiles*, who suggests that the barbarians are blocked in their communications because their hearts are "ocupados con la ira y la venganza [preoccupied by anger and vengeance]" (69). Cervantes's barbarians are, in short, characterized by a wildly exhibitionist discourse, accompanied, at the same time, by a kind of angry aphasia. Psychoanalytic thinkers would argue that such impoverished verbalization may lead toward other displacements, specifically toward the kind of psychotic violence that is seen lurking under any nonverbal society.[42]

Walter Ong, on the other hand, would regard Latin language study in the Renaissance, a nonvernacular if not exactly nonverbal pursuit, as similarly fostering a psychology of violence. Indeed, it is most instructive to examine Cervantes's heart-swallowing barbarians in the light of Ong's view of Latin language learning as a "Renaissance puberty rite." This elitist learning once involved, for isolated all-male pockets of European culture, the following rituals: forcible removal from the maternal world of the vernacular, close segregation within a male environment, and corporal punishment in order to instill "corage" [ME, OF]—strength of heart or "heartiness"—into young men.[43] There would seem to be little difference, in sum, between the exegetical frames of learned Latin and its traditional opposition, "barbarolalia," for hatching male violence. Both Latin and its barbaric countertongue may be also, in turn, "like two concurrent lines" that "end up in one place." It is a dark and violent place, where the maternal discourse does not fit, where it is silenced.

What is especially prescient about Cervantes's germinal narrative is that it allegorizes, at the threshold of his text, not only an exclusionary symbolic system in crisis but also a Western subject being "born" into that fractured system, into the realm of unconscious language, into an encounter with sexual difference. Working out of a pre-Cartesian, pre-

---

[42] For the French intelligentsia's somewhat arrogant idea of a nonverbal culture, see the discussion between Marcelin Pleynet, Julia Kristeva, and Philippe Sollers in "Why the United States?" first published in 1977 in *Tel Quel* 71/73. Toril Moi has included an excellent new translation of this compelling and irritating exchange in her edition of *The Kristeva Reader* (New York: Columbia University Press, 1986), 272–91.

[43] Ong, "Latin Language Study," 113–41.

Freudian, pre-Lacanian model of the psyche, Cervantes uncannily seems to prefigure elements of that notion of the order of discourse articulated today as the "Law of the Father." He also chooses to represent that symbolic order as brutal, childish, and imperative. To read the *Persiles* in the light of the child's induction into Western culture is to see its hero poised on the threshold of a symbolic order dominated by patriarchal law, by a law that Cervantes inscribes, preconstitutes, as the "Barbaric Law." Lacanians define the Law of the Father as those "manifestations through which the father, possessor of the phallus, represents language and culture."[44] The Lacanian association of the symbolic order with a phallocratic community, with the Reign of the Phallus, may afford adept readers a radiant perspective on Cervantes's Barbaric Isle narrative. Like the female sexuality Freud and his followers have tried to chart, however, Cervantes's Barbaric Isle remains a terra incognita requiring further exploration. For now, all we know about that "place" of narcissistic closure is that Cervantes allegorized it as the Barbaric Isle, because, unlike Montaigne, he understood that what we call "barbarous" was *not* so "contrary to our own habits."

[44] The "Ley del Padre" is defined as those "manifestaciones por las que el padre, poseedor del falo, representa el lenguage, la cultura, e instaura la configuración familar de tres individualidades" (Jean-Baptiste Fages, *Para comprender a Lacan*, trans. Matilde Horne [Toulouse: Privat, 1986], 156). That the symbolic order associated with the phallus in the *Persiles* is more of a code than a language underwrites the Lacanian notion that the unconscious is structured *like* a language, that it is formed by the agency of language and its effects. It may be fruitful to envision the Barbaric Isle as the realm of unconscious language, as Cervantes's pre-Lacanian map of the unconscious, adumbrating and perhaps even further problematizing the Lacanian theory of the paternal metaphor. See Jacques Lacan, *Speech and Language in Psychoanalysis*, trans. Anthony Wilden (Baltimore: Johns Hopkins University Press, 1968), 270–72, 299. See also Ellie Ragland-Sullivan's *Jacques Lacan and the Philosophy of Psychoanalysis* (Urbana: University of Illinois Press, 1986); and *Lacan and Narration: The Psychoanalytic Difference in Narrative Theory*, ed. Robert Con Davis (Baltimore: Johns Hopkins University Press, 1983).

Chapter Six

PLOT AND AGENCY

And they are gone: aye, ages long ago
These lovers fled away into the storm.
—Keats, *The Eve of St. Agnes*

ON SOME fictive date in or around the 1560s, two young people, a man and a woman, embark on a two-year, thousand-mile journey from "Tile" (Thule, Iceland) to Rome, arriving in the Eternal City in its jubilee year.[1] Only in chapter 12 of the fourth and last book of the *Persiles*—"donde se dice quién eran Periandro y Auristela [where it is revealed who Periandro and Auristela were]" (464)—do we learn that their rightful names are Persiles and Sigismunda. At that point we also learn the real motives for the trip. Ostensibly, Auristela is fulfilling a vow to travel to Rome for Catholic instruction; in fact, she is fleeing Iceland in order to avoid an arranged marriage with Prince Magsimino, a young man whose "barbaric" habits have repulsed his own mother. At the close of the pilgrimage, in other words, readers discover that it was actually founded on a stratagem devised by this widowed queen mother, Eustoquia, to save Auristela for Magsimino's younger brother, her beloved son Periandro. Erotic escape, then, the perennial stuff of romance, fuels the beginnings of Cervantes's main plot.

[1] In 3.18, the prophet Soldino, who claims to have served under Carlos V, foresees certain feats at Lepanto by Don Juan of Austria (1572), as well as the death of Don Sebastián of Portugal at Alcazarquivir (1578), thereby dating the plot as earlier than 1572. The Spaniard Antonio mentions in 1.5 that he had fought under Carlos V in Germany (in his wars, c. 1547, against the Elector of Saxony and other Protestants); the Irishman Mauricio claims in 2.19 to have seen this king after he retired to his monastery at Yuste (1557–1558); and the Frenchman Sinibaldo communicates in 2.21 the death of Carlos V (1558), which dates the plot as later than 1558. In 3.10, two counterfeit captives feign a story of their sufferings in Algiers under the renegade Turk Dragut, a famously cruel Turkish corsair who died in 1565. But just before and after this episode, there are two surprising references to Philip III: one in 3.6 to his newly established court in Madrid (1606) and another in 3.11, albeit prophetic, to his expulsion of the Moors (1609). Searching for an exact chronology is futile: the *Persiles* is not historically rigorous because Cervantes was not aiming for a historical reconstruction. He was simply doing what Gabriel García Márquez claims "all writers do": using historical elements "poetically" (see Raymond Leslie Williams, "The Visual Arts, the Poetization of Space and Writing: An Interview with Gabriel García Márquez," *PMLA* 104 [March 1989]: 136).

Quoting from the *Georgics* during the belated revelations in book 4, the hero's old tutor discloses that Thule—"que agora vulgarmente se llama Islanda |which nowadays people call Iceland]" (469)—was once Virgil's "última Thule" (465). As the plot of the *Persiles* internalizes the move from pagan to Christian worlds, it represents a curious blend of geographical precision and dreamlike *fantasía*. For the first half of the work, Cervantes deploys the icy cold wastes of the northern European seas, with their enshrouding mists and—as novels like *Frankenstein* and *Jane Eyre* would later attest—enduring Arctic romance. But the pilgrims of the *Persiles* are not always at sea: they sometimes drop anchor in what Spenser's *Faerie Queene* had earlier called "the six Islands"—Iceland, Norway, the Orkneys, Ireland, Gotland, and Dacia (Denmark) (3.3.32). Many scholars have concluded that Cervantes was thoroughly familiar with contemporary northern geography, and that even his most bizarre-sounding sites (the Isle of the Hermits, for instance) may be found in maps of the era.[2] The mid-nineteenth-century English translator of the *Persiles* lamented, however, that Cervantes "should know so little of England, considering how much his own country had been connected with her." Louisa Dorothea Stanley then went on to question his representation of "a perfect land of Romance" whose northern European inhabitants affect "utterly unknown and barbarous" customs and manners: "Yet Elizabeth or James the 1st was reigning in England; the queen of James the 1st was a Danish princess, and Denmark and Sweden were assuredly not un-known to fame." Stanley's carping, which may appear nationalistic in its defense of northern European interests, actually echoes the sentiments of an early nineteenth century Italian scholar. Simonde de Sismondi spoke of the *Persiles* as "the offspring of a rich; but at the same time of a wan-dering imagination," chiding Cervantes for "his complete ignorance of the North, in which his scene is laid, and which he imagines to be a land of Barbarians, Anthropophagi, Pagans, and Enchanters."[3]

The above critiques of Cervantes's errant imagination reveal a sturdy ignorance of the genre of allegorical romance. Cervantes's "northern

---

[2] In his edition of the *Persiles*, between pages 144 and 145, Avalle-Arce includes a facsim-ile of the title page of Olaf Magnus's *Historia de gentibus septentrionalibus*, newly trans-lated into Italian in 1565 and available to Cervantes. This *Historia* included maps that would have helped Cervantes with his itineraries for the *Persiles*. See also Ricardo Beltrán y Rózpide's "La pericia geográfica de Cervantes demostrada en la *Historia de los trabajos de Persiles y Sigismunda*," *Boletín de la Real Sociedad Geográfica* 64 (1923–1924): 270–93. Several critics have noted that Cervantes may have selected the Arctic landscape for the *Persiles* on the strength of Tasso's recommendation that poets seek their materials in, tell-ingly, the far-off and exotic lands "di Gotia e di Norveggia e di Suevia e d'Islanda" (*Discorsi del poema eroico*, 109). On Norway as a literary symbol, see Américo Castro, "Noruega, símbolo de la oscuridad," *Revista de filología española* 6 (1919): 184–86.

[3] Stanley, "Preface," *Wanderings*, x–xi. Sismondi is cited by Stanley on p. viii.

story"—announced as an "historia septentrional" in the subtitle of the *Persiles*—is not staged in the England of Elizabeth I but on a *paysage moralisé*, a scenic landscape against which the characters act or react, either kindling or burying their erotic fires in its icy realms. While the elderly Rosamunda "burns" for the young Antonio on the Isla Nevada (Snowy Island)—"aquí entre estos yelos y nieves, el amoroso fuego me está haciendo ceniza el corazón [here amidst this ice and snow, an amorous fire is turning my heart to ashes]" (142)—the hermits Renato and Eusebia willfully bury their passion in the snows: "Enterramos el fuego en la nieve [We buried our fire in the snow]" (264). Cervantes's so-called wandering imagination is strategically errant: "Jamás se hace mención de la brújula [There is never any mention of a compass]," as Schevill and Bonilla remind us, noting the logic of Cervantes's dismissiveness toward history or cartography.[4] The errancy of the ships themselves across the northern seas shows that, for the first half of the journey of the *Persiles*, Cervantes's "wandering imagination" was en-compassed by romance.

THE MAIN PLOT

The first installment of the journey across these cold climates is not mentioned until book 2, when Periandro's ten-chapter narration furnishes it as a deferred prologue (2.10-20). Glossing over their royal lineage and falsifying their kinship, Periandro begins by recounting how he and his "sister" Auristela, having escaped from a band of pirates and taken refuge with a community of fisherfolk, expedite a double wedding by rearranging the couples. During the wedding festivities, a band of brigands, shades of Heliodorus, swoops down to steal both Auristela and the new brides (2.12). Periandro and the fishermen become pirates themselves, for a season, during which they comb the North Seas for their lost women. During this watery quest, Periandro has encounters at sea with the aged Danish king Leopoldio, a suffering cuckold, and, soon after, with the Lithuanian widow Sulpicia, an avenging pirate woman (2.13–14), both of whom insert their stories into that of the hero. Periandro also narrates the dream-vision discussed in chapter 3 of the present book, with its parade of personifications (2.15); his vessel's slow drift toward, and ultimate congealment in, the icy Arctic seas, where his party is marvelously rescued by a squadron of Lithuanian skiers (2.16–18); his taming of King Cratilo's barbaric horse (2.20); his springtime sea voyage back to Denmark and, finally, via the Irish coast, to the Barbaric Isle, whose inhabitants imprison him (2.20).

At this juncture we are back to the in medias res beginnings of the *Per-*

---

[4] Schevill and Bonilla, "Introduction," *Persiles*, xii.

siles, with the hero being hoisted up from an underground dungeon in preparation for the barbarians' ritual sacrifice, which requires, as noted in the preceding chapter, that his heart be charred and pulverized in accordance with the Barbaric Law (1.1). Periandro escapes both executioners and a watery death, this last thanks to Arnaldo, a princely rival who will also pursue Auristela to the very ends of the *Persiles*. Both men sail back to the Barbaric Isle, Periandro disguised as a female this time, in order to rescue the captive Auristela (1.2–3). When the hero's cross-dressed beauty attracts the desire of a barbarian, an erotic explosion foments a civil war and an insular holocaust (1.4). The protagonists are offered refuge from the flames in the sea-cave of Antonio, a Spaniard who interrupts the main narrative with his life story, the first of the *Persiles*'s many interpolations (1.5–6). Antonio and his family will accompany the protagonists on most of the journey to Rome, sharing a series of Northern adventures with them that includes an encounter with the Italian dancing-teacher Rutilio, whose inset story discloses his torpid sexual biography to the pilgrims (1.8–9); a meeting at sea with the dying Portuguese lover Manuel de Sosa Coitiño, whose fatal erotic rejection is related at bemused length (1.10–11); and a reunion of the Irish family of the Mauricios (Fitzmaurices), who narrate their own calamities in tandem (1.12–14).

Book 2 narrates the protagonists' tediously overlong visit, reminiscent of Don Quixote's visit to the Duke and Duchess, with the Irish king Policarpo, an old man who runs about his palace distractedly muttering the Pauline dictum that "es mejor casarse que abrasarse [it is better to marry than to burn]" (1 Cor. 7:9). During their regal captivity, the main personages become involved in a mesh of palace intrigue, largely the result of the old king's grand passion for Auristela, and his daughter's similar desires for Periandro (2.3–17). A narrow escape from Policarpo's burning palace moves the party to the snowy Isla de los Ermitas (Isle of the Hermits), whose resident ascetics Renato and Eusebia recount their former amorous travails within French chivalric court circles (2.18–21). At the close of book 2, the pilgrims bid farewell to the northern latitudes and sail southward to Portugal (2.21).

Their joyous arrival in Lisbon, where the party is feted by the governor and enjoys a pleasant holiday of tourism, marks the beginnings of the Southern adventures and of the second half of the *Persiles* (3.1), which takes place in Portugal, Spain, Provence, and Italy. Wearing pilgrims' habits purchased in Lisbon and taking only one beast of burden for their necessities, the party sets off across Spain on foot, aiming to cover two or three leagues per day. At an inn in Badajoz, they lodge with a cry of players, whose resident poet tries to talk Auristela into becoming a *farsanta* (comedienne), even though his discourse betrays all the cruelty, hypocrisy, and greed that distinguished the politics of the Golden Age theater.[5] As the pilgrims enter an oak forest in Extremadura, en route to the shrine of Guadalupe, an encounter with an infant suddenly involves them in the misfortunes of Feliciana de la Voz, an unwed mother who recounts her *caso*, and in their felicitous resolution several days later (3.2–5). From Guadalupe, the pilgrims walk through Trujillo and Talavera, on whose outskirts they witness a horseman being thrown by his horse: the shaken victim, a Pole called Ortel Banedre, shares with them the two great crises of his sexual and violent life (3.6–7). Near Toledo, the pilgrims witness a squadron of dancing *villanas*, one of whom is Tozuelo, the male stand-in for his pregnant girlfriend, whose "in-drag" representation we discussed in chapter 4, and whose impromptu wedding the pilgrims help celebrate (3.8). From Aranjuez, the pilgrims walk on to Ocaña, where the long-exiled Antonio reveals his identity in considerate stages to his aged parents (3.8–9). Having dropped off Antonio and his wife Ricla in Ocaña, the remaining pilgrims now head toward "un lugar . . . de cuyo nombre no me acuerdo [a place . . . whose name I have forgotten]" (3.10), a place forever fixed by the opening sentence of *Don Quixote*. In the plaza of this nameless town, the travelers witness a typical Golden Age scam when two fast-talking students from Salamanca, disguised as recently ransomed Algerian captives, pressure the crowd for alms by narrating the false history of their captivity (3.10). On the road again to Valencia, the pilgrims experience a hairbreadth escape from the hands of some *moriscos* who, as a community, are about to flee Spain aboard Turkish vessels (3.11). When the pilgrims finally arrive in Barcelona, they encounter an Aragonese lady whom they had earlier succoured on the road, Ambrosia Agustina, who narrates the tale of her own cross-dressed quest for her husband (3.12). Although she offers the pilgrims the use of her brother's galleys, the travelers, deferring to Auristela's fear of the sea, continue their journey overland, entering into France through Perpignan (3.12).

While in Provence, three French beauties, all potential brides for a certain Duke of Nemurs, join their entourage (3.13), and while dining alfresco the party is disturbed by the violent drama of the mad Count Domicio, whose wife recounts the tragic results of his mistress's poisoned shirt (3.14–16). Since Periandro's active involvement in this domestic tragedy costs him a near-fatal fall from a tower, the pilgrims must wait out his month-long convalescence before resuming their journey. When

[5] Cervantes's failure to succeed "in the cruel patio" of Golden Age theater is instructive: "At a time when largely pre-proletarian audiences were eager to identify themselves with the powerful, the wealthy, the aristocratic—in short, with the fortunate—Cervantes offered them themselves, sometimes idealized, as often not. He was turning up a side street while the parade went straight ahead, to where Lope was preparing to lead it" (Byron, *Cervantes: A Biography*, 288–89).

they take to the road again, they find themselves lodging in the same inn as a Scottish countess called Ruperta who, while on the road seeking vengeance for her husband's murder, ends up marrying the murderer's son. In the same inn, the pilgrims also encounter the adulterous wife of the Pole Ortel Banedre, who moves them to pity and assistance by a recital of her picaresque wanderings from one man to another (3.16–17). An octogenarian sage called Soldino, a Spaniard who had once served under Carlos V, comes to the inn to predict a kitchen fire which, before long, consumes the entire dwelling. Afterward he conducts the pilgrims to a hidden meadow where he lives in Prospero-style retirement, having, like the hero of Shakespeare's *Tempest*, also forsworn his books (3.18–19). Cervantes's travelers then cross through the Piedmont into Milan, proceeding from there to Lucca, where they participate in the drama of Isabela Castrucha's feigned demonic possession that closes book 3 (3.20–21).

When the party finally arrives on the outskirts of Rome in book 4, their dinner in a local *mesón* is interrupted by a Spanish man of letters, the pilgrim-editor whose verbal *resumé* identifies him as a surrogate of Cervantes himself (4.1). The next day in a wooded area near Rome, the party happens upon two of Auristela's admirers, the constant prince Arnaldo and the Duke of Nemurs, both wounded from a duel over her picture (4.2–3). After tending to the victims, the travelers enjoy a climactic vision of Rome (4.3) before descending to the city itself, where they soon learn that their muleteer Bartolomé and Ortel Banedre's wanton wife Luisa have been sentenced to hang for a street brawl that took the Pole's life (4.5). While the pilgrims busy themselves bailing out the prisoners (who eventually marry and fare badly in Naples), Auristela begins taking Catholic instruction in all the mysteries, catechism lessons which daily reinforce her ascetic leanings. Apart from visiting Rome's seven churches, a pious custom of all Renaissance pilgrims, the party hears about a curious museum there, whose empty canvases await the portraits of famous future poets, among whom Torquato Tasso is singled out by a Cervantine *vaticinatio ex eventu*.[6]

During their Roman holiday, Periandro is invited to visit a woman from Ferrara, a courtesan ironically called Hipólita, who wishes to show him a storeroom of treasures that includes paintings by Rafael and Michelangelo. Because Periandro flees from her embrace, Hipólita first

---

[6] Beneath the empty canvas with Tasso's name is printed *Jerusalén libertada*, which Tasso "había de cantar . . . con el más heroico y agradable plectro que hasta entonces ningún poeta huviese cantado [was to sing . . . with the most heroic and pleasing plectrum used by any poet until then]." Cervantes's "after the fact" prediction of fame here also extends to the Spanish poet Francisco López de Zárate, who wrote a Christian epic on Constantine and the discovery of the True Cross (4.6).

falsely accuses him of robbery; then recants and publicly confesses her mad passion for him; and, lastly, hires a sorceress to inflict a disfiguring disease upon Auristela (4.7–10).[7] When she recovers, Auristela asks to be released from her vow to marry Periandro, a request that drives Periandro to leave town in a despondent state, wandering south until, in a wood outside of Naples, he overhears a Norwegian conversation between his old tutor and the reformed dancing-master Rutilio. This crucial exchange provides the reader with all the regal politics of Tile and Friesland that led to the pilgrimage in the first place (4.12). Since this conversation also reveals the news that Prince Magsimino has just anchored his ships at Naples in quest of his betrothed Auristela, Periandro returns to Rome instantly. He meets up with a repentant Auristela before the Basilica of Saint Paul, where the lovers undergo their final series of trabajos: first Periandro is seriously wounded in the shoulder by Hipólita's jealous lover, one of Cervantes's gallery of *rufianes*; then Periandro and Auristela both prepare to confront the dreaded Magsimino. When the latter pulls up in a carriage, he is already dying of a fever endemic to the Mediterranean, and the last gesture of this formerly repugnant person is surprisingly magnanimous: he personally joins the protagonists' hands in marriage and then dies. After Periandro recovers from his wound and Auristela kisses the Pope's feet, the couple returns to Thule for a long and fruitful life that—according to an aftertext projected by the closing line of the *Persiles*—even includes "biznietos [great-grandchildren]" (4.14).

The Biblical Pattern in the Plot

What has not been rehearsed in the foregoing synopsis of the *Persiles*, of the main plot of its two-year journey, is the narrative's prefiguration by the story of Israel: Israel captive, wandering and, finally, restored. Let us thicken the plot by retelling it through the grid of Christian typology. The pilgrimage in the *Persiles*, the anxious and vicissitude-filled progress of its protagonists, is from Iceland to Rome, but it may also be read allegorically as a journey from Egypt to the New Jerusalem. There is manifold internal evidence that the Exodus story subtends—or "pennes," to use George Herbert's verb—the main plot of Cervantes's last romance.[8] Allusions to the Exodus event are obtrusive throughout the *Persiles*, as

[7] See Lapesa's "En torno a *La española inglesa* y el *Persiles*." For a magisterial historicist reading of *La española inglesa*, see Johnson, "*La española inglesa* and the Practice of Literary Production," 377–416.

[8] "For as the Jews of old by Gods command / Travell'd, and saw no town; / So now each Christian hath his journeys spann'd: their storie pennes and sets us down" ("The Bunch of Grapes," in *The Poems of George Herbert*, ed. F. E. Hutchinson [London: Oxford University Press, 1961], 118).

when Clodio promises to liberate Auristela "deste Egipto [from this Egypt]" and take her to "la tierra de promisión [the Promised Land]" (191); or when Lisbon is itself described as "la tierra de promisión" (277); or when Hipólita is labeled as a "nueva egipcia [new Egyptian]," an allusion to Potiphar's wife in Genesis 39 (446). The text's depiction of itself as a pilgrims' progress toward "the Promised Land" has inspired a number of Christian allegorical readings.[9] The remarks that follow, focused on the *Persiles* as Christian allegory, are meant to supplement these interpretations. My own organizing interest in the *Persiles* as Christian allegory has a psychological rather than doctrinal end: in order to understand the strange affectlessness of Cervantes's protagonists, it is crucial to understand the ritualistic nature of the text they motivate, with its special orderliness and repetition of parts.

Three landmarks across the main plot function as vehicles of a kind of typology, in the looser literary, if not desanctified, sense of the word.[10] These are three poems, two religious sonnets framing a hymn: Rutilio's sonnet on Noah's flood, sung near the beginning of the journey (1.18); Feliciana de la Voz's hymn to the Virgin, sung at the midpoint of the pilgrimage (3.5); and the unknown pilgrim's sonnet to Rome, recited near the end of the journey, at a climactic moment, during the pilgrims' epiphanic vision of the Eternal City (4.3).[11] Sandwiched in between these three poems are two episodes of a markedly typological character, representing both Old and New Testament events: the pilgrims' entrapment in the "belly" of their capsized vessel in part 1 of the *Persiles* (2.2); and their betrayal and near-destruction by a dissembling community of moriscos in part 2 (3.11).

The first religious sonnet, which Rutilio sings in Tuscan aboard ship, during an unusually serene night in the North Sea, links the pilgrims in their perilous wanderings to the "reliquias del linaje humano [remnants

[9] Inarguably the most sophisticated is Forcione's archetypal study of the *Persiles* in *Cervantes' Christian Romance*, where he links the cycle of catastrophe and restoration in the quests of the characters with the orthodox Christian myth of the Fall and Redemption.

[10] Typology in its strict sense—as argued by theologians who find it inappropriate to literature—means God's historical design in which New Testament persons and events (antitypes) recapitulate and fulfill Old Testament persons and events (types). A. C. Charity, who acknowledges the tense relation between the currently available meanings of *typology*, sees it, in its least dogmatic sense, as "either the broad study, or any particular presentation, of the quasi-symbolic relations which one event may appear to bear to another—especially, but not exclusively, when these relations are the analogical ones existing between events which are taken to be one another's 'prefiguration' and 'fulfillment' " (*Events and Their Afterlife* [Cambridge: Cambridge University Press, 1966], 1). In its loosest sense, typology may offer "a kind of symbolic thought without any necessary Christian presumptions" (Earl Miner, "Afterword," *The Literary Uses of Typology*, ed. Earl Miner [Princeton: Princeton University Press, 1977], 393).

[11] See 1.9 and 2.3 for two other interpolated sonnets in the *Persiles*.

of the human race]" who found asylum within Noah's ark. The sonnet evokes the ark itself as an "excelsa máquina [sublime machine]" that breaks the laws of Fate ("los fueros de la Parca"). This particular Fate, one of the three Moirae, is evidently Atropos, who cuts the thread of human lives with her shears, and whose decrees were held to be inexorable. Cervantes has Rutilio picture this Fate as she must have appeared in Noah's day, as "fiera y licenciosa [ferocious and dissolute]" in her destruction of human life (132). In celebrating the ark that subverts the Parca, Rutilio is reiterating what A. C. Charity calls the long and gradual process by which Israel "must deny the mythical cosmos of her neighbours, with its concomitants of eternal repetition, manipulative magic, manipulative ritual."[12] Rutilio, whose exemplary story will be more fully developed in the following chapter, had himself been manipulated by magic while imprisoned in Rome for the sexual kidnapping of one of his dance students. His story about this *hechicera* (witch) represents her as an angel who promised that she would break his chains if he agreed to marry her. After conveying him on a magic carpet to Norway, she turns into a wolf while embracing him, during which metamorphosis he stabs her dead (1.8). Although Rutilio wants to turn his back on the whole magical cosmos his wolfwoman represents, the language of his sonnet shows that she has been displaced onto another "fiera"—projected onto a Parca—and that only the "ark" he is sailing on, the pilgrims' boat, can break her powers. By the end of his sonnet, the analogues between the occupants of Noah's ark and those of the pilgrims' drifting vessel begin to break down, and the romance conventions quickly eclipse the biblical ones. The sonnet itself, however, stands out obtrusively as the first major sign of a prefigurative pattern that has been programmatically drawn across the main plot of the *Persiles*.

Some three months and several shipwrecks later, a tempest completely overturns the pilgrims' vessel, which washes up to an island off the coast of Ibernia (Ireland) with all the passengers trapped within. When the islanders first see the capsized vessel floating into harbor, "creyeron ser el de alguna ballena o de otro gran pescado [they thought it was that of some whale or other great fish]" washed ashore by the recent storm (162). While workmen are busily trying to right the ship, a spectator remarks that he witnessed a similar accident in Genoa with a Spanish galley, "y aun podría ser viviesen agora las personas que segunda vez nacieron al mundo del vientre desta galera [and the people who were born a second time from the belly of that vessel may still be living]." The king responds that it would be a miracle indeed "si este vientre vomita vivos [if this belly vomits up live people]," and the narrator speaks of the great desire of

[12] Charity, *Events and Their Afterlife*, 18.

everyone on the beach "de ver el parto [to see the delivery or birth]" of the pilgrims, later described as "resucitados [returned to life]." All of this, of course, adds up to an extended allusion to the biblical captivity of Jonah in the whale (Jon. 1:17–2:10), linking Cervantes's pilgrims to the Leviathan story. The ship's hull is insistently called a "vientre," corresponding to the "belly of the fish" in Jonah's story, and the notion of being "vomited" out of captivity is common to both the *Persiles* and its biblical subtext.

This pattern across the main plot, however, a passage across biblical linear time, is shown to be in constant tension with verisimilitude (to wit, the deliverance of the pilgrims "need not be taken as a miracle" because a similar rescue occurred in Genoa once). A pilgrims' progress is not an easy story to write in the late Renaissance, and Cervantes feels obliged to tell us so. The chapter begins with a criticism of its own fictionality, when the narrator, in one of his increasingly obtrusive eruptions,[13] confides to us that it cost "el autor desta historia [the author of this story]" some four or five false starts to get this chapter under way, "casi como dudando que fin en el tomaría [almost as if he doubted his purpose in it]" (162). Cervantes's hyperactive narrator here calls attention to the "author's" resistance to a typological pattern that is at odds with the progress of his own pilgrims toward love and intimacy: writing plausibly about "born-again" Christians who still have miles to go in their pilgrimage would make any author hesitate.

Close to the center of the *Persiles*, and soon after the pilgrims have arrived in the so-called "tierra de promisión [Promised Land]," Cervantes inserts into the main narrative Feliciana de la Voz's long hymn to the Virgin of Guadalupe. It is a discourse that spans the whole of Old Testament history, from Genesis to an imaginative point in time just prior to the Annunciation. In twelve stanzas of *octava real* meter, the hymn establishes Mary as the antitype of the gardens of Jericho, the temple of Solomon, and Esther. Mary is also pictured as the "brazo de Dios [arm of God]" which detained Abraham from his sacrifice, in order to give the world the true sacrificial Lamb ("Cordero"). The closing stanza of this long poem depicts that moment in biblical history when the angel Gabriel first flutters his wings prior to visiting Earth for the "embajada honesta [chaste mission]" of the Annunciation (3.5).[14] Ending as it does in the

---

[13] On the inconsistency of the narrator's role in the *Persiles*, see Forcione, *Cervantes, Aristotle, and the* Persiles, chaps. 6–8.

[14] Forcione's description of Feliciana's hymn multiplies the typology: "The celestial palace with its gardens is simultaneously Eden, the imperfect temple of Solomon, and the New Jerusalem. Christ is both the lamb of God, the 'true sacrifice,' prefigured imperfectly in Abraham's sacrifice of Isaac, and the Messiah of the Apocalypse. The serpent is both the

temporal center of biblical history—in the moment between both testaments—and in the virtual center of the text, the hymn reveals the rigid sequence of events that funds the main narrative of the *Persiles*. Cervantes's choice of an unwed mother to sing this hymn to the Virgin Mother will be the organizing interest of chapter 9 of this book. In the present context, it is sufficient for our purposes to show the high degree of organization, rarely acknowledged by critics, that subtends Cervantes's main narrative.

Typology is at work again when the pilgrims, after crossing through Castilla and La Mancha, arrive in "un lugar de moriscos [a place of moriscos]"[15] in the kingdom of Valencia (3.11). The hospitality of the inhabitants there masks their treacherous intentions, a conspiracy to destroy the pilgrims that is virtually foreseen by Periandro, who prefigures the event with a New Testament abstract: "Con palmas . . . recibieron al Señor en Jerusalén los mismos que de allí a pocos días le pusieron en una cruz [The same people who received Christ in Jerusalem with palms were to crucify him several days later]" (354). And several days later, in point of fact, Cervantes's pilgrims recapitulate Christ's betrayal when the moriscos turn on them; they are saved by some Christian moriscos from being murdered, and after the town is burned to the ground by visiting Turks in "el nombre de Mahoma [the name of Mohammed]," the pilgrims continue their journey. When, after numerous adventures in France and northern Italy, the pilgrims arrive at a hill from where they can look down at the city of Rome, they kneel in adoration to it, "como a cosa sacra [as if to a sacred thing]" (426). At that moment, an unknown pilgrim breaks out into a spontaneous sonnet to Rome, whose closing line establishes it as the great model "de la ciudad de Dios [of the city of God]."[16] This allusion to Augustine's *De civitate Dei*, a work that itself uses the term *city* as a symbolic mode of designation, reminds us of the traces, in the main narrative of the *Persiles*, of the Augustinian theme of

---

corrupter of Adam and the dragon slain by the Messiah" (*Cervantes' Christian Romance*, 88).

[15] A morisco, also known as a *musulmán converso*, is a convert from the Muslim religion to Christianity. Philip III expelled them as a nation from Spain in 1609, a shameful historical event recalled in the Ricote episode in *Don Quixote* (2.54).

[16] Cervantes was correct in saying that poetry was "la gracia que no quiso darme el cielo [the grace that heaven did not wish to give me]." This last sonnet is the most mechanical of the poems he included in the *Persiles*. One wishes it could have been of the stature of Petrarch's *In Vita* no. 14 ("Movesi il vecchiere canuto e bianco"), about an ancient, white-haired pilgrim, broken down with age ("rotto de gli anni"), who leaves his anxious family to make this same pilgrimage, obviously his last, to Rome. Also far superior to Cervantes's poem is Dante's sublime simile of a Croatian pilgrim who visits Rome during a Jubilee Year (*Paradiso*, 31).

human desires and God as their point of repose.[17] Cervantes's fictive Rome, built on soil mixed with martyr's blood ("con la sangre de mártires mezclada"), is the symbolic goal of all Christian pilgrims and the equivalent of their Promised Land. Rome closes the prefigurative pattern established throughout the *Persiles* by strategically placed spots of typology, of which I have selected five: three religious poems—the central one spanning the whole of Old Testament history—and two incidents recapitulating Old and New Testament events. These analogical relations establish a symbolic spread across the *Persiles* from the Flood up to the Papacy. They also reveal a remarkable degree of literary organization, one must conclude, for a writer accused of having produced in the *Persiles* "a farrago of helterskelter fantasy."[18]

THE PRODUCTION OF CHARACTER

The formal controls in the main narrative extend to the character—or more accurately, the agency—of each of Cervantes's titular protagonists, Persiles/Periandro and Auristela/Sigismunda. Because beauty does as beauty is in allegory, these protagonists are predictably beautiful. Modern readers may be dismayed at the frequency of the narrator's panegyrics to the physical beauty of Cervantes's heroes. The opening chapter of book 3, when the entire party of pilgrims is described as they appear to the admiring eyes of Lisbon, may serve to instance this formulaic homage: "En efeto, todos juntos y cada uno de por sí, causaban espanto y maravilla a quien los miraba; pero sobre todos campeaba la sin par Auristela y el gallardo Periandro [In short, both as a group and as individuals, they all excited amazement and wonder in their onlookers; but the peerless Auristela and the graceful Periandro outdid them all]" (279). Schevill long ago lamented the "repetition *ad nauseam*" of the heroine's beauty: "Words seem to fail to express how beautiful Auristela is. The result is that she is nothing else."[19] Except when she is poisoned by Hipólita's hired witch in book 4, during which disease she is colorfully uglified—"se le parecían . . . verde el carmín de sus labios [the rose of her lips seemed green]" (458)—we are never suffered to forget that Auristela's beauty is "sin par." And only when Periandro has fallen from Count Domicio's tower and is spilling quantities of blood "por los ojos, narices y boca [through his eyes, nose, and mouth]" (3.14) does he appear less graceful than normal. The Victorian translator of the English *Persiles* (1854),

[17] See chap. 15 on "The Two Cities in Early Biblical History," where Augustine distinguishes between the earthly city of Babylon and the heavenly city of Jerusalem.

[18] Lewis, *The Shadow of Cervantes*, 188.

[19] Rudolph Schevill, "Studies in Cervantes. I. 'Persiles y Sigismunda': The Question of Heliodorus," *Modern Philology* 4 (1907): 700.

Louisa Dorothea Stanley, speculates on Cervantes's creation of a fair Periandro: "For assuredly those blue eyes and golden ringlets must have been most unlike the visions of beauty that dwelt around him, in his own land of Spain."[20] Lovers of Cervantine realism may miss Sancho's unbeglamoured description of the peerless Dulcinea with her "olorcito hombruno [slightly mannish odor]," or of Don Quixote's dream of Belerma's "mal mensil [monthly periods]." These endearing biological realities remain occulted in an allegorical hero, however, whose physical appearance is cogently depicted as a declaration of what he or she is so that the depiction itself may suffice for identification without any further amplification. Honig succinctly explains the strategy behind the beautification of the allegorical hero: "Before we know *who* he is, we know *what* he is."[21]

Even more than for their beauty, Cervantes's heroes have been critically reviled for their moral perfections. The norm for characterization that crystallized in the eighteenth century has dominated the discursive practices of writers of prose fiction until very recently, although even the characters of a contemporary author like John Updike have been dismissed for lacking "the stubborn selfhood and waywardness of the truly memorable figures in literature."[22] The same kind of critics who exalt "stubborn selfhood"—with all its fictions of consistency and closure—have ritually deplored the characters of Persiles and Sigismunda. Entwistle, for instance, accuses them of embodying what he calls "the exemplary fallacy." "The spectacle of unrelieved virtue in the main persons proves intolerable," he laments, adding with remarkable condescension that, had Cervantes lived longer, "he might have agreed that the novel, like tragedy, needs the saving human touch of imperfection." Because Entwistle sees the protagonists as "figures rendered pallid by their aureoles," he speculates that Cervantes himself "must have tired of their perfection." Trying to explain the grounds of his argument—which I believe belongs to "the perfection fallacy"—Entwistle concludes that "the portrait of the perfect prince fails to excite admiration because it is monotonous."[23] In the same critical vein, E. C. Riley regards perfection in the *Persiles* as a quality that does not make "for great character-creation."[24] And Byron, too, having pronounced the *Persiles* as a splendid failure—"a Magnificat, a great cantata to the joyous complexity of life"—sees the protagonists "as wooden, rolled out on schedule to strike the hours," hewn from a material, that is, even denser than the so-called cardboard characters ritually damned by

[20] Stanley, "Preface," *Wanderings*, xii.

[21] Honig, *Dark Conceit*, 85, 81.

[22] Robert Towers, Review essay of *Problems and Other Stories*, by John Updike, *The New York Review of Books*, 8 November 1979, 19.

[23] Entwistle, "Ocean of Story," 166, 163.

[24] Riley, *Theory of the Novel*, 54.

advocates of neorealism. Not only are Cervantes's main personages "wooden," but also, in Byron's overloaded criticism, they are chaste and stupid: "Auristela-Sigismunda drifts erotically throughout the book exciting desire in the men she meets while remaining as chaste as a holy image. It is hard to think of Periandro-Persiles without recalling comedienne Anna Russell's description of Siegfried as 'very big, very strong, very stupid.'" After confidently predicting extratextual "lives of unflinching rectitude" for the protagonists, Byron feels obliged to conclude that Cervantes "did not love the population of the *Persiles*," possibly echoing the earlier and similar judgment of Matilda Pomes.[25]

A robust complacency emerges from the above descriptions, or rather judgments, of the character of the protagonists of the *Persiles*. The punchy conjectures regarding Cervantes's immaturity, or his feelings of tiredness with his own characters, even border on arrogance. The critical reification of "unflinching rectitude"—entailing various ideological assumptions that privilege the individual over the collective—turns out, in fact, to be a myth. The virtue of Cervantes's protagonists, as all close readers will attest, is by no means "unrelieved." Auristela, in particular, regularly displays for us that "saving touch" of imperfection. Not only are her chronic fits of gratuitous jealousy throughout book 2 worth citing (El Saffar writes that "Auristela's jealousy of Sinforosa nearly overwhelms her, and literally provokes yet another storm at sea"),[26] but also the more fraudulent traits she has inherited from her Greek romance predecessor, the heroine of the *Aethiopica*. Chariclea's similar dedication to virginity, as Northrop Frye reminds us, "certainly does not imply that she is also truthful or straightforward; in fact a more devious little twister would be hard to find among heroines of romance."[27] Auristela's own deviousness, painfully apparent in her untruthful dealings with the guileless Policarpa in book 2, is by no means her only flaw. Her obsession with her chastity, a quality that critics other than Bandera have noted with disapproval, often has a narcissistic edge to it: "¡Oh hermano!, mires por mi honra [O my brother, look after my honor!]" (296) is her egotistical response to the sexual sufferings of Feliciana de la Voz, which she largely takes as cautionary. Auristela is also something of a worrier, even a whiner, and in a refrain that gathers negative momentum as the book continues, she frets about how she and Periandro will fare when "un mismo yugo oprima nuestros cuellos [one and the same yoke burdens our

---

[25] Byron, *Cervantes: A Biography*, 513–19. Pomes had come to the same conclusion: "Cervantes no les ha cobrado afecto ni a Persiles ni a Sigismunda ni a ninguno de sus compañeros [Cervantes did not love either Persiles or Sigismunda or any of their companions]" ("Interés del *Persiles*," *Cuadernos de Ínsula*, Homenaje a Cervantes [1947]: 136).

[26] El Saffar, *Beyond Fiction*, 140.

[27] Frye, *Secular Scripture*, 73.

necks]." Directly upon her arrival in Rome, she peremptorily declares her intentions to go to heaven "sin rodeos, sin sobresaltos, y sin cuidados [with no delays, no unpleasant surprises, and no anxieties]" (4.10). Auristela has always wished to escape the sea, that symbol of mutability, and even to avoid "los caminos torcidos y las dudosas sendas [the twisted roads and the doubtful paths]" (4.11). At times she even sounds pertly egotistical: "Que más me debo yo a mi que no a otro [I owe more to myself than to anyone else]" is the curt reason she gives for wanting to be released from her engagement (461). Otis H. Green is not alone in his vision of Auristela as "a self-centered young woman whose only concern [is] for her *pudor* [modesty]."[28] And as for Periandro, his refreshing fallibility has been noted by more than one critic: "Periandro es un llorón [Periandro is a crybaby]," declares Stanislav Zimic emphatically, adding for good measure that, in the horse-taming episode, the hero is "un sujeto jactancioso de la peor especie [an arrogant boaster of the worst kind]."[29] Criticism has also often pointed out Periandro's representation as an insensitive, even defensive, storyteller. Cervantes strategically surrounds Periandro, during his long, serial narration in book 2, with an alert audience of narratees given to censoring many of his narrative procedures. Noting that a reader's attention will be "naturally caught by any suggestion of imperfection in such a hero," Riley asks the blunt critical question: "What critical devil prompted Cervantes to make Persiles a bit of a bore to his companions?"[30]

The frequent critical complaint about the lack of great character-creation in the *Persiles* shows how difficult it is to dislodge character as the touchstone of narrative criticism. It is a given that Persiles and Sigismunda cannot compete with Don Quixote and Sancho for that "stubborn selfhood" ingredient that Cervantes himself gave to Western fiction, but there are other discursive practices—ones that do not oppose the individual to the collective—that critics conditioned by realism seem to have difficulties envisioning. To invoke a conception of character based on the tenets of nineteenth-century realism, as the above critics do, is to forget that the novel works, as Lennard Davis explains, "by turning personality into controlled character": "Like a desirable commodity that seems to offer the promise of an improved life, or like an objectified fashion model who beckons the user of the targeted product into the frame of an advertisement, character holds out the possibility of personal fulfillment in a world that is increasingly making such fulfillment inconceivable."[31]

[28] Green, *Spain and the Western Tradition* 1:201.
[29] Zimic, "Novela bizantina," 60, 62.
[30] Riley, *Theory of the Novel*, 121.
[31] Lennard J. Davis, *Resisting Novels: Ideology and Fiction* (New York: Methuen, 1987),

Whether Cervantes may have conceived "the possibility of personal fulfillment" in the closing years of his life, he chose to experiment with the
kind of writing in which character was not, as the great novelistic myth
would have it, universal. Persiles/Periandro and Auristela/Sigismunda are
not wayward and memorable characters because they are allegorical
agents, self-divided figures (as their names show). As incomplete personages, they are acting in consort with other agents, the entire cast created
to solve a given set of problems. Had Cervantes worked harder to "hu-
manize" his protagonists, they may have eclipsed the generic intent of his
allegorical romance. As allegorical agents, Cervantes's protagonists do
not have solid and memorable characters because, to borrow a phrase
from C. S. Lewis, character is what they have "to produce."[32] What is
valid for the cluster of heroes of *The Faerie Queene* is also valid for each
of Cervantes's titular protagonists: "The moral obligation of a central
character may simply be . . . to pull himself together."[33] Allegorical heroes seem to be thinly characterized because they are being *serially* characterized: their cognitive integration is achieved piecemeal in a quest
which is a kind of collective self-creation. This may explain, in part, why
Cervantes's protagonists are never called by their real names until the last
book of the *Persiles*: the "real" Persiles and Sigismunda are by then a kind
of composite picture of all the lovers whose exemplary stories they have
internalized during a journey of seventy-nine chapters.

Cervantes's rigid control over the behavior of his titular protagonists is
generically motivated by his uses of allegorical romance. If Periandro and
Auristela have been denied true individualizing character, it is not because
Cervantes disliked them or tired of them, but because he envisioned them
as representative types with characteristically limited ways of behaving.
Fletcher may help readers to imagine a "real-life" analogue of Periandro:
"If we were to meet an allegorical character in real life, we would say of
him that he was obsessed with only one idea, or that he had an absolutely
one-track mind, or that his life was patterned according to absolutely
rigid habits from which he never allowed himself to vary. It would seem
that he was driven by some hidden, private force."[34] Cervantes's protagonists are driven agents, with characteristically compulsive behavior pat-

---

128. Davis sees novel reading as "the process of falling in love with characters or making
friends with signs" (127).

[32] Lewis's context bears quoting: "No man is a 'character' to himself, and least of all
while he thinks of good and evil. Character is what he has to produce; within he finds only
the raw material, the passions and emotions which contend for mastery (*Allegory of Love*,
61).

[33] Barney, *Allegories of History*, 43.

[34] Fletcher, *Allegory*, 40. I am indebted to Fletcher's study of "daemonic agents" in allegory for a number of my conclusions about Cervantes's heroes.

terns: Periandro is obsessed with the idea of getting to Rome and to "la dulce posesión esperada [the sweet, long-awaited possession]" of Auristela (413), and Auristela with the idea of getting there *intacta*. Both lovers seem to be acting under compulsion and, despite long colloquies or soliloquies on the subject of their respective desires, rarely do they manifest any evidence of either inner control or active freedom of choice.

Instead of criticizing the protagonists for not being what they are not—that is, novelistic characters—we might try to see them as allegorical agents, as creatures strategically remote from realism and mimesis. Setting aside the chivalric dimensions, Periandro in many ways resembles an allegorical hero like Spenser's Redcrosse Knight, whose identity is revealed to him only after he has endured the trials that attend his sign. Redcrosse "is not so much a real person as he is a generator of other secondary personalities, which are partial aspects of himself."[35] These other secondary personalities then tend to react, either against or with the hero, in a kind of syllogistic manner. Ruth El Saffar suggests a similar dynamics for the *Persiles* when she writes that "through the new secondary characters, Periandro and Auristela once again meet images of themselves."[36] Secondary or subcharacters have long been considered a standard feature of the allegorical repertoire. An understanding of the fragmented conceptual hero in Spenserian allegory is useful for reading Cervantes's protagonists, who may each be said to generate a great crowd of subcharacters—aspects, essentially, of themselves—who then help the heroes to "produce" character. Unaware of the *Persiles*, Fletcher actually mentions "the servant Sancho Panza" as belonging to the type of "subcharacters who arise to help the hero," not an outrageous but an unfortunate example, I think, since it wrenches *Don Quixote* into the category of allegorical romances like *The Faerie Queene* and the *Persiles*. The steady generation of subcharacters across allegory, the refraction of the allegorical protagonist into composite chips of his personhood, has its modern "real-life" analogue in people who "project," who run about, as Fletcher explains, "ascribing fictitious personalities to those whom they meet and live with." By analyzing the projections of such people—the needs, desires, fears, and hates they generate—we determine what is going on in their minds. Similarly, allegorical agents project their selves into refracted "chips of composite character," into personifications that help us to read them.[37]

Apart from the personifications projected by Periandro in his dream of "SENSUALIDAD," earlier discussed in chapter 3, we might consider Auris-

[35] Ibid., 35.
[36] El Saffar, *Beyond Fiction*, 138.
[37] Fletcher, *Allegory*, 35–38.

tela's "projection" of a subcharacter in Leonora, the deified and depriving female protagonist in the episode of the "enamoured Portuguese" (1.10) who, in an elaborately staged Christian ritual, rejects and essentially kills her despairing lover. Cervantes manipulates Leonora into service as an "expression," a negative example, of Auristela's potential sexual powers: the conclusion of Auristela's marriage-versus-the-nunnery dilemma in book 4 is predetermined by Leonora's toxic solution to a comparable psychomachia in book 1. Auristela's final destiny as Periandro's wife has been preordained from the first episode of the *Persiles*, where the subcharacters of Antonio and Ricla jointly relate the beginnings of their conjugal love and its resultant fruitfulness. If Auristela seems wooden and pallid to many critics, it is not because she is too virtuous but because she is not free. Her role is not to represent a memorable and convincing individual, but to internalize, through a kind of shuffling technique, the personhood of the female subcharacters. She is like Spenser's Britomart, who internalizes Amoret, the subcharacter she has rescued from the House of Busyrane in *The Faerie Queene* (3.12). As an allegorical character, Auristela's agency is prefabricated.

Periandro is in a similar modal bind. All his erotic desires, as the text slowly reveals, are either personified in his dreams or enacted by his subcharacters. The sexual feelings repressed by the devoted Periandro are expressed for him by the Tuscan dancing-master Rutilio, a "facet" of Periandro. As one of those "subcharacters who arise to help the hero," the reformed Rutilio strategically materializes in Rome during Periandro's final erotic crisis. Another subcharacter who helps to "express" the hero is Isabela's lover: when she describes him as "ese putativo Ganimedes [that so-called Ganymede]" (409), we know him to be a "facet" of Periandro, the man whom Clodio earlier in the book called "este Ganimedes" (182). By working with facets of the protagonist's composite character, in other words, authors can better control the meanings their heroes are meant to carry: but that control implies, of course, some severe limitations on the "humanity" of allegorical heroes. As Fletcher notes, "the idea that the hero undergoes a change as a result of a psychomachia in which he battles, or of an agony, a progress, a voyage to the moon, or whatever typical story we choose, should not blind us to the real lack of freedom in all these stories."[38] Cervantes's protagonists, in other words, are governed by a rigid destiny, a kind of authorial control that makes us rethink our conventional notions of allegory as a "pilgrim's *progress*." Although they have perhaps seen, and certainly they have heard, everything, Periandro and Auristela seem scarcely changed at the end of their two-year pilgrimage: their characters, as it were, remain predictable and underdeveloped.

---

[38] Ibid., 64.

Psychoanalysis has assisted literature, and vice versa, in understanding that allegorical heroes are like certain kinds of neurotics, people with patterns of behavior that are anxious, rigid, authoritarian. These modern insights allow us to recognize the "wooden" portrayals of Periandro and Auristela, their one-track minds, as a kind of "frozen agency."[39] The psychoanalytic analogues for allegory are obsession and compulsion, the first as an *idée fixe*, the second as an act, although the two are often closely related. It was via caricature—a mode not unfamiliar to Cervantes—that Freud himself equated compulsion and religion: "It might be maintained," he writes in *Totem and Taboo*, that "an obsessional neurosis is a caricature of religion."[40] The equation of religion—with or without its caricature in the compulsion neuroses—and literary allegory is of course an ancient one: we need only invoke the *Psychomachia*, the *Commedia*, *Everyman*, and *The Faerie Queene* as examples. Allegory, whose natural theme is temptation, is "the most religious of the modes," Fletcher reminds us, "obeying, as it does, the commands of the Superego, believing in Sin, portraying atonements through ritual."[41] Cervantes's allegorical agents may be seen obeying, believing, and atoning across the text of the main narrative, a "compulsive" fiction of Christian romance—with both agents *driven* to reach Rome, the heavenly city, in a quest whose "progress" is repeatedly halted by "digressions." Throughout this laborious process, the *trabajos* of the title, the protagonists are finally disclosed to us through a multitude of generated subcharacters.

Cervantes's discursive practice of subordinating character to agency throughout the *Persiles* is revealed by his own surrogate storyteller, the protagonist Periandro. In a mysterious remark that strongly militates against novelistic individualism, Periandro defends his storytelling techniques by constituting himself as a "place" open to Otherness: "Yo soy como esto que se llama lugar, que es donde todas las cosas caben, y no hay ninguna fuera del lugar [I am like that which is called *place*, where all things fit and nothing is out of place]" (227). This improbable site of coalescence—a narrating self as a locus of attraction for all perceptions, a kind of "one-size-fits-all" narrator—belongs to a quintessentially rhetorical discourse.[42] The question of what constitutes place, however, is

---

[39] "The tendency of agents to become images, which allowed agents to represent the 'cosmic' order of allegories," as Fletcher notes (ibid., 289) is also played out in the *Persiles*, where images—canvases and portraits and miniatures—are very much in evidence.

[40] Freud, *SE* 13:73.

[41] Fletcher, *Allegory*, 283. But see the whole chapter on "Psychoanalytic Analogues: Obsession and Compulsion," *Allegory*, 279–303.

[42] Cervantes's energized predication here is the work of what Juan Luis Vives would call "ingenium," that passionate faculty of the rational soul which discovers new and apt resemblances. See *De anima et vita*, in *Opera omnia*, 8 vols. (1782; rpt. London, 1964), 3:372, 374.

especially pertinent to ontological speculations regarding character. We may be led, for example, to cross-discipline rhetorical notions of *lugar* with the "physics" of place, problematized as early as Aristotle, who queried the accepted notion that extant beings had to be in *some* place, if only because nonbeing was in *no* place: where, he asked, with pointed literary flair, were the Goat-stag and the Sphinx? (208a)[43] In comparing himself to "that which is called place," the hero of the *Persiles* embraces not only Aristotle's sphinxes and goat-stags but also all *other* notions of Otherness. This embrace of Otherness, in its inclusion of the disparate and the incongruent, seems peculiarly postmodern. "I am like that which is called place" would seem to anticipate some of the insights of modern psychoanalysis, which has an interest in the concept of place as well as the logic of place (topology). One pioneering instance might be the Lacanian notion of the "margins" of psychoanalytic discourse—"where the ego seems to speak almost at the cost of disintegrating." This place, reminiscent of the subject's origins, is a place Lacan ambiguously calls the "limit experience of the non-existent," of what is *not* created by language.[44] An even more promising gloss on Cervantes's *lugar* may be found in Julia Kristeva's theoretical description of the semiotic chora, which addresses the pre-Oedipal state marginal to language.[45] Kristeva's theory is grounded on Plato's representation, in the *Timaeus*, of the chora, the "nurse of all Becoming": "a Kind invisible and unshaped, *all-receptive*, and in some most perplexing and most baffling way partaking of the intelligible." And so we are led backward, courtesy of revisionary psychoanalysis, to the "baffling and obscure" model for the *place* to which Periandro compares himself, to Plato's "ever-existing Place, which admits not of destruction, *and provides room for all things that have birth*, itself being apprehensible by a kind of bastard reasoning by the aid of non-sensation, barely an object of belief; for when we regard this we dimly dream and affirm that it is somehow necessary that all that exists should exist *in* some spot and occupying some *place*."[46] As one of the central texts used to assimilate both Greek and Judeo-Christian

[43] Aristotle, *The Physics*, trans. Rev. Philip H. Wicksteed and Francis M. Cornford, 2 vols. (Loeb Classical Library, 1929–1934), 1:277.

[44] For this exposition of part of the seminar *Encore* (1972–1973), which addresses the "inexpressible" realm of feminine sexuality, see Bice Benvenuto and Roger Kennedy, *The Works of Jacques Lacan: An Introduction* (New York: St. Martin's Press, 1986), 185–86.

[45] Julia Kristeva, "Revolution in Poetic Language," in *The Kristeva Reader*, 93–95. Kristeva's depiction of the *chora*, which avoids fixing it in terms of any sign or position, is as "a non-expressive totality formed by the drives and their stases in a motility that is as full of movement as it is regulated." She sees these drives predominantly as "oral and anal drives, both of which are oriented and structured around the mother's body" (93–95).

[46] Plato, *Timaeus, Critias, Clitopho, Menexenus, Epistulae*, trans. R. G. Bury (Loeb Classical Library, 1929), 7:113–27; emphasis added.

traditions, Plato's *Timaeus* represents the unformed chaos or "nurse" of all material things as unambiguously feminine. In our time, then, through the framing discourses of Plato and revisionary psychoanalysis, we may begin to dimly enlighten (and be enlightened by) Cervantes's outrageous simile for the all-receptive storyteller. Out of the "place" that resembles both his hero and himself, Cervantes fashions a large and wayward population of subcharacters for his interpolated tales, and it is time to hear their side of the story.

Chapter Seven

THIRTEEN EXEMPLARY NOVELS

... of delicious love, he fabled, yet with stainless virtue.
—Coleridge, "Cervantes: A Lecture" (1818)

THE FOCUS of this chapter will be on Cervantes's inset stories (also known as interpolations, intercalations, or episodes), those fables "of delicious love" that, depending on who is reading, either "make" the *Persiles* or break it.[1] One eighteenth-century reader even felt that they swallowed it up. Warning contemporary writers to curb their episodes, Gregorio Mayáns y Siscar pointed to the episodes in the *Persiles* as a negative example of overload: "No deven ser tantos, que por ellos desparezca el assunto principal, como sucedió a Miguel de Cervantes en su *Persiles i Segismunda* [sic] [They should not be so many that they eclipse the main narrative, as happened to Miguel de Cervantes in his *Persiles and Sigismunda*]."[2] Other, more impatient, critics have seen the episodes as "incidental," "interminable," and even "tedious." Louisa Dorothea Stanley, the 1854 English translator of the *Persiles*, speaks for this last school: "I fear the modern reader will find the numerous episodes tedious; and story after story, which every additional personage we meet, thinks it necessary to relate, will perhaps try his patience; yet there is great beauty in many of these, at least in the original language." The history of the modern reader's reception of these multiple stories—of how "*his* patience" has been tried by their numbers—belongs to a study of Western hermeneutics.[3] In the present context, it is sufficent to note that Cervantine scholarship has either reiterated the uneasy fit of these stories within the main narrative or theorized each tale as a "miniature analogue" of its Christian allegory.[4] The recent English translators of the *Persiles*, Weller and Co-

---

[1] "It is . . . the inset stories that make the *Persiles*" (Entwistle, "Ocean of Story," 166).

[2] See Schevill and Bonilla, "Introduction," *Persiles*, xliv. The judgment of Mayáns y Siscar is iterated, to a large extent, in Riley's remark that Cervantes "overloads the structure" of the *Persiles* (*Theory of the Novel*, 130).

[3] The adjectives "incidental," "interminable," and "tedious" belong, respectively, to Philip Ward, ed., *The Oxford Companion to Spanish Literature* (Oxford: Clarendon Press, 1978); Wyndham Lewis, *Shadow*, 188; and L. D. Stanley, "Preface," *Wanderings*, x; emphasis added.

[4] The more hospitable reading is Forcione's in *Cervantes' Christian Romance*, 31.

lahan—who claim that the story line is "as branching and intertwined as a Spanish wrought-iron balcony"—see the interpolated stories as tied together in a way "related to the later Romantic use of recurring themes, or the *leitmotivs* of musical composition."[5]

Whether they make, break, eclipse, miniaturize, or thematize the main plot, however, the interpolations are generally acknowledged to be realistic narratives: mimetic antiromances that differ from the reified, often ossified, allegorical idealization of the main plot chronicled in the last chapter. It is too easy to say, however, that Cervantes wished to reprimand romance by incorporating reality within it. His particular "novelization" of allegorical romance seems closer to Bakhtin's view of the same historical process as embattled but liberating: "In the presence of the novel, all other genres somehow have a different resonance. A lengthy battle for the novelization of the other genres began, a battle to drag them into a zone of contact with reality . . . [but] the novelization of other genres does not imply their subjection to an alien generic canon; on the contrary, novelization implies their liberation from all that serves as a brake on their unique development."[6] By the same token, in the presence of the inset stories, the main narrative of the *Persiles* has "a different resonance": they allow its development into a new kind of secular and sexual allegory, one that Freud, the neo-Freudians, and now even the anti-Freudians are still trying to teach us to read. It is through the interpolations, in short, that we can best access Cervantes's understanding of female desire; of the blend of power and subordination that characterizes male desire; and, above all, of the shaping power of social discourse in constructing the genders—the normative Renaissance Man and Woman whose ideological traces are still with us. Seen from this perspective, each of the interpolations, the so-called digressions, loses its digressive onus and turns out to be crucial to Cervantes's whole work.

In 1914, Schevill and Bonilla noted in passing that the inset stories in the *Persiles* were "exemplary": "Tienen el carácter de novelas ejemplares [They have the character of exemplary novels]," they noted, in a glancing judgment that coincided with Ortega's description of the *Persiles* itself as "una larga novela ejemplar [a long exemplary novel]."[7] Echoing Ortega's judgment, Tilbert Diego Stegmann has, more recently, called the *Persiles* a "huge exemplary novella."[8] None of these critics, however, has enlarged

---

[5] Weller and Colahan, *Persiles*, 7.

[6] Bakhtin, *The Dialogic Imagination*, 38–39.

[7] Schevill and Bonilla, "Introduction," *Persiles*, xxxv; see Ortega y Gasset's "meditation" on the *Novelas ejemplares*, in *Meditaciones del Quijote* (Madrid: Aguilar, 1967, 186–93.

[8] Tilbert Diego Stegmann, *Cervantes' Musterroman* Persiles, cited and trans. by Alban K. Forcione in his review for *MLN* 88 (March 1983): 438.

on the issue of exemplarity. Schevill and Bonilla even qualified their editorial remark, by allowing that not all of the interpolations "fit" the case ("no siempre vienen al caso"). The example they suggested as a misfit was the story of "the enamoured Portuguese" who dies for love in book 1, a partial suicide who appears to have destabilized their notions of moral exemplarity.[9] Following in their wake if not their intention, Forcione also excluded this enamored Portuguese from his roster of episodes, stories he constituted as analogues to a "catastrophe and restoration" cycle.[10] A chapter-long autobiographical tale told by a dying man to the pilgrims as a solicited bedtime story, this is an episode that critics as diverse as Entwistle and El Saffar have included in their own mini-canons of the interpolated tales.[11] My reading of the episodes as exemplary novels invites the enamored Portuguese (and all other behavioral misfits) back into a circle of exemplarity. I would define an exemplary novel within the *Persiles* as a "true" story or confession of personal experience, of varying length (from one page to two chapters), told by a subcharacter, sometimes as part of a joint narration, about his or her own past erotic history. The story is told to subjects prepared to use it as a template for their own input, to characters and readers ready to fulfill its narrative potential. As such, an exemplary novel is an "imitable" rather than inimitable story, a model that invites imitation or rejection by both its audience within and its readers without.

The odd notion that such an audience is suffering from a "pestilencia de la curiosidad [pestilence of curiosity]" has been aired by at least one modern critic, Stanislav Zimic, who castigates the characters of Byzantine novels as "buscavidas [seekers-of-lives]": "Demuestran una patológica curiosidad por las experiencias ajenas y, a la vez, un irresistible deseo de revelar las proprias [They demonstrate a pathological curiosity about the experiences of others and, at the same time, an irresistible desire to reveal

---

[9] Schevill and Bonilla, "Introduction," *Persiles*, xxxv.

[10] Forcione accounts for his exclusion as follows: "Sosa Coitiño's function in the symbolic movement of the romance is limited to the plane of the main plot; hence I do not treat him below among the figures whose quests constitute analogues of the protagonists' quests." Forcione also includes as episodes two incidents that my reading confines to the plane of the main plot: an unknown *villana*'s brief revelation, scarcely adding up to a story, that María Cobeña cannot dance because she is pregnant by Tozuelo (3.8); and the feigned "historia" of the counterfeit captives from Algiers, who themselves recant it as a lying scam (3.10). Forcione chooses to call both of these events "episodes" because they recapitulate the major theme of "trabajos" in a playful way: "near death," he argues, is followed in each case by "salvation" (*Cervantes' Christian Romance*, 65n, 136–39).

[11] Entwistle writes that bk. 1 of the *Persiles* contains "a group of four" inset stories: "*Antonio the Spanish Barbarian, Rutilio the Italian Dancer, Manuel de Sousa Coutinho or the enamoured Portuguese,* and the history of *Transila or jus primae noctis*" ("Ocean of Story," 166). El Saffar's discussion of the "enamoured Portuguese" story is found under the rubric of "The Interpolated Tales" in *Beyond Fiction* (135–37).

their own]."[12] This critical fastidiousness is scarcely shared by the characters of the *Persiles*, who repeatedly stress the healing properties of communicating their woes. As the hero puts it, in one of his earliest exchanges, "las desgracias y trabajos cuando se comunican suelen aliviarse
[adversities and trials are eased when they are communicated]" (55). The
character Rutilio uses the noun *alivio*, meaning an alleviation or mitiga-
tion of pain, to reinforce the same idea: "Que es alivio al que cuenta sus
desventuras ver o oír que hay quien se duela dellas [It is a comfort to those
who relate their misfortunes to see or hear that there is someone else who
shares their sorrows]" (88). And, in book 2, Cervantes's heroine endorses
the same practice: "Los males comunicados, si no alcanzan sanidad, alcanzan alivio [Misfortunes told to others may find relief if not cure]"
(170). A desire to know the other, and to reveal oneself to the other, is
indeed operative across the *Persiles*. But at what point such a desire becomes pathological—or such curiosity becomes impertinent—is arguable.
It is true, as Zimic notes, that the most accidental contact in these novels
produces an "intercambio de confidencias [exchange of confidences]," for
him a sign of "indiscreta curiosidad [indiscreet curiosity]," but it is also
true that Cervantes was curious about alterity, about the experiences of
others. Indeed, he even introduces himself that way in book 4 of the *Persiles*: "Yo, señores, soy un hombre curioso [I, sirs, am a curious man]"
(415–16).

INTEGRATION

In view of the above critical orientations—which pronounce certain stories as misfits and certain narrative techniques as pathological—it would
seem fitting and even necessary here to address the hoary theoretical issues of integration and exemplarity before returning our focus to the stories themselves. All Cervantists remember that self-conscious moment in
Don Quixote, part 2, when the narrator casts a cold eye on the stories he
has earlier interpolated into part 1. Cervantes represents him retrospec-
tively regarding these tales as flaws in the narration (*El curioso impertinente* is one example), either because they were "sueltas [detached]" from
the main narrative or merely "pegadizas [tacked on]" to it. Because nothing in these tales, Cide Hamete laments, ever "happened" to Don Quixote
himself, part 2 would rectify such inorganic interpolations: instead of any
autonomous or ill-fitting narratives, the Arab historian would include
only those episodes "nacidos de los mesmos sucesos que la verdad ofrece
[born out of the very events that truth offers]" (2.44). Cide Hamete's
abrupt and formal retraction of past practices within the same novel

---

[12] Zimic, "Novela bizantina," 56–57.

shows us an ongoing process of revision "born out of the very events" that El Pinciano, if not "truth," had been offering as the ruling literary codes of the age. Or at least the diction of Cide Hamete's resolutions gestures directly to El Pinciano's Aristotelian precepts. Participles like *nacidos* (born) and *pegadizas* (tacked on), used by Cervantes's penitent narrator to disown his former compositional techniques, suggestively reiterate El Pinciano's formulas: "Los episodios han de estar *pegados* con el argumento de manera [que] si *nacieran* juntos, y se han de *despegar* de manera que si nunca lo huvieran estado [Episodes must adhere to the main narrative as if they had been born together, and they must be detachable as if they had never been together]." The serene fixity of this monstrous birthing metaphor, guaranteed to put most Golden Age writers into a double bind, splendidly reflects the paradoxical nature of so much of the theorizing of the period.[13]

In the *Persiles*, however, there are no palinodes or recantations or self-corrections, no narrator looking back to disown portions of his former creation. What Cervantes gives us instead is a confrontation between an audience of carping neo-Aristotelians and a digressive storyteller, the hero Periandro, who refuses to be daunted by their repeated criticism, their frequent expressions of incredulity and tedium at his narrative techniques (2.10–20).[14] As if anticipating his own future critics, Cervantes creates this fictional cluster of auditors who produce a significant undercurrent of critical complaint. But although Periandro appears defensive about his digressions, he recants nothing. When, after an especially fatiguing session of storytelling, Arnaldo begs Periandro to stop, he retorts with the curious simile discussed in the previous chapter, whose import is the subjection of the text to its creator: "Yo . . . soy hecho como esto que se llama lugar, que es donde todas las cosas caben, y no hay ninguna fuera del

[13] López Pinciano, *Philosophía antigua poética* 3:173. In the long quarrel over Ariosto's and Tasso's *romanzi*, much theoretical energy was given over to the definition of episode and to the poet's proper uses of episode. For a history of these quarrels, see Weinberg, *Italian Renaissance* 2:954–1073. In Aristotle's discussion of episodes, unity of action is recommended *as well as* diversity within it by means of episodes. Aristotle praises Homer because "he detaches a single portion [of the whole war of Troy], and admits as episodes many events from the general story of the war—such as the catalogue of the ships and others," by which he diversifies his poem (*Poetics*, chap. 23, trans. S. H. Butcher, in *Critical Theory Since Plato*, ed. Hazard Adams [New York: Harcourt Brace Jovanovich, 1971], 62).

[14] Editor Avalle-Arce sees Periandro's long narration as "un relato *in fieri*, con todas las críticas, amonestaciones y correcciones del caso, hechas en caliente, al rodar las palabras [a narration *in fieri*, with all its criticisms, warnings, and corrections made on the spot, as the words emerge]" (*Los trabajos*, 207n.). Forcione sees the narration as tribute to sixteenth-century neoclassical theorists, Cervantes having created a fictional audience to enforce "the scrupulous prohibition of any episode not subordinated to and integrated in the plot of the epic poem and its empirically oriented interpretation of the Aristotelian principle of mimesis" (*Cervantes' Christian Romance*, 79).

lugar [I . . . am made like that which is called *place*, where all things fit and nothing is out of place]" (227). If all things "fit" in the "place" that is the artist, then none of his productions can be labeled a "misfit." This is an explicit critique of the neo-Aristotelian precepts of integration that governed both the age and Periandro's noisy critics. Cervantes seems to be straining here to articulate a new theoretical position, or "lugar," for artistic creation—the subordination of the fragmentary, the flawed, and the ill-fitting under the agency of a hospitable and integrative narrator. Cervantes's hero is teaching us here how to read not only the episodes in his own narration but also the ones in the narration that includes him, the *Persiles*.

Exemplarity

Discussing what is or is not an interpolation, despite all the critical variance, may be an easier task than addressing the pawed-over subject of exemplarity. For centuries there has been a peaceful (although tense) coexistence between the various meanings of the word: between *ejemplar* as in *exemplarity* (the quality of acting as an example or warning) and *ejemplar* as in *exemplariness* (the quality of being worthy of imitation). In Castilian, this tension is suggested by the different meanings available to *exemplarizar*, a verb only recently equated with *exemplificar*.[15] In the prologue to the *Novelas ejemplares*, Cervantes recognizes the term *ejemplar* in its precise derivation from the Latin verb *eximere*,[16] meaning *sacar* or *extraer*: "Heles dado el nombre de *Ejemplares* y si bien lo miras no hay ninguna de quien no se pueda sacar algún ejemplo provechoso [I have given them the name of *exemplary* and, looked at properly, there is not one from which a profitable example cannot be extracted]." As he baptizes the *novelas* in his prologue with the term *ejemplares*, he assures readers that an *ejemplo*[17] can be extracted from each of them, and, moreover,

[15] In 1984, the *Diccionario de la Real Academia Española* legitimated *exemplarizar* as a verb, equating it with *exemplificar*. María Moliner defines *exemplarizar* as "edificar con el ejemplo," as well as "demonstrar o autorizar alguna cosa" (*Diccionario del uso del español* [Madrid: Gredos, 1986]), two meanings which echo Cervantes's phrase, "de ejemplo y aviso" (*Rinconete y Cortadillo*). Juan Corominas informs us that *exemplo* was used as early as A.D. 1140 as *enssiemplo*; that *exemplificar* was a compound word by 1495; and that the adjective *exemplar*, derived from the Latin *eximere* (= *sacar*, *extraer*) was used in 1541.

[16] "*Exemplum*: de *eximere*, eximir, separar, sacar fuera o al exterior, c. de *ex* y *emere*, obtener, adquirir" (Dr. Pedro Felipe Monlau, *Diccionario etimológico de la lengua castellana*, 2d ed. [Buenos Aires: Librería "El Ateneo," 1944], 631).

[17] Covarrubias sums up the meanings of *ejemplo* available to Cervantes: "EXEMPLO. *Latine exemplum, est virtus vel vitium, vel aliud quiduis, quod in alio nobis imitandum vel vitandum proponitur; ex Valla*, lib. 6. Absolutamente exemplo se toma en buena parte, pero dezimos dar mal exemplo. Exemplo, la comparación que traemos de una cosa para apoyar

that he would, if he could, give us a free home demonstration—"si no fuera por alargar el sujeto [if it were not to dilate the subject]." At the very portico to his *Novelas ejemplares*, then, Cervantes resists decoding his intention for us. And so we are left with a collection of *novelas* labeled *ejemplares* that has often been theorized as inconsistent.[18] Readers in quest of exemplar*iness* (the virtuous life) in Cervantes's work are disturbed, even offended, when they find only exemplar*ity* (a smorgasbord of good *and* bad lives). Yet base exemplarity was a popular rhetorical practice in Cervantes's age. In the *Rhetorica ad Herennium*, for instance (which Riley claims Cervantes must have read), "an Example is defective if it is . . . base, and hence not to be imitated."[19] This "inimitable" example, however, is still exemplary—if only of baseness. A quaint example of one of these "base" and "hence not to be imitated" examples occurs in *El curioso impertinente*, where Lotario sanctimoniously invokes the easily seduced Danae in order to discourage Anselmo from wife-sharing: "Que si hay Danaes en el mundo, / hay pluvias de oro tambien [If there are Danaes in this world, / there are also showers of gold]" (1.33). Various sixteenth-century theoreticians seem to have no problem with the notion of base exemplarity, and their answers to the old question—recently reposed by Hillis Miller as "Must We Do What We Read?"[20]—are instructive. The neo-Aristotelian Lodovico Castelvetro instructs us in 1570, through a scarcely disinterested rectification, that "Plato supposes that poetry was invented for no other reason than to teach by means of examples and that whatever is found in poetry, be it good or bad, can and must of necessity be followed by others. This is false; for what is con-

---

otra. Exemplo, lo que se copia de un libro o pintura, y exemplar, el original. Hombre exemplar, el que vive bien y da buen exemplo a los demás. Dexemplar a uno, vale deshonrarle, en lengua aldeana. Estar dexemplado, estar infamado. Exemplificar, traer exemplos para declarar mejor alguna cosa" (*Tesoro*, 575).

[18] Ortega, who did not think it possible to include *El amante liberal* and *Rinconete y Cortadillo* in one and the same genre, regarded Cervantes's use of the term *exemplary* as a sop for the Counter-Reformation (*Meditations*). Miguel de Unamuno, similarly, regarded the title of the collection as an afterthought, as the strategy of an author who, having morally strayed, was now resorting to "face-saving" allegory: "Lo de llamarlas ejemplares fue ocurrencia posterior a haberlas escrito [Calling them *exemplary* occurred after writing them]" (*Tres novelas ejemplares y un prólogo*, 11th ed. [Madrid: Espasa-Calpe, 1964], 11). More recently, Albert Sicroff has argued for "the demise of Exemplarity" *if* the novels are read seriatim, in the order they were published: *La gitanilla*, for example, would be exemplary but *El casamiento/coloquio*, "anti-exemplary" because it represents so much human perversity ("The Demise of Exemplarity in Cervantes's *Novelas ejemplares*," in *Hispanic Studies in Honor of Joseph H. Silverman*, ed. Joseph V. Ricapito [Newark, Del.: Juan de la Cuesta Press, 1988], 345–60).

[19] [Cicero], *Rhetorica ad Herennium* 2.29.46.

[20] Hillis Miller, Paper delivered at the annual meeting of the Modern Language Association, New Orleans, La., 29 December 1988.

tained in poetry is proposed . . . so that we might have examples of all kinds—to frighten the wicked, and to console the good, and to learn about the nature of men and women." Along similar lines we have Andrea Menechini's 1572 oration, in which he views poetry as "the corrector of life," largely through the examples it furnishes of monstrous things that we must avoid and of desirable things that we must follow. Jacopo Zabarella's 1578 tractate furnishes yet another example of taking exemplarity "in the broad sense of actions, characters, and passions presented to the audience for imitation or rejection."[21]

All of the above Renaissance examples in defense of base exemplarity are fortified and updated in Michael Riffaterre's description of *Madame Bovary*, which he calls "a template for the *exemplary* story of the adultress." Riffaterre claims that *Madame Bovary*, with its plot supported by all the sociolectic clichés about the fallen woman, functioned as an "exemplary novel" because it struck such "dire forebodings" into the collective psyche of nineteenth-century France.[22] In the light of *Madame Bovary*'s well-known intertextuality with *Don Quixote*, one is moved to consult Cervantes for a similar Fallen Woman "template." The *Persiles*, in fact, contains one, and it is explicitly described as exemplary: the description of Feliciana de la Voz's premarital pregnancy as "un caso que puede servir de ejemplo a las recogidas doncellas que le quisieren dar bueno de sus vidas [a case that may serve as an example to decent young women who wish to give a good account of their lives]" (296).

Can we have an exemplary novel of a virtuous woman (say, Preciosa) as well as an exemplary novel of a fallen woman whose tale is presented to its readers for rejection? By the same token, but in the light of the *Persiles*, can we have an exemplary novel about a mother's forgiveness of her son's slayer (Ortel Banedre's story) as well as an exemplary novel about a love suicide (Manuel de Sosa Coitiño's story)? Can the term *exemplary* signify both a paradigmatic example (to be imitated) *and* a deterrent example or *aviso* (to be avoided)? If the term begins to seem radically blurred, a kind of "vulnerable signifier" (to use Thomas Greene's phrase) from which stable meaning seems to leak away, it bears noting

[21] Castelvetro, Menechini, and Zabarella are all cited by Weinberg, *Italian Renaissance* (1:58–59, 190–91, 21–23).

[22] Michael Riffaterre, "Relevance of Theory/Theory of Relevance," *The Yale Journal of Criticism* 1 (Spring 1988): 172. My argument is indebted, in part, to Riffaterre's modern definition of *exemplarity*: "As for *exemplarity*, I mean by that the apodeictic, self-evident appearance of truth conferred upon the text by descriptive or narrative representations such that the characters, situations, or settings and circumstances represented are models or types, or, more precisely, classemes, representative of a class or category. They eventually become templates for the reader's individual input, exemplars in which that reader may fit his own personal experience, however imperfect or incomplete it may be with regard to the model" (170–71).

that this vulnerability was already evident in Covarrubias's *Tesoro* (1611). Trying to pin down the notion of exemplarity, to give it some definitional stability, Covarrubias wrote (shortly before Cervantes published his *Novelas ejemplares*): "Absolutamente exemplo se toma en buena parte [An example is taken in the absolute sense of good]," he begins, only to conclude lamely, "pero dezimos dar mal exemplo [but we say 'to give a bad example']."[23] By the following century, however, the *Diccionario de autoridades* (1732) was moving toward the *Madame Bovary* paradigm of exemplarity: "El *exemplar* malo nunca se ha de tomar, pero puédese tomar de los malos el bueno [The bad example should never be followed, but one can take some good from the bad ones]" (679). This is the paradigm that Cervantes had in mind, I believe, for the reading of all his "novelas ejemplares," good or bad, with or without a frame. He wished to push his readers into interpretation—into extracting (*eximere*) some "delicioso fruto" that would fit their own lives. To read these novels was to understand and use them, not to imitate them parasitically. The examples are there for the picking, or, as Harry Sieber sums it up in the context of the frameless *Novelas ejemplares*: "Los ejemplos . . . existen cuando quiere el lector. Un ejemplo del tipo de que habla Cervantes está en el texto solo cuando el lector aporta con su lectura una situación, un punto de vista, que realiza la potencialidad de tal ejemplo [Examples . . . exist whenever the reader wishes. An example of the kind Cervantes refers to is in the text only when the reader contributes, through his or her reading, a situation, a point of view, which fulfills the potential of such an example]." Sieber's vision of exemplarity, based on the paradigmatic sense of the term, allows him to see Cervantes's *Novelas ejemplares* as themselves providing models, as setting an example for future literary works: "No es exageración pensar que una novela ejemplar cervantina es, para Cervantes, el punto de partida de otras novelas escritas en castellano [It is not an exaggerated notion to think that an exemplary novel is, for Cervantes, a point of departure for other novels written in Spanish]."[24] To Sieber's "exemplary" reading of this whole murky issue, I would only add that Cervantes's *Novelas ejemplares* are also points of departure for works written in English, to wit, Fletcher's *The Custom of the Country* (1621), or Aphra Behn's *The Amorous Prince* (1671), or Southerne's *The Disappointment* (1684), or Crowne's *The Married Beau* (1694). All signs, then, point to Cervantes's knowing what Riffaterre suggests about exemplary stories—that they "become templates for the reader's individual input, exemplars in which that reader may fit his own per-

[23] Covarrubias, *Tesoro*, 575.
[24] Harry Sieber, "Preliminar," *Novelas ejemplares*, by Miguel de Cervantes, 10th ed., 2 vols. (Cátedra: Letras Hispánicas, 1988), 1:14.

sonal experience, however imperfect or incomplete it may be with regard to the model." In Cervantes, however, unlike in Riffaterre, it is clear that a reader or listener could also fit *her* own personal experience into the template, as does Auristela, in the quotation cited above, into Feliciana's story.[25]

The common denominator of all of the "templates" or exemplary novels interpolated into the *Persiles* is erotic love—fables of "delicious love" for their readers or listeners, if not always for their protagonists. Love in Cervantes's work is presented not as a quality but as an ability, one that cannot be defined and so must be instanced or enacted. In each of these tales, parodic or broken nuptials, premature or deferred consummations, anger, lust, adultery, alcohol, fetishized violence, and greedy or offended kinsmen repeatedly interrupt the main narrative's movement toward marriage. All the sex and violence of these interpolations gives a new resonance to—or, in Bakhtin's parlance, "takes the brakes off"—the idealized, Christian, morally uplifting allegory of the main narrative, with its rigid ideology of chastity, fidelity, and prudence. Edwin Honig suggests another way of articulating these two worlds—the *"as-if"* world "universally assumed to be remote from possibility" and the *"as-is"* world "proposed [as the] norm in all types of symbolic fiction."[26] In the *Persiles*, the *"as-if"* world of the main allegorical narrative is both complicated and liberated by the *"as-is"* world of the mimetic interpolations: it is the juxtaposition of the two, however, that makes possible the radical exploration of gendered sexuality that each fictional world alone could not comprehend. Yet another way of putting this is to emphasize, as does Ruth El Saffar's reading, the interpolated tales as "voices from the unconscious," with the heroes of the main narrative opening themselves to this unconscious.[27] Two texts—two disparate generic forms—problematically coexist here: the romance world of the main narrative and the novelistic one of the interpolations.

Shakespeare's negotiation of disparate worlds in his own late romances affords an interesting parallel here. When Leontes is confronted with Hermione's "statue" in the closing scene of *The Winter's Tale*—Shakespeare's own imitation of Greek romance—he is aghast at the change in his wife's countenance: she was, he swears aloud, "not so much wrinkled, nothing / So aged as this seems." "This," of course, is the "real" Hermione some sixteen devouring years later, and, as Howard Felperin sug-

---

[25] Riffaterre, "Relevance of Theory," 170–71. I would recall, in this context, Barbara Johnson's observation that "the very notion of the self, the very shape of human life stories, has always, from St. Augustine to Freud, been modeled on the man" ("My Monster/My Self," *Diacritics* 12 [Summer 1982]: 10).

[26] Honig, *Dark Conceit*, 169.

[27] El Saffar, *Beyond Fiction*, 145.

gestively argues, "a lesser romancer than Shakespeare would have produced an unwrinkled Hermione, as Lyly had produced an unwrinkled Endymion more than two decades earlier." Good romancers, then, use the technique "of shadowing or qualifying or problematizing the triumphs" of romance by incorporating strong antiromantic dimensions in their work: "What the best romancers have done with a mode that opens the door to infinite possibility is to fasten a chain on it, to impose strict limits on the capabilities of their heroes and on the success they enjoy, in Freudian terms, to establish a reality principle firmly within their work that holds the pleasure principle in check."[28] By these standards, the inset stories of the *Persiles*, with their strong antiromantic dimensions, would be tantamount to Hermione's wrinkles. But they would be "exemplary" wrinkles, too: worthy of imitation.

THE NORTHERN EXEMPLARY TALES

The first inset story (1.5–6) is told to the pilgrims by the Spaniard Antonio, in the asylum of a sea-cave while the Barbaric Isle burns and smolders. Antonio begins his narrative in the 1540s, recalling his return home to Spain from the wars that Carlos V was waging in Germany. The tale turns on a swordfight with some local nobleman who addressed him as *vos*, as an inferior.[29] Forced to flee the country, Antonio then sailed for England aboard a ship which became the setting for yet another brawl, this one with an English sailor. Angered with Antonio, the mariners put him out to sea in a small boat with provisions and, after many nights and various nightmares on the high seas, he was washed ashore on the Barbaric Isle. He saw—from the same cave where he now, some fifteen years later, narrates his story—a barbarian girl looking for shellfish by the shore. Antonio pulled the terrified girl (who dropped all her fish) into the cave, where he kissed her hands and face until she lost all her fear. She, in turn, touched his body with her hands, laughed, hugged him, and fed him some strange unwheaten bread ("que no era de trigo") (80). Frequent encounters of this kind, unobserved by the inhabitants of the Barbaric Isle, resulted—as Ricla herself finishes the tale—in physical intimacy: "Es, pues, el caso . . . que mis muchas entradas y salidas en este lugar le dieron

---

[28] Howard Felperin, *Shakespearean Romance* (Princton: Princeton University Press, 1972), 50–53.

[29] The nucleus of this episode is taken from Juan Huarte de San Juan's *Examen de ingenios* (1575), wherein a duel is described as the result of some social offense. Avalle-Arce discusses the episode at length in chap. 2 of *Nuevos deslindes cervantinos* (Esplugues de Llobregat: Ariel, c. 1975). See also the Schevill and Bonilla discussion of the possible relation of this episode to the historical Cervantes, who may or may not have been condemned to have his right hand cut off for offending a courtier named Antonio de Sigura ("Introduction," *Persiles*, xxxviii–xlii).

bastante para que de mí y mi esposo naciesen esta muchacha y este niño [It so happened . . . that my many comings and goings into this cave were enough to produce this boy and this girl]" (82). Ricla goes on to relate how Antonio promised to become her husband, how he taught her Spanish, and how he baptized her and instructed her in the Catholic faith, a religion whose credo she carefully recites for her audience.

In what way does Antonio's story—and Ricla's also, for she appropriates it midway—serve as an exemplary template for the protagonists? In the opening chapters of the main narrative, Periandro and Auristela have observed (and narrowly avoided involvement in) marriage Barbaric Isle style—an arranged marriage whose messianic offspring, predictable by legalized sacrificial rites, is destined to become a world conqueror. In Antonio's story, however, the protagonists observe marriage Adam-and-Eve style—a marriage whose male offspring functions as a salvific figure, rescuing the pilgrims from the Barbaric Isle holocaust. It may seem that Antonio's story provides a corrective to the demonic and elemental world of the barbarians, who, "ocupados con la ira [possessed by their anger]," burn down their entire island in a petty civil war. But Cervantes suggests that there is no clean opposition between the barbarians and Antonio, who, for his inability to control his rages, was twice exiled from the society of two different nations. Antonio's trip to the Barbaric Isle has all the hallmarks of expiation. Adrift in a lifeboat for six days and nights, he sleeps fitfully, only to dream about "mil géneros de muertes espantosas, pero todas en el agua [a thousand kinds of hideous deaths, and all of them in water]" (76). The text makes it clear that anger, and only anger, is Antonio's governing sin. As a youth he had been continent, even repressed, as he now confesses to the pilgrims: "En mí siempre estuvo Venus fría [Venus had always been cold within me]" (72).[30] The fire that destroys the whole of the Barbaric Isle reifies Antonio's burning anger, which enters the fiction as a palpable thing, flaring and smoldering outside his cave as he recalls the sins of his youth. The whole episode invokes Dante's representation of anger as a smoke screen of the mind, and of the terrace in the *Purgatorio* as a kind of smog belt, enwrapped by "un fummo . . . como la notte scuro [a smoke as black as night]" (canto 25). Antonio's episode, in short, is the exemplary story of a man who spends fifteen years in Barbary learning how *not* to be a barbarian, how to substitute love for that formerly "cold" Venus, as well as for the hot rage that had once dominated his life.

The second inset story of the *Persiles* (1.8–9) has been anticipated by our discussion, in the last chapter, of the sonnet on Noah's ark, fictionally

---

[30] Antonio's diction here reveals Terence's proverb as its precursor: "Sine Cerere et Baccho, friget Venus" (*Eunuchus* 4.5).

sung in Tuscan though represented by Cervantes as a Spanish translation. The author and singer of that sonnet, the Italian dancing-master Rutilio, tells his life story to the sleepless pilgrims while they are anchored near an icy and mountainous island. Rutilio's story is a painful and imaginative projection of a man's degradation, and ultimate isolation, through lust. He begins by identifying himself as a citizen of Siena, where he was a celebrated dancing-teacher. The habit of loveless sexuality is still framing his speech, as he recalls his casual seduction of one of his pupils, whom he describes as "más hermosa que discreta [prettier than she was prudent]" (89). This nameless girl's lack of prudence, twice noted by Rutilio, was disclosed by her inability to withstand his seduction: hired to teach her "los movimientos del cuerpo [the movements of the body]," he moved instead "los del alma [those of her soul]," and she yielded him both (89). In his present narrative, it is "la suerte [his bad luck]" that made Rutilio carry the girl off to Rome—"para que los dos nos gozásemos [so that we two might enjoy each other]." At the instigation of the girl's father, the couple was seized on the road and Rutilio sentenced to death by a Roman judge, a punishment he now lightly glosses with an aphorism: "El amor no da baratos sus gustos [Love doesn't give its pleasures cheaply]" (89).

While in prison awaiting death, however, Rutilio was approached by an "hechicera [witch]," who offered to save him if he would marry her. He readily consented and, that very night, the witch conducted him out of prison and onto a *manto* or magic carpet, her conveyance for a four-hour flight to the wilds of Norway. As soon as they landed on this "tierra no conocida [unknown land]" (90), the witch began to embrace Rutilio, not very "honestamente [chastely]," he tells his auditors, once again distancing himself from his lust. Upon pushing her away, however, he discovered that his witch had become a wolf ("una figura de *lobo*," that is, a male wolf) (91). This metamorphosis is rationalized later in the text, precisely in the context of whether Rutilio's story is truth or fiction. In a passage worth quoting at length, if only because it shows the medicalization of lycanthropy occurring in the late sixteenth century,[31] Cervantes's Mauricio enlightens the whole party on the wolf "mania":

Lo que se ha de entender desto de convertirse en lobos, es que hay una enfermedad a quien llaman los médicos manía lupina, que es de calidad que al que la padece le parece que se ha convertido en lobo, y aúlla como lobo, y se junta con otros heridos del mismo mal, y andan en manadas por los campos y por los montes, ladrando ya como perros, o ya aullando como lobos; des-

---

[31] The French physician Jean de Wier (1515–1588) regarded lycanthropy as a real disease—as a "melancholie Louviere" or a "folie Louviere" (Julio Caro Baroja, *Vidas mágicas e inquisición*, 2 vols. [Madrid: Taurus, 1967], 2:124).

pedazan los árboles, matan a quien encuentran y comen la carne cruda de los muertos. (134)

[What should be understood about this business of turning into a wolf is that there is a sickness that doctors call *lupine mania*, in which sufferers think they have turned into wolves, and they howl like wolves, and they join with others suffering from the same disease, and they prowl in packs through the fields and woods; they tear apart trees, they kill whom they meet and eat the raw flesh of the cadavers.]

When illusions become manias, early modern Europe begins the long march from demonology to science that would find its modern articulations in Freud's famous Wolfman. In the infantile formation of phobia in the Wolfman, "what became conscious was fear not of the *father* but of the *wolf*."[32] In Rutilio's adult disorder, what becomes conscious to his readers and listeners, if not yet to himself, is fear not of the *lobo* but of the *loba*, the female wolf. Rutilio's wolfish, suffocating lust undergoes a striking gender change *in fieri*—from male to female wolf—as he stabs through the heart "a la que pensé ser loba [she whom I thought to be a wolf]" (91). The projection of male lust onto the female, who is then "projected" as a demonic wolfwoman, has rarely been represented with such imaginative power. One wonders whether Golden Age readers, at least those alert to the gender-coding of Cervantes's story, could see Rutilio's wolfwoman as we see her today: as the projection of a repentant Renaissance playboy who knows little or nothing about the women he seduces. Even Freud's famous description of female sexuality as a terra incognita is adumbrated here by Cervantes's description of the "tierra no conocida" of Norway—that dark place where evil witches "abound" (90).

After killing off his wolfwoman, Rutilio explains how he found himself isolated in darkest Norway, and with scant means of livelihood, there being little call for dancing-teachers in those Arctic zones. Taking up employment as a goldsmith, a career with traditionally demonic connotations, Rutilio was eventually tempest-tossed, while selling his wares, on the Barbaric Isle. There he "borrowed" some clothing from a hanged man and, posing as a deaf-mute, he entered the capital of the barbarians doing cartwheels ("haciendo cabriolas en el aire"), in a caricature of his former dancing career (94). After three years on the Barbaric Isle, he was rescued from the scorched island just after the holocaust, and by the very pilgrims

---

[32] Both Olaf Magnus in his *Historia de gentibus septentrionalibus* (1555) and Antonio de Torquemada in his *Jardín de flores curiosas* (1570), cited as subtexts for the *Persiles*, narrate cases of lycanthropy in their works. In the modern case of the Wolfman, Freud saw the "anxiety-animal" as a symbolic substitution for the most threatening aspects of sexuality (*SE* 17, esp. 32 and 112).

who are now hearing his *caso*. The template in Rutilio's exemplary story is designed for Periandro, whose own flight with Auristela to Rome is a battleground between his love for a chaste woman and his own sexual needs, a psychomachia played out in the dream vision of "SENSUALIDAD" (2.15) discussed in chapter 3.

En route to yet another frozen island, the pilgrims overhear a singer across the waters, whom they greet and approach. As he passes over into their boat, he abruptly informs them that he is a terminal case: "Tengo la vida en sus últimos términos [My life is in its final stages]" (97). That sunset, while they all sit around a campfire, the singer, a Portuguese character called Manuel de Sosa Coitiño,[33] relates the story of his mortal sufferings. This third inset story (1.10), which represents unrequited love as mortal, may have triggered in many Golden Age readers the kind of skepticism Shakespeare gave to Rosalind in *As You Like It*: "Men have died from time to time, and worms have eaten them, but not for love" (4.1.101–2). That the story of the enamored Portuguese is not meant to be read entirely straight is revealed to us two books later, when the pilgrims visit Manuel's epitaph in Lisbon and learn there that his death, described as "la enamorada muerte [his loving death/his death in love]," was regarded as enviable.[34] Among the Portuguese, as Cervantes fictionalizes it, such a death was a common event—"por tener casi en costumbre el morir de amores los portugueses [since dying for love is virtually a Portuguese custom]" (280–81). Whether it was the custom of the country or Leonora's rejection that killed Manuel, the pilgrim-protagonists who hear his exemplary story are easily drawn into its template. Manuel recounts all the details of how his beloved rejected him, in a gratuitously public manner, to become a bride of Christ. One of the more painful moments in Manuel's story occurs when Leonora first emerges from church, having earlier agreed to meet him there; splendidly dressed and opulently bejeweled, her strategy is to undeceive Manuel even as she cheats him of his expectations. At that moment an unidentified passerby, as deluded as Manuel in his expectations of a betrothal ceremony, shouts out a blessing to the couple, wishing them a long and happy life: "Coronen presto hermosísimos hijos vuestra mesa, y a largo andar se dilate vuestro amor en

---

[33] A Portuguese poet named Manuel de Sosa Coitiño shared Cervantes's years of captivity in Algiers. He was ransomed in 1579 and married soon thereafter. In 1613—perhaps near the time Cervantes was writing this episode—he and his wife, by mutual consent, entered religious orders.

[34] The closing lines of the epitaph read, "Procura saber su vida, / y envidiarás su muerte, / pasajero [Try to learn about his life, / and you shall envy his death, / passerby]." Portuguese epitaphs, in their sentimentality and verboseness, amounted to a literary subgenre in the Golden Age. For a reading that finds humor and satire in this episode, see Zimic, "Novela bizantina," 49–64.

vuestros nietos [May the most beautiful children soon grace your table and, after many years, may your love extend unto your grandchildren]" (102). Leonora, however, stubbornly opts for the chaste life: "Yo no os dejo por ningún hombre de la tierra [I am not leaving you for any earthly man]," she addresses her stunned suitor, just as the prioress and nuns begin cutting off her long hair (103).[35] Manuel's only response to this cold comfort is a recitation of Luke 10:42, "Maria optimam partem elegit [Mary chose the best part]" (104). Addicted to the scene of his rejection, however, he is slowly driven mad. An extended Northern journey, meant to court forgetfulness, is all in vain, although it allows Manuel the temporary *alivio* of unburdening his sorrows to the protagonists and their party. The moment he finishes his story, however, the sickened man falls dead to the ground. The pilgrims bury him under the ice and snow, a fitting reification of the chilling and killing rejection that finished him.

Manuel's tale foreshadows the protagonists' own amorous situation upon their arrival in Rome, where Auristela, after a near-fatal illness and a series of intensive catechism lessons, tries to imitate Leonora's argument for avoiding marriage: "Yo no te quiero dejar por otro; por quien te dejo es por Dios [I do not wish to leave you for another man; I leave you only for God]" (459). But the text does not allow Auristela to model herself after the chaste Leonora: the narrator's voice closes the *Persiles* with the pointedly satisfied observation that, after all, the protagonists lived a long and happy life, "hasta que biznietos le alargaron los días [until great-grandchildren lengthened their days]" (475). Whatever comically Portuguese elements invade this love-suicide—in certain ways an avatar of Grisóstomo in *Don Quixote*, part 1, who also "ha muerto de amores [has died for love]" (1.12)—Manuel's icy death cannot be excused by regarding Leonora's spiritual marriage as a healthy sublimation (or, for that matter, as even her own business, given that she is a subcharacter of Auristela). The template her story affords Auristela is unambiguously cautionary, since Leonora herself dies, soon after she learns about Manuel's fate: "o ya por la estrecheza de la que hacía siempre, o ya por el sentimiento del no pensado suceso [either from her austere mode of living, or from the emotion of this unexpected event]" (281). "Reader, you decide," as Cervantes himself would put it, though the tale points to the nunnery as a sign of maladjustment. The ascetic solution, for Cervantes's main protagonists, is no solution: it is not love but *estrecheza* that kills.

As the fourth and fifth interpolated stories in the *Persiles*—the episodes of Transila and Sulpicia—will be jointly addressed in the following chap-

---

[35] The parallels here with *La española inglesa* are obvious, as is the contrasting closure: Isabela, also on the point of taking the veil, chooses at the last moment secular instead of divine love.

ter, let us here turn to the sixth: a mini-tale of cuckoldry that serves as a kind of postscript to *El celoso extremeño*.[36] Narrated by Periandro as indirect discourse, this is the second tale within a tale in the *Persiles*. A short inset story, it plots the sufferings and reconsidered vengeance of the aged King Leopoldio of Danea/Dinamarca (Denmark) upon his betrothed queen-to-be and her young lover (2.13). When Periandro encounters the desperate king, he is on the high seas in pursuit of the faithless pair. As in *La Galatea*, *El celoso extremeño*, and *El viejo celoso*, the popular Cervantine theme of the May-January marriage erupts once more in the *Persiles*. "May," however, is treacherous and even murderous here. And "January" is anxious to talk about it: "Escúchame un poco, que en breves razones te contaré cosas grandes [Listen to me a while, and in a few words I'll relate some great things]" (231). The old king confesses his loss of honor to Periandro in figurative language:

> Ésta, pues, pareciéndole no ser injusto anteponer los rizos de un criado mío a mis canas, se envolvió con él, y no solamente tuvo gusto de quitarme la honra, sino que procuró, junto con ella, quitarme la vida. (232)

> [She, therefore, thinking it no great injustice to put my servant's curls ahead of my white hair, became involved with him, and he not only had the pleasure of destroying my honor, but he also attempted, together with her, to destroy my life.]

The tension between *rizos* (curls) and *canas* (gray hair) here—with hair metaphorizing youth and age—offers a template to King Policarpo in the audience, whose own gray hair is, on the plane of the main plot, competing with Periandro's curls for the love of Auristela. In both stories, main plot and inset tale, the curly heads win, further reinforcing Cervantes's consistently negative view of intergenerational marriage. In the end, Periandro dissuades the king from taking vengeance on the treacherous couple, thus furnishing further evidence that the *Persiles* is a "continuation" of the unfinished *Galatea*, where granting pardon leaves one "más rico y satisfecho [richer and more satisfied]" than exacting vengeance (2.165).

The last of the Northern episodes is narrated on the Isle of the Hermits, where "los limpios y verdaderos amantes [the chaste and true lovers]" Renato and Eusebia have extended the hospitality of their hermitage to the wanderers (2.18–19). The aging French hermit Renato explains to the pilgrims that, about a decade earlier, a fellow courtier had wrongly ac-

---

[36] Alison Weber has argued for a vindication of the affect of cuckolds, moving the coded assumptions of the cuckold's tale from derisive object to articulate subject. The tale of Leopoldio in the *Persiles* bears out her claims for Cervantes's humanization of the *senex* ("Cervantes and the Italian Connection," Paper delivered at the annual meeting of the Modern Language Association, New Orleans, La., 28 December 1988).

cused him of having illicit sexual relations with Eusebia, then a lady-in-waiting to the French queen. Since Renato wished to defend both himself and Eusebia from this accusation, he agreed to a duel with the slanderer. The king dispatched both men off to duel in Germany, Catholic law forbidding it in France, and Renato lost the match. He returned home greatly dishonored, and his melancholy reached such devastating proportions as to drive him into self-exile. Renato's problem here, a case of depleted chivalric honor, recalls Don Quixote's defeat, on the beach in Barcelona, by the Knight of the White Moon, where in his melancholy he laments that Dulcinea "es la más hermosa mujer del mundo . . . y no es bien que mi flaqueza defraude esta verdad. . . . Quítame la vida, pues me has quitado la honra [is the most beautiful woman in the world . . . and it is not just that my weakness should discredit that truth. . . . Take away my life, since you have robbed me of my honor]" (2.64). Instead of going home to die, however, Renato lit out for the northern territories, trusting their remoteness to bury both his dishonor and his name. Upon arriving at the Isle of the Hermits, where the pilgrims are now hearing his story, he dismissed his few servants, requesting only yearly visits from them. The following year they returned with the maligned Eusebia, who had elected to become his "compañera en la pena [companion in hardship]" (264). Her flight, of course, confirmed all vulgar suspicions of her being, as her accuser had earlier put it, "impúdica [shameless]" (261).

Cervantine irony functions here to make the *soledades* (wasteland) the couple has chosen for exile—where a philosophy of *carpe diem* might make good sense—have a chilling effect on their sexuality. Renato relates their common decision to marry and not to burn: "Dímonos las manos de legítimos esposos, enterramos el fuego en la nieve, y en paz y en amor, como dos estatuas movibles, ha que vivimos en este lugar casi diez años. [We exchanged vows of legitimate man and wife, we buried our fire in the snow, and in love and peace, like two mobile statues, we have lived in this place for almost ten years]" (264). The "mobile statues" emblematize the *contemptus mundi* the wronged couple has decided to profess: "Dormimos aparte, comemos juntos, hablamos del cielo, menospreciamos la tierra y confiados en la misericordia de Dios, esperamos la vida eterna [We sleep apart, we eat together, we talk of heaven and despise earth, and confident of God's mercy, we await eternal life]" (264). Just as Renato assures the pilgrims that he and Eusebia are in daily expectancy of Paradise, a ship pulls into the harbor to wrench them back to earth, to the world of the Renaissance French court. Renato's brother brings the good news that the gentleman who defamed Eusebia has recanted everything on his deathbed. As a result, the French king has officially restored Renato's "honor," and he has declared Eusebia to be just what she had always been—both in court and in the hermitage—"honesta y limpia [chaste and clean]" (271).

Schevill and Bonilla have briefly noted that "la extraña historia de Renato constituye un episodio genuinamente caballeresco [the strange story of Renato constitutes a genuinely chivalric episode]."[37] I would say that the story constitutes a genuine *parody* of a chivalric episode, with aging ex-courtiers, now ascetic lovers, in flight from the erotic entanglement thrust upon them. The parodic linkages between this chivalric tale and the world of Don Quixote are evident, but it is the ascetic dimension that serves as a template for Renato's audience, especially for Auristela, who throughout the pilgrimage begs Periandro to mind her honor ("mires por mi honra") (296). As was earlier thematized in the episode of "the enamoured Portuguese," the celibate life does not appeal to Cervantes, whose work repeatedly affirms sexuality as sanctioned by God, and rejects, often with wry humor, the ascetic alternative for everyone, it would seem, except the unchaste Rutilio. "As always in Shakespeare," writes Marjorie Garber, "the alternative of a celibate life in a nunnery is presented as a wrong path, an infertile solution which denies the fundamental nature of humanity."[38] The same may be said of Cervantes's attitudes toward the nunnery.

THE SOUTHERN EXEMPLARY TALES

The first of the six inset stories in part 2 of the *Persiles* is the tale of Feliciana de la Voz, treated separately in chapter 9 of this study. The subsequent interpolation (3.6–7), narrated by a Pole named Ortel Banedre, is modeled on a novella from Cintio's *Hecatommithi* (1565). Cervantes has manipulated his model almost beyond recognition, however, in order to make his own story serve the erotic concerns of his larger text. Whereas Cintio's novella is largely concerned with a mother's forgiveness of her son's slayer, the vengeance/forgiveness contrariety, Cervantes's adaptation focuses on the subsequent erotic fortunes of the slayer himself, who, some fifteen years later, after his return from the Indies, is being asked to temper his own desires for vengeance. The object of Ortel Banedre's avenging mania is a certain Talavera wanton, a woman who marries him only to run off, fifteen days later, with his money, his jewels, and her own former lover. Eventually, Ortel will be killed during a Roman street brawl, stabbed in the kidneys by his wife, a debased version of Doña Estefanía from *El casamiento/coloquio*. Luisa appears both in and out of Ortel Banedre's story, making his episode appear as what El Pinciano

---

[37] Schevill and Bonilla, "Introduction," *Persiles*, xxxi.
[38] Marjorie Garber, *Coming of Age in Shakespeare* (London: Methuen, 1981), 39.

would have called loosely "tacked on." In her repeated surfacings across the last two books of the *Persiles*, Luisa is described by a variety of characters in deprecatory terms: as "atrevidilla [daring]"; "libre [free]"; "desenvuelta [loose]"; a "ramera [whore]"; "una mujer loca [a crazy woman]"; and the "sepultura [sepulchre]" of her husband's honor. Without even seeing her, the prophet Soldino manages to characterize Luisa as a "soiled" woman: "más del suelo que del cielo [closer to the soil than to the heavens]" (397). She herself recounts her side of the story with an abrupt first-person opener—"Yo, señora, soy esa adúltera [I, Madam, am that adultress]" (382)—locating her episode squarely in the female picaresque tradition that originated, about a decade earlier, with Francisco López de Úbeda's *La pícara Justina* (1605). Luisa's portion of Ortel Banedre's tale, notable for its antiromance dimensions, represents a riveting portrait of the physical abuse of lower-class women in Renaissance Spain, and their own abuse, in turn, of kindlier men. Luisa's attachment to a young brute of a *mesonero* called Alonso is graphically represented by another worker in the inn at Talavera: "Se atreve Alonso a molella a coces todas las veces que se le antoja [Alonso dares to beat her to a pulp whenever he feels like it]" (321). Luisa's own later description of life as a Spanish soldier's camp follower—"comiendo pan con dolores [eating bread with sorrows]"—opens the text to a degree of anxiety rarely found in allegorical romance (383). Cervantes allows Luisa, more than any other character in the *Persiles*, to drag his romance into Bakhtin's so-called "zone of contact with reality." When Luisa and her muleteer lover, both sentenced to death by hanging, describe the horrors of jail life in Renaissance Rome, where prisoners are eaten alive by bedbugs and other insects, the *Persiles* becomes firmly emplaced in the zone of reality (434). Luisa's tale of "base exemplarity," then, begun by Ortel Banedre and continued by her own serial mini-narratives, offers listeners and readers a class-conscious Renaissance version of Emma Bovary's "fallen woman" template.

The inset story which follows Ortel and Luisa's story, Ambrosia Agustina's narrative (2.12), returns us to the ruling class and to the more frivolous issues of gender disguise. Ambrosia is secretly married to Contarino de Arbolánchez, a gentleman belonging to the Knights of Alcántara. The marriage cannot be consummated, however, because her husband is immediately after the wedding dispatched by the king to fight the Turk in Malta: "Obedeció Contarino con tanta puntualidad lo que se le mandaba, que no quiso coger los frutos del matrimonio con sobresalto [Contarino obeyed the King's order with such alacrity, that he did not wish to pick the fruits of matrimony as a sudden assault]" (362). Her despondency at the absence of her new husband moves Ambrosia to seek him out. She takes to the road in male clothing and, at one point, further disguises herself with a heavy facial anointment of mud and axle grease, an imitation of Heliodorus's Chariclea, who, trying to hide her identity in the sixth book of the *Aethiopica*, rubs mud and soot on her face. Ambrosia recounts her adventures as the servant of a military drummer, her involvement in a brawl about lodgings in La Mancha, and her consequent arrest and sentencing to the king's galleys—adventures that have the flavor, if not the piquant intelligence, of Berganza's recital of his "perruno" wanderings in *El coloquio*. Ambrosia's disguise game comes to an end, however, when a ship's barber in Barcelona pronounces her unfit to row in the galleys. The desired husband, however, suddenly materializes in Barcelona to reclaim her, calling her "mitad de mi alma [half of my soul]" (364), a precise echo of Periandro's address to Auristela when he encounters her, also disguised in male clothing, on the Barbaric Isle. The template of transvestism here invokes the earlier "strange metamorphosis" of Auristela and Periandro in the opening scenes of the *Persiles* (1.2–4). What Auristela hears in Ambrosia's story, however, is the erotic desire thus far wanting in her own.

Count Domicio's story, the fourth tale interpolated into the Southern adventures, is told to the pilgrims somewhere in Provence by his widow Claricia (3.15), the "mujer voladora [flying woman]" who, having been pitched from a tower by her mad husband, "flies" down to the ground safely on her billowing skirts. Periandro rushes up the tower to rescue the count's children from their crazed father, and, after a violent wrestling episode, they fall down together from the tower, the count impaled on a knife. Periandro's interference is heroic, and nobody seems distressed by the count's death. Later that day, back at the count's manor, his wife gives an account of the origins of all the violence. Her husband's lunacy, she explains to the pilgrims, stemmed from an earlier love affair with a kinswoman. In anger at the count's marriage to Claricia, the woman sent her lover a poisoned linen shirt that, after producing a two-day coma, left the count with a malignant psychosis: after the coma lifted, all his actions were "no de loco manso, sino de cruel, furioso y desatinado [not of a tame madman, but rather a cruel, furious, and extravagant one]" (378). Claricia herself, in a display of classical erudition, compares the poisoned shirt to the one sent to Hercules by "la falsa Deyanira [the false Deianeira]" (377), forgetting that it was Hercules himself who was false to his wife when he took on Iole as his concubine. Whether or not Domicio's ex-mistress was "false," she was certainly "poison," a notion that Cervantes reifies through the linen shirt that destroys the count.

The curious feature of this episode is that the sexually toxic atmosphere hardly touches the count's wife, who sails safely down on the wings of her skirts, whereas it almost kills Periandro—"como no tuvo vestidos anchos que le sustentasen [because he had no wide skirts to break his fall]" (373). Different readers will read Periandro's fall from a tower differ-

ently: as a fall from pride, a fall from grace, or even as a "fortunate fall."
On the interpretation of falls within dreams, Freud himself insists that it
is "impossible to give a general reply" as to the meaning of such dreams:
"They mean something different in every instance," he writes. This poly-
valence, however, seems oddly exclusive to male dreamers: "If a woman
dreams of falling," Freud elsewhere writes, "it almost invariably has a
sexual sense: she is imagining herself as a *fallen woman.*" [39] Freud's remark seems to be fortified in *Don Quixote* by the innkeeper Juan Palo-
meque's daughter, who mentions, just prior to the sexually charged garret
episode, that she has often dreamt of falling off a tower and never reaching the ground, but that, when she woke up, she was bruised and bumped
("molida y quebrantada") as if she had really fallen (1.16). To conceive
of a "fallen man" in the sexual sense suggested by this episode is difficult,
however, even given Cervantes's explicit allusion to Periandro's unfortunate lack of sustaining skirts. What is clear here is that the "mujer voladora [flying woman]" uses hers to survive. The whole story, and its near-
tragic postscript outside the interpolation, is an exemplary one for
Periandro, whose "quixotic" response to the situation costs him a
month's convalescence. His fall, however, immunizes him for a later encounter with his own "Deyanira," the false Roman courtesan Hipólita,
who will try to poison Auristela in order to win Periandro for herself.

Unlike the domestic tragedy of Count Domicio, the last interpolated
story to be discussed in this chapter is a kind of "revenger's comedy"
(3.16–17). It is a tale of a triangle, although the heroine, a Scottish countess called Ruperta, is the only survivor when the story opens. A female
revenger, she is obsessed with securing blood vengeance for the murder
of her husband, Lamberto de Escocia, treacherously slain by another
Scots nobleman, Claudino Rubicón, who had once been a rival for her
hand. Directly after her husband's burial, the grieving widow orders his
corpse to be decapitated and the head unfleshed by appropriate chemicals
("se le cortó la cabeza, que en pocos días, con cosas que se le aplicaron,
quedó descarnada y en solamente los huesos") (385). The clinical details
of the preservation of a spousal body part for veneration by a widow
invoke Cervantes's ultimate parody of a bankrupt chivalric order: the
Cave of Montesinos episode in *Don Quixote* (2.23), in which the salting
and mummifying of Durandarte's heart ("un corazón de carnemomia")
as a token for his wife Belerma is carefully documented.

In the *Persiles* episode, the heroine carts the grisly relic of her husband's
skull all around Europe in a silver chest, together with the blood-stained

[39] Freud, *The Interpretation of Dreams*, trans. James Strachey (1953; rpt., New York:
Avon Books, 1965), 428, 235. On the associations between flying and sexual power, see *SE*
5.410 and 394; see also "Leonardo da Vinci and a Memory of his Childhood," *SE* 11.125–
27.

shirt he died in and the bloodied sword that killed him.[40] She uses the skull as a prop for her secret rites of blood vengeance, a tirade of vivid rhetorical threats. Until she accomplishes what she confesses is her "no cristiano deseo [unchristian desire]," Ruperta swears to remain, Hamlet-style, in all "the trappings and the suits of woe" (1.2.86): "Que mi vestido será negro, mis aposentos lóbregos, mis manteles tristes y mi compañía la misma soledad [My dress shall be black, my dwellings dark, my table sad and my only company, solitude itself]" (386). This *juramento* or ritual swearing belongs to the archaic formulas of the oaths of vengeance found in chivalric literature. Ruperta's words famously recall Don Quixote's version of the Marquéz de Mantua's oath, beginning with the memorable resolution "de no comer pan a manteles, ni con su mujer folgar [not to eat bread at table, nor to sleep with his wife]" (*DQ* 1.10).

The highly parodic episode of the avenging Scottish countess intersects with the main plot when, en route to Rome to seek political aid for her plotted revenge, Ruperta takes rooms in the same Italian inn where Periandro, Auristela, and their entourage are lodging. Because Ruperta, in her projected vengeance, has enlisted the sympathy of her manservant, he invites the whole party of pilgrims to her bedchamber as voyeurs, allowing them to spy on her dark and secret rites. In a wild soliloquy intoned over her relics, Ruperta commands herself to forget that she is a woman in preparation for the task of blood vengeance (388), a mandate that recalls Lady Macbeth's gender-coded invocation to the infernal powers, her request that they "unsex" her for the work of murder (*Macbeth* 1.5.42).

Cervantes's precursor here is not Shakespeare, however, but Apuleius, whose Psyche also undergoes a sex change when on the verge of killing Cupid: "Sexum audacia mutatur."[41] But this parallel is the least notable of the many signs in Cervantes's tale that gesture to *The Golden Ass* as his model, a work available to the age in Diego López de Cortegana's Spanish translation (1513).[42] So well disseminated was this *Asno de oro* that, even a century later, Cervantes's witch Cañizares would be moved, in *El coloquio de los perros*, to cite "Apuleyo," his *Asno de oro*, and his antidote of roses.[43] I have argued elsewhere—on thematic, structural, and

[40] María Rosa Lida de Malkiel situates the traveling skull as "probably" in the Arthurian tradition and suggests, as analogues, the *Perlesvaus*, where a maid carts the head of a knight about in a rich ivory vessel, and the *Mabinogion*, where two maids carry a man's head about on a large dish ("Dos huellas del *Esplandián* en el *Quijote* y el *Persiles*," *Romance Philology* 9 [November 1955]).

[41] Apuleius, *The Golden Ass: Being the Metamorphoses of Lucius Apuleius*, with an English trans. by W. Adlington (1566) (Loeb Classical Library, 1965), 230.

[42] Diego López de Cortegana's *El asno de oro* is now available to us in a splendid edition by Carlos García Gual, including a long and instructive introduction (Madrid: Alianza Editorial, 1988); my citations are to this edition and will be parenthetically documented.

[43] Cañizares laments that the recipe for disenchanting Cipión and Berganza from their

rhetorical grounds—that *The Golden Ass* is a major and determinate subtext in Cervantes's episode of Ruperta. To my thinking, the basic revenge
structures of Apuleius's tale of Charites and Tlepolemus—the frame for
the drunken crone's tale of Cupid and Psyche—play a constitutive part in
Cervantes's story.[44] Even the feverish rhetoric of his avenging widow
would seem to return us to what Menéndez y Pelayo condemned as "la
violenta y atormentada latinidad [the violent and tormented Latinity]" of
Apuleius.[45]

Unknown to Cervantes's vengeful Ruperta, her intended victim, Claudino Rubicón, is already dead. His son Croriano, however, seeking her
throughout the Continent to make atonement for his father's crime, co-
incidentally puts up at the same inn where she is lodging. When Ruperta
learns of his presence there, she gains access to his bedroom, lantern and
knife in hand, in order to exact vengeance on him as a surrogate for his
father. Cervantes's frenetic narrator tries to alert Ruperta to avoid looking at the sleeping "Cupid" she is about to kill ("Mira . . . que no mires a
ese hermoso Cupido"), but his Apuleian warning is put forward in such
a way as to make it entirely unreceivable. When the narrator says *don't*
he means *do* look: if you look at "Cupid," he explains, "se deshará en un
punto toda la máquina de tus pensamientos [the whole machinery of your
thoughts will be dismantled]" (389). Because Ruperta's mental machinery is fueled by a morbid, quirky, and bloodthirsty desire for revenge,
looking at "Cupid" turns out to be a wise move. In Cervantes's dialectical
imitation of Apuleius, the cost of sight is not Cupid's flight but his cap-
ture. Ruperta is so overcome by her intended victim's physical beauty that
she stays her hand: "¡Cuán mejor eres tú para ser mi esposo que para ser
objeto de mi venganza! [How much better might you be for my husband
than for the object of my vengeance!]" (389). Croriano/Cupido awakens
when Ruperta/Psyche drops the lantern on his chest, Apuleius's oil lamp
having metamorphosed into Cervantes's *lanterna*. In the ensuing ruckus
in the bedchamber, the heroine renounces all thoughts of vengeance, and
the hero asks her to marry him. When she assures him that she is not a
deceiving phantom—"este mi cuerpo no es fantástico [this body of mine
is not fantastic]"—the couple embrace. After a hugger-mugger pre-Tri-

---

animality could not be "tan fácil como el que se dice de Apuleyo en *El Asno de oro*, que
consistía en sólo comer una rosa [as easy as the one mentioned by Apuleius in *The Golden
Ass*, which only consisted in eating a rose]" (*Novelas ejemplares*, ed. Rodríguez Marín,
2:294).

[44] Diana Wilson, "Apuleius as Subtext of Cervantes's *Persiles* 3.16–17" (Paper delivered
at the Second International Conference on the Ancient Novel, Dartmouth College, Hanover,
N.H., 26 July 1988).

[45] Cited by Adolfo Bonilla y San Martín, "Advertencia," *Orígenes de la novela*, Nueva
Biblioteca de Autores Españoles, vol. 4 (Madrid: Casa Editorial Bailly//Baillierie, 1915),
149.

dentine marriage, with servants as their only witnesses, the newlyweds fall back into bed (391). The next morning finds them still in each other's arms.

The florid, self-conscious, and highly artificial prose of this eccentric tale—with its rhetorical set-pieces and extravagant diction—advertises its filiation with Apuleius's extravagant stylistic mannerisms. The unstable narration of the tale, however, is recognizably Cervantine: it is begun by Ruperta's manservant, a senile squire dressed in mourning; then taken up by the anonymous narrator of the *Persiles*, who intervenes vigorously in the events, addressing both the heroine and the reader in the second person; and, finally, closed by the indirect discourse of the same woman-hating squire. The story, in short, is "framed" by a misogynist, a kind of Golden Age Juvenal who is given the last word in the tale.[46] This aged manservant generalizes about women as he removes the grisly relics—skull, sword, and shirt—from the inn: "Murmuró de la facilidad de Ruperta, y en general, de todas las mujeres, y el menor vituperio que dellas dijo fue llamarlas antojadizas [He carried on about the easy sexuality of Ruperta and, in general, of all women, and the least vituperation he expressed was to call them all capricious]" (392). His *vituperio* is an echo of a similar moment of vituperation about the easiness of women in *The Golden Ass*, when the hero Lucius, misjudging a woman's response, concludes that "todo el linaje de las mujeres merecía ser vituperado [the whole lineage of women deserved to be vituperated]." Apuleius's narrator distances himself from Lucius by explaining that the character of the whole female sex was hanging upon "the judgment of an ass"—in the Cortegana translation, "del juicio de un asno" (203). Ruperta's misogynist manservant is also constituted as an asinine judge, a figure of ridicule who venerates the chivalric codes of vengeance that his mistress happily recants.

The template here for the auditors of this tale is the exemplary issue of women's anger, an issue invoked, at different points, by the heroine, her squire, and the narrator. Ruperta compares herself to an angry Judith ("Judic") taking vengeance on Holofernes (388).[47] Ruperta's manservant appoints himself as the impresario for her ritual shows of anger. And the hyperactive narrator persuades himself that the anger of women is limitless ("que la cólera de la mujer no tiene límite") (386), a topos he reinforces with three rhetorical questions: "¿Qué no hace una mujer enojada?

[46] James Tatum writes of the tradition, "beginning with Semonides in the mid–seventh century B.C., of cataloguing the vices of women. In Latin literature the longest example of this kind of dispraise is Juvenal, *Satires* 6 (written ca. A.D. 116)" (*Apuleius and* The Golden Ass [Ithaca: Cornell University Press, 1979], 74).

[47] Freud saw the biblical Judith as "the woman who castrates the man who has deflowered her" (*SE* 11:207).

¿Qué montes de dificultades no atropella en sus disignios [*sic*]? ¿Qué in-
ormes [*sic*] crueldades no le parecen blandas y pacíficas? [What will an
angry woman not do? What jungle of difficulties will she not trample in
her designs? What enormous cruelties will not seem to her gentle and
peaceful?]" (389) Between a hysterical narrator and a misogynist manservant, in sum, Ruperta is represented as either too angry or too easy. These
Renaissance notions of woman are addressed and redressed in the three
inset stories that I have saved for star billing, and it is time now to turn to
the first.

PART THREE

The Woman in the Text

Chapter Eight

A ROMANCE OF RAPE:
TRANSILA FITZMAURICE

What's to prevent human beings from similarly
agreeing among themselves to legalize certain types
of rape . . . ?
—Thomas More, *Utopia*

As ALL READERS of *La fuerza de la sangre* know, Transila's inset story
(1.12–13) is not Cervantes's first representation of rape. But the narrative
in the *Persiles* is a tale of *foiled* gang rape and, therefore, a kind of romance *in ovo*. It may even be called a "kidnapped" romance, in that the
heroine violently wrenches the tale out of her father's mouth in order to
make it her own: "Quitándole a su padre las palabras de la boca, dijo las
del siguiente capítulo [Taking the words out of her father's mouth, she
said those of the following chapter]" (113). "The word in language,"
writes Bakhtin, "exists in other people's mouths, in other people's con-
texts, serving other people's intentions: it is from there that one must take
the word, and make it one's own."[1] Luce Irigaray both reiterates and genders Bakhtin's advice: "Let's take back a bit of our mouth to try to
speak," she exhorts women, whom she regards as still "(d)raped" in the
words of others.[2] A similar parenthetical metaplasmos operates in Cervantes's tale, which enacts the attempted "(d)raping" of a woman in the
name of the law. Not allowing her own desire to go unrepresented, however, the woman will "try to speak" other-wise, interrupting the account
of her own wedding night begun by her father.

What readers confront, then, is a joint father/daughter narrative of
rape set in Ireland some time before the in medias res beginnings of the
Persiles. The daughter belongs to a tradition of women warriors who enjoyed a small revival during the Renaissance. The father belongs to the
well-known lineage of the Irish Fitzmaurice family, having been modeled,

[1] Bakhtin, "Discourse in the Novel," in *The Dialogic Imagination*, 293–94.

[2] Luce Irigaray, "Quand nos lèvres se parlent," in *Ce sexe qui n'en est pas un* (Paris:
Minuit, 1977); "When our lips speak together," trans. Carolyn Burke, *Signs* 6 (Autumn
1980): 69–79.

perhaps, on the Irish rebel "Jaime Fitzmauricio," who, as Cervantes would surely have known, offered the crown of Ireland to Don Juan of Austria in 1577.[3] Within this fictional father/daughter dyad, "the seduction of the daughter," to borrow the modishly psychoanalytic term, is less the issue than the seduction of the father by the so-called "custom of the country": the *ius primae noctis* or Law of the First Night, a Latin circumlocution for the custom of legislated rape. The aim of this chapter is to contextualize Cervantes's literary use of this curious custom by looking both at his precursors—including *himself* as precursor—and at his imitators.

We first meet the daughter—aptly called "Transila"—in her official role as interpreter-in-residence of the Barbaric Isle, the extended metaphor of the opening chapters of the *Persiles*. In chapter 5, we noted how Cervantes's barbarians manage to immolate themselves in a bloody civil war, suffering "mil diferentes géneros de muertes, de quien la cólera, sinrazón y enojo suelen ser inventores [a thousand different kinds of deaths, of which rage, unreason, and anger tend to be the inventors]" (84). After the destruction of the Barbaric Isle, translator Transila, saved from the holocaust in the company of the protagonists, heads south with their party. When the ex-captives arrive at the Baltic island of "Golandia" (Gothland)—an island some ninety-five kilometers east of Sweden—she surprisingly encounters, in its bustling seaport (the unnamed Visby?), both her aged father Mauricio (Fitzmaurice) and her young husband Ladislao. Husband and father, both Irish subjects, have been combing the North Sea for her, and the father has predicted, through "astrología judicaria [judicial astrology]," this joyous reunion to the very hour. After some rest and nourishment at a local inn, Mauricio begins to relate the story of the catastrophe of his daughter's wedding night, the event that separated her from father, husband, and country.

Mauricio opens this double-voiced discourse by identifying himself as an Irish-Catholic astrologer. A conventional Renaissance literary widower, he reared his daughter until she was of marriageable age, at which time he chose Ladislao for her husband, but only after consulting her wishes. The father's enlightened vision of an excellent match for his daughter, however, was marred by the barbarous custom of his country, the ius primae noctis, whereby a new bride must suffer the nocturnal visits of all her husband's kinsmen, "a manosear los ramilletes que ella quisiera guardar intactos para su marido [to paw at the flowers she would have wished to keep intact for her husband]" (112). The father's decorous use of floral metaphorics for this group defloration is meant not to mollify but to lament this violent wedding protocol. Mauricio had attempted,

---

[3] Schevill and Bonilla, "Introduction," *Persiles*, xxxvi.

many times, to persuade his countrymen ("había yo intentado de persu-
adir") to give up this custom, but with no luck. And so he had resigned
himself to believing that custom is a "second nature" ("la costumbre es
otra naturaleza") and that changing it feels like death ("el mudarla se
siente como la muerte") (113). It is suggestive, I think, that Mauricio here
echoes sentiments similar, in their resigned passivity, to Saint Augustine's:
"O thou torrent of human custom, who shall be able to resist thee?"[4] As
it turns out, Mauricio's own daughter is able to resist the "custom of the
country," a custom he had supported because, as he now confesses, he
had been trained early in self-interest. When this or that cultural custom
seemed unjust to him, Mauricio was not given to making a fuss:

> Seguí las costumbres de mi patria, a lo menos en cuanto a las que parecían
> ser niveladas con la razón, y en las que no, con apariencias fingidas mostraba
> seguirlas, que tal vez la disimulación es provechosa. (111)

> [I followed the customs of my country, at least insofar as they appeared to
> be reasonable, while I gave the appearance of following those that did not,
> for sometimes dissimulation can be beneficial.]

But dissimulation is scarcely beneficial to a sexual scapegoat, the "custom"-designed role for his daughter. Describing her ferocious confrontation of all the wedding guests, Mauricio represents her as emerging, lance
in hand, into the great hall where everyone was congregated, "hermosa
como el sol, brava como una leona y airada como un tigre [as lovely as
the sun, as angry as a lion and as wrathful as a tiger]" (113). Just as
Mauricio arrives at this point in the story, Transila leaps up to her feet,
and with her face flushed and her eyes afire, breaks into his discourse and
continues to narrate her own epic of resistance.

She recalls how she accused her persecutors, "en alta y colérica voz [in
a loud and angry voice]," of being a lascivious community who, under
the guise of vain ceremonies "queréis cultivar los ajenos campos sin licen-
cia de sus legítimos dueños [wish to cultivate other people's fields without
the license of their legitimate owners]" (113–14). Moving the trope of
cultivation from a bouquet of flowers to a ploughed field, Transila addressed the wedding guests on the impertinence of having her own "field"
cultivated without her license. After brandishing her lance at these would-
be "cultivators," she managed to escape out of the wedding hall, and ran
down to the marina, where she threw herself into a small boat. The wind
carried her out to sea and then back to a neighboring coast, where some
profiteering fisherman sold her to the barbarians as a candidate for their
next queen. The coming of the protagonists to the Barbaric Isle finally

---

[4] *The Confessions of St. Augustine*, trans. Sir Tobie Matthew (Glasgow: Fontana Books,
1923), 49.

released her to follow them in their wanderings. In her spirited rebellion against the Law of the First Night, Transila had at least the tacit support of her husband Ladislao, who now crowns her narration by praising her legendary escape from the communal institutions of his own kinsmen (114).

That is all that happens in this narrative of a rape that never happened. It is enough, however, to show us that rape is here framed by Cervantes as an affair between men: legislated by them, piously yoked to their religious ceremonies, scarcely contested even by caring fathers. And it may be enough to serve as retrospective commentary on Cervantes's prior fiction of rape in *La fuerza de la sangre*. This problematic "exemplary novel" is a text which, until recently, traditional criticism has managed to allegorize, to displace onto Christian interpretive systems, latching their readings onto the silver crucifix that Leocadia steals from her rapist—"no por devoción ni por hurto [neither for devotion nor theft]" but as evidence that will later corroborate her rape. In an excellent revisionary study of this episode, Marcia Welles shows how this iconic crucifix has allowed interpretive history to drain meaning away from the violence of the rape by imposing on it the reading of a *felix culpa*. Such readings, for Welles, amount to an objectionable "elision of gender," one that occults the "truth of the matter that it is the bonding between women that allows the plot to unfold, for they resist by breaking the silence of shame imposed by son and father, and risk the resolution."[5] The correspondences between this reading and the events represented in the *Persiles* are startling. We have earlier noted that it is the bonding between women— the two mothers of the protagonists, the queens of Thule and Friesland— that allows the plot of the *Persiles* to unfold. But another notable linkage between *La fuerza de la sangre* and Transila's episode in the *Persiles* is the presence of a loving father whose passivity endorses the status quo. Leocadio's father, for instance, counsels his raped daughter not to try to use the crucifix to publicly identify her violator: "Lo que has de hacer, hija, es guardarla [the image of the crucifix] y encomendarte a ella, que pues ella fue testigo de tu desgracia, permitirá que haya juez que vuelva por tu justicia [What you must do, daughter, is save the crucifix and commend yourself to it, and because it was a witness to your disgrace, it will permit that some judge return to grant you justice]."[6] This could be Mauricio, in the later *Persiles*, counseling silence as the wisest response to rape. The issue of rape is advanced in the Transila episode, however,

[5] Marcia Welles, "Violence Disguised: Representation of Rape in Cervantes's *La fuerza de la sangre*," *Journal of Hispanic Philology* [Special Issue: *Feminist Topics*, ed. Alison Weber] 13 (Spring 1989): 240–52.

[6] Miguel de Cervantes, *Novelas ejemplares*, ed. Juan Bautista Avalle-Arce, 3 vols. (Madrid: Castalia, 1982), 2:155.

by representing "justice" as always already tied up by legislation, by the preexisting law of the land, the Law of the First Night.

Between the Leocadio and the Transila stories, then, Cervantes not only moves rape from the private into the public domain—exposing the dangerous sophism of a rape law—but also, by remotivating the curious custom of the ius primae noctis, makes a polemic and agonistic gesture to all of his conjectured sources. We know that the practice of ritual defloration was reported by various sixteenth-century chroniclers and travel writers, from Johann Boehme to Inca Garcilaso de la Vega. Boehme's *Repertorium . . . de omnium gentium ritibus* (1520), of which there were several sixteenth-century editions, gave the following account of the practice in the Balearic Isles: "Mirandum vero quod in nuptiis de more servant . . . primus secundusque et deinceps secundum aetatem reliqui nuptam cognoscunt: ultimus sposo locus ad sponsam datur [In truth, what they observe as a custom in nuptials . . . ought to be wondered at: one man and then a second and then the rest, according to age, knows the bride: the final place is given to the groom for his bride]."[7] Boehme's account had been adapted into Spanish by Francisco Thámara as *El libro de las costumbres de todas las gentes del mundo* (1556), a text Cervantes seems to have used for his description in the *Persiles* of the fabulous birds called *barnaclas*. In keeping with Boehme, Thámara attributes, in his chapter 8, the custom of ritual defloration to the inhabitants of the Balearic Isles, as alluded to by Diodorus Siculus in his Greek history of curiosities. Why Cervantes chose to represent the practice in Ireland, in the oddly pagan Hibernia of the 1560s, may bear further historicist researches. Avalle-Arce thinks it probable that Cervantes, reading about other, more ordinary, Irish customs further on in Thámara's text, conflated them with the Balearic practices.[8] Legislated rape is also discussed in Pedro Cieza de León's *La chrónica del Perú nuevamente escrita* (1554), a text that Schevill and Bonilla regard as "rarísimo" and therefore unlikely to have been seen by Cervantes.[9] Jean Leon l'Africain also discussed ritual defloration in his *description de l'Afrique* (1556).[10] López de Gomara notes in his Amerindian history the practice of both polygamy and group defloration: "Casaban con muchas mujeres, y los señores y capitanes rompían las novias por honra o por tiranía [They married many women, and the lords and captains "ruptured" the brides either for honor or for tyr-

---

[7] See the chapter entitled "De Anglia, Scotia, Hybernia, allisque multis insulis et insulanorum moribus," in Boehme's *Repertorium*, bk. 3, chap. 26, fol. 78.

[8] Avalle-Arce, "Introduction," *Los trabajos*, 14–15n.

[9] Schevill and Bonilla, "Notes," *Persiles*, 337.

[10] Jean Leon l'Africain, *Description de l'Afrique* 1:405; cited by W. D. Howarth, "Cervantes and Fletcher: A Theme with Variations," *Modern Language Review* 56 (1961): 563n.

anny]."[11] But the version of the custom that tallies most closely with Cervantes's text—at least in its use of the phrase "los parientes más cercanos [the nearest kin]"—may be found in chapter 24 of the *Comentarios* of Inca Garcilaso de la Vega, who characteristically distances the practice away from the Inca nation: "En otras provincias corrompían la virgen que se había de casar *los parientes más cercanos* del novio y sus mayores amigos, y con esta condición concertaban el casamiento, y así la recebía después el marido [In other provinces, the groom's *nearest kinsmen* and his best friends would "corrupt" the virgin who was to be married, and with this condition they settled the marriage, and in that way her husband would receive her later; emphasis added]."[12] W. D. Howarth assures us that ritual defloration—which he calls "a harmless anthropological curiosity"—was not regarded by these sixteenth-century primitive societies as "tyrannical or cruel," that, on the contrary, it was "considered a source of honor to the bride." Since Howarth withholds from us the ablative of agent who "considered" the practice a "source of honor," we must assume that it was "custom" speaking.[13] Whether or not the primitive brides themselves regarded their multiple defloration as "harmless" is beyond the scope of this chapter, but speculations on the matter need no longer, I think, be consigned to French high theory of the female body. What is pertinent to the present study, however, is Cervantes's own attitude toward the ius primae noctis, which his text explicitly regards as a "costumbre bárbara y maldita [barbarous and wicked custom]" (1.12).

The representation of Transila throughout the *Persiles* is, consistently, that of a gendered, even a cross-gendered, subject. Three of her subject-positions are especially remarkable, in that they help to explicate the strange name Cervantes gives to this Irish heroine. As a ritual rape candidate, as the daughter of a "seer," and as a polyglot interpreter of the codes of the Isla Bárbara, Transila leaves us little room for doubting that her own "trabajos" in Cervantes's text—to borrow a phrase from Robert ter Horst's reading of a learned Tirso heroine—are to provide both "a deed of translation and a theory of translation."[14] Her response to the role imposed upon her as the community's sexual scapegoat is, as mentioned earlier, to fend off her would-be rapists with a lance, to dash down to the local marina, and to row herself out to sea. Remembering, no doubt, the reigning neo-Aristotelian premium on plausibility, Cervantes

[11] López de Gomara, *Hispania victrix* 1:294.

[12] Inca Garcilaso, *Comentarios reales* (Mexico City: Editorial Porrúa, 1984), 27. Inca Garcilaso adds that Pedro de Cieza says the same thing in chap. 24 of his chronicle.

[13] W. D. Howarth, "Cervantes and Fletcher: A Theme with Variations," *Modern Language Review* 56 (1961): 563–64.

[14] Robert ter Horst, "Aspects of Love and Learning in *El amor médico*," *Revista canadiense de estudios hispánicos* 10 (Winter 1986): 287.

had to create a tough heroine, one who could physically defend the proprietary rights to her own body. The solution was to represent Transila as a virago, in the earlier exemplary and not later pejorative connotation of the word.

The term *virago*—literally "I make or do [like a] man"—meant a "manlike woman" in the classical tradition, and was used by Ovid, for example, to describe Minerva transformed by rage into a "metuenda virago [frightening amazon]" (*Met.* 2.765). This kind of masculinizing, apparent elsewhere in the *Persiles*, stands out in Cervantes's representation of Transila as "menos tierna, más animosa [less tender, more animated]" than the pilgrims, whom she follows "con varonil brío [with a manly brío]" (1.4). An oddly feminine use of the term *virago* by Leone Ebreo bears citing here, deployed for the androgynous Eve discussed in chapter 4 of the present book.[15] The unambiguous sign of Transila's status as a virago or woman warrior is the lance she assumes in her confrontation with her new husband's "lascivious" kinsmen. Cervantes's depiction of this agile, strong, valiant, and virginal warrior maiden[16] evokes a cluster of her literary sisters, characters from Renaissance epic who had been modeled on the figures of Greco-Roman epic. Boiardo's Marfisa in *Orlando Innamorato* is one of these conventional viragos. Ariosto's Bradamante in *Orlando Furioso*, also the precursor for Spenser's Britomart, is another. And Tasso's Clorinda in *Gerusalemme liberata* (canto 12), modeled closely on Heliodorus's heroine Chariclea, is yet another. Behind all these Renaissance women warriors stand three hardy classical models: the Amazon queen Hippolyta; the other bare-breasted Amazon, Penthesilea, mentioned by Virgil in the *Aeneid* (1.491) and appearing in numerous minor epics; and Virgil's own Camilla (*Aen.* 7.803ff., 11.532ff.).

Heroic, intrepid, and seaworthy, Cervantes's Transila reminds us that his main heroine, Auristela, is tender, skittish, and pathologically afraid of sea voyages, the sea being explicitly equated in the *Persiles* with the insecurities of life: "Que la inconstancia de nuestras vidas y la del mar simbolizan en no prometer seguridad ni firmeza alguna largo tiempo [The inconstancy of our lives and that of the sea symbolize the unlikelihood of any long-term stability or security]" (253). Forcione has interpreted Transila's role as "very similar to that of Auristela in the main plot," largely on the grounds that each woman is "a heroic virgin, separated from her beloved and harassed by various lustful antagonists."[17] Apart from the

---

[15] León Hebreo, *Diálogos de amor* 2:220.

[16] On the motif of the warrior maiden, see Petrarch's intriguing letter (23 November 1343) about his meeting in Pozzuoli with "a mighty female soldier." This letter to Cardinal Giovanni Colonna (*Le familiari*, bk. 5.4) is excerpted in *Letters from Petrarch*, trans. Morris Bishop (Bloomington: Indiana University Press, 1966), 52–54.

[17] Forcione, *Cervantes' Christian Romance*, 119.

stock romance roles they assume as harassable virgins, however, there is a strategic nonconvergence between these two heroines. Transila's role is actually closer to that of Sulpicia, the pirate woman whose own story is interpolated into Periandro's ten-chapter-long narration in book 2 of the *Persiles* (2.14). As this later episode presents a grisly supplement to Cervantes's fictional reflections on rape, it is worth a few remarks here.

Sulpicia's story was undoubtedly inspired by Olao Magno's book of Northern customs, in which he recalls various women warriors, among whom was one Alvida: "que se hizo corsario, y recorría los mares en traje masculino [who turned herself into a corsair, and sailed the seas in masculine dress]."[18] Being pushed to speculate, for his story, on why any woman would become a corsair, Cervantes created the horrific fiction of Sulpicia, a Lithuanian widow who turns into an avenging pirate in response to her husband's murder. When Periandro first encounters her at sea, Sulpicia has just avenged herself on a whole shipload of lecherous drunkards who, intent on rape, had committed murder. As her ship first comes into view, some forty men are seen hanging from its tackle and yards, like "fruto" on "árboles" (237). When Periandro's men visit its decks, they stumble over the remainder, or rather the remains, of the other murderers. The Nabokov who complained about the degree of cruelty represented in *Don Quixote*[19] would have found the following scene of mass killing in the *Persiles* even more repellent:

> Hallaron la cubierta llena de sangre y de cuerpos de hombres semivivos, unos con las cabezas partidas, y otros con las manos cortadas; tal vomitando sangre, y tal vomitando el alma; éste gimiendo dolorosamente, y aquél gritando sin paciencia alguna. (236)

> [They found the deck awash in blood and filled with the bodies of semi-alive men, some with their heads asunder, and others with their hands cut off; this one vomiting blood, and that one his soul; this one whimpering painfully, and that one screaming with no patience whatsoever.]

Stepping over all this dreadful carnage—no doubt a haunting residue of Cervantes's own experience at sea during the ferocious Battle of Lepanto—Periandro's sailors make their way to the poop of the ship, where they discover some dozen women being instructed by a "capitana" dressed in a spotlessly white tunic. She interrupts her drill to tell them her story, which, although wanting the romance ending of Transila's episode, shares with it the marital theme: both Transila and Sulpicia are married women when they confront the threat of rape, but only Transila will be

---

[18] Schevill and Bonilla, "Introduction," *Persiles*, xxiv.

[19] See chapter on "Cruelty and Mystification" in *Lectures on* Don Quixote, ed. Fredson Bowers (New York: Harcourt Brace Jovanovich, 1983), 51–88.

reunited with her husband. Tapping into the rare Renaissance genre of the Oaristys or poem on married bliss, the young widow describes herself as a woman "que ayer se vio en la cumbre de la buena fortuna, por verse en poder de su esposo [who yesterday saw herself on the crest of good fortune, for seeing herself in possession of such a husband]" (238). During a sea voyage to visit her uncle in Lithuania, however, the couple's servants run amuck because of drinking too much wine: "Borró las obligaciones de la memoria, y en su lugar les puso los gustos de la lascivia [It wiped out all sense of obligation from their memories, replacing it with the pleasures of lust]" (237). After these drunken men kill Sulpicia's husband—but before they can go into their "rape-or-else" routine[20]—the women on the ship, with the help of four servants who were "libres del humo de Baco [free from the fumes of Bacchus]," cut their assailants to pieces and hang them up on the rigging. Cervantes no doubt worried here about the verisimilitude of this whole skirmish, since twelve women cutting down forty drunken men brings to mind the Canon of Toledo's dismissal of those romance heroes who cut giants in half like marzipan. As a corrective, however, Cervantes gives Sulpicia a long speech that ends with how the anger of endangered women could extend to all this cruelty: "Cuarenta son los ahorcados, y si fueran cuarenta mil, también murieran, porque su poca o ninguna defensa, y nuestra cólera, a toda esta crueldad, si por ventura lo es, se estendía [The hanged men amount to forty, and had there been forty thousand, they too would have died, because their little or no defense, and our rage, could extend to all this cruelty, if indeed it *is* cruelty]" (237).

The differences between this method of rape prevention and Transila's nonviolent resistance would appear to depend on the differences between criminal passions and legislated pressures: whereas the lust is alcohol-induced in one episode, it is communally legislated in the other. In the context of the *Heptameron*, Lucien Febvre writes about men's rage to satisfy their lustful passions in the violent sixteenth century (which he sees as a period during which love was a sickness "closely akin to rabies"): "Victory is the one aim. And the means? Any and every possible one. Including murder. No false sense of decency. Women are forewarned. It is up to them to be on their guard."[21] Both of the rape episodes in Cervantes's last work, written almost a century after the *Heptameron*, show women still "on their guard"—a condition literalized in the case of Sulpicia as drill sergeant. In her violent story, Cervantes reifies all forty would-be rapists into hanging "fruit"—suggesting a figurative likeness to

[20] Northrop Frye's phrase in his discussion of romance heroines as beleaguered virgins (see *Secular Scripture*, 65–93).

[21] Lucien Febvre, *Amour sacre, amour profane, autour de l'Heptameron* (Paris: Gallimard, 1971), 276.

the very grapes whose fumes helped to unhinge them. The excessive carnage operates as allegorical "fruto" in a moral sense, too, suggesting the degree of "cólera [rage]"—a key word also in the Transila story—that rape could invoke in women, not simply in virginal maidens but in married women too. In the Transila story, the would-be rapists are left behind in Ireland, minus two of their kinsmen, the father and husband who follow her out to sea. It is important to see that Cervantes has depicted Transila's "varonil [manly]" spirit as one entirely capable of deeply feminine love for her husband Ladislao. It is he who ecstatically declares that her resistance would be celebrated "por siglos [for centuries]" (114). Of perhaps even greater significance here, however, is Cervantes's subversion of the conventional Renaissance narrative of rape, generally subtended by the cherished paradigm of Lucretia, where death is the price a loving wife pays for having been raped. The Roman matron Lucretia was tirelessly invoked throughout the sixteenth century for her pudicity, for having prized her honor more than her life. Such a masochistic concept of honor, introjected by countless women of the period, is never endorsed by Cervantes. The closest he ever comes to the Lucretia paradigm of death is in *La fuerza de la sangre*, where he metaphorically describes the bed upon which Leocadia is raped as the "tumba de su sepultura [tomb of her sepulcher]." But Leocadia's only real entombment is her ensuing "recogimiento" or social retreat, a kind of self-exile iterated in the *Persiles* by Transila's season in the Barbaric Isle.

In Transila's role as the daughter of a seer, she plays out Cervantes's intertextuality with Virgil's *Aeneid*, participating in an ongoing critique of Virgil's use of magic that Michael McGaha correctly reads as a form of agonistic imitation: "Not content to imitate Virgil, Cervantes sought to surpass him. He achieved this objective by eliminating the flaws in Virgil's work which had diminished its credibility: the reliance on magic and divine machinery."[22] Cervantes represents the seer Mauricio as a passive interpreter of portents of disaster, as helpless to avert them. Later in the text he will predict though be unable to prevent the sinking of their ship by two Renaissance terrorists (1.18). Unlike his daughter, Mauricio is a *seer* but not a *doer*. When he finally locates Transila in accordance with his astrological signs, she oddly tries to resist the encounter by asking for a veil to hide her identity. This locus of resistance in the text yields its richest meaning, to my mind, as the daughter's ambivalence: her wish to break, in the mode of the Moorish Zoraida of *The Captive's Tale*, with the more pernicious values of her father's culture, with the patriarchal

[22] Michael D. McGaha, "Cervantes and Virgil," in *Cervantes and the Renaissance*, Papers of the Pomona College Cervantes Symposium, 16–18 November, 1978, ed. Michael D. McGaha (Easton, Pa.: Juan de la Cuesta Press, 1980), 49.

ideology that he had dis-simulated as his own. By taking "the words from his mouth" in midnarration, however, Transila, unlike Zoraida, will perform this psychic surgery far more humanely.

Finally, and most radically, Cervantes represents Transila from the position of woman as interpreter, as subject or knower. Our first image of Transila in his text is that of a woman being carried up to an anchored ship on the shoulders of the barbarians, for whom she functions as "la intérprete [the interpreter]" (62). As a translator-in-captivity, she speaks alternately in Polish ("en lengua polaca") and in "barbarolalia," the barbarian language, using the European tongue to lament the prospect of becoming the "queen" of a culture that imports and commodifies its women (63). Later we discover that Transila is a polyglot, speaking also Swedish (Gothland) and Celtic (Hibernia). As a gendered subject of knowledge, Transila can interpret the barbarian discourses of power, can call into question their knowledge. She sees through their messianic mission as yet another pious legitimization of customs that she dismisses as "más lascivos que religiosos [more lascivious than religious]" (1.13), of customs, in other words, strategically similar to those in Ireland, the country she has fled. Transila's attack on the "bárbara e insolente [barbarous and insolent]" law of the Barbaric Isle echoes Preciosa's similar response to the "bárbara e insolente" legality of the gypsies in *La gitanilla*. In ter Horst's reading, Preciosa outlaws herself from the jurisdiction of the gypsies: "Her refusal to obey imbues the decision with its sacred or sacramental character. As she does so, a central tenet of the old compact shatters."[23] Transila, who has outlawed herself from the ius primae noctis of her home country, becomes the interpreter of a jurisdiction where women are merchandizable. Her task is now a *translatio*, a carrying across (*translatus*, past participle of *transferre*) of the original barbarian language to the other characters and, by extension, to the scene of our reading. And as there can be no translation without interpretation, the figure of Transila functions to reveal the covert relations of power and knowledge inherent in an all-male rhetorical culture ritually hatching its world conqueror.

These labors of interpretation may express the central feature of signification in the *Persiles*. Transila's plurivocity would seem to be exemplary of a text that begins with the word "VOCES" and that relentlessly invokes the interpretation of speech acts. Although she is described as having a

[23] On Cervantes's gypsies as "primitive and barbaric legislators," see Robert ter Horst, "Une saison en enfer: *La gitanilla*," *Cervantes* (Fall 1985): 102. This essay—which argues that "legality is the universal of *La gitanilla*" (105)—shows many affinities with my reading of the Transila episode. According to ter Horst's suggestive reading, "the core event in Cervantine fiction comes to be what it will be in later fiction—a transaction, an instrument of exchange, a deal" (111).

"lengua a quien suele turbar la cólera [a tongue which rage tends to
tongue-tie]" (113), Transila's narrative concludes by leaving all her listeners "colgados de la suavidad de su lengua [hanging onto the smoothness
of her tongue]" (1.13). The tongue as "woman's weapon" is an ancient
topos and, as Jean-Paul Debax reminds us, "women's will to revolt necessarily passes through the use of language, the tongue [*la langue*]."[24] The
tongue would seem to be a programmatic feature of the *Persiles*, however,
a text where everyone and everything seems to be speaking in tongues—
where wolves speak (77), fame speaks (114), and even silence speaks
(110); where tongues become as loose as thought itself (121), or, con-
versely, stick to the roofs of mouths (100) or stammer in shame (113);
where they choose to play mute (94), are like double-edged swords (120),
are muzzled (135), are tied by prisons (118), or are pierced by arrows
(68). As we suggested in chapter 5, the Barbaric Isle, where Transila
works as translator, represents not only a hegemonic culture of domination and submission, but also a discursive system which begs for interpretation. With the character of Transila, interpretation is both personified
and gendered. By contesting the cultural codes that legislate sexual customs, whether on the Barbaric Isle or back home in Ireland, Transila informs—may perhaps even reform—the subjectivities of her readers. Alert
to the "muchas injuriosas plumas [many offensive pens]" ever ready to
rewrite one's narratives (227), Transila labors through language first to
gain and then to maintain control of her own representation. What her
tongue speaks is, at least for the Renaissance, a new order of things: essentially, she asks to participate in the production of knowledge about
herself.

These labors seem modern, or in any event scarcely confined to Golden
Age damsels: Transila must confront, in turn, the family (her kinsmen),
the terrifying forces of nature (the sea), and the self (alone at sea). In terms
of narrative energy, her tale moves from captivity to confrontation and,
finally, toward deliverance. Although her story constitutes yet another of
Cervantes's many "captives' tales," we are not told whether during her
captivity Transila discovers—as Cervantes did during his Algerian im-
prisonment—the great virtue of "patience in adversity." We only know
that she learns, as Derrida would put it, "to speak the language of the
other without renouncing [her] own."[25] I would interpret Cervantes's interpreter, in short, as one of the most complex embodiments of both the
power *and* the incompleteness of interpretations. Transila takes the word
out of "other people's mouths" and makes it her own, the narrative pro-

[24] Jean-Paul Debax, "Et voila pourquoi votre femme est muette," cited and trans. by
Christine Brooke-Rose, "Woman as Semiotic Subject," in *The Female Body in Western Culture*, ed. Susan Rubin Suleiman (Cambridge, Mass.: Harvard University Press, 1986), 310.
[25] Jacques Derrida, "Racism's Last Word," *Critical Inquiry* 12 (Autumn 1985): 294.

cedure recommended by Bakhtin at the beginning of this chapter. As the remainder of it will argue, John Fletcher's much-cited imitation of her episode utterly fails to do the same. To explore this imitation is to understand the transhistorical clairvoyance of Cervantes's ius primae noctis text, its susceptibility to our own historical moment.

When the censor to King Philip III wrote his approbation for the *Persiles*, availing himself of the venerable topos of literary paternity, he cited Cervantes as the "padre ilustre de tantos buenos hijos [illustrious father of so many good children]" (41). Censor José de Valdivieso (himself a "fecund" religious poet and author of *autos sacramentales*) was no doubt thinking of Cervantes's former "good" children and/or stepchildren, perhaps some of his "exemplary" offspring: *Galatea, Don Quixote, La gitanilla*, to name only a few. There was no thought in our worthy censor's mind that the last of Cervantes's tested and approved "children" would soon be generating some naughty progeny abroad. Yet just a few years after his fulsome approbation, around 1620, there suddenly materialized on the London stage a drama loudly advertising itself as an imitation of the Transila episode: *The Custom of the Country*.[26] And if the title of this Jacobean drama failed to conjure up Cervantes to most literary Englishmen, some dozen characters in the play unabashedly proclaimed him as their legitimate pregenitor. This was an unfortunate intertextuality, given that the drama—as *The Oxford Companion to English Literature* even today laments—was "disfigured by the indecency of its scenes." Along the same disapproving lines, *The Cambridge History of English Literature* judges *The Custom of the Country* as "a drama of considerable merit, but unfortunately marred by grosseness [*sic*] in some of the scenes."[27] Hispanists, as might be expected, are scarcely kinder in their judgments. Schevill and Bonilla speak of it as a "grosera farsa [gross farce]" using two or three episodes from the *Persiles*, including "la historia de Transila [the story of Transila]," and adding to them "lo que de ningún modo merece recuerdo en la historia literaria [what in no way merits a memorial in literary history]." Osuna, in turn, speaks of Fletcher's play as "de harto mal gusto [in supremely bad taste]."[28] This much-impugned English play invites us to speculate on whether its Cervantine model—the ius primae noctis episode of Transila Fitzmaurice—was itself "disfigured by the in-

[26] E.H.C. Oliphant dates *The Custom of the Country* to 1620 in *The Plays of Beaumont and Fletcher: An Attempt to Determine Their Respective Shares and the Shares of Others* (New Haven: Yale University Press, 1927), 235–36.

[27] *The Oxford Companion to English Literature*, 3d ed. (Oxford: Clarendon Press, 1946), 202. G. C. Macaulay's judgment in *The Cambridge History of English Literature*, vol. 6 (Cambridge: Cambridge University Press, 1961), chap. 5.

[28] Schevill and Bonilla, "Introduction," *Persiles*, xliii; Osuna, "El olvido del *Persiles*," 66.

decency" of its English imitation, which was both a linguistic and generic *translatio*.[29]

Invoking a justly discarded system of similitude used by many Renaissance humanists—that the proper resemblance between a text and its model is analogous to the likeness between son and father—we are moved here to wonder about Cervantes's most prodigal son, John Fletcher. Remembered primarily as the great collaborator of the English Renaissance, Fletcher is permanently linked to a fellow playwright called Francis Beaumont, thanks to their famous division of labor. Theirs was literally a labor of love, because all of the fifty-two plays in their canon—the largest single corpus of dramatic poetry in the Jacobean period—deal with erotic love. Beaumont and Fletcher actually collaborated on fewer than twelve of these plays, the hands of at least six other authors having been traced in the canon. Fletcher was probably (or characteristically) co-parent to Beaumont's first creation, *The Woman Hater*, a play which shows some traces of Hispanic irony, if only because it features an epicure with the unlikely name of Lazarillo. But Fletcher collaborated promiscuously: *The Custom of the Country*, for instance, is officially in the Fletcher-Massinger canon. As one critic amusingly puts it, "there is no sign in Fletcher's work that he needed to be alone."[30]

Cervantists may recall Fletcher as a possible contributor to Beaumont's masterpiece of mock-heroic drama, *The Knight of the Burning Pestle*, a play whose subtext is probably *Don Quixote*.[31] Fletcher is also conjectured to have written *The History of Cardenio* in conjunction with Shakespeare, or at least critics have ascribed to him a share of that lost play. Not only has Fletcher's use of Hispanic sources been well documented but, as William Appleton assures us, he probably suffered few scruples about "looting" Golden Age texts: "The Elizabethans took a tolerant view of piracy in general—particularly from the Spanish."[32] We now

[29] Fletcher may have himself worked from the English translation of the *Persiles*, entered in the Stationer's Register on 22 February 1618–1619 (Oliphant, *The Plays of Beaumont and Fletcher*, 224). On the vexed issue of Fletcher's "command of Spanish," see William W. Appleton, *Beaumont and Fletcher: A Critical Study* (London: Allen and Unwin, 1956), 72–73.

[30] For characteristics of the Beaumont and Fletcher canon—as well as the lament that "the test of staging has been consistently withheld from their work"—see Ian Fletcher, *Beaumont and Fletcher*, ed. Geoffrey Bullough (London: Longmans, Green and Co., 1967), 14 and 49. Ian Fletcher cites Clifford Leech on Fletcher's collaborative mania (9).

[31] Alfred Harbage's *Annals of English Drama* designate the authorship of the 1613 quarto of *Knight* as "B (and F?)"; cited by Appleton, *Beaumont and Fletcher*, 120. Ian Fletcher ascribes the play to Beaumont, adding that "it is possible that the love scenes are by Fletcher."

[32] Appleton, who sees Fletcher's use of Spanish sources as oddly confined to prose works instead of drama, notes that "comparative studies of Elizabethan drama and the drama of

smile at the self-conscious rectitude of Fletcher's Victorian editor, George Darley, as he documents the mischievous influences brought upon Jacobean England by her "intercourse with foreign kingdoms"—notably with "Spain, whose corrupt practical ethics, less primitive pastimes and less earnest literature, began to find much favor among us under the Stuarts." The fraught question of England's "intercourse" with Spain's Golden Age literature is an issue that continues to interest scholars alert to the colonialism of language. This kind of nineteenth-century defense against Spain's Golden Age literary models echoes the prefatory panegyrics to Beaumont and Fletcher's 1647 Folio, which pronounced it—"without flattery"—as "the greatest monument of the scene that time and humanity have produced, and must live, not only the crown and sole reputation of our own, but the stain of all other nations and languages."[33]

Although Beaumont and Fletcher's work achieved a respectable canonicity, *The Custom of the Country* became, in fact, a kind of "stain" on Fletcher's reputation. What is remarkable about his particular "piracy" from Cervantes, however, is the meretricious manner in which Fletcher wrenched a narrative of rape into a comedy of errors. Fletcher's play *Rule a Wife and Have a Wife*, itself traced to an untranslated Spanish novel called *El sagaz estacio*, has been called "less a comedy than an olla podrida of comicalities."[34] Fletcher's *Custom of the Country* is yet another "olla podrida," this one cooked up, unfortunately, from Cervantine ingredients. To read in recent criticism about the "misogynistic abuse of women" as a "commonplace" of Fletcher's later work is to recall Coleridge's observation that Fletcher's heroines were "either strumpets or virgins with the minds of strumpets."[35] Even Fletcher's nineteenth-century editor George Darley allowed that, throughout his comedies, woman "is degraded into a mere object of voluptuous pursuit—a hare to be coursed, or a trout to be tickled, for supper." Far from being repelled by Fletcher's degradation of women, however, Darley concluded by applauding Fletcher for having caught "one deep truth of nature": namely, that his

---

Spain's golden age abound with perils and temptations" (*Beaumont and Fletcher*, 73). For a comparative study of the drama that abounds with cogent and learned commentary but regrettably excludes Fletcher's imitation of Cervantes, see Walter Cohen, *Drama of a Nation: Public Theatre in Renaissance England and Spain* (Ithaca: Cornell University Press, 1987).

[33] George Darley, "Introduction," *The Works of Beaumont and Fletcher*, ed. George Darley (London: George Routledge and Sons, 1876), 1:xxiii and xliv. All subsequent citations from *The Custom of the Country* are to this edition and will be parenthetically documented by page number.

[34] Darley, "Introduction," *Works*, xxiv. See E. M. Wilson's "*Rule a Wife and Have a Wife* and *El sagaz estacio*," *Review of English Studies* 24 (1948): 189–94.

[35] See Appleton, *Beaumont and Fletcher*, 12–13.

women characters were "either far more angelical or diabolical" than his men. Indeed, this delineation Darley considered a mark of Fletcher's "feminine genius, if we must not call it effeminate or feeble." My main argument here is that Fletcher did not catch that "deep truth of nature" from his model Cervantes, whose own writing progressively destabilizes the Baroque view of woman as either angelic or diabolic. It would seem that Cervantes's mature genius was indeed "feminine," whereas Fletcher's was only "feeble."[36]

The plot structures of Fletcher's imitation bear rehearsing here, however, if only to understand its cross-cultural linkages with Cervantes's work. An Italian governor in Fletcher's play invokes the "custom of the country," namely, that when a woman is contracted to be married, "the governor, / Must have her maidenhead" (106). The incumbent count who invokes the custom at the play's opening is variously described as a "maiden-monger" and as a "cannibal that feeds on the heads of maids" (107). Because this governor refuses to lose any gubernatorial privileges ("I will not lose my custom"), the alert heroine escapes from the country by sea. Unlike Transila, however, she is not alone but accompanied by the hero, her new husband, and his brother. She is captured by a Portuguese captain and sold to a brothel in Lisbon, where the hero eventually turns up. The madam of the brothel falls violently in love with him and, trying to eliminate her rival, arranges to have the heroine first strangled and then poisoned by a witch. In a fit of fifth act remorse, however, the brothel owner cancels the charm and marries an old suitor, leaving the lovers to enjoy their freedom and each other. Of the drama's secondary and even tertiary plot-strands, easily the most memorable is concerned with the adventures of the above-mentioned brother as an exhausted stud in a male house of prostitution in Lisbon, servicing an endless stream of "young fillies"—of female clients who "are mad on him" (130, 124).

In his prologue, whose opening note is spectacularly commercial, Fletcher himself advertises his play as "neat, and new / Fashion'd like those, that are approved by you" (105). "You" was, in all likelihood, the epicene court of James I, for which Fletcher's erotics of misogyny had great topical appeal.[37] What is "new" if not "neat" here is the representation of the "male stews," Fletcher's very own pornographic addenda. What is not new—that is, whatever he borrowed from Cervantes—is never acknowledged by Fletcher. His prologue's claims to novelty show

[36] Darley closes the long "Introduction" to his edition of Beaumont and Fletcher's *Works* with that "deep truth of nature" (29, 43). On Cervantes's "feminine" genius, see El Saffar's *Beyond Fiction*, whose main thesis is his progressive "recovery of the feminine."

[37] "So free this work is, gentlemen, from offence / That, we are confident, it needs no defence, / From us, or from the poets" (105). Appleton notes the topical misogyny in Fletcher's work (*Beaumont and Fletcher*, 12–13).

him practicing the recommended art of dissimulation (*dissimulatio*), a praxis recommended by Renaissance humanists under the adage of "ars est celare artem." It would seem that Fletcher introjected Petrarch's advice to Boccaccio on the need to conceal (*celare*) one's models in order to "seem to have brought, from the old, something new to Latium [*Latio intulisse*]."[38] What he brought that was new to London, if not Latium, was a play that has been regularly stigmatized as obscene: as Dryden would write in his preface to *Fables* (1700), "there is more bawdry in one play of Fletcher's, called *The Custom of the Country*, than in all ours together." But although Fletcher conventionally concealed that his model was Cervantes, even the most superficial glance at *The Custom of the Country* reveals at least five categories of imitation from the *Persiles*.

First and foremost, Fletcher imitated from Cervantes the theme of ritual defloration—the ius primae noctis—reducing the deflowering agents from *all* the groom's kinsmen in Cervantes's work to *one* incumbent governor in his own. Not only does Cervantes's masculine plural agency become Fletcher's singular, but Cervantes's Northern latitudes are safely and conventionally distanced by Fletcher to the South, to Italy, in keeping with the English Renaissance view of that country as "the Academie of manslaughter," Thomas Nashe's trope for Italy in *The Unfortunate Traveler* (1594). The first gesture in Fletcher's drama "that signals the intent of reanimating an earlier text,"[39] however, is the notion of legislated or institutionalized rape.

Secondly, Fletcher pirated all but one of his fourteen *dramatis personae* from Cervantes, not strictly from the narrative of rape in question, the Transila episode, but from all over the *Persiles*. Fletcher's poetics of naming follows the norms of imitation that Alejandro Ramírez calls "mera coincidencia onomástica [mere onomastic coincidence],"[40] a judgment that I would extend from "mere" to "lamentable," given that often in Cervantes, and always in allegory, the naming of characters fixes their functions irrevocably. Fletcher's rewriting of the *Persiles* uses all nomination arbitrarily because, as what follows will show, "the custom of the country" is a screen for his real intentions.

Thirdly, Fletcher kept Transila's escape by sea, but—true to his own psychobiography as a relentless collaborator—he added two men to her boat. One of them, the heroine's brother-in-law, he consigned into that

---

[38] See Petrarch's letter to Boccaccio, *Fam.* 23.19.10 (excerpted in *Letters from Petrarch*, trans. Bishop, 198–200).

[39] Greene, *Light in Troy*, 37.

[40] Alejandro Ramírez, "Cervantes y Fletcher: El *Persiles* y *The Custom of the Country*," in *Homenaje a Sherman H. Eoff* (Madrid: Castalia, 1970), 209. See Ramírez's helpful three-page summary of who's who in both texts (208–11).

male brothel in Lisbon, largely in order to furnish his Jacobean audience
with the obligatory stage misogynist.

As a fourth item, I would note Cervantes's modeling behind Fletcher's
gender-role reversals. In Cervantes, however, this confounding of sexual
differences is an iconoclastic gesture with a challenging *figura* of meanings. As Mary Gaylord has argued, "the most challenging interpretive
task" of the *Persiles* is "reading" the protagonists, because all the essential facts about them remain in doubt: "origin, identity, names, relationship to one another, sometimes even their sex."[41] The "essential facts"
about Fletcher's revision never remain in doubt: they turn on the comically intended *contrapasso* of a stud being sexually abused by his own
"fillies" (130).

Finally, let me point to the "outdoing topos" hard at work in Fletcher's
imitation of Cervantes's romance ending, a happy ending for the protagonists whose felicity Fletcher extends to all the characters, including various ad hoc repentant evil figures. Having abruptly extended this degree
of moral hospitality, however, Fletcher must then lace his closure with
numerous time-bound pieties—with such fatuous lines as, "a mother / So
pious, good, and excellent in sorrows!"; or even, "The hand of Heav'n
still guides such as are good" (130–31). Even Ramírez, an admiring critic,
is forced to allow that Fletcher here, "como de costumbre [typically],"
has "suavizado la situación para que todos los personajes participen del
feliz desenlace [smoothed over the situation so that all the characters may
participate in the happy denouement]."[42]

Criticism on Fletcher's *Custom of the Country* instructively bears out
George Steiner's dictum that "anything can be said about anything." The
modern commentary of Hispanists ranges from Schevill's dismissal of
Fletcher's play as a "grosera farsa [gross farse]" to Ramírez's defense of
it as a kind of Fletcherian psychomachia: "la lucha entre las virtudes y los
vicios [a struggle between the virtues and the vices]" whose finale foregrounds "el triunfo del bien [the triumph of the good]."[43] Although Celia
E. Weller and Clark A. Colahan oddly choose to underwrite Ramírez's
defense of Fletcher's binarism, they provide a cogent exploration of sex-
role reversal issues in *The Custom of the Country*.[44] Beyond a nod to the
happy management of its plot, English criticism of Fletcher's play has also
been divided: the Cavalier poet Lovelace loved it for its "loose thought

---

[41] Mary Gaylord [Randell], "Ending and Meaning in Cervantes' *Persiles y Sigismunda*,"
Romanic Review 74 (March 1983): 158.

[42] Ramírez, "Cervantes y Fletcher," 211.

[43] Schevill and Bonilla, "Introduction," *Persiles*, lxiii; Ramírez, "Cervantes y Fletcher,"
220.

[44] Celia Weller and Clark Colahan, "*The Custom of the Country*," *Cervantes* 5 (1985):
27–43.

said with such a grace"; Dryden, as mentioned earlier, hated it for its excessive "bawdry"; Swinburne mounted a "shrill and adolescent" defense of it, at least in Appleton's view, who maintains that "most critics" have condemned or disregarded the play.[45]

What has gone unremarked in the interpretive history of this play, however, is how Fletcher's male brothel has drained all meaning from his own titular theme, from what he occasionally remembers to denounce as that "barbarous, most inhuman, damned Custom" (106). Fletcher's secondary plot—the antics in and around his Lisbon male brothel—has regrettably determined much of the interpretation of his play: critics either play "Cato Major" to its scurrilousness or they feel obliged to defend it. What appears to have been forgotten, however, is that "the custom of the country"—in Fletcher as in Cervantes—*is not male whoring but the ritual defloration of women*. Fletcher employs the custom of legislated rape largely to motivate his lover's flight from Italy to Lisbon at the close of act 1. But then he dismisses the issue in order to highlight, indeed to fetishize, the vicissitudes of male sexual depletion at the hands of "these unsatisfied men-leeches, women!" The serious issue of female rape is nicely eclipsed by entertaining scenarios of male rape:

> I had a body once, a handsome body,
> And wholesome too: Now, I appear like a rascal,
> That had been hung a year or two in gibbets.
> Fie, how I faint!—Women! keep me from women!
>
> (125)

My concerns here are not with Fletcher's so-called "coarseness," with his "indelicacies and indecorums," or with his "too-frequent use of scavenging words and offal images"—the complaints of his fastidious Victorian editor.[46] Cervantes was also capable of "indelicacies," as Anson C. Piper's masterly study of the clawing cats episode in *Don Quixote* (2.46) testifies.[47] Nor am I disturbed, as was Coleridge, by Fletcher's promiscuous poetics. Coleridge's accusation—a vegetable version of Horace's animalized caution at the start of his *Ars poetica*—reminds us that Cervan-

---

[45] See Lovelace's "To Fletcher Revived," one of over twenty-five long Commendatory Verses in Darley's edition of *Works* (liii–liv); see also Dryden's preface to *Fables* (1700); on both Swinburne's admiration and Appleton's critique of it, see Appleton (*Beaumont and Fletcher*, 85–86).

[46] Darley, "Introduction," *Works*, xxx.

[47] For an exploration of Cervantes's parodic use of a libidinous "bag of cats" to punish Don Quixote—that sexually unresponsive object of Altisidora's female desire—see Piper's "A Possible Source of the Clawing-Cat Episode in *Don Quijote* (Part Two)," *Revista de estudios hispánicos* (October 1980). See the section on "Anson C. Piper: Man, Teacher, Scholar" in the *homenaje* volume, *From Dante to García Márquez*, ed. Bell-Villada, Giménez, and Pistorius, xvii–xxxi.

tes in the *Persiles* also worked by "gross contradictions to nature," fitting together the kind of generic "monster" discussed in the opening chapters of the present study.[48] What does provoke me to this critique of Fletcher's imitation is that it reinscribes Cervantes's powerful narrative of organized violence against women—both biological and epistemic—into a functionally witless comedy about a "universal rutter." The real *grosería*, which seems to have been lost in the interpretive shuffle, is "the custom of the country" itself, the issue of institutionalized rape. Cervantes's ius primae noctis narrative is moved by one graceful two-step into *droit de seigneur* status in Fletcher's imitation and then all but dismissed. Where Cervantes attempts to legitimate an attack on legislated rape, Fletcher attempts only to be jocular. The tone of his play, indeed, might be forecasting one of those *Jocular Customs of some Manors* documented by T. Blount—the custom of wedding fines paid to the lord of the manor in lieu of the "*mercheta mulierum*, or first night's lodging with the bride, which the lord anciently claimed in some manors"—that survived in Suffolk, England, as late as 1679.[49] Fletcher's exploitation of the diverting possibilities of the fictional subject of legislated rape would find its echo, over a century later, in Beaumarchais's *Mariage de Figaro*.[50] And it would find a more serious echo, over two centuries later, in Coleridge's own interpretation of Fletcher's play, a piece of wildly imperialist criticism that comes very close to legitimating rape: "I cannot but think that in a country conquered by a nobler race than the natives, and in which the latter became villeins [*sic*] and bondsmen, this custom [droit du seigneur], may have been introduced for wise purposes—as of improving the breed, lessening the antipathy of different races, [or] producing a new bond of relationship between the lord and the tenant."[51] Although it is easy to see why Roberta Florence Brinkley suppresses this passage in her edition of *Coleridge on the Seventeenth Century*, it seems more difficult to determine how Fletcher's attitudes may have funded Coleridge's. Although *The Custom of the Country* has various characters who noisily deprecate the custom of ritual defloration, Fletcher's easy dismissal of the ritual victim shows their phi-

---

[48] S. T. Coleridge accuses Beaumont and Fletcher of working by "gross contradictions to nature," that is, "just as a man might fit together a quarter of an orange, a quarter of an apple, and the like of a lemon and of a pomegranate, and make it look like one round diverse colored fruit" (lec. 7 in *Coleridge's Miscellaneous Criticism*, ed. Thomas Middleton Raysor [London: Constable and Co., 1936], 42–43).

[49] See T. Blount's *Fragmenta antiquitatis: Ancient Tenures of land, and Jocular Customs of some Manors. Made public for the diversion of some, and instruction of others* (1679); cited by Howarth, "Cervantes and Fletcher," 566.

[50] See W. D. Howarth, "The Theme of the *Droit du Seigneur* in the Eighteenth-Century Theatre," *French Studies* 15 (1961): 228–40.

[51] *Coleridge's Miscellaneous Criticism*, ed. Raysor, 72–73. Brinkley's edition is *Coleridge on the Seventeenth Century* (Durham, N.C.: Duke University Press, 1955).

lippics to be purely conventional and thoroughly inert. Why Fletcher and his followers made a fundamental change in the material borrowed from Cervantes is open to speculation. Howarth, for one, thinks that "the sub ject of the *droit du seigneur* attracted the authors of the English play on account of its romanesque possibilities, and not because of any moral implications. It is even quite likely that they entertained a healthy scepticism as to whether the custom had ever existed."[52] The healthiness of Fletcher's skepticism aside, his jocoseness is only one of his more appalling swerves from the text of his model. Did he willfully misunderstand the revolutionary work of Cervantes's ius primae noctis narrative? Are we to see Fletcher's revivalist initiative as abortive, as a failure, or just in plain bad faith? The contrast of value between Fletcher's surface text and Cervantes's subtext is, as all of the above shows, strikingly disproportionate. Indeed, Cervantes appears to have been read so ineptly by Fletcher that the possibility of any vital passage from the Transila episode to the Jacobean farce, from model to imitative text, was killed outright.[53] We must conclude, in sum, that Cervantes—whose focus throughout the *Persiles* is sexual custom *as an object of interpretation*—was too powerful a precursor for Fletcher. Although he tried to "take the word" out of Cervantes's mouth, it was still "serving other people's intentions." Fletcher, unlike Transila, could never make that word his own.

[52] Howarth, "Cervantes and Fletcher," 565.

[53] The intertextual concerns expressed here are indebted to Greene's *Light in Troy*, a model study of imitation in the Renaissance.

Chapter Nine

SOME PERVERSIONS OF PASTORAL:
FELICIANA DE LA VOZ

Neque habent sua verba dolores . . .

[The birth pains cannot voice themselves . . .]

—Ovid, *Metamorphoses*

THE CRITICAL QUESTION of what's in a name, always a fertile one for Cervantes's work, remains for the character of Feliciana de la Voz not only unanswered but unasked. As the heroine of the central episode of the *Persiles*, this young Estremaduran woman can explain only the social derivation of her odd cognomen: that all who have heard her sing acknowledge her to have "la mejor voz del mundo [the best voice in the world]" (299). But the figurative operations at work in Feliciana's depiction suggest forces well beyond the range of such provincial singing talents. The tale she relates, a nativity story with complicated intertextual relations, is preoccupied with three questions: female desire, its interdiction by patriarchal law, and its flight into elemental nature as a place for coming into voice. Cervantes's episode, indeed, remits us to a central postmodern insight, one cogently summed up by Rachel Jacoff in an essay on Dante's *Commedia*: "What theology, and literature too, make it difficult to uncover is an image of female desire that is not in and of itself *transgressive.*"[1] Cervantes's heroine uncovers, through her own compelling narrative, various images of transgressive desire: her illicit sexuality and occulted pregnancy; the freakish delivery of her infant; and her desperate flight into a crude pastoral world where she finds asylum in a sheepfold. Here she is enclosed and nurtured, within a "pregnant" tree, by an aged shepherd, a rustic clown who sees no difference at all "del parto de una mujer que del de una res [between the parturition of a woman and that of a cow]" (299). Why the representation of such anti-

---

[1] Rachel Jacoff, "Transgression and Transcendence: Figures of Female Desire in Dante's *Commedia*," *Romanic Review* 79 (January 1988): 142. I am indebted to this essay—which focuses on Semiramis and Myrrha, the two "framing females" of the *Inferno*, as well as on Pasiphae, in the *Purgatorio*—for its helpful researches into the exegetical tradition that linked Mary to Myrrha, as well as for its extraordinary insights into the transition from the transgressive to the transcendent.

poetic events? What is their relation to the main plot of the *Persiles*? And how, in turn, do they intersect with the Golden Age anthropology of female desire? The constituents of this rich and crucial narrative, with its pronounced acoustic and rhetorical qualities, reveal Cervantes, once again, in the act of imitation. The prime model this time is Ovid, the "narigudo poeta" (Publius Ovidius *Naso*) whom the narrator of *La ilustre fregona* alluded to in the context of the "transformaciones [metamorphoses]" of the two young aristocrats in that story.[2] This chapter aims to bring into focus certain forces in the text and subtexts of Cervantes's story that may enrich our growing epistemology of childbirth.

That this episode qualifies for the spatial and symbolic center of the *Persiles* has been remarked by various critics. Casalduero, for instance, tries to explain why Cervantes must intone his song in the center ("el centro") of the *Persiles*:

> Necesita el espacio inmenso de su novela, necesita todo el tiempo de su vida y la vida, todo el tiempo del hombre, para que su voz llena de escuela y de estilo, radiante de belleza, voz en donde se ha acumulado la tradición de una noble cultura, se eleve en una armonía plena para cantar el misterio de caridad.

> [He needs the immense space of his novel; he needs all the time of life and of his life, all the time of man, so that his voice, filled with style and erudition, radiant with beauty, a voice which the tradition of a noble culture has accumulated, elevates itself in full harmony to sing the great mystery of charity.][3]

From a rather different perspective, Forcione argues that Feliciana's hymn—"placed at the center of the *Persiles*"—discloses the work's biblical shape.[4] Given the remarked centrality of this episode, then, an exploration of Cervantes's strategies of representation at that center, with all its fissures and formal complexities, should illuminate the entire text.

When Feliciana's father, en route to kill her for dishonoring the family, overhears her singing, he remarks, "O aquella voz es de algún ángel de los confirmados en gracia, o es de mi hija Feliciana de la Voz [Either that voice belongs to some angel among those confirmed in grace, or to my daughter Feliciana de la Voz]" (306). Collapsed into this remark is the very either/or opposition, between a fallen woman and an *un*fallen angel, that Cervantes's text—by granting the voice of an angel to a fallen woman—radically destabilizes. Cervantes chooses the character of an

---

[2] *La ilustre fregona*, in *Novelas ejemplares*, ed. Rodríguez Marín, 1:255.

[3] Casalduero, *Sentido y forma de* Los trabajos, 184.

[4] Forcione, *Cervantes' Christian Romance*, 88; see also 19–21 and 123–28. In *Cervantes and the Humanist Vision*, Forcione reads this episode as a powerful expression of the traditional miracle narrative (328–35).

unwed and sexually discredited mother to sing a long, centrally positioned hymn to the Virgin Mother, a choice that at least one modern critic finds remarkable: "The novel of Feliciana and Rosanio is an adventure, through the lands of Extremadura, in which the most opposed circumstances are to be found: the voice of an angel in a newly-delivered woman, a hymn to the Virgin by a mother not yet married in the eyes of the Church."[5] Amazed at the literary conflation of what are supposed to be "opposed circumstances"—a hymn to the Virgin sung in church by a "not yet married" nonvirgin—this critic mirrors and repeats the logic of Feliciana's enraged father, who appears to have anticipated future misreadings of his daughter's story. This critical binarism also reveals the tenacity of some ancient, perhaps deeply unconscious, misogynist notions. Canon law had once decreed, for example, that no new mother could enter a church to pray until forty days after childbirth. The attitudes behind such taboos had intricate linkages with the scholastic infrastructures of thought so pervasive in Renaissance texts, notions whose pedigree could be traced back to Lev. 12:2: "According to the days of the separation from her infirmity shall *she* be unclean." Parturition, as well as the blood accompanying it, made woman "unclean" or impure. The ideology behind the notions of ritual impurity after childbirth is shown in *The Book of Jubilees* (c. 150 B.C.) to be partial to gender: the impurity lasts for two weeks if a woman gives birth to a female, for one week if to a male child.[6] Such biblical abominations[7] and their secular echoes are implicitly critiqued by Feliciana's story, which gives the voice of an angel to a newly delivered woman. As for the hymn to the Virgin sung by a "not yet married" mother, Cervantes deploys the Virgin/Fallen Woman pairing—one of the most stubborn polarities informing the Renaissance notion of woman—in order to dismantle it. The interpolated story of Feliciana "of the Voice" not only questions this ossified hierarchy, but also, in the process, explores the channels through which Renaissance women, both fallen and unfallen, could "come into voice."

This tale of the consequences of "not yet married" motherhood in Golden Age Spain, an elaboration of the maternal position unusual for its time and place, exhibits profound disjunctions between Virgin and Fallen Woman. The tension is between "icons and fallen idols," to use Beth Miller's title for a study addressing the "consensus that misogyny [fallen idols] and idealization [icons] have been two aspects of a single tendency

[5] Francisco López Estrada, "La novela de Feliciana y Rosanio en el *Persiles* o los extremosos amores de la Extremadura," *Anales cervantinos* 6 (1957): 341.

[6] *The Book of Jubilees* 3:8–14; cited by Pagels, *Adam, Eve and the Serpent*, 12.

[7] See Julia Kristeva's instructive chapter, "Semiotics of Biblical Abomination," in *Powers of Horror: An Essay on Abjection* (New York: Columbia University Press, 1982).

through centuries of literary production in Spanish."[8] But Cervantes's story also sets up a visible tension between what may be called natural and unnatural childbirth. His narrative invites us to distinguish between a character and her discourse—between a "calumniated Mother" and her own song about the world's most venerated mother. It also invites us to reflect on a *third* literary maternity, sedimented into the text through a sequence of oddly arresting elements: a pregnant and suicidal girl; her knife-wielding father; her escape into pastoral; a "pregnant" tree; a mother's inability to nurture her infant; its fosterage by pitying caretakers. These elements, to be taken up in what follows, advertise their derivation from Ovid's myth of Myrrha, transformed into a pregnant myrrh tree for her "criminal" incest.[9]

What is the meaning of the ironic intertextuality of these three nativities, textual and subtextual, at the heart of Cervantes's posthumous work? Forged out of such conflictual materials, the episode of Feliciana de la Voz presents an interpretative challenge of special appeal to critics awakened to the significance of sexual codes in literature. The interweaving of these three mothers—Feliciana, Mary, Myrrha—has to my mind a complex of institutional aims: to expose and conceptually restructure the Golden Age mythology of motherhood; to rescue female desire from the scapegoating mechanisms of patriarchy; and to represent the rise, as it were, of the fallen woman. "Alzar a los humildes abatidos [To raise the downtrodden]" was, we recall, one of the revolutions that Cervantes's sententious dogs, Berganza and Cipión, had to witness in order to attain their "true" human form. The category of fallen woman, Casalduero assures us, is by no means reserved for the sexually transgressive woman: "En el Barroco toda mujer es la mujer caída, hija de Eva, cuyos ojos llenos de lágrimas tienen que elevarse hacia el paradigma de gracia y virtud: La Virgen [In the Baroque period, *every* woman is a fallen woman, daughter of Eve, whose tear-filled eyes must elevate themselves toward the paradigm of grace and virtue: the Virgin]."[10] As an exemplary model of this Baroque Everywoman, then, Feliciana would represent the privative half of the Mary/Eve opposition, a hierarchy whose separability might be called the credo of scholastic sexual theory. Cervantes's strategic use of this polarity enables him to explore, at a centrally figurative space in his last work, the darker sides of the female psyche: the beguiling relations

[8] Beth Miller, *Women in Hispanic Literature: Icons and Fallen Idols* (Berkeley: University of California Press, 1983), 8.

[9] Ovid, *Metamorphoses* 10.298–518 (trans. Frank Justus Miller, 2 vols. [Loeb Classical Library, 1916], 2:84–101; all subsequent citations are to this edition and will be parenthetically documented).

[10] Casalduero, *Sentido y forma de* Los trabajos, 17.

between voice and sexuality, between maternity and desire, between purity and incest.

Let us rehearse the plot of Feliciana's "exemplary" novella before we address the resonant issue of its "exemplarity." Feliciana's path interthreads with that of the protagonists five leagues outside of Badajoz, Extremadura, and halfway through their pilgrimage to Rome. Her episode, over three chapters long (3.2–5), involves the main characters as listeners, exegetes, and agents. In the middle of the pilgrims' journey and as they are traversing a dark, Dantean wood, a horseman suddenly confronts them and begs from them a boon: the transport of an infant, for the reward of a gold chain, to the nearby city of Trujillo. The text refers to this apparition, in free indirect discourse, as "el caballero de la criatura" (290), meaning "the gentleman with the infant," but remitting us to other chivalric parodies in Cervantes, such as "el Caballero de la Triste Figura [the Knight of the Sad Countenance]." The horseman hands over the infant to the party of travelers and gallops off into the night, returning briefly to inform them that the child is still unchristened. Soon after this strange encounter, the pilgrims arrive at a sheepfold at about the same time that a weeping, disheveled young woman stumbles forward to beg asylum. An aged shepherd lines the hollow of a huge oak tree with sheepskins, lifts the traumatized girl into it, nourishes her with milksops and wine, and covers the aperture with more skins. The pilgrims guess the woman to be the mother of their infant and, when a troop of menacing horsemen arrives in search of her, do not reveal her whereabouts. All the following day the old shepherd attends to the fugitive, quietly convalescing within her tree, while he also arranges for the baby to be tended by his sister in a nearby village. By the third day, the newly delivered mother emerges from her enclosure ready to tell her story to the curious pilgrims.

Beginning her narrative with a currency metaphor, Feliciana opts to forgo "el crédito de honrada [the credit of a chaste woman]" (292) in order to gratify an audience eager to hear her "caso." The eagerness of the protagonists is structurally understandable: Feliciana will be advancing *their* story as she narrates her own. The genesis of her caso—imposed triangulation—is a repetition in a Mediterranean key of the original drama of the *Persiles*. Like the heroine Sigismunda, Feliciana is forced to choose between two suitors and, by her choice, subverts the institutionalized mechanisms of sexual control. Unlike Sigismunda, however, Feliciana gives herself sexually to her lover. Out of this irregular sexual liaison,[11] Feliciana becomes pregnant, or as she herself puts it, swerving the

[11] See Américo Castro's vast footnote on Cervantes and free love, which includes brief mention of the "natural" morality of Feliciana de la Voz (*El pensamiento de Cervantes* [Madrid: Casa Editorial Hernando, 1925], 349–52).

language of a popular ballad, "se acortó mi vestido y creció mi infamia [my dress shrank and my infamy grew]" (293). We must assume that her dress was, in the best Renaissance fashion, commodious and concealing, because two days before her due delivery date her father decides, peremptorily, to hold a betrothal ceremony for his daughter and the suitor of *his* choice. Earlier in the *Persiles* the practice of forced marriages is critiqued by another father, the sage Mauricio, who declares it to be "just and even convenient"

> que los padres casen a sus hijas con su beneplácito y gusto, pues no les dan compañía por un día, sino por todos aquellos que les durare la vida, y de no hacer esto ansí, se han seguido, siguen y seguirán millares de inconvenientes, que los más suelen parar en desastrados sucesos. (112)

> [that fathers marry their daughters with their consent and for their pleasure, as they are not giving them company for a day but for all the days of their lives, and from not proceeding in this manner there have followed, follow, and will follow thousands of difficulties, the majority of which tend to come to disastrous ends.][12]

Feliciana's father evidently does not proceed in the textually recommended manner and, in a state of shock over his wedding announcement, the daughter retires to her chamber. There, between hysterical weeping and thoughts of suicide, she suddenly delivers "una criatura en el suelo [an infant onto the floor]"—a "nunca visto caso [an unheard-of event]," as there had been no warning labor pains. Looking back on the event from her pastoral haven, Feliciana is now able to describe such a crisis in markedly "literary" language: "el deposado en la sala, esperándome, y el adúltero, si así se puede decir, en un jardín de mi casa [my betrothed down in the drawing room, awaiting me, and the adulterer—if he can be called such a thing—in a garden outside my house]" (294). Feliciana's trustworthy maid gives over the newborn infant to the putative "adulterer," who runs off with Feliciana's father at his heels. Feliciana herself manages to escape into the street, running from there into the countryside and, finally, coming to rest in the sheepfold which now serves as the setting for her confessional narrative. She concludes it by leaving the ending to heaven ("cuyo fin dejo al cielo") (295), an intervention which indeed materializes several chapters after her self-disclosing narrative.[13]

---

[12] Basing himself on Marcel Bataillon's "Cervantes y el matrimonio cristiano," *Varia lección de clásicos españoles* (Madrid: Gredos, 1964), 238–55, editor Avalle-Arce regards Mauricio's words as expressing Cervantes's constant attitude toward marriage ("la actitud constante de Cervantes ante el matrimonio") (*Los trabajos*, 112n).

[13] In his reading of the Feliciana episode as a traditional miracle tale, Forcione explains that the emphasis in this literary form falls "on the intervention of a divine agency, which

Before that, however, there occurs a radical interruption within Feliciana's episode, a deep fissure which offers readers a revealing glimpse of its structuring. Having decided to turn her back on her country—"a la tierra donde quedaba enterrada su honra [on the land where her reputation was buried]" (298)—Feliciana asks to accompany the pilgrims into Italy. En route to Cáceres, their afternoon siesta in a meadow is disrupted by the figure of a young man, impaled by a sword, who darts abruptly through the bushes to collapse dead in their midst. It is clear that "traidoras manos [treacherous hands]" have killed him, since the sword pierces his body from back to front. Upon carefully searching the corpse, the pilgrims discover the picture of a woman surrounded by four circular lines of Petrarchan verse, evidence which moves Periando to conjecture an obvious motive for the murder: "De causa amorosa debía de haber nacido su muerte [His death was probably born from some amorous affair]" (303). While the party is trying to determine the identity of the corpse, a posse of the Santa Hermandad, the Holy Brotherhood or institution of Castilian justice, breaks into the picnic to arrest the pilgrims as highwaymen and murderers. This arrest ironizes the words of the heroine at the episode's beginning, in which she gives thanks for their finally having reached Spain, because its fame throughout all regions "de pacífica y de santa [as a peaceful and holy nation]" promised them a safe journey (297). After a complicated whirl on the machines of Spanish justice in Cáceres, the pilgrims are acquitted when a local innkeeper produces a letter written by the dead man. Identifying himself as Don Diego de Parraces, this exemplary masochist accuses his kinsman, with honorable belatedness, of his murder: "Creo que me llevan a matar; si esto sucediere, y mi cuerpo se hallare, sépase que me mataron a traición, y que morí sin culpa [I think he's planning to kill me; should this happen, and should my body be found, let it be known that they killed me treacherously]." For his collusion in the codes of blood vengeance, the murdered man gets what he asks for and nothing more: his kinsman, as it turns out, is never caught and the crime remains forever unpunished ("sin castigo").

What is suggestive about this interpolation within an interpolation is that Cervantes loudly fictionalizes all its unresolved questions *as* unresolved: an unknown motive, an unquestioning victim, an uncaught murderer. Why is Don Diego's death—a death "born" out of an amorous triangle—incorporated into the center of the central inset story of Feliciana? Why must her story of coming to voice contain, at its problematic core, his story of silence? Within Cervantes's controlled disruption of narrative, the meaning of Don Diego's familial victimization invites displace-

---

comes to the aid of heroes who are usually helpless, quite unheroic, and frequently even fallen" (*Cervantes and the Humanist Vision*, 329).

ment onto Feliciana: both characters are persecuted by kinsmen whose
sense of honor demands a blood vengeance. Never once voicing *his* side
of the story, Don Diego marches off to sacrifice like the proverbial lamb
to the slaughter: or as his posthumous letter puts it, "fiándome en mi
inocencia, di lugar a su malicia, y acompañéle [trusting in my innocence,
I yielded to his malice and accompanied him]" (303). Although this same
dynamic, as we shall see, will be imaged within Feliciana's hymn, her own
life story both corrects and criticizes it. Diego de Parraces' revealing meta-
text, in short, functions to expose the structures and strategies of a text
which it appears simply to interrupt. Feliciana is saved from being slaugh-
tered by her kinsmen—"que parecían mas verdugos que hermano y padre
[who seemed more like executioners than brother and father]" (307)—
who catch up with her at the famed shrine of Guadalupe. Having dragged
their victim out into the street because of their scruples about murder in
a cathedral, the would-be "executioners" are restrained from wreaking
vengeance on the "traitor" by villagers, the police, and, finally, the parodic "Knight of the Infant," who, masked in black taffeta, gallops into
the square in the nick of time. As Feliciana's secret lover and the father of
her illegitimate child, he asks her kinsmen to be given by consent what he
knew how to take "por industria [by ingenuity]"—a phrase that remits
the reader to Basilio's self-congratulatory cries of "¡industria, industria!"
in *Don Quixote*, part 2, in response to the ingenious trick that recovers
his love Quiteria back from Camacho, the chosen husband of the establishment (2.22). In the finale to Feliciana's story, a wildly paratactic reconciliation scene follows, with tears and swoonings and the noisy intervention of onlookers, during which the furious kinsmen are defused. The
ex-victimizers even manage to gain the reputation, as the text wryly puts
it, "de prudente el padre, de prudente el hijo [of being a prudent father
and a prudent son]" (308). When Feliciana's father eventually holds his
grandson—again, three allusive days later—it is to edit his nativity story:
"¡Que mil bienes haya la madre que te parió y el padre que te engendró!
[A thousand blessings on the mother who bore you and the father who
engendered you!]" (309).

It is not the redeemed grandfather, however, but the Madonna of Guadalupe who has the last word in this episode. For Cervantes reproduces
the hymn to the Virgin not when Feliciana sings it but a few days later,
when she gives a written draft of its dozen stanzas to the heroine. These
verses are "más estimados que entendidos [more esteemed than under-
stood]" by Auristela, whose inability to read Feliciana's hymn seems less
connected to her deficient Spanish than to her inability to read Feliciana
herself as other than a paradigmatically "fallen woman." The discourse
of Feliciana's long hymn, which spans the whole of Old Testament history—from Genesis to an imaginative point in time just prior to the An-

nunciation—has been enlightened, typologically and archetypally, by various modern readings.[14] I would add to these rich commentaries two observations, the first in response to the opening four stanzas of the hymn—the only stanzas which Feliciana is allowed to sing before she is interrupted by her brother brandishing a dagger. These stanzas focus, through metaphors of architecture, on the building of an edifice which represents Mary. The opening stanza thrice depicts the genesis of Mary as an event occuring "before" Genesis ("Antes . . . y antes . . . y antes"), a conception which stands counter to the patriarchal tradition of Genesis, whose repeated anatomies in the postmodern have revealed, among other things, how "the repression of the mother is the genesis of Genesis."[15] Equally pertinent to my reading of Feliciana's story is her own direct address, in the hymn's tenth stanza, to Mary as an *interruptor* of sacrifice— as "el brazo de Dios, que detuvistes / de Abrahán la cuchilla rigurosa [the arm of God, who detained / Abraham's rigorous knife]" (311). She who detained Abraham from sacrificing Isaac, in short, intervenes once again, this time at her own shrine, to detain Feliciana's father from sacrificing his child. The rigorous patriarchal code motivating him and his son to become "executioners" of a sexually transgressive woman is prefigured by Abraham in the Old Testament. Once again Cervantes exposes, as he did through his Barbaric Isle narrative at the beginning of the *Persiles*, the conflations of violence with the sacred.[16]

If the happy ending of Feliciana's story does not deafen us to the rhetoric of her kinsmen's fury, we shall hear its affiliation—by a resonant formula metaphorizing voice—to the opening words of the *Persiles*: "VOCES daba [He shouted]" (51). In the height of their anger and confusion, Feliciana's kinsmen are described by the text as "dando voces [shouting]" for their victim (307), an echo of Cervantes's barbarians as they bark out orders for yet another sacrificial victim. The opening words of the *Persiles*, as we noted in chapter 5, forge the equation of voice with sacrifice. And the behavior of Feliciana's kinsmen in this central episode replicates, in a civilized key, the behavior of the inhabitants of the Barbaric Isle: a violent, all-male sacrificial community whose "Law" or ritual idolatry dictates, as it does for Feliciana's family, the circulation of women as commodities. The story of Feliciana de la Voz attempts to rescript the sexual economy of the Barbaric Isle, Cervantes's emblematic

[14] See Forcione, *Cervantes' Christian Romance*, 87–89; also El Saffar, *Beyond Fiction*, 153–54.

[15] Christine Froula, "When Eve Reads Milton: Undoing the Canonical Economy," *Critical Inquiry* 10 (December 1983): 337. See also Stephen G. Nichols, "Rewriting Marriage in the Middle Ages," *Romanic Review* 79, 1 (January 1988): 42–60.

[16] A conscious echo of René Girard's *Violence and the Sacred*, trans. Patrick Gregory (Baltimore: Johns Hopkins University Press, 1977).

landscape of patriarchal legitimacy. It is Feliciana's voice that questions a legitimacy only recently understood, in Alice Jardine's terms, as the basis of patriarchal culture: "part of that judicial domain which, historically, has determined the right to govern, the succession of kings, the link between father and son, the necessary paternal fiction, the ability to decide who is the father."[17] Although Feliciana's male kinsmen take for granted the ability to decide who the father of her child should be, her tale entirely subverts their assumed legitimization through the device of an illegitimate child. As such, the episode functions to iterate Cervantes's analysis, lamentation, and critique of the institution of patriarchy.

The plot of Feliciana's episode parallels the story germ of the *Persiles*: escape from captivity in a barbaric sacrificial culture into elemental nature as the locus for a birth or rebirth. Feliciana's episode, as we shall see, is a nativity story whose focus is not on an infant's birth but rather on his mother's *rebirth* into the symbolic order, her acquisition of narrative voice and authority. Although my own reading of Feliciana's episode contrasts sharply with that of Casalduero, we seem to agree on the identity of its true protagonist: "El protagonista de este episodio no es ni el recién nacido ni ninguno de los otros personajes, el protagonista es la voz de Feliciana [The protagonist of this episode is neither the newborn child nor any of the other characters; the protagonist is the voice of Feliciana]." Casalduero, however, seems content to pronounce that protagonist-voice as "el sentimiento de la mujer-madre [the sentiment of the woman-mother]," thereby glossing over the explicit *absence* of that sentiment in Feliciana, a psychologically tantalizing feature of this episode to be discussed later in this chapter.[18] In my own darker reading, that protagonist voice is the voice of female desire, muted on Cervantes's Barbaric Isle as well as in many of the traditional readings of the *Persiles*. It is that same voice, "born" with Feliciana into a place of narrative authority, that contests the sacrificial paradigms of voice represented on the Barbaric Isle. Voice is so crucial in the *Persiles* that when a near-fatal poisoning destroys Auristela's appearance in book 4, she can no longer be recognized "sino por el órgano de la voz [except through the organ of the voice]" (456). Voice, for Cervantes, means the ability to generate signs.

Feliciana's voice finds its chorus within the *Persiles* itself, wherever the fetishizing of women as property, a conspicuous hallmark of patriarchal history, is attempted. In the last chapter we focused on the story of the ius primae noctis, that "barbarous custom" (112) of an insular Irish culture which legally obliged all new brides to satisfy sexually their male

[17] Alice Jardine, *Gynesis: Configurations of Woman and Modernity* (Ithaca: Cornell University Press, 1985), 24.

[18] Casalduero, *Sentido y forma de Los trabajos*, 183.

in-laws. In the next chapter we shall explore an episode of more sophisticated barbarism, an uncle's foiled attempts to force his niece into a cross-cousin marriage in order to keep the wealth in the family (402–12). There would seem to be little difference, in short, between the male traffic in women practiced on the Barbaric Isle, the legislated rape in Ireland, and the forced nuptials in Spain and Italy. These interpolated tales all subvert patrilineal descent systems in which female desire is conveniently scapegoated, in which women lose their "credit" when they determine their own sexuality. As such, these "exemplary novels" may be read as a critique of the limitation of these systems. Centuries later, writing of a Spanish woman called Paquita in "The Girl with the Golden Eyes," Balzac has his protagonists dismiss her with a brutally revealing observation: "She comes from a country where women are not beings, but things— chattels, with which one does as one wills, which one buys, sells, and slays."[19] Cervantes came from that country, too, and if a number of his tales suggest Balzac's portrait of the Spanish woman as chattel, they also rewrite Paquita. The bulk of the *Persiles*, in other words, is a quest for a re-creative narrative tradition. Both the main plot and its dozen interpolations seem to be working toward a regeneration of genres that seek to survive the destruction of patriarchal fictions. How might language and literature remotivate the old genres? One way to proceed, the "exemplary" way shown in the *Persiles*, is by exhibiting a profound concern for all the mechanisms of generativity—*of* children, *in* adults, and *for* texts.

In chapter 7 we discussed Ortega's notion of the *Persiles* as "una larga novela *ejemplar* [a long exemplary novel]," a judgment fortified by Schevill and Bonilla, who both suggested and evaded the idea that the interpolations had "el carácter de novelas *ejemplares* [the character of exemplary novels]." Internal evidence suggests that the tale of Feliciana de la Voz functions as an "exemplary novel," specifically when Auristela describes the premarital pregnancy of Feliciana as "un caso que puede servir de ejemplo a las recogidas doncellas que le quisieren dar bueno de sus vidas [a case that may serve as an example to proper maidens who wish to give a good account of their lives]" (296). Auristela here clearly reads Feliciana's "caso" as a deterrent example, as an "aviso" or cautionary tale. Obsessed with her chastity, Cervantes's main protagonist fits her own personal experience into the template of Feliciana, for her a paradigm of terrifying sexuality. But Feliciana's "exemplary novel" also serves as a template for our own readerly input, which will of course vary, depending not only upon our own race, class, or gender, but also on our

---

[19] Honoré de Balzac, *The Thirteen*, trans. Ellen Marriage and Ernest Dowson (London: Society of English Bibliophiles, 1901), 356.

ability to recognize the complex intertextuality of this Cervantine tale of childbirth.

What is there to say about literary childbirth in the Golden Age? At least one of Cervantes's rustics has something to say about the childbirth of Eve, whom he exalts as a model postpartum patient: "Yo [estoy] seguro . . . que cuando Eva parió el primer hijo, que no se echó en el lecho, ni se guardó del aire, ni usó de los melindres que agora se usan en los partos [I am certain . . . that when Eve bore her first son she did not take to her bed, nor protect herself from the outdoors, nor affect any of those niceties nowadays used in deliveries]" (299). Despite this shepherd's obstetrical clowning,[20] the narratives that subtend Feliciana's nativity story open out the range of literary childbirth in order to reconceptualize the maternal position. The felicity of this position, the story implies, hangs on the nature of one's kinsmen's ties to the patriarchal order. In Feliciana's case, the rigor of these ties is exacerbated by an absent mother, a Golden Age topos here openly lamented by the daughter: "Que madre no la tengo por mayor desgracia mía [To my great misfortune, I have no mother]" (293). It may be argued that Feliciana involves herself in the pilgrimage to the Black Madonna of Guadalupe as a mother-quest, since Black Madonnas—those hermetic wonder-workers who preside over sex, pregnancy, and childbirth in Catholic countries—are especially venerated as the maternal aspect of Mary.[21] The intertextuality of Feliciana's tale— the ostensible presence within it of both biblical and Ovidian elements— moves us to inquire into their structural function within such a mother-quest. What kind of model mothers, in short, subtend the surface text of Feliciana's narrative?

The Virgin Mary pervades the whole of Feliciana's episode, most visibly as the vocative of the above-mentioned hymn, whose subject is Mary's life, but also as an object of the text's deliberate allusiveness to the Nativity and Resurrection stories. The underlying Christian configuration of Feliciana's story includes, too, the Lucan Magnificat, even though Mary's triumphant hymn of praise (her longest speech by far in the Bible) has a bellicose character not found in Feliciana's song. Mary's Magnificat, as Warner explains, "is not a psychological poem on the mystery of the conception of Christ, or even on the miracle of the virgin birth—which she does not mention at all—but a rousing cry that the Jewish Messiah prom-

---

[20] Evidently Cervantes chose to ignore Tasso's suggestion, in his Discorsi, that if a poet simply had to use shepherds, goat-herds, or pigherds in his work, he should somehow manage to show them the way they would appear at palace ceremonies and solemnities. See Tasso's Discorsi del poema eroico, bk. 2 in Scritti sull'arte poetica, ed. Ettore Mazzoli, 2 vols. (Turin: Einaudi, 1977), 1:211. I owe this reference to Walter Stephens of Dartmouth College.

[21] On Black Madonnas, see Warner, Alone of All Her Sex, 273–75.

ised by God has arrived to vanquish his enemies."[22] Cervantes's hymn *to* Mary, then, may be said to supplement the biblical hymn *by* Mary. Forcione's catalogue of the Christian allusions in this text justly supports his claim that "Cervantes had Christ in mind at this point in the composition of the work": "the infant menaced by the knife of the enraged father (Herod), the flight of the parents toward Portugal, the shelter given them by shepherds, the triumphant reappearance of the missing child 'on the third day,' the allusion to baptism, and the approach of Easter."[23] Cervantes must also have had Mary in mind, as a woman who, like Feliciana, was forced to deliver her son under traumatic circumstances. What is missing from the above catalogue of allusions—the mother's story—is supplied, as a personal agency narrative, in Cervantes's text of Feliciana. Indeed, I would argue that the recovery of this suppressed story is part of Cervantes's imitative strategy in this episode. The interplay between Feliciana and the Virgin Mary in Cervantes's text, however, is not posited on a fallen woman's need for an elevating paradigm of asceticism (pace Casalduero), but rather on her need for a salvific mother figure. What Freud could argue about his "hysterical" patient Dora—that "the notion of the Madonna is a favourite counter-idea in the mind of girls who feel themselves oppressed by imputations of sexual guilt"[24]—cannot in any form be applied to Feliciana, who appears throughout the tale remarkably free of guilt about her "hurtos amorosos [amorous escapades]" (293). If she feels herself "oppressed," it is less by "imputations" than by the very real threats of death from "dos hombres que decían ser su hermano y su padre [two men who claimed to be her brother and her father]" (307).

Far more than the ascetic paradigm is turned on end in Cervantes's depiction of a very flesh-and-blood heroine. His portrait of Feliciana, in fact, inverts with curious precision the traditional female virtues projected onto the image of the Virgin by Counter-Reformation Mariolatry: humility, obedience, and silence. Feliciana is not humble: "Tengo la mejor voz del mundo [I have the best voice in the world]," she notes as the opinion of all who have heard her sing (299). She is not obedient: "Me entregué por suyo a hurto de mi padre y mis hermanos [I yielded myself to him in concealment from my father and brothers]" (293). And she is not silent, especially not in church: "Soltó la voz a los vientos [She let loose her voice to the winds]" (306). To put it summarily, it is not the image of Mary as an ascetic and speechless ideal that the text of Feliciana exploits. Ian Maclean has shown how this image, despite Mary's redemp-

[22] Ibid., 13.

[23] Forcione, *Cervantes' Christian Romance*, 127.

[24] Sigmund Freud, *Dora: An Analysis of a Case of Hysteria* (New York: Collier, 1963), 125n.

tive role in medieval and Counter-Reformation literature, presented a
"questionable advantage to womankind." Citing from innumerable Renaissance writings—theological, mystical, occult, medical, political, social, and legal tractates—Maclean regards Mary as a sexually remote
model: "Far from being the glory of her sex, she is *not of her sex* in its
malediction, tribulation and imperfection." Along these same exclusionary lines, Marina Warner notes that her historical research into the cult
of the Virgin Mary grew out of an intimation "that in the very celebration
of the perfect human woman, both humanity and women were subtly
denigrated."[25] If women were denigrated by Mary, however, it was
largely by an image that had been studiously desexualized by over a millennium of church fathers—men such as Augustine, Jerome, and Gregory
the Great—who were at one in viewing the female libido as a constant
and collective threat. There was—there *is*—another view of Mary to consider. Implicit in Feliciana's story is the story of Mary's maternity: her
anguished concealment of her pregnancy, her flight from the patriarch
Herod's knife, and her delivery within the cold pastoral world of Christ's
Nativity. Cervantes's text, in short, may be seen as trying to recover
Mary's *story* as opposed to her *image*.

The other side of Mary's story, as we suggested earlier, is the Ovidian
myth of Myrrha. It was a myth of incest well known to Cervantes's age,
although the entry in Covarrubias's *Tesoro* (1611) characteristically suppresses the reason for Myrrha's metamorphosis:

> MIRRA. Es un árbol pequeño que nace en Arabia, de altura de cinco codos,
> algo espinoso, del qual, abriéndole la corteza, mana una lágrima o licor que
> llamamos también *myrrha*. La principal virtud que tiene es conservar los
> cuerpos de los muertos sin corrupción. *Vide Plinium*, lib. 12, caps. 15 *et* 16.
> *Los poetas cuentan aver sido nombre de una donzella, hija de Cinira, rey de
> Cipro, que se convirtió en este árbol*. Verás a Ovidio, lib. 10, *Metamorpho-
> sen*.

> [MYRRHA. A small tree that grows in Araby, of the height of five elbows,
> somewhat thorny, which, upon opening its bark, distills a tear or liquor we
> call *myrrh*. Its principal virtue is to conserve the bodies of the dead without
> corruption. *See Pliny*, book 12, chaps. 15 *and* 16. *The poets say that it was
> the name of a maiden, daughter of Cinyras, King of Cyprus, who was con-
> verted into this tree*. See Ovid, book 10, *Metamorphoses*.][26]

Numerous signs indicate that Cervantes did indeed "see Ovid" for his
composition of Feliciana's story, that he had not only Christ but also
Ovid in mind throughout its composition. If "the sweete wittie soule of

---

[25] Maclean, *Renaissance Notion*, 23–24; Warner, *Alone of All Her Sex*, xxi.
[26] Covarrubias, *Tesoro*, 807; emphasis added.

Ovid lives in mellifluous and hony-tongued [*sic*] *Shakespeare*," as the Elizabethan critic Francis Meres once remarked,[27] it also lives on in the sharper-tongued Cervantes. The final word of Ovid's *Metamorphoses* is "vivam"—the egotistic first-person future verb for "I shall live"—a literary claim that Cervantes was also happy to advance, most explicitly in the chapter on the scrutiny of Don Quixote's library, where he gave Ovid the last word: "Ovidio."[28]

The first ostensible allusion to Ovid in the episode of Feliciana opens the chapter containing her own narration (3.3). Under the chapter heading "La doncella encerrada en el árbol [The Young Woman Enclosed in the Tree]," Cervantes anxiously proffers his reader one of the most deliberately allusive tropes in his opus: "Preñada estaba la encina—digámoslo así ['Pregnant was the oak tree'—let's say it that way]" (291). Should the hortatory construction ("digámoslo así") which here enlists readers into approbation of this odd uterine metaphor seem a bit defensive, it may be in defense of Ovid, regarded in many Renaissance quarters as a perverse literary influence.[29] The narrator's "I"—who, after all, *is* saying the phrase—has been transformed here into the first person *plural*: "Let *us* say it that way." This rhetorical dissolution of egotism reveals the discourse as a source of anxiety for the writer, one eloquently recognized in Terence Cave's study on Renaissance imitation theory, which he claims "recognizes the extent to which the production of any discourse is conditioned by pre-existing instances of discourse; the writer is always a rewriter, the problem then being to differentiate and authenticate the rewriting. . . . Rewriting betrays its own anxiety by personifying itself as the product of an author; it imprints on itself—one might even say *forges*—an identity."[30] Rewriting Ovid would gesture, generally, toward metamorphosis. Rewriting a "pregnant" tree, even one growing in the green world of Christian pastoral, gestures very ceremonially toward one peculiarly resonant Ovidian metamorphosis. "Media gravidus tumet arbore venter [The pregnant tree swells in mid-trunk]," Ovid writes in one of the most moving depictions of childbirth in Western literature—a "vegetable" parturition, assisted throughout by a "pitying Lucina," that provides powerful metaphors for the human event (*Met.* 10.503–18). The

---

[27] Francis Meres, "A Comparative Discourse of Our English Poets with the Greeke, Latine, and Italian Poets," in *Palladis Tamia, Wits Treasury* (1598), rpt. in *Elizabethan Critical Essays*, ed. G. Gregory Smith, 2 vols. (London: Humphrey Milford, 1904), 2:316–17.

[28] During the scrutiny of the library (*DQ* 1.6), the Curate refers glowingly to Luis Barahona de Soto's Spanish translation of Ovid ("fue felicísimo en la tradución de algunas fábulas de Ovidio"), doubtless Cervantes's source here.

[29] See Rudolph Schevill, *Ovid and the Renascence in Spain* (Berkeley: University of California Press, 1913), 134.

[30] Terrence Cave, *The Cornucopian Text: Problems of Writing in the French Renaissance* (Oxford: Clarendon Press, 1979), 76–77.

"pregnant" tree in the *Persiles* functions as an organic, if profoundly unsettling, allusion to Myrrha's childbirth, the scene from Ovid which Cervantes here wishes to advance.

Myrrha, as we recall, becomes pregnant as the result of an incestuous affair with her unsuspecting father Cinyras, who drunkenly enjoys a bed partner while his wife is away at the annual festival of Ceres. After many meetings, Cinyras becomes curious about the identity of his sexual partner. Speechless with horror at the discovery that it is his own daughter Myrrha, Cinyras snatches his sword to kill her. Myrrha flees into the night and begins a fugitive existence across the broad lands of Arabia and beyond. Her exhausted wanderings are mercifully terminated when the gods, at her own request, encase her laden womb with bark. The goddess Lucina helps the pregnant "tree" to deliver, through a fissure in its bark, the beautiful infant Adonis. The price of Myrrha's transgression is that she must suffer in silence the pains of childbirth: "Neque habent sua verba dolores, / nec Lucina potest parientis voce vocari [The birth pangs cannot voice themselves, nor can Lucina be called upon in the words of one in travail]" (*Met.* 10.506–7). In the context of Cervantes and the pastoral, William Byron notes, parenthetically and in passing, that "the scene in the *Persiles* . . . in which shepherds make a bed in a hollow tree trunk for Feliciana, newly delivered of a child, has the true country flavor along with the mythical quality of a divine myth."[31] Although *which* "divine myth" underlies this scene is not Byron's concern, its identity is of crucial import to any close reading of Feliciana's episode and even, perhaps, of the larger novel that contains it. Ovid's myth of incestuous female desire reveals its subterranean outlines at strategic points within Feliciana's episode.[32] The interplay of the Ovidian subtext with Cervantes's surface text urges readers to confront what can only be called a perversion of pastoral.[33] How do we unperplex these three profoundly interrelated maternities?

I have suggested that the text of Feliciana strategically sets up a network of differences between itself and its two constitutive subtexts: one Christian and one pagan nativity story. Each of the three nativities sheds light on the others. At the level of the subtexts, a dialogue takes place between the infancy Gospels of the New Testament (with all their histor-

[31] Byron, *Cervantes: A Biography*, 270–71.

[32] Apart from the "pregnant tree" motif, cf. the passage in Cervantes which begins "El resplandor del cuchillo [The gleaming of the sword]" (294) with the passage in Ovid beginning "He snatched his gleaming sword" (*Met.* 10.475ff.).

[33] In his essay on *La gitanilla*, which he views as a "fallen pastoral," Robert ter Horst writes that "Cervantes deliberately corrupts and perverts the pastoral with the tale's gypsy personnel, a band of thieves who in some ways live nobly with nature" ("Une saison en enfer," 105).

ical repercussions) and the Ovidian myth of the birth of Adonis. No two conception accounts would appear more dichotomous. Whereas the Virgin Mary did not "know . . . a man" (Luke 1:34), Myrrha knew only the one man forbidden her by "pietas [natural love]" (*Met.* 10.333). Whereas Mary was impregnated by voice (through the ear, according to literalist interpreters of Origen)[34] and was thereby hailed as "plena gratia [full of grace]," Myrrha was impregnated by her father's seed and was depicted as "plena patris [full of her father]" (*Met.* 10.469). It was the issue of female pleasure, however, that most distinguished Mary from Myrrha. That Mary had felt no physical pleasure during her conception of Christ was famously argued by Francisco Suárez, a Marian theologian who died in 1617, the same year the *Persiles* was published. Father Suárez reassured an anxious clerisy—many of whom still believed in Saint John Crysostom's equation of sexual coupling with death[35]—that "the Blessed Virgin in conceiving a son neither lost her virginity nor experienced any venereal pleasure." How did Father Suárez know that Mary had so categorically eschewed pleasure? Because sexual pleasure, he argued, was not "fitting": "It did not befit the Holy Spirit without any cause or utility to produce such an effect, or to excite any unbecoming movement of passion."[36] In contrast to this canonical image of a passionless Mary, the Ovidian Myrrha legend glaringly focuses upon "venereal pleasure." By having Myrrha declare her wish that her father feel a "similis furor" (*Met.* 10.355) to her own, Ovid articulates some distinctly "unbecoming" movements of passion.

It would seem that the virginal Mary and the venereal Myrrha function within Cervantes's story of Feliciana as a repetition, in a much soberer key, of the comic opposition that Sancho's slip of the tongue establishes between a "soberana señora"—a sovereign lady—and a "sobajada señora"—a pawed-over lady, one soiled from too much handling (*DQ* 2.23). Both of these ladies are understood, even by first-time readers of

[34] Conflating spontaneous generation and divine impregnation, the Greek exegete Origen (d. 254) suggested that Mary had conceived Jesus the *Logos* upon hearing the angel's voice. Origen's Alexandrine argument was taken literally in certain quarters, so that a hymn later attributed to Fortunatus (d. 609?), marveling that "aure virgo concepit [the virgin conceived through her ear]," would find its echo centuries later, in medieval English lyrics that reminded Mary how "through thine ear thou were with child" (Warner, *Alone of All Her Sex*, 34–49).

[35] According to Saint John Crysostom, sexual desire was a consequence of the Fall: "[Thus] marriage . . . springs from disobedience, from a curse, from death. For where death is, there is marriage" (*On Virginity*, chap. 14, sec. 6; from *On Virginity; Against Remarriage*, trans. Sally Rieger Shore, in *Studies in Women and Religion*, vol. 9 [New York: Edwin Mellen Press, 1983]).

[36] Francisco Suárez, s.j. "The Dignity and the Virginity of the Mother of God"; cited by Warner, *Alone of All Her Sex*, 39.

Don Quixote, to be projections of Dulcinea by men who refuse to confront her in person. The moment of reversal between female oppositions of this kind takes place in the Cave of Montesinos, where it is revealed to the "dreaming" hero that even "sovereign" ladies like Belerma can lose their teeth, have bags under their eyes, or experience monthly periods (*DQ* 2.23).

Is the opposition of Mary and Myrrha, between the sacred and the sacrilegious, similarly negotiable? Since it is now possible, at least without tumbling into heresy, to bring up some provocative connections between Mary and Myrrha, let me begin with the gloomiest one: the linkage between Myrrha's tears—"stillataque robore murra [the myrrh which drips from her tree trunk]" (*Met.* 10.501), with which her son Adonis is anointed at his birth—and the myrrh carried by the wise men to Bethlehem (Matt. 2:1–12), its perfume foreshadowing Mary's own later sorrows as a *mater dolorosa*. Another surprising correspondence is etymological: the name of Mary is elusive and has been derived from the words for *light-bearer*, *ocean*, *stubborn*, *corpulent*, and, more to our point, the Hebrew word for *myrrh*. Yet another linkage is anatomical: Mary's "intact" postpartum condition, debated for centuries by churchmen, is a feature that, in its unnatural perfection, separates her from the rest of her sex as much as Myrrha's bark does.[37]

The exegetical tradition that linked Mary with Myrrha was motivated, no doubt, by the association of the myrrh tree with Christ's birth and death in a number of key biblical passages: Matt. 2:11, Mark 15:23, and John 19:39–40. Within this tradition, the Myrrha story was glossed both *in bono* and *in malo*, imitating Ovid's own treatment of Myrrha from two very different perspectives: the salacious one, shown by Orpheus as he begins her tale with a reference to her impiety; and the sympathetic one, shown from the moment Myrrha's father discovers her identity and she must flee his rage. In Pierre Bersuire's *in bono* reading, for example, Myrrha "is the blessed virgin who conceived through the father and was changed into myrrh." Bersuire even interprets Myrrha's parturition as a figure of Mary's uncontaminated maternity: "She therefore conceived a son by her father: that is, Christ: and she contained him within the wood and the bark, that is, within a pure and untouched womb without corruption, and afterwards she bore him, existing not as flesh but as wood, that is not a carnal being but a perpetual virgin."[38] The author of the *Ovide*

[37] On Mary's name, see Warner, *Alone of All Her Sex*, 40n. For a précis of the debate about Mary's virginity both *in partu* and *post partum*, see 43–49.

[38] Pierre Bersuire, *Metamorphosis ovidiana moraliter . . .* (Paris, 1515), fol. 83; cited and trans. by Noam Flinker in an essay tracing the exegetical traditions of the Myrrha legend, "Cinyras, Myrrha, and Adonis: Father-Daughter Incest from Ovid to Milton," *Milton Studies* 14 (1980): 63.

moralisé allegorized not only Myrrha as a figure of Mary, but also Adonis as a figure of Christ.[39] Colard Mansion's French prose paraphrase of the *Metamorphoses* (1484) even more programmatically linked Myrrha to Mary: "This virgin, then, conceived a son with her father, that is to say, Jesus Christ, and bore him between the wood and the bark."[40] Closer to Cervantes's time, Spenser's *Faerie Queene* represents the myrrh tree as "bleeding" its prized resins of perfume and incense—"The Mirrhe sweete bleeding in the bitter wound"—in an association of the tree with Christ's death (1.1.9). These allegorical relocations of Myrrha in Christian history wildly destabilize the categories of virgin and desiring woman.

Another line of coincidence between Mary and Myrrha, although one scarcely remarked by the exegetical tradition, is their shared silence concerning the experience of childbirth: neither woman—unlike Feliciana—is allowed to tell her story. Mary rarely speaks throughout Matthew and Luke, the two infancy narratives that provide the quarry for Marian knowledge. And Myrrha's birth pangs are explicitly depicted as not having "sua verba [their own words]" (*Met.* 10.506). But the opposition between Mary and Myrrha becomes most charged when we confront the issue of the paternal relation, which is, after all, the main problematic of Feliciana's episode. Both Mary and Myrrha, again in contrast to the surface text of Feliciana, are patriarchal women: each of them conceives—the one divinely, the other incestuously—the father's child. Where Mary obeys and Myrrha seduces the patriarchal order, Feliciana fractures it, shattering its order of representation, exploding its cherished binaries. By showing that—*like* the rest of her sex—she cannot be firmly situated in either pole of the Mary/Myrrha dualism, Feliciana opens possibilities for a new conceptualization of maternity. Mediating between the virginal and desiring subtexts of her story, Feliciana reforms various scholastic distortions concerning childbirth. Cervantes's notable departure from his maternal models is in allowing his heroine a voice in fidelity to her own experience. By narrating her own delivery—in both senses of that word—Feliciana breaks through the limits of a symbolic order that for millennia has had comparatively little to say concerning childbirth.

"Born again" after her own embodiment within the "pregnant" oak, Feliciana acquires the voice of authority to render a story that is remarkable for its reflective intelligence. As she recounts the genesis of her "fall," she employs various conditional clauses to rewrite the language naming her dishonor: "mi infamia, si es que se puede llamar infamia la conversación de los deposados amantes [my infamy, *if* the conversation of be-

---

[39] Cf. *Ovide moralisé*, ed. Martina de Boer, 5 vols. (Wiesbaden: M. Sandig, 1936), 4:99–100.
[40] Cited by Flinker, "Cinyras," 65.

trothed lovers can be called infamy]" (293); "el adúltero, si así se puede
decir [the adulterer, *if* that is how one would put it]." The pure conventionality of each of these signifiers—*infamy, adulterer*—is observable under the control of a self-conscious narrator who contests the linguistic
structures used to condemn her. Feliciana's ironic rewriting here anticipates the character of Mari Cobeña, also given to figurative language in
defense of her own premarital pregnancy. This peasant parody of Feliciana—depicted by her exasperated father as "nada muda [nothing
mute]"—coolly assures the civil authorities of Toledo that she is neither
the first nor the last woman to have stumbled and fallen "en estos barran-
cos [into these ravines]" (330).

That Feliciana has moved beyond the maxims of the age that defined
the maternal nature is shown when she first meets up with her infant,
whom she has never really seen. Critics expecting the overblown responses of an Unamuno to the maternal impulse are amazed to read that
Feliciana experiences, instead, a kind of vacuum—a marked (and textually *re*marked) absence of the sympathetic swellings conventionally de-
manded of new mothers. Calling into question the sentiments of his acknowledged model Heliodorus—who pronounced the "maternal nature"
as "a knowledge which cannot lie"—Cervantes chooses to depict Feliciana's maternal nature as eclipsed by her sufferings. She cannot "recognize," for some time, the creature which the text, in what might seem to
be a superfluous coda, identifies as a boy-child:

> Lleváronsela, miróla y remiróla, quitóle las fajas; pero en ninguna cosa pudo
> conocer ser la que había parido, ni aun, lo que es más de considerar, el na-
> tural cariño no le movía los pensamientos a reconocer el niño, que era varón
> el recién nacido. (297)

> [They took it to her, she looked it over again and again, she removed its
> swaddling clothes; but by no sign could she recognize it as the child she had
> delivered; nor even—which is more significant—did any natural love move
> her feelings to recognize her child, which was a boy.]

Heliodorus's representation of the maternal nature as biological and instinctual does not find its way into the Feliciana story because Cervantes
is trying to represent not received opinion but "the soul's hidden
thoughts," as he put it in the prologue to his *Ocho comedias*. He is thinking presciently, intuiting what many psychoanalysts today believe: that
evidence for the biological basis for parenting is difficult to establish, because physiological changes in mothers can be radically distorted by psychic upheaval.[41] Cervantes conceptualizes the mother-infant bond in the

---

[41] For a sample of modern research on the "maternal instinct," see Nancy Chodorow's

Feliciana episode as temporarily undermined by her shocking postnatal circumstances. This implicit critique of a model for whom maternal love swells up naturally, "through a secret conformity and convenience of nature," reveals Cervantes's modernity and the force of his challenge to the classically correct Greek romancer Heliodorus.

When, toward the close of her episode, Feliciana finally gives her companions a sample of "the best voice in the world," she raises it in church, in the place where for centuries women had been debarred from teaching, preaching, or even speaking, on the grounds, as Peter Martyr Vermigli's collection of "commonplaces" authorized, that Eve's words had once beguiled Adam.[42] The conjunctions of voice with sexuality are ancient and, in Cervantes's final work, radically exposed. The voice that once beguiled Adam is here allowed to narrate the maternal implications of that once and future fall. The trajectory of that voice across Cervantes's canon is slow but steady. It begins perhaps with Marcela, whose economy of desire, stoutly defended by Don Quixote, disdains any masculine object but then, in a moment of notable gender reversal, appropriates the conventionally masculine ethic of autonomy. Unlike Feliciana's flight, Marcela's lends itself to depiction, in Poggioli's demeaning phrase, as a "pastoral of the self."[43] The burial of the love-suicide Grisóstomo at the close of Marcela's story is replaced, in Feliciana's episode, by the reunion and reconciliation of a family. And in the place of Marcela's defensive "Knight of the Mournful Countenance" we have Feliciana's industrious "Knight of the Infant." The most salient feature of Feliciana's story, however, is that it returns female desire to the reproductive site, exposing the duplicity apparent within—as well as the duplicity necessary to maintain—the opposition of the "virgin" mother and the "fallen woman." In *Des chinoises*, Julia Kristeva examines the binary opposition mother–wife/"other woman"–mistress as a useful ideological assumption of the bourgeois family, since such an opposition locates disruptive female desire in the mistress or prostitute—in any case, at the margins of the family scene. By this tactic, desire is split off from the mother, who cannot be imagined as having participated in an act of coitus or "primitive scene" of the kind inscribed exclusively for fallen women.[44] Cervantes's story of Feliciana—

The Reproduction of Mothering: Psychoanalysis and the Sociology of Gender (Berkeley: University of California Press, 1978), 17–19, 21–23.

[42] Vermigli, *Loci communes* 4.1.588–89; cited by Maclean, *Renaissance Notion*, who notes that the biblical *locus* is 1 Tim. 2:14 (18).

[43] Renato Poggioli, *The Oaten Flute: Essays on Pastoral Poetry and the Pastoral Ideal* (Cambridge, Mass.: Harvard University Press), 173ff.

[44] Julia Kristeva, *About Chinese Women*, trans. Anita Barrows (New York: Urizen Books, 1977), 26.

by its steady refusal to sublimate the erotic into the maternal—would seem to be anticipating similar kinds of psychoanalytic insights.

If throughout *Don Quixote* Cervantes was working out the problem of woman's voice within a masculine position of desire—conceptualizing feminine desire as either absent, disruptive, or entirely split off from the maternal body—with the marginal *Persiles*, a missing text is restored. To extend the quixotic trajectory of masculine desire proleptically is to arrive at the Barbaric Isle, that paradigmatic locus of sacrifice whose custodians self-destruct. Plotted as a quest for new paradigms of voice, Cervantes's last romance moves its large, fluid, and fragmentary cast of characters away from the charred structures of the Barbaric Isle and toward a series of regenerative places—caves, hermitages, bowers—where these new paradigms might fit. Antonio's uncouth cave, a generative retreat in which a Spanish soldier expiates the sin of anger and conceives his children, is one of these places (71–83). The island hermitage where Renato and Eusebia live, "como dos estatuas movibles [like two moving statues]," for ten years is another (264). Soldino's cave, where an aged prophet retires to seek enlightenment before death, is yet another (392–98). In this chapter we have focused on Feliciana's creative enclosure, that place in midtext where new life and language meet: the "pregnant" tree. Having earlier negotiated the Ovidian world invoked by so generative a metaphor, it now seems appropriate to close with some response to the narrator's plea for our collusion with his rhetoric: " 'The oak tree was pregnant'—let *us* say it that way" (291).

If as readers we take up Cervantes's exhortation to co-create, we would move from the plot of Feliciana directly into the "plot" of her metaphor—into the figurative or "dialogical" space created by that metaphor, a space in which all plotting is suspended while a new meaning or "issue" is being recreated. This conception of metaphor as creating a privileged space—brilliantly traced within the English critical tradition by Patricia A. Parker[45]—may be usefully applied to the figurative "womb" into which Feliciana is returned before she can generate her story. Here at the spatial center of the *Persiles*, Cervantes's uterine trope emblematizes his long brooding on issues of female sexuality: pregnancy, childbirth, and the loss of "credit" suffered by women like so many of his own female relatives, women involved in repeated extramarital liaisons.[46] One of the

[45] Patricia A. Parker, "The Metaphorical Plot," in *Metaphor: Problems and Perspectives*, ed. David S. Miall (Sussex: Harvester and Humanities Presses, 1982), 148–55 (rpt. in *Literary Fat Ladies*, 36–53).

[46] In Byron's discussion of the loss of "credit" of most of Cervantes's female relatives, he writes that "of the six children Doña Leonor de Cortinas raised to adulthood, Miguel was the only one known to have married. Every one of the women of her progeniture—Andrea and her daughter Constanza, Magdalena, Miguel's daughter Isabel—would turn out to be

most remarkable features of the *Persiles* is the dominance in it of the language of female parturition. The work represents women, trees, ships, a love triangle, and even the text itself—as it "delivers" its hero out of the "estrecha boca de una profunda mazmorra [narrow mouth of a deep dungeon]" (51)—in the act of giving birth. In this last structural sense, the *Persiles* is a book (like Feliciana within her tree) enclosed by its own contents. The configurations used by Cervantes to organize his nativity narratives show that he was experimenting with new structures of desire, that he was laboring to generate a nonlinear, nontriangular, nonsacrificial paradigm of a plot—essentially a critique of the limitations of his prior works. Unlike his earlier writings, the *Persiles* attempts to voice—after long silence and with all its gaps and interruptions—the mother's story.

---

what pre-liberation morality would unhesitatingly have described as a whore" (*Cervantes: A Biography*, 52). See also Rosa Rossi's chap. 2 on "Aquel extraño inquilino del piso de abajo," *Escuchar a Cervantes* (45–66).

Chapter Ten

THE HISTRIONICS OF EXORCISM: ISABELA CASTRUCHA

No Exorcisor harme thee . . .
—Shakespeare, *Cymbeline*

ALONG WITH hermaphrodites and colonialism, exorcism has become a seductive Renaissance topic in the postmodern period, its interest for us perhaps culturally rooted in the increasing "bewitchment" of rationalist thought by new articulations of knowledge. During the 1980s, for instance, a complex and resonant intertextuality was established between Shakespeare's *King Lear* and a savage contemporaneous English satire aimed at a group of Roman Catholic exorcists, "Papists" involved with the Babington Plot (1586). Trying to show us how exorcism and theater converge in *Lear*, at least two critics nominated as Shakespeare's source the Protestant polemicist Samuel Harsnett, who, while domestic chaplain to the Bishop of London in 1603, wrote a scathing attack on the practice of exorcism by English Jesuits.[1] Harsnett's polemic was used to document that, even as early as 1600, Shakespeare had "clearly marked out possession and exorcism as frauds."[2] An earlier Catholic version of these and other spectacular clandestine English exorcisms may have reached Cervantes,[3] Shakespeare's contemporary, through Philip II's own domestic chaplain, Fray Diego de Yepes. In his vast *Historia particular de la persecución de Inglaterra* (1599), a long and outraged history of the perse-

---

[1] See John L. Murphy, *Darkness and Devils: Exorcism and* King Lear (Athens: Ohio University Press, 1984), and Stephen Greenblatt, *Shakespearean Negotiations* (Berkeley: University of California Press, 1988). Samuel Harsnett's *A Declaration of Egregious Popish Impostures* (London: J. Roberts, 1603) was concerned with the clandestine exorcisms conducted under the Jesuit priest William Weston (Father Edmunds), largely in the home of Sir George Peckham of Denham, a recusant from Buckinghamshire. I am grateful to John L. Murphy for his comments on an earlier version of this chapter.

[2] Greenblatt, *Shakespearean Negotiations*, 115. Greenblatt argues that Harsnett's intentions were to marginalize the ceremony of exorcism, to present it as "emptied out" (113–14, 119).

[3] Cervantes's awareness of the plight of Catholics in Jacobean England would later be fortified by popularized accounts of such dispatches as the "Carta de don Juan de Tassis, Conde de Villamediana, al rey Felipe III, noviembre de 1604," cited by Carroll B. Johnson, "La Española Inglesa and the Practice of Literary Production," 386–87.

cution of English Catholics during the Elizabethan period, Diego de
Yepes celebrates such prodigious feats as those of Father Dibdal, who
forced the devil to eject "por la boca de una persona endemoniada, ovillos
de pelos, y pedazos de hierro, y otras cosas semejantes [through the
mouth of a possessed person, balls of hair, pieces of iron, and other similar things]."⁴ Although Cervantes may indeed have read the *Historia particular*, he had other, equally riveting, accounts of possession and exorcism to turn to for his fictions. Exploiting many of the same issues
surrounding the rite of exorcism as Shakespeare, a decade or so later and
on the other side of the Channel, Cervantes also seems to have marked
out the practice, if not as a fraud, at least as a ritual that had already been
exhausted—"emptied out"—and therefore one that could be refilled.

In the story of Isabela Castrucha, the last of the inset stories in the
Persiles (3.20–21), Cervantes ridicules exorcism as the monopoly of credulous and pretentious, although not necessarily insincere, men. A cross-
cultural study of Shakespeare and Cervantes on the question of exorcism
might underline the old dictum that sincerity is a Protestant ethic. Both
writers see exorcism as a dramatic performance, as high theater, but Cervantes's convergence of theater and exorcism in the *Persiles* comically
celebrates its own protagonist for simulating the state of demonic possession. For a similarly fraudulent act, "two maydens" in London were punished in 1574, a few years after the fictional time of the *Persiles*.⁵ Under
Cervantes's representation of exorcism lies no singular and identifiable
Harsnett figure but rather a cluster, even a clash, of subtexts. There is, to
begin with, the model of Heliodorus's *Aethiopica*, specifically the short
passage in which Calasiris, the Memphian priest of Isis, performs a mock
exorcism—"a piece of play-acting"—over the love-sick Chariclea (4.5).
Less remote than the pagan exorcism in Heliodorus is the model of Erasmus, the Catholic humanist whose comic reflections on exorcism served
as a satire of superstitious credulity. Like both Heliodorus and Erasmus,
Cervantes's tale acknowledges the *theatricality* of the ritual. The tale may
be read as a "reiteration"⁶ of Erasmus's humanist expose of exorcism

---

⁴ Diego de Yepes' Spanish version of these events is in bk. 2, chap. 13 of a long, untranslated work, the *Historia particular de la persecucción de Inglaterra, y de los martirios
más insignes que en ella ha avido, desde el año del Señor. 1570* (Madrid: Luis Sánchez,
1599), 97. I have consulted this edition at the Biblioteca Nacional in Madrid, under the
"Signatura" of "Raro [rare]" 26.921.

⁵ See *The Disclosing of a late Counterfeyted Possession by the Devyl in Two Maydens
within the Citie of London* (1574), cited by Keith Thomas in *Religion and the Decline of
Magic: Studies in Popular Beliefs in Sixteenth and Seventeenth Century England* (London:
Weidenfeld and Nicolson, 1971), 482–83.

⁶ The term is borrowed from Greenblatt, who reads *King Lear*'s relation to Harsnett's
expose of *Popish Impostures* as "one of reiteration, a reiteration that signals a deeper and
unexpressed institutional exchange" (120).

save that, unlike Erasmus, Cervantes *genders* the whole issue of demonic possession. He explicitly represents it as a displacement of erotic love, a representation that looks ahead to the later Freudian equation of medieval possession with sexuality. For her confidants and readers, if not for the exorcising clerisy around her bedside, Cervantes's heroine frankly equates her *demonio*—"el que me atormenta [he who torments me]" (403)—with her libido. Such a representation, for all its playfulness, distances Cervantes from the Erasmist theater of exorcism and aligns him with various contemporary treatises and handbooks, texts where demonic possession appears more sexualized. After a historicized discussion of the tale of Isabela Castrucha, this chapter will consider Erasmus's *Exorcismus, sive Spectrum* (1524) as the theatrical precursor for Cervantes's tale of spurious possession. Following this, we shall glance at two treatises on demonology that acknowledge the sexuality, if not the theatricality, of demonic possession: Kramer and Sprenger's *Malleus maleficarum* (1484) and Pedro Ciruelo's *Reprobación de las supersticiones y hechicerías* (c. 1530). Finally, we shall close as we opened, with a comparison of Shakespeare and Cervantes on the fictions of fictionalizing possession.

Cervantes's episode, essentially a panegyric of histrionic skills, focuses on the simulated demonic possession of Isabela Castrucha, unequivocably the most vocal and desiring woman in the Cervantine canon, a kind of "older" sister to those clever Doroteas and Camilas who manipulated their way through adversity in *Don Quixote*. Isabela appears in the *Persiles*, perhaps with positional significance, in the last of its interpolated tales. In the fashion of formal allegories, the text signifies her emblematic role of desiring woman by her clothing. When the protagonists first see Isabela, in an earlier chapter, she is one of a party of eight horsemen, all galloping toward Milan: "una mujer sentada en un rico sillón y sobre una mula, vestida de camino, toda de verde, hasta el sombrero, que con ricas y varias plumas azotaba el aire, con un antifaz, asimismo verde, cubierto el rostro [a woman seated on an expensive saddle over a mule, dressed for the road, all in green, even her hat, whose rich and various feathers beat the air, and the veil, similarly green, that covered her face]" (398). As a Green Woman ("dama . . . de lo verde"), Isabela is a distant relation of the European Green Man, himself identified as "a descendant of the Vegetation or Nature god of almost universal and immemorial tradition (whatever his local name)." If Isabela's green clothing has any "expressionist dimension," it involves deception rather than, as Helena Percas de Ponseti convincingly argues for Don Diego de Miranda, "self-deception."[7]

---

[7] John Speirs, *Medieval English Poetry: The Non-Chaucerian Tradition* (New York: Macmillan, 1957), 219. Helena Percas de Ponseti, *Cervantes y su concepto del arte*, 2 vols. (Madrid: Gredos, 1975), 2:386–87. See also John G. Weiger on Isabela in *The Individuated*

Isabela's guardian-uncle wishes to marry her off to a cousin whom she despises—"hombre no de mi gusto, ni de mi condición [a man neither to my liking nor suited to me]" (406). This impending cross-cousin marriage, a union that would facilitate the passage of inheritable property within a patrilineal descent system, is designed, as Isabela herself remarks, to keep the wealth within the family. Cervantes's allegory of the Barbaric Isle has alerted us to the mechanisms of social control in the Renaissance, when, in legal, economic, and political discourse, woman is regularly produced as a category of property, is conceptualized as a possession. We have seen how Cervantes's cannibals construct women, by law, as entirely within the economic discourses of useful commodities. Here in Lucca, two fictional years and two real books later, Isabela will contest the similar construction of a normative "woman" within the discursive practices of the Golden Age ruling elite. The signs of this idealized woman, as Cervantes had parodied her in the Barbaric Isle narrative, were a closed mouth and an enclosing body, one emblematic of the messianic container. Cervantes's Isabela, however, negates all those ideological boundaries without which property could not be constituted. In order to subvert her uncle's plans and to gain time until the man of *her* choice arrives—a foreigner whom *she* has proposed to by letter—Isabela decides to feign demonic possession, "fingir[se] endemoniada" (406).

The first commentary on her condition is by a "médico," an unnamed stage figure whose diagnosis, a kind of interpretive supplement, reminds us that theories of possession were beginning to compete, in the late Renaissance, with theories of insanity: "Yo, señora, no me acabo de desengañar si esta doncella está loca o endemoniada, y por no errar digo que está endemoniada y loca [I, madam, can't make up my mind as to whether this young woman is crazy or possessed, and so as not to err, I'll say that she's both possessed and crazy]" (402–3). About a half-century before Cervantes was writing these lines, the idea of demonic possession was being systematically weakened in Spain by dissenters like Teresa of Ávila, who, in a reversal of her former views, was demystifying *arrobamientos* or ecstatic trances, and offering sixteenth-century Spain alternative theories to demonic possession.[8] Outside of Spain, a number of medically minded skeptics who equated demoniacs and lunatics had begun to surface: thinkers like Johann Weyer, who argued in *De praestigiis daemonum* (1563) that many so-called witches were in reality innocent melancholics; or like Reginald Scot, who in *The Discoverie of Witchcraft* (1584) reinterpreted the New Testament cases of possession as instances

---

Self: Cervantes and the Emergence of the Individual (Athens: Ohio University Press, 1979), 159 n. 33.

[8] Alison Weber, *Teresa of Avila and the Rhetoric of Femininity* (Princeton: Princeton University Press, 1990), 139–47.

of madness or epilepsy; or like Edward Jorden, who in 1603 saw possession as a form of psychosomatic illness for which supernatural explana-
tions were vain.[9] By 1621, Robert Burton could categorically state that
there were "never any strange illusions of devils amongst hermits," but
that "immoderate fasting, bad diet, sickness, melancholy, solitariness, or
some such things were the precedent causes, the forerunners or concomitants of them."[10] Isabela's doctor, choosing to be ideologically safe, embraces the possibilities of *both* devils and melancholy: she is, for him,
both "endemoniada y loca [possessed and crazy]," at least until her pol-
ished performance convinces him that there is a devil within her. But even
the doctor's original ambivalence, as it turns out, could have been taken
as an "indication" of certifiable demonic possession. Vincentius von Berg,
for one, in his famous manual of exorcism, the *Enchiridium* (1748), regarded it as "especially significant if skilled physicians are not sure what
the affliction is, and cannot form an opinion about it."[11]

The second commentary in Cervantes's tale is by the innkeeper's wife,
whose idea of possession as theater is underlined by her open invitation
to the spectacle: "de cien leguas se podía venir a ver lo que está en esta
posada [people might well come from a hundred leagues away to see what
is in this inn]" (403). Michel de Certeau's narrative about demonic possession among the Ursuline nuns of Loudun in 1634 stresses the same
notion of the demoniac as a public spectacle for tourists, for an influx of
spectators who kept the inns of Loudon filled: "As word of the possession
spread, crowds of the curious arrived not only from the region but from
all over France and from as far away as England and Scotland."[12] Greenblatt's fertile conjunction of "Loudon and London" may be further allit-
erated to include Cervantes's "Lucca," where demoniacs were evidently
also great cause for spectacle. Other contemporaneous texts reveal that
exorcisms were a regular tourist attraction in Rome: Joachim Du Bellay
included a satirical sonnet on the matter in his sequence *Les regrets*, writ-

[9] J. Weyer, *De praestigiis daemonum* (1563); R. Scot, *Discoverie: A Discourse upon Di-*
vels and Spirits (1584), chap. 14; E. Jorden, *A Briefe Discourse of a Disease called the*
Suffocation of the Mother (1603); cited by Thomas, *Religion and the Decline of Magic*,
580.

[10] Robert Burton, *Anatomy of Melancholy* (3:393), cited by Lawrence Babb, *The Eliza-*
bethan Malady: A Study of Melancholia in English Literature from 1580 to 1642 (East
Lansing: Michigan State University Press, 1951), 49.

[11] Rossel Hope Robbins, *The Encyclopedia of Witchcraft and Demonology* (New York:
Bonanza Books, 1981), 181–83.

[12] *La possession de Loudon*, Collection Archives Series, 37 (Paris, 1980), cited and trans.
by Stephen Greenblatt, "Loudun and London," *Critical Inquiry* 12 (Winter 1986): 326. The
mass possession at Loudon is widely known through Aldous Huxley's notorious account in
his *Devils of Loudon*.

ten while in Rome in the 1550s; and Montaigne's *Journal* of his journey to Rome in 1581 documents the notion of exorcism as public spectacle.[13]

When the pilgrims first meet Cervantes's Isabela, she is stretched out on a brass bed, with her arms extended and tied with rags to the balusters of the headboard. Two women, evidently serving as her nurses, are searching for her legs under the bedclothes, aiming, not very successfully, to tie them down also. Although Isabela has been wildly biting herself in a manic impersonation of the Devil, she tries to convey to the visitors that she is not as crazy as she seems, that her "tormentor" is not what they think: "Que con cuatro o cinco bocados que me dé en el brazo, quedaré harta y no me haré más mal, porque no estoy tan loca como parezco, ni el que me atormenta es tan cruel que dejará que me muerda [With four or five bites of my arm I'll be satisfied and won't do myself any further damage, because I'm not as crazy as I seem, nor is my tormentor cruel enough to let me bite myself]" (403). Isabela's uncle Castrucho, however, walking into this conversation, announces Isabela's self-inflicted bites as the agency of the Devil: "ese que dices que no ha de dejar que te muerdas [he whom you say will not allow you to bite yourself]." Indeed, throughout this opening scene, the uncle seems acutely concerned about Isabela's diet of Isabela: "Encomiéndate a Dios, Isabela, y procura comer, no de tus hermosas carnes, sino de lo que te diere este tu tío, que bien te quiere [Commend yourself to God, Isabela, and try to eat, not your own lovely flesh, but rather what your uncle, who loves you well, gives you]" (403–4). Isabela's self-mutilation—a language without words for the guardian-uncle entrusted to her care and feeding—is the most violent of her symptoms, a rather decorous one compared to the spectacular fits and convulsions the age came to expect from its demoniacs:

> A person into whom an evil spirit had entered could be recognised by the strange physical and moral effects of the intrusion. He would suffer from hysterical fits, wild convulsions and contortions, analgesia, strange vomitings, even total paralysis. From his mouth would come the voices of demons, emitting obscene and blasphemous ravings, or talking fluently in foreign languages previously unknown to the victim.[14]

Within the consensus of the demonologists that possession should show itself via supernatural symptoms, vocal eccentricities were frequently cited. In the group epidemic of possession in Xante, Spain, in 1560, which Johann Weyer documented in *De praestigiis daemonum*

---

[13] See Sonnet 97 of Du Bellay's *Les Regrets et autres oeuvres poetiques, suivis des Antiquitez de Rome. Plus un Songe ou vision sur le meme sujet*, ed. J. Joliffe and M. A. Screech (Geneva: Droz, 1966), 170; and Montaigne's *Journal de voyage en Italie*, ed. Maurice Rat (Paris, Classiques Garnier, 1955), 111–12.

[14] Thomas, *Religion and the Decline of Magic*, 477–78.

(1563), the nuns were said to have suffered convulsions in church, to have torn off their veils, and to have bleated like sheep. Similarly strange vocal symptoms were noted in Reginald Scot's *The Discoverie of Witchcraft* (1584), which documents, along with contortions, vomitings of pins, and displays of supernatural strength, the weird voices of the "possessed," whom the skeptical Scot regarded as mentally ill: "It is indifferent or all one, to saie; He is possessed with a divell; or He is lunatike or phrenetike: which disease in these daies is said to proceed of melancholie."[15] In Cervantes's tale, we know that the prescribed remedies have begun, that clerical intervention has been sought for Isabela's weird, and even obscene, "voices," when her uncle enters the room carrying in one hand a cross and in the other "un hisopo bañado en agua bendita [an aspergill containing holy water]." In Castrucho's train are "dos sacerdotes [two clergymen]" who have come to sprinkle Isabela's face with holy water: "Creyendo ser el demonio quien la fatigaba, pocas veces se apartaban della [Believing it to be the Devil who was fatiguing her, they stayed very close to her]" (404). Much of the Cervantine humor of this tale comes from Isabela's expert ventriloquism, her assumption of the gendered subjectivity of the Devil and her mastery of the idiom of demonic possession. Her "demonio," wildly libidinized, is amazingly vocal about such unfeminine topics as lice ("animalejos") in men's breeches, and about the classes of men who scratch or delouse themselves (408). The doctor in attendance even chastizes Isabela's "demon" for his sexual coarseness: "Todo lo sabes, malino . . . ; bien parece que eres viejo [You know everything, Evil One . . . ; it certainly shows that you're an old man]" (409). This demon, whom all the company are eager to exorcise, has the effrontery to dictate the conditions of his own emergence: "Yo saldré presto; pero no ha de ser cuando vosotros quisiéredes, sino cuando a mí me parezca [I'll emerge soon; but it won't be when you wish it, but rather when I feel like it]" (404). As Isabela's spokes-demon, he refuses to be officially exorcised until the arrival in Lucca of one Andreas Marulo, the heroine's secret lover. No one regards this demonic qualification as strange. Young Marulo's father even prides himself that "cosas mías [things of mine]" have been chosen as "paraninfos de tan buenas nuevas [harbingers of felicity]" (408).

Although the institutional logic of exorcism is ridiculed throughout Cervantes's representation, the official guardians of mystical ideology, the clerics who busy themselves reciting from the Book of Hours, are represented as unquestioning believers. All of Isabela's male bedside visitors—uncles, fathers, doctors, priests—see her as "indubitablemente . . .

---

[15] Reginald Scot, *The Discoverie of Witchcraft . . . Hereunto is added a treatise upon the nature and substance of spirits and diuels* (1584; rpt. London, 1886), 430.

endemoniada [undoubtedly . . . possessed]" (405). They are also convinced that the Evil One is "spread out" in her "angelic" body, that it has become a container for the demon who has collectively enchanted them all. Once again the doctor testifies, this time to the authenticity of Isabela's possesion: "Vea . . . la lástima desta doncella, y si merece que en su cuerpo de ángel se ande espaciado el demonio [Note . . . the pity of this young woman, and whether her angelic body deserves to have the demon expatiate himself in it]" (408). The doctor's reference to Isabela's writhing body, as well as her uncle's to her "lovely flesh," remind us that in this tale the "unnaturall venereans" are not, as Harsnett would have it, the clergy.[16]

Unlike the men in Isabela's sickchamber, the four women visiting her are represented as knowing the whole truth about her counterfeiting. These female conspirators position themselves on her bed, in programmatically evangelical fashion, in order to hear the reasons for her feigned possession. Born in Spain of Italian parents, Isabela was orphaned and left in the custody of her uncle Castrucho, a courtier in the Emperor's retinue. While in his care, she crossed paths with a young man in church, thereby ironizing Luis Vives's prohibition about *doncellas* never stirring abroad except to church, a recommendation still in effect a century later: "La doncella cristiana no haga más que orar y callar, y obrar con sus manos, y obedecer a sus padres, y vivir en recogimiento y honestidad [The Christian maiden should do nothing but pray and be silent, and work with her hands, and obey her parents, and live in withdrawal and chastity]."[17] Isabela stared at this man in church so purposively ("tan de propósito") that she must now, in her representation, invoke her gender to defend the unseemly as seemly: "Y no os parezca esto, señoras, desenvoltura, que no parecerá, si consideráredes que soy mujer [And this should not seem to you, ladies, looseness, when you consider that I am a woman]" (405). Isabela's female audience here would have known that she was admitting to what Juan Espinosa, among countless other sixteenth-century writers, had codified as indecorous female behavior: "A las mugeres de honra no basta la abstinentia sola del peccado, mas aun para librarse de la sospecha del, les conviene huir todos aquellos inconvenientes e indicios que pueden causarla [It is not enough for honorable women to abstain from sin, but even, in order to free themselves from any suspicion of it, to avoid all those occasions and indications that might

---

[16] Harsnett, *Declaration*, 160–61.

[17] Gaspar de Astete, *Tratado del gouierno de la familia, y estado de las viudas y donzellas* (Burgos, 1603), 183; cited by Edward Glaser, "Nuevos datos sobre la crítica de los libros de caballerías en los siglos XVI y XVII," *Anuario de estudios medievales* 3 (1966): 407.

cause it]."[18] Having discovered that the object of her gaze was a university student at Salamanca, Isabela writes him a proposal of marriage, urging haste because of the impending marriage already arranged for her. Andreas responds eagerly, promising to become her husband as soon as he returns from Salamanca. Isabela's prehistory concludes here with an equation between demonic and *daimonic* possession that exposes exorcism as a misplaced ceremony: "Una legión de demonios tengo en el cuerpo, que lo mismo es tener una onza de amor en el alma [I have a legion of demons in my body, which is the same thing as having an ounce of love in one's soul]" (407). Her problem, in other words, is not demonic possession but daimonic desire. Writing in the context of French seventeenth-century drama, Greenblatt notes that "the greatest image of possession" was "Vénus tout entière à sa proie attachée [Venus entirely attached to her prey]," a form of possession for which "there is no exorcism."[19] There is no exorcism for Isabela's form of possession either, whose source is also Venus. Even the narrator feels compelled to share this insight with the reader: "Porque se vea quién es el amor, pues hace parecer endemoniados a los amantes [See who Love is, who can make lovers seem possessed]" (407).

As the would-be exorcists begin to activate the remedies prescribed by the church against her incubus devil, Isabela's task, Cervantes's text makes clear, is to "revalidar su demonio [revalidate her demon]" (407). She begins to urge on her demon to wilder antics, trying to confirm that it is indeed the Evil One speaking from her body. The text distinguishes between her so-called "secretarias [secretaries]," who can understand all this diabolic "doublespeak," from all the men in her chamber, who cannot: "Ellas las interpretaban verdaderamente, y los demás como desconcertados disparates [The women interpreted her words as the truth, the others, as disconcerting nonsense]" (408). Isabela's uncle, especially gratified about the forthcoming exorcism, addresses Isabela's demon directly, in the old Catholic manner, conjuring him to depart with the Latin conjuration "*vade retro, exi foras* [Go back! Get out!]" (409). This is a longer version of the same formula employed by the protagonist of Cervantes's *El rufián dichoso*, Fray Cristobal de la Cruz, when he exorcises some half-dozen screaming demons from an infernal, and highly eroticized, vision with a cry of "*Vade retro!* Satanás."[20] A great menu of published exorcisms from which to choose one's formula was available to the late Renaissance: Cervantes may have been writing this episode around the same

---

[18] Juan Espinosa, *Diálogo en laude de las mujeres* (1580), ed. Ángela González Simón (Madrid: CSIC, 1946), 268.

[19] Greenblatt, "Loudun and London," 343.

[20] *El rufián dichoso*, ed. Dr. Florián Smieja (Madrid: Editorial Ebro, 1977), 88. Further citations will be parenthetically documented.

time that Paul V's *Rituale romanum* of 1614 was attempting to standardize its exorcizing liturgy.[21] Many of these conjurations had been modeled upon the Roman judicial system, which meant that exorcists would be pressuring demons into confessing the truth in a version of a formal *quaestio*.[22] Although Castrucho, pedantically indulging in a dress rehearsal for the forthcoming exorcism, is officially commanding Isabela's demon to depart, he does not confine his lore of exorcism to learned Latin. He also employs a vernacular metaphor for exorcism, popular among the superstitious, of "sweeping the house" ("barrer la casa"), when he rejoices at the prospect of Isabela's unpossessed body as a "cleanly swept" habitation.[23] Earlier in the *Persiles*, marriages "de concierto y conveniencia [of convenience]," such as those arranged to favor inheritance patterns, were likened to "renting out" a house—"como . . . alquilar una casa" (325)—a similitude that reveals the unconscious motives behind Castrucho's later "housekeeping" metaphor.

In response to her uncle's pre-exorcism counsel, Isabela produces another string of her gibberish, of her "razones equívocas [equivocal statements]" (408). Karl-Ludwig Selig has noted how, "in the feigned madness scene, Ysabela Castrucho expresses herself very much by design with ambiguities and double talk, a manner which is rather reminiscent of Tómas Rodaja's frequent mode of expression in the *Licenciado*."[24] The description by Isabela's putative demon of her lover-exorcist as "ese putativo Ganimedes [that so-called Ganymede]" (409) is strikingly ambiguous, given that the Romans had often corrupted the name of Jupiter's cupbearer to "Catamitus," which gave origin to the term "catamite." Covarrubias breathes not a word of these homosexual suggestions in his definition of "Ganimedes," but foregrounds instead the elevated Platonic sense—"muy recibida entre Católicos [well received among Catholics]"—of a spiritual and contemplative man.[25] And, indeed, we read in

[21] See D. P. Walker, *Unclean Spirits: Possession and Exorcism in France and England in the Late Sixteenth and Early Seventeenth Centuries* (Philadelphia: University of Pennsylvania Press, 1981), 6.

[22] Peter Brown, *The Cult of the Saints: Its Rise and Function in Latin Christianity* (Chicago: University of Chicago Press, 1981), 109–11.

[23] See F. Rodríguez Marín, *Ensalmos y conjuros en España y América* (Madrid, 1927), 18–19.

[24] Karl-Ludwig Selig, "*Persiles* (Book III, chapts. xx–xxi) and *El Licenciado Vidriera*," in *Studia Hispánica in Honorem R. Lapesa* (Madrid: Gredos, 1974), 2:594. In Isabela's wordplay on *rodaxa/rodaja*, Selig finds yet another link, an "amusing" one, between Cervantes's two texts.

[25] According to Covarrubias, "GANIMEDES . . . en sentido más levantado, según la dotrina de los platónicos, sinifica el hombre espiritual y contemplativo, el ánima del varón prudente y justo, cuya hermosura parece a los ojos de Dios tan bien, que la lleva para sí" (*Tesoro*, 628).

the Protestant Harsnett that Catholic exorcists, specifically Jesuits, were called, among countless other vilifying names, "Ganimedeans."[26] That Cervantes's heroine has her counterfeit "demon" indulge in similarly puritanical name-calling may bring the text to the borders of blasphemy. One should stress here, however, that Cervantes is no Harsnett, who sees exorcisms as stage plays fashioned by cunning clerics, by Catholics who seek to make the misrecognition of reality both permanent and invisible, in short, by "self-conscious professionals."[27] Although Cervantes, too, wishes to debunk exorcism, it is *not* to identify any sleazy moves or traitorous designs of the Catholic church, whose spokesmen are here represented as credulous but not fraudulent. The fraud here, as will be explored in what follows, is Isabela herself, whose stage tricks Cervantes represents as by no means contemptible. Harsnett explains how Catholic exorcists, about to practice their craft on the possessed, "doe tell them" how to behave—how to "fall to their fittes, and play their prankes point by point exactly, according as they haue beene instructed."[28] The Catholic exorcists in Cervantes's tale never instruct Isabela, who falls to her spectacular biting "fittes" under no clerical prodding. The only person instructed in this theater of exorcism, and by certified mail, is Isabela's lover, "que era discreto y estaba prevenido, por las cartas que Isabela le envió a Salamanca, de lo que había de hacer si la alcanzaba en Luca [who was by nature discreet and who had been thoroughly instructed by Isabela's letters of what he had to do upon catching up with her in Lucca]" (3.21). Unlike Harsnett's anti-Jesuitical agenda, Cervantes's chief concern in this episode is erotic love, not holy wars.

When Isabela's lover finally enters her sickroom, it is to play the role of exorcist in discreet collusion with her own histrionic imposture. As if in a trance ("atontado y loco"), he shouts at Isabela's "demon" some tropes of repetition lifted from a ballad cited by Ginés Pérez de Hita in his *Guerras civiles de Granada*: "¡Afuera, afuera, afuera; aparta, aparta, aparta . . . ! [Out, out, out! Depart, depart, depart . . . !]" (1.6).[29] The original ballad follows these triple imperatives with the speaker's identification of himself as "el valeroso Muza / cuadrillero de unas cañas . . . [the valiant Muza / commander of the gun chases . . .]." Cervantes's hero, however,

---

[26] "Dissemblers, iuglers, impostors, players with God, his Sonne, his angels, his saints: deuisers of new deuils, feigned tormentors of spirits, vsurpers of the key of the bottomlesses pit, whippers, scourgers, batfoulers of fiends, Pandars, *Ganimedeans*, enhaunsers of lust, deflowrers of virgins, defilers of houses, vncivil, vnmanlie, vnnaturall venereans," and many more names along these same vehement lines (*Harsnett, Declaration*, 160–61; emphasis added).

[27] Greenblatt, *Shakespearean Negotiations*, 106–7.

[28] Harsnett, *Declaration*, 62.

[29] See Schevill and Bonilla, "Notes," *Persiles*, 313, nn. 196–97.

outdoing that "valiant Muza," identifies himself as "cuadrillero mayor de
todo el infierno, si es que no basta de una escuadra [chief commander not
merely of a squadron but of all the legions of hell]" (3.21). This bellicose
self-presentation taps into a scholastic tradition of the Devil as a military
chief. From the mid–twelfth century onward, as Jeffrey B. Russell notes,
"Christian writers began to place greater emphasis upon the Devil's
power as the chief of an army of demons who roamed the world actively
attempting to undermine the saving mission of Christ and tempting people to sin."[30] It is at this point—when the long-awaited "exorcist" identifies himself with the Devil—that the text loudly advertises Cervantes's
intentions: to demystify exorcism as a theatrical ritual that, like a stage
play, can be scripted and rehearsed. Where one actor can play the con-
flicting roles of both exorcist and demon, where the demon is located
within the very figure designed to erase him, the opposition between the
two is radically destabilized. Even the doctor admits testily that it is all
probably play-acting ("esto debe ser burlando") so that the Devil can
emerge (410).

During the ad hoc marriage rite between the lovers, Andreas asks for
the glory of being lifted "de la humildad de ser Andrea Marulo a la alteza
de ser esposo de Isabela Castrucho [from the humility of being Andreas
Marulo to the heights of being the husband of Isabela Castrucho]." Anyone wishing to disturb this "sabroso nudo [delicious knot]" is, in Andreas's eyes, also to be equated with "los demonios [demons]." When
Isabela's uncle extends an impediment, it is to ask whether it is the custom
in Lucca "que se case un diablo con otro [for one devil to marry an-
other]." Isabela finally confesses that she was never "endemoniada," forc-
ing her credulous spectators to see themselves as manipulated (410). At
this point the lovers join hands and, as the narrator puts it, "con dos síes
quedaron indubitablemente casados [with two 'yeses' they remained in-
dubitably married]" (411). Although this marriage reiterates the earlier
marriage of Ruperta and Croriano (3.17), in that both unions were canonically irregular in the post-Tridentine period, Avalle-Arce justly defends them as "artísticamente impecables [artistically impeccable]."[31]
One might add the wedding of Persiles and Sigismunda to all this "irreg-
ularity," since a similarly uncanonical "sí" joins them in marriage at the
book's close, in a rite conducted, by the dying Magsimino and without
benefit of clergy, on a field in front of Saint Paul's, "witnessed" by friends
as well as by the wounded Periandro's dripping blood ("la sangre que
estás derramando") (474). Américo Castro's judgment of Cervantes's

[30] Jeffrey B. Russell, A History of Witchcraft: Sorcerers, Heretics and Pagans (London:
Thames and Hudson, 1980), 66.
[31] Avalle-Arce, "Introduction," Los trabajos, 391n.

aversion to legal and religious marriage rites seems borne out by both Isabela Castrucha's marriage and that of the *Persiles*'s main protagonists: "Es innegable que a Cervantes le encanta este amor libre y espontáneo, sin fórmulas legales ni religiosas [It is undeniable that Cervantes is enchanted by this free and spontaneous love, without legal or religious formulas]."[32]

In faking possession, then, Isabela exposes not only exorcism as a fraudulent drama but also herself as a fraud. The diabolic little drama of her marriage to Andreas Marulo—produced, directed, and even acted by Isabela—completely undoes her uncle, who, feeling himself dishonored by this match, dies on the spot in a "mortal parasismo [mortal paroxysm]" of rage (411). One may recoil from the virtual "murder" of a character who seems to be merely the proverbial obstacle. Readers of "The Captive's Tale" in *Don Quixote*, part 1, however, will remember that this is not the first "heavy father" figure that Cervantes has done away with.[33] What is instructive about this one, however, is that the dead Castrucho, courtesy of a rhetorical zeugma, replaces Isabela in bed, in the very *lecho* where her incubus had confined her: "Lleváronle sus criados al lecho, levantóse del suyo Isabela . . . [His servants carried him to his bed, Isabela arose from hers . . .]" (411). Cervantes's rhetorical wordplay invites us to equate Isabela's uncle with her demon, a strategy that decreases the readerly impulse to mourn the dead: he who wished to exorcise her is now exorcised. Within a few days of old Castrucho's death, Isabela and Andreas are married again, this time canonically, in the same holy church whose exorcism had seemed so unavailing.

In Cervantes, then, the theater of exorcism is appropriated by a female *hysteron* and represented as erotic possession, as the theme of the demon-lover that would resurface, all humor spent, in such later European authors as Goethe, Coleridge, Emily Brontë, T. Gautier, and others. If the sexual discourse of a culture plays a crucial part in the shaping of identity, Cervantes's tale reveals some of the more outrageous ways that women had to negotiate the reality of their desire during the Golden Age. Con-

[32] Castro cites some seven examples of "amor libre" from Cervantes's works, four of them from the *Persiles* (*El pensamiento de Cervantes* [Madrid: Casa Editorial Hernando, 1925], 349n). Regarding the ambiguities surrounding the marriage institution in Europe prior to the Council of Trent, Erwin Panofsky writes that, until 1563, "two people could contract a perfectly valid and legitimate marriage whenever and wherever they liked, without any witness and independently of any ecclesiastical rite, provided that the essential condition of a 'mutual consent expressed by words and action' had been fulfilled" ("Jan van Eyck's Arnolfini Portrait," in *Renaissance Art*, ed. Creighton Gilbert [New York: Harper Torchbooks, 1970], 6–7).

[33] For an excellent psychoanalytic study of *El cautivo*, see María Antonia Garcés's "Zoraida's Veil: The Other Scene of *The Captive's Tale*," *Revista de estudios hispánicos* 23 (January 1989): 65–98.

testing the received ideas of her culture about demonic possession, Isabela also rewrites their notion of desiring woman. If Dulcinea is their ideally desirable and always inaccessible object, a cruel fair lady doomed ever to be desired "through the Other"—in the Girardian scheme, through the external mediation of Amadís of Gaul and his countless chivalric clones—then Isabela furnishes us Dulcinea's precise antithesis.

She also meticulously counterpoints the cultivated prudery of Sigismunda, the work's titular and more conventional romance heroine, who begins her career of trabajos as a Dulcinea-figure, desired by all men but—and this by her own admission—with no desires of her own: "que ella no tenía voluntad alguna [she had no will of her own]" is her response to the revelation that the hero is passionately in love with her (467). When, later in the text, Sigismunda muses about people who, unlike herself, regard love as "una vehemente pasión del ánimo [a vehement passion of the soul]" (401), we understand that there is a strong allegorical polarity between her worried chastity and Isabela's unrepressed libido, what she chooses to masquerade as her *demonio*. Although Cesáreo Bandera reasonably maintains that "we cannot truly hope" through the pure Sigismunda—through a woman "ready to die rather than be soiled"[34]—he might be able to regain hope through her subcharacter Isabela, whose eroticism Sigismunda must absorb before she can entertain the idea of marriage. The allegorical character of Sigismunda is being mosaically "produced," as we argued in chapter 6, by a series of subcharacters, the last of which is Isabela, certifiably the most libidinal of all of Cervantes's interpolated heroines. We know there is hope for the bloodless Sigismunda when she loudly, and uncharacteristically, endorses Isabela's stratagem for marrying her "exorcist" (410).

Apart from her libidinal stripes, Isabela is also wily and clever. Toward the end of the *Persiles*, a minor character recalls that "en Luca se hablaba mucho en la sagacidad de Isabela Castrucha [in Lucca there was much talk of Isabela Castrucha's sagacity]" and of her "demonio fingido [feigned devil]" (452). Isabela's feigning makes her, like Odysseus, a sympathetic literary liar. Her stratagems also shift the romance foundations of the *Persiles* temporarily into the comic realm, where the triumph of *froda* is often a driving force.[35] Cervantes has regularly employed froda figures in his narratives, sometimes himself taking on the *burlador* or trickster role. Ruth El Saffar sees many of the male characters in Cervantes's later narratives as using froda in order to "win minus conflict." Her explanation of the trickster's relationship to his prescribed role—that instead of letting it manipulate him, he will take possession of that

---

[34] Cesáreo Bandera, "An Open Letter to Ruth El Saffar," *Cervantes* 1 (1981): 104.
[35] See Frye, *Secular Scripture*, 68ff. for a discussion of the role of fraud in romance.

role[36]—seems to me, given a pronominal gender change, equally apt for Isabela's theatrical tactics.

For the plot structure of Isabela's episode, Cervantes borrows and inverts the centuries-old formula of Greek New Comedy, whose "normal" narrative is that "a young man wants a young woman, that his desire is resisted by some opposition, usually paternal, and that near the end of the play some twist in the plot enables the hero to have his will."[37] With an exchange of genders, this antique comic formula could furnish an abstract for Cervantes's tale of Isabela. In Cervantes's version, a young woman wants a young man, but she cannot wait for "some twist in the plot" to help her. She cannot remain the *muta persona* which Greek comedy labeled its heroines. She must create that "twist" herself in order to revise the social grammar of a powerful core of adult males who see her as an object of circulation, as their possession. Isabela must shift her grammatical position, in short, from object to subject of barter. Because Isabela's uncle, a surrogate of the formulaic *senex iratus* or "heavy father" in the Latin tradition of these comedies, wishes to "rent out" her body, Isabela's stratagem is to beat him to it—to rent it out herself to the Devil. By feigning demonic possession, she triumphs over a culture so mesmerized by the Evil One that it confounds him with women in love. Already "possessed" economically by this culture, Isabela simply translates that bondage into a charade of supernatural possession. She not only resists possession, she rescripts it. Instead of her being sacrificed to a marriage arranged by the Law of the Father, the surrogate father who would have bartered her is snuffed out—exorcised—from the text.

It is the presence of erotic love that reveals the considerable psychic distance traveled between the fiction of exorcism in the *Persiles* and the work of so cultivated a skeptic as Erasmus, who also ridiculed exorcism in *Exorcismus: sive Spectrum* (1524). Erasmus's colloquy ostensibly celebrates the histrionic skills of Polus and Faunus, the former "the author of this play as well as an actor in it," the latter "an actor for the play."[38] Although the whole colloquy is a rationalist satire on credulity, Erasmus generically transforms it by depicting the events as a five-act play: Anselm shares with Thomas "a delightful story," one which he divides into acts ("There you have Act I of the play"; "Let this be, if you like, Act III of the play") (45). In act 1, a credulous priest called Faunus prepares to ex-

---

[36] See Ruth El Saffar, "Tracking the Trickster in the Works of Cervantes," in *Cervantes: Modern Critical Views*, ed. Harold Bloom (New York: Chelsea House Publishers, 1987), 151–68.

[37] Frye, *Anatomy of Criticism*, 170.

[38] "Exorcism," *Erasmus: Ten Colloquies*, trans. Craig R. Thompson (Indianapolis: Bobbs-Merrill, 1957), 38, 39. All further references to this colloquy are from this edition and will be parenthetically documented.

orcize not a person but a place, a little bridge near a briar patch supposedly inhabited by devils. Faunus prepares for "the proper ritual" by marking off a circle "to hold the numerous crucifixes" and other various signs: "A large vessel filled with holy water was brought. In addition, a sacred stole (as it's called), with the opening verses of St. John's Gospel hanging from it, was draped over Faunus' shoulders. In his pockets he had a waxen image of the kind blessed annually by the pope and known as an Agnus Dei. Long ago—before a Franciscan cowl became so formidable—people used to protect themselves by this armor against harmful demons" (40). Exorcism, for Erasmus, was already drained of its earlier doctrinal significance. In his genial colloquy, he irreverently cites "the bowels of the Blessed Mary" or "the bones of Blessed Winifred" as instances of effective new verbal exorcisms. This was the kind of learned fun that earned Erasmus the kind of reputation still lingering, almost a century later, in Covarrubias's *Tesoro* (1611): "Fue doctísimo . . . [pero] . . . no le hizo ningún provecho ser tan libre como fue [He was extremely learned . . . [but] . . . it did not profit him to be as liberal as he was]."[39] Erasmus saw the whole rite of exorcism as passé by 1524, in other words, a date that tellingly squares with the beginning of the end of the publishing "boom" of the *Malleus*. For Erasmus the "formidable" weapon against demonic possession was "the Franciscan cowl"—symbol of the redemptionist order of poverty and humility that Cervantes himself, as a lay Franciscan of the Tertiary Order, would officially join at the end of his life.

What is Isabela to Faunus or he to her? I have called Isabela's episode a "reiteration" of Erasmus because in Cervantes, as in Erasmus, the protagonist is the author of as well as an actor in the play; because the play itself ridicules credulity in Christians; and because it turns on the device of a duped character who himself becomes a ghost. The "play" Erasmus rehearses turns out to be a practical joke played on Faunus, who becomes so obsessed with the empty signs of exorcism that "you would have said he was a ghost, not a man" (46). In this last technique of inversion, Erasmus seems very close to Cervantes, with his narrative of "the exorciser exorcised." Indeed, the astoundingly similar dynamics of the two moves us to pose, once more with feeling, Marcel Bataillon's unanswerable question: "¿Habrá leído Cervantes a Erasmo? [Could Cervantes have

[39] Covarrubias's whole entry under "ERASMO ROTHERRODAMO" reads as follows: "Fue doctísimo y dexó escrito mucho, como a todos es notorio; no le hizo ningún provecho ser tan libre como fue, y assí estan defendidas algunas de sus obras y expurgadas las demás [He was very learned and he left many writings, as is notoriously known; it did not profit him to be as liberal as he was, and thus some of his books are prohibited and the rest expurgated]" (*Tesoro*, 529).

read Erasmus?]"[40] Cervantes may, in fact, have ferreted out some censored translations of Erasmus, or he may have absorbed Erasmist thought indirectly, through either his old schoolmaster López de Hoyos or other like-minded worthies. By whatever means Erasmus's *Exorcismus* came into Cervantes's orbit, it seems highly likely that this humanist critique of uninspired ceremonies—a colloquy serenely free of any psychological concerns—inspired Cervantes to attempt his own irreverent parody of exorcism. No servile imitator of Erasmus, Cervantes regenerates the comic structures of *Exorcismus* by moving the representation away from the religious toward the psychosexual, away from the masculine toward the feminine. In the context of the *Novelas ejemplares*, Francisco Márquez Villanueva has brilliantly assessed Erasmus's lack of sensitivity (the creation of "Folly" notwithstanding) toward the feminine:

> No hay en Erasmo especial sensibilidad para la mujer entendida en sus propios términos, ni planteamientos de aun lejano sentido feminista. [. . .] Ni tampoco se ve en Erasmo ninguna apertura hacia la dignificación del erotismo femenino, como de un modo algo más que implícito hace Cervantes a través de la figura de Dorotea en el *Quijote*.

> [There is no special sensibility in Erasmus toward woman as such, nor any arguments of an even remotely feminist sense. (. . .) Neither does one see in Erasmus any move toward dignifying the feminine erotic, as Cervantes, in a more than implicit mode, achieves through the figure of Dorotea in the *Quixote*.][41]

Nowhere in Cervantes does the feminine erotic invite more astute commentary, including internal commentary from the characters themselves, than in the episode of Isabela Castrucha. Of all the interpolations in the *Persiles*, Isabela's episode most resembles a psychoanalytic case history. Freud himself called attention to the uncanny resemblance between the psychoanalyst and the exorcist when, in a letter to Fliess, he suggested that the whole of his "brand-new" theory of the origins of hysteria was already familiar and, centuries before his own theory, had been "pub-

[40] Bataillon, *Erasmo y España*, 799. The vexed question of the imprint of Erasmus in Cervantes's fiction begins with Américo Castro, who, having aligned several pages of what he regards as direct imitations, roundly concluded, in 1925, that it was undeniable ("innegable") that Cervantes was directly influenced by Erasmus (*El pensamiento de Cervantes*, 281–83). Alban Forcione's main argument in *Cervantes and the Humanist Vision*—that Cervantes's *Exemplary Novels* can be "appreciated properly only if they are situated in the cultural context of Christian Humanism"—is a response to his hearing Castro say, in a 1960 recantation, that "there is absolutely nothing of Erasmus in Cervantes's work!" (x). Francisco Márquez Villanueva reminds us of the dangers of reducing Cervantes's intellectual formation to "un virtual monopolio erasmista [a virtually Erasmian monopoly]" ("Erasmo y Cervantes, una vez más," *Cervantes* 4 [Fall 1984]: 132).

[41] Márquez Villanueva, "Erasmo y Cervantes," 136.

lished a hundred times over." "Do you remember," Freud jogs Fliess, "that I always said that the medieval theory of possession held by the ecclesiastical courts was identical with our theory of a foreign body and the splitting of consciousness?" Freud then poses the key question about his hysterical patients: "Why did the devil who took possession of the poor things invariably abuse them sexually and in a loathsome manner?"[42] Years later, in his study of "A Neurosis of Demoniacal Possession in the Seventeenth Century," Freud flatly declares that "the states of possession correspond to our neuroses," and that, in our eyes, "demons are bad and reprehensible wishes, derivatives of instinctual impulses that have been repudiated and repressed."[43] In yet another letter to Fliess, Freud tells us about the reading project that was to test his theories: "I have ordered the *Malleus maleficarum*, and ... I shall study it diligently."[44] If the "medieval theory of possession" was, as Freud put it, "identical" with his theory of hysteria, then the *Malleus maleficarum* (*Hammer of Witches*), a codification of that medieval theory that includes various chapters on the "Lawful Exorcisms of the Church," allows us to take a closer look at the phenomenon that Freud remotivated and Cervantes exploited.

One of the most influential of all of Europe's early printed books, the *Malleus* appeared in no less than fourteen editions between 1484 and 1520 and became the casebook on every Renaissance magistrate's desk.[45] It acquired especial authority from the scarcely innocent papal document that generated and prefaced it—the famous bull of Pope Innocent VIII— in which the pontiff appeared to have delegated two Dominican inquisitors, Heinrich Kramer (Henricus Institoris) and James Sprenger, the duty of combating witches throughout northern Germany. "The burthen of Our bull," in the Pope's words, was that "the Catholic Faith should especially in this Our day increase and flourish everywhere, and that all heretical depravity should be driven far from the frontiers and bournes of the Faithful." The spiritual "errors" that were to be "uprooted by Our

---

[42] See Letter of 17 January 1897, in *The Complete Letters of Sigmund Freud to Wilhelm Fliess, 1887–1904*, ed. and trans. Jeffrey Moussaieff Masson (Cambridge, Mass.: Harvard University Press, 1985), 224–25.

[43] *SE* 19:69–105. The "demonological case history" of a seventeenth-century painter called Christoph Haizmann is brilliantly analyzed by Freud, who sees the devil who appears to Haizmann—on one occasion with two pairs of female breasts and "a large penis ending in a snake"—as a father-substitute. Haizmann's "demonological illness" has an economic meaning for Freud: the painter had "wanted all along simply to make his life secure" (104).

[44] Freud, Letter of 24 January 1897, in *Complete Letters*, 227.

[45] "Introduction to 1928 Edition" of the *Malleus maleficarum* of Heinrich Kramer and James Sprenger, trans. Rev. Montague Summers (New York: Dover Publications, 1971), xi–xl. Further citations from the *Malleus* are from this edition and will be parenthetically documented.

diligent avocation as by the hoe of a provident husbandman" included the practices—and sometimes, indeed, the persons—of persons who had "abandoned themselves to devils, incubi and succubi." That in 1495 Fr. Joaquín de Torres, O.P., the master general of the order of Saint Dominic, summoned Institoris to Venice for a series of crowded public lectures shows the institutional spread of the *Malleus*.[46]

Immunity from the fiend—a kind of Renaissance preventative medicine—could be secured via church bells, holy candles, consecrated herbs, and other such talismans. Once possessed by either incubi or succubi, however, one of the remedies prescribed by the holy church—the "means by which these devils may be driven away"—was exorcism. Other possible cures were sacramental confession, the sign of the cross, moving to another place, or excommunication, although incubus devils could also be driven away by the Lord's Prayer or sprinkling with holy water. The *Malleus* regularly refers to "bewitched" persons, and devotes various chapters to the method of exorcising them: witches, after all, could rob a man of his "male organ," or make him think he had been robbed, and replace it with an illusory "glamour" (58–61).[47] The text, however, tries to distinguish between bewitchment and possession: "Let the reader pay attention to the six impediments [to successful exorcism] mentioned above, although they refer to *Energoumenoi*, or men possessed, rather than to men bewitched" (186). Cervantes's Isabela, it would seem, is a mock *Energoumen*, a Greek term whose derivatives the *Malleus* considerately furnishes readers: "from *En*, meaning In, and *Ergon*, meaning Work, since they labour within themselves" (184). Cervantes would have been familiar with the Greek term, courtesy of Covarrubias, in whose *Tesoro* it is translated as *ergumenus*, under the rubric of "ENDEMONIADO."[48] Although it is easier, the *Malleus* allows, to cure a possessed than a bewitched person (186), the "lawful exorcisms of the Church" are cited as the "most often considered" verbal remedies for liberation from either state.

But exorcisms, as the *Malleus* warned early modern Europe, were "lawful" only on three conditions: the authority of the exorcist (whether laymen, or secular clerics, or even devout persons "may lawfully exorcise devils" is pondered at length); the presence of "unknown names" in the benedictions or charms; and the use of any kind of "lie" during the incan-

[46] Montague Summers, "Introduction to 1948 Edition," *Malleus maleficarum*, viii.

[47] "Thou shalt not suffer a witch to live"—rendered in the Vulgate translation in the masculine plural "Maleficos non patieris vivere" (Exod. 22:18)—was the Mosaic maxim behind the *Malleus*. Kramer and Sprenger codified for Cervantes's age, and not only for his age, all the processes by which witches—especially female ones, who were declared more carnal than men—were not suffered to live.

[48] Covarrubias, *Tesoro*, 517.

tation (such as the "jingling doggerel" used by "old women") (179–91). As we recall from Isabela's story, all of the above conditions are broken in Cervantes's representation of exorcism. There is a "flaw in the exorcist" (185), or at least his authority is illegal, given that he identifies himself as the commander of the legions of hell, explicitly countering Saint Thomas Aquinas's prohibition that "there must be nothing in the words [of the benediction] which hints at any expressed or tacit invocation of devils" (180). The "unknown name" of the exorcist, a not-very-pious university student at Salamanca called Andreas Marulo, is unlawfully invoked in the benediction, disregarding Saint John Chrysostom's explicit warning that unknown names "are to be regarded with fear, lest they should conceal some matter of superstition" (181). And, finally, the secular romance formulas of the exorcist's incantation—"¡Afuera, afuera, afuera; aparta, aparta, aparta!"—if not precisely doggerel, are a far cry, both vernacular and secular, from the formulaic Latin charms canonized by the church. Pointing to the great significance of the words that are used in the charms, the *Malleus* expressly forbade any tampering with the language of exorcism: "And let no one meddle with such sacred offices by any accidental or habitual omission of any necessary forms or words" (183–85). Within man himself and in sinful matters brought about by him, the *Malleus* assured inquisitors, lie the sources of the Devil's power: "This then is the significance of the words that are used in exorcism, as when it is said, 'Depart, O Satan, from him' " (183). Of the many authorities on exorcism cited by the *Malleus*—including Saints Augustine, Gregory, Benedict, Isidore, John Chrysostom, and Thomas Aquinas—perhaps none is more pertinent to Cervantes's rendering of Isabela's demonic possession than Origen, who notes in a gloss that "this sort of devil, that is, the variability of carnal desires induced by that spirit," is resistant to healing grace, and can be conquered only by prayer and fasting (185). Several years before "this sort of devil" appeared to Isabela, it bears noting, he had visited the saintly Dominican priest in Cervantes's *El rufián dichoso*, masquerading as six dancers "vestidos como ninfas lascivamente [lasciviously dressed like nymphs]" (87).

The institutional spread of the *Malleus*, it would appear, affected not only Renaissance magistrates but also Sorbonne-trained humanists. If the Hieronymite Pedro Ciruelo took his information on pacts with the Devil from the *Malleus*, as William A. Christian suggests,[49] he may also have taken from that notorious text some of his information on exorcism. Ciruelo's astonishingly popular treatise, *Reprobación de las supersticiones y hechicerías*, appearing in Alcalá around 1530, was one of the earliest of

---

[49] William A. Christian, *Apparitions in Late Medieval and Renaissance Spain* (Princeton: Princeton University Press, 1981), 196.

the Spanish handbooks for combating witchcraft.[50] In his *Reprobación*, Ciruelo devoted an entire chapter to exorcisms, but his approach to the diabolic arts was vastly different from Kramer and Sprenger's. Unlike the authors of the *Malleus*, Ciruelo is an unfanatic humanist, a Thomist philosopher who did not participate in the tribunals of the holy office. Although a demonologist, his tolerant prose and his search for "una explicación natural [a natural explanation]" anticipate, according to Francisco Tolsada, some "modernas y muy avanzadas teorías" [modern and very advanced theories]."[51] Ciruelo's stance on the practice of exorcism is basically cautionary, and his repeated warnings against "vanas supersticiones [vain superstitions]," or "cerimonias vanas [vain ceremonies]" (105, 114) would seem to foreshadow Cervantes's own language in the *Persiles* for the ceremonies of his cannibals.

At least two of Ciruelo's five "reglas [rules]" for proper exorcisms move us to think that Cervantes may have known his treatise on demonology. The first rule may even have given Cervantes the idea for his fraudulent exorcist:

> Que cuando alguno puro lego . . . se muestra por sacador de espíritus malos de los hombres endemoniados y usa este oficio públicamente, hay grande sospecha . . . que lo haga por pacto de amistad que tiene con el diablo, o claramente o solapada y encubierta. (104–5)

> [When a simple layman . . . claims to be an exorcist of evil spirits from possessed men and uses this role publicly, there is great suspicion . . . that he is doing it through a pact of friendship he has with the Devil, either openly or artfully and surreptitiously.]

Cervantes's use of the "purely lay" figure of Andreas as a public exorcist who loudly reveals a manifest pact of amity with the devil is squarely in the representation forbidden by the first of Ciruelo's rules.

But Cervantes is even more subversive of Ciruelo's rule that demons be kept silent: "No debemos oír las palabras del demonio [We should not listen to the words of the demon]" (110). Ciruelo, in fact, repeatedly laments the Spanish practice of encouraging demons to speak aloud. On

---

[50] Others were Castañega's *Tratado de las supersticiones y hechicerías* (1529); Peréz de Moya's *Philosophia secreta* (1585); Horozco y Covarrubias's *Tratado de la verdadera y falsa astrología* (1588); Martín del Río's *Disquisitionum magicarum liber sex* (1612); and Torreblanca's *Epitome delictorum* (1618).

[51] Introductory material in *Reprobación de las supersticiones y hechicerías* (facsimile; Madrid: Collección Joyas Bibliográficas, 1952), xxvii–xxviii. My citations from this text's eighth Chapter, which focuses on demoniacs, will be parenthetically documented. See also Pedro Ciruelo's *A Treatise Reproving All Superstitions and Forms of Witchcraft Very Necessary and Useful for All Good Christians Zealous for their Salvation*, trans. Eugene A. Maio and D'Orsay W. Pearson (London: Associated University Presses, 1977).

the contrary, he writes, "el bueno y católico conjurador . . . manda en nombre de Jesucristo al demonio que no hable, y por eso no le pregunta cosa alguna a que el diablo haya de responder [the good Catholic conjurer . . . orders, in the name of Jesus Christ, the demon not to speak, which is why he asks the devil no questions whatsoever]" (107). In Cervantes's burlesque representation, the whole party chats with Isabela's demon and even takes his "sign" of coming out very seriously. The very idea of a demon's making the rules for his own exorcism, selecting his own exorcist, and even fixing the date for his "coming out" would have been regarded as outrageous in Ciruelo's handbook. To converse with the Devil and to ask him anything at all ("cosa alguna") is actually fixed as a mortal sin by Ciruelo: he reproves people who, wishing to know "cosas ocultas [occult things]," actually ask the possessing demon "cosas curiosas [curious questions]" (111–12). This is precisely what Cervantes dramatizes in his tale of exorcism, when he presents Sr. Marulo asking the "possessed" Isabela about her knowledge of his son, who in a curious revelation is pictured as picking cherries in Illescas; or when the doctor calls the demon himself a "know-it-all"; or when Isabela's uncle directly addresses him as a "demonio maldito [malign demon]" and tells him not to dream of returning to visit her body. It would seem, then, that Ciruelo's *Reprobación* provided at least some of the rules of exorcism for Cervantes's fiction to break.

Can we deduce from all this subversiveness what Cervantes's private views were on these explosive religious issues? Claudio Guillén once mentioned, in an altogether different context, that Cervantes was "no doubt . . . capable, even in his old age, of holding several opinions at once."[52] This would seem to be the case with his "opinions" regarding possession, whose long Roman Catholic tradition—based on Mark 5:1–19, where Christ drove a legion of unclean spirits out of a possessed man and into the Gadarene swine—had been developed into a sophisticated demonology by generations of medieval theologians. Cervantes had regularly represented bewitchment or possession in his fictions, as, for example, in *La española inglesa* or *El licenciado Vidriera* or *El rufián dichoso*. Whatever Cervantes thought of possession, as real or as a demonic illusion or as something in between, in the *Persiles* he provides a mordant parody of the canonically prescribed remedies of *dis*possession, that is, the lawful exorcisms of the church that had been the target of skeptical Roman Catholic satire from Boccaccio to Erasmus. And although Cervantes is not above satirizing the clergy (one thinks, for instance, of that clerical parasite who serves as resident chaplain of the Duke and Duchess in *Don*

[52] Claudio Guillén, "Truth and Illusion," Review of *Cervantes: A Biography*, by William Byron, *The New York Times Book Review*, 8 April 1979, 22.

Quixote, part 2), he does not choose to portray Isabela's exorcists as either sleazy or contemptible, a role he reserves only for the guardian-uncle who calls them in. One might say tentatively, then, that Cervantes recognizes demonic possession as a rich trope but dispossession as an empty ritual. Exactly what Cervantes's private religious beliefs were is impossible to determine, although speculation ranges from Castro's portrait of the artist as an "enlightened believer" constrained by post-Tridentine orthodoxies, to Forcione's picture of him as holding "extremely complex" and perhaps even "troubled and unstable" views.[53]

What is clear to us about Cervantes's reiteration of the theme of exorcism is that he both gendered and psychologized the narrative. It is instructive to address Erasmus's colloquy on exorcism with the modern question, "Is there a woman in this text?" Woman is absent in *Exorcismus*, and the presence of her absence seems not eccentric in a text so relentlessly focused on male humanist pranks. Woman is present in Cervantes's tale of exorcism, however, a woman who rescripts Erasmus's comic skit about exorcism into a kind of New Comedy, produced and directed by her, about women in love. By taking possession of the role of demonic possession, Cervantes's Isabela generates a loud critique of the patriarchal economy of desire—where women must seem to *be* possessed in order to resist *being* possessed, where they must feign lunacy in order to express desire. The Isabela of the *Persiles* recalls the earlier Isabela of *La española inglesa*, who enters Cervantes's text as a *despojo*, as Carroll Johnson observes: "dehumanized, reduced to the level of an object, a spoil of war."[54] In the *Persiles*, the dehumanization from which the later Isabela suffers is emblematized as fetters, as those *ligaduras* tying her to the bedposts which she begs to have removed: "Lo que quiero es . . . que me quiten estas ligaduras que aunque son blandas, me fatigan, porque me impiden [What I want is . . . that you remove these fetters which, although soft ones, fatigue me because they impede me]" (405). The very first speech by a woman in the *Persiles*, Taurisa's lament, is an analogous cry of freedom: "Libre pensé yo que gozara de la luz del sol en esta vida; pero engañóme mi pensamiento, pues me veo a pique de ser vendida por esclava: desventura a quien ninguna puede compararse [I thought I would be free to enjoy the sunlight in this life; but I was deceived, because I see myself on the verge of being sold as a slave: a catastrophe compared to none]" (55). Isabela Castrucha, who also sees herself "on the verge of being sold," takes control of her own erotic destiny and gives herself where she chooses, becomes an independent arbitrator of her desire. Like

[53] On Castro, see Bataillon, *Erasmo y España*, 785; Forcione, *Cervantes and the Humanist Vision*, 351.

[54] Johnson, "*La española inglesa* and the Practice of Literary Production," 400.

Don Quixote, Isabela challenges a worldview by means of her craziness. Unlike Don Quixote, however, hers is a *simulated* dementia. By producing and directing the whole script of her possession, she reinforces the Renaissance similitudes between theater and exorcism, thereby foreshadowing Freud's vision of hysteria as not only "identical" with the medieval theory of possession, but also as "a caricature of a work of art."[55] But such clinical futurism aside, what is perhaps most illuminating to Cervantes's poetics is that Isabela's artistic labors assimilate her to no less an "author" than Cide Hamete Benengeli. As a magician descended from a whole race of "liars," Cide Hamete not only enjoyed mingling truth with falsehoods in the process of artistic creation, but also, like the "possessed" Isabela, he appeared to be on speaking terms with the Devil.

The literary character whom Isabela most resembles appears not in Cervantes, however, but in Shakespeare: Edgar in *King Lear*, who is also forced by domestic circumstances to mime demonic possession. A closing glance at Shakespeare's representation of a sham demoniac, his "poor Tom-o-Bedlam," helps us to see what the theater of exorcism was struggling to articulate throughout the sixteenth century. By the time Edgar was simulating possession, exorcism had been officially banned in Anglican England, a cultural abdication that lends fuel to the notion that Shakespeare's attack on the practice may have had politico-religious aims: according to the new church canons of 1604, no minister, without his bishop's special permission, was henceforth to attempt "upon any pretence whatsoever whether of possession or obsession, by fasting and prayer, to cast out any devil or devils, under pain of the imputation of imposture or cozenage and deposition from the ministry."[56] The Catholic rite of exorcism continued unabated, however, both among England's recusant clergy and in numerous Continental epidemics of possession—such as the twenty-five nuns in Madrid (1628–1631)[57] and the notorious affair several years later in Loudon (c. 1634). The Protestant *Lear*, then, was a work that, unlike the Catholic *Persiles*, could more safely brood upon the idea of spurious exorcism.

Like Shakespeare's Edgar, Cervantes's Isabela is a feigning demoniac, but because she is an essentially comic heroine, her tale has none of the elements of terror we experience in *King Lear*. Like Edgar, Isabela would seem to be trying to substitute dramatic illusion for the "miracles" of exorcism. Edgar's response to his father's aborted suicide attempt—"Thy

---

[55] Freud, *SE* 13:73.

[56] Thomas, *Religion and the Decline of Magic*, 485.

[57] For the frank testimony of the Spanish abbess involved in this mass possession in Madrid, see Calmeil, *De la folie*, ii, pp. 3 sq., cited by T. K. Oesterreich, *Possession, Demoniacal and Other Among Privitive Races, in Antiquity, the Middle Ages, and Modern Times* (New Hyde Park, N.Y.: University Books, 1966), 41.

life's a miracle" (4.6.55)—belongs to the same Cervantine "naturalizing" of miracles discussed in an early chapter of this book. Also like Edgar, Isabela is not superstitious, but she is identified throughout her narrative with deceit, illusion, and manipulation through madness. Her entire project of marriage ultimately rests on a kind of stage trickery, one that is validated by Cervantes because her illusion-making supplants a cozening reality (quite literally, in the prospect of a dreaded cross-*cousin* marriage). In both Edgar's and Isabela's stories, evil is represented as coming not from demons but from the structure of the patriarchal family. The most powerful "demons" in both these works would seem to be the demoniacs' kinsmen. Shakespeare's Edgar assumes the role of demon-ridden Tom-o-Bedlam in order to survive the persecutions machinated by his illegitimate brother, the greedy Edmund. Among the clutch of demons he claims are possessing him—Modo, Manu, Turleygod, Flibbertigibbet—Shakespeare slyly includes one "Fraterreto," an apt name for a diabolic brother. Cervantes's Isabela similarly fabricates her own demon as a ploy to ward off the intolerable marriage arranged for her by her uncle, the greedy Castrucho. Both Edgar and Isabela are marked out as entirely sympathetic characters, and their histrionic manipulations are fictionalized as essentially ethical labors. It is striking, moreover, that the demons assumed by both young people drive them to acts of sham masochism, or self-inflicted punishment, but never to acts of villainy or viciousness. Even as pretend demoniacs, Edmund and Isabela take upon themselves, as it were, the pains of their respective family dynamics.

Finally, the texts of both Shakespeare and Cervantes, separated only by perhaps a decade, are heavily *gendered* narratives, fictions that focus on the engendering and transfer of power. Edgar feigns the role of a possessed man because he has fallen from his father's graces, the power of love and patrimony succeeding to the brother begotten in a "dark and vicious place." Faking possession out of the need to survive in a world of unredeemed evil, the unjustly persecuted Edgar fabricates a population of demons who turn out to be salvific figures. If Edgar seems to be feigning "overtime," notably in the "deceit-therapy" he gives his suicidal father, it may be because *Lear*, as John Murphy argues, chooses the "illusions" of theater against "the consolations of philosophy." But if the *Lear* of Murphy's illuminating study is, as he claims, "very close to the dramatic world of Calderón," it is also, in its convergence of possession and sexuality, close to that of Cervantes.[58] When theatrical "illusions" are seen not as deceits but as artistic strategies, they become prescient explorations of the patrilineal ideology Renaissance men lived by, as well as of the "glamours" that tended to foil them.

[58] Murphy, *Darkness and Devils*, 11–12. On Edgar as an "energumen," see 197–202.

EPILOGUE

This would not be only a man's story from now on.
A presence (my presence . . .) will alter the story.
—Carlos Fuentes, *The Old Gringo*

NOTHING has been more difficult than writing this epilogue you are now reading. Many times I fed my disk into the computer, and many times I took it out again, not knowing what I would write. One of these times, seated at my desk thinking of what to say—the screen blank, my elbow on the keyboard, my cheek in my hand—an essay on Cervantes unexpectedly arrived, via Federal Express. It was from a lively, clever friend of mine who, intuiting my difficulty, helped me to understand why books in the postmodern age must be abandoned rather than finished. "We can't say it all, do it all, know it all," my *amiga* wrote, sweeping away my anxieties over the deficiencies of this present book, but we can, "according to the shaping of our own consciousness," try to "illuminate something." What her own work has illuminated in Cervantes is "a universe that questions—radically questions—all received norms, categories, theories, beliefs, and structures." Because Cervantes "saw the world differently from his contemporaries," it is important to hear, my friend suggests, the voices he gives to "deviants" from the social norms.[1]

Cervantes's sympathy toward deviants and marginals has been lately remarked, from a considerably different perspective, by a contemporary European scholar: "No hay nadie que no vea cuanta simpatía e interés lleno de respeto mostró siempre Cervantes frente al mundo de 'los otros': los golfillos, los gitanos, los moriscos, los protestantes, y en especial frente a los musulmanes [There is no one who cannot see how much sympathy and interest, filled with respect, Cervantes always showed toward the world of 'the others': petty thieves, gypsies, Moorish converts, Protestants, and especially toward Muslims]." Although women are not included in this catalogue of Golden Age Otherness, this critic has elsewhere acknowledged the extraordinary autonomy that Cervantes—who alone, in his day, placed himself "on the margins of the systems of difference"—could imagine for his female characters.[2]

[1] Ruth El Saffar, "Confessions of a Cervantes Critic," *Journal of Hispanic Philology* [Special Issue: *Feminist Topics*, ed. Alison Weber] 13 (Spring 1989): 269, 263.

[2] Rossi, *Escuchar a Cervantes*, 60, 74. On the vexed issue of the Muslims, and on Cervantes as "la voz de su tiempo," see Rafael Osuna's essay "La expulsión de los moriscos en

My study has addressed the systems of difference in the *Persiles* from multiple angles—from the role of "Otherness" as a code in Greek romance (chap. 1) to its travesty in Renaissance exorcisms (chap. 9). In between, I have spotlighted Cervantes's various agents of liminality— witches, magi, hermits, pirates, bandits, psychotics, flying women, talking wolves, army prostitutes, and transvestites—characters who counter or derail the structures of official discourse. In the last third of the present study, however, the world of *las otras* is more prominent than that of *los otros*. I examine, in these closing chapters, a trio of representations of femininity by Cervantes that counters most Renaissance notions of woman. In each case—and each subject relates what she considers her "caso"—the woman's sexuality has been co-opted by her kinsmen, by more or less loving patriarchs fortified by the working myths of their respective pan-European cultures. Cervantes's liberatory plots bear out at least the spirit of Catherine A. MacKinnon's observation that sexuality, for women in certain oppressed cultures, is "that which is most one's own, yet most taken away."[3] Yet Cervantes's women never internalize the dominant ideology of the cultures that would both idealize and marginalize them. Refusing to be fixed in the condition of the ornamental or the contingent, they produce texts that challenge, and even move beyond, the Law of the Father allegorized in the opening chapters of the *Persiles*.

To the extent that Cervantes resists the symbolic order—the order from which women and other marginals are excluded as subjects of discourse—his writing is revolutionary. It is part of the general dethroning of authority commonly thought to have been initiated by Marx, Freud, and Saussure, but that really began, as all Cervantists know, with the prologue to *Don Quixote*, part 1, whose inimitable parody seems closer to a manifesto for our time. The increasing decanonization of novelistic values, however, may be moving us beyond our fixation with *Don Quixote* toward a new interest in romance forms, and not only in romance forms: "It is to be hoped," Forcione remarks, "that the new interest in the *Persiles* is the healthy sign of a new respect for literary forms of all types, of a literary catholicity admirably exemplified by Cervantes himself, who apparently saw in nearly every book he could lay his hands on a fascinating, challenging invitation to his genius."[4] I would add to Forcione's my own hope that future practitioners of such a literary catholicity will see

---

el *Persiles*," *NRFH* 19 (1970): 388–93. See the episode in "un lugar de moriscos" in the *Persiles* (3.11).

[3] Catherine A. MacKinnon, "Feminism, Marxism, Method, and the State: An Agenda for Theory," in *Feminist Theory: A Critique of Ideology*, ed. Nannerl G. Keohane, Michelle Z. Rosaldo, and Barbara C. Gelpi (Chicago: University of Chicago Press, 1982), 1.

[4] Alban K. Forcione, Review of *Cervantes' Musterroman* Persiles, by Tilbert Diego Stegmann, *MLN* 88 (March 1983): 444.

in the *Persiles* more than a return to a conservative and reassuring framework of the traditional pieties. Anthony J. Cascardi, for instance, has recently proposed that "the *Persiles* represents not a reactionary or conservative effort, as many have taken it to be, but a vanguard attempt that rejects the return to the moral order elsewhere dominant in early modern Spain"—an order of "fixed essences, social hierarchies, and universal moral truths."[5] How fiercely Cervantes's last work rejects that dominant moral order has been the burden of this study. Its overarching aim has been to present the *Persiles* as stories of men and women rather than as embodiments of Man.

When I first read the *Persiles* some years ago—"in the dark backward and abysm of time" before women became resistant readers—I could not articulate any of the conclusions of the present book. Even then, however, in my early encounters with Cervantes's last work, I was "surprised by Otherness."[6] I was surprised to find, for one, that Cervantes had opened the Golden Age signifying world to its conventionally absent mothers, that he did not allow them to remain outside representation. When I began writing about the *Persiles*, I did not understand, as I do now, that "the name of the Father" requires the repression of the mother. In their wild attempts to legislate this kind of repression, Cervantes's cannibals produce a holocaust instead. But on the margins of that barbaric community, Cervantes strategically places a man and a woman who will be saved from destruction: a Spaniard called Antonio and a Northern woman called Ricla, who programmatically figures as Eve throughout the text—a "serpentless Eve," to use Casalduero's alert qualification.[7] A de-

---

[5] Anthony J. Cascardi, "Reason and Romance" (Paper delivered at the Second International Conference on the Ancient Novel, Dartmouth College, Hanover, N.H., 26 July 1989), 3, 6. Countering Américo Castro's disparaging view of the *Persiles* as a retraction of the valorized perspectivist stance of *Don Quixote*, Cascardi concludes that "the *Persiles* seeks to establish what is essentially a new law, and new conditions for moral discourse. These do not depend, as in the *comedia*, on a sublimation of those sacrificial demands through an idealist reshaping of the past, but require instead the projection of a reconciled community of mankind. In the *Persiles* this community is modeled in the relations of the virtuous couple" (13).

[6] My earliest encounters with the *Persiles* were enriched through endless formative conversations with Rachel Jacoff, whose work on Dante offered me the first model of the feminine as speculative and vice versa. "Surprised by Otherness" is Barbara Johnson's admirable phrase, in *A World of Difference*, 15.

[7] Casalduero, *Sentido y forma de Los trabajos*, 42. Ruth El Saffar writes in *Beyond Fiction* that "Antonio and Ricla, in their faith and natural prosperity, resemble Adam and Eve" (135). In the *Persiles*, the myth of Eve is redeployed for purposes quite different from the sexualized Augustinian reading of Genesis that engendered the concept of Original Sin. Although Augustine's interpretation prevailed in the western Christian tradition, and is still orthodox in many Christian churches, Cervantes seems much closer to the views espoused by Clement of Alexandria (c. A.D. 180), the early Christian Neoplatonist who regarded

fector from the barbarians, this new Eve explains to the Europeans how she became a mother: "Entreguéle mi cuerpo, no pensando que en ello ofendía a nadie, y deste entrego resulto haberle dado dos hijos [I gave him my body, not thinking that I would offend anyone in doing so, and this affair resulted in my giving him two children]" (82). Kristeva has called for a reformulation of a contemporary ethics that would require, specifically, the contribution of mothers: "Of women who harbour the desire to reproduce (to have stability). Of women who are available so that our speaking species, which knows it is moral, might withstand death." One might say that Cervantes's Ricla—in both her desire to reproduce *and* her desire to represent her reproduction—qualifies as one of the rare Renaissance foremothers of Kristeva's projected *herethics*, "an heretical ethics separated from morality."[8]

What I find most striking about the representation of Ricla, however, is that she enacts the epigraph cited above from Carlos Fuentes, a kind of retrocursor to Cervantes. As Antonio is relating his history, Ricla's presence alters it: she appropriates and concludes the man's story, courteously, affectionately, but "in a different voice." This technique of appropriation is common in the theater of Calderón, where, as one critic argues, a speech is made "más ameno y movido [more pleasing and moving]" for being divided up.[9] In Cervantes's hands, however, the joint tenancy of a discourse not only moves and pleases but also makes pervious both gender and cultural oppositions. As this European man and barbaric woman—Cervantes's new Adam and Eve—collaborate in a long narration, we discover that they have both learned new languages: "Hame enseñado su lengua y yo a él la mía [He has taught me his language, and I (have taught) him mine]" (82). The kind of verbal barter Cervantes depicts here—a dialogue between a Spanish male subject and a non-Spanish female Other—is rarely found in representations of love in Golden Age prose, where alterity is dimly understood.[10] Indeed, in most Renaissance fictions, the verbal exchange between the sexes may be exemplified by Hermione's words to Leontes in *The Winter's Tale*: "You speak a language that I understand not" (3.2.80). More recently, Nietzsche, reflecting on "marriage as a long conversation," worried whether his male readers could find mates who spoke the same language: "When marrying, one

conscious participation in procreation as "cooperation with God in the work of creation" (Pagels, *Adam, Eve, and the Serpent*, xxiii; see also 26–31).

[8] Kristeva, "Stabat Mater," 185.

[9] Navarro González, *Cervantes entre el* Persiles *y el* Quijote, 29.

[10] Daniel Eisenberg glosses "el amor entre dos interlocutores [love between two interlocutors]" as a rarity in Golden Age prose. See the thorough treatment given to Cervantes and "el amor" in chap. 15 of *Las semanas del jardín de Miguel de Cervantes* (Salamanca: Ediciones de la Diputación de Salamanca, 1989), 81–91.

should ask oneself this question: Do you believe that you will be able to converse well with this woman into your old age? Everything else in marriage is transitory, but the most time during the association belongs to conversation."[11] Nietzsche's prudent warning seems scarcely the stuff of romance, which he in any case loathed. But knowing and acknowledging the problem of other minds—not merely in conversation but also in language without words—remains the central preoccupation of Cervantes's last romance. At the threshold of the *Persiles*, and at the close of his life, Cervantes's primal couple shows readers how men and women can become "bilingual." It is this kind of collaboration that signifies the real "labors" of Cervantes's title—learning the language of the Other.

[11] Cited as an epigraph by Michael Ragussis, *The Subterfuge of Art: Language and the Romantic Tradition* (Baltimore: Johns Hopkins University Press, 1978), 172.

INDEX

WIDENER UNIVERSITY WOLFGRAM LIBRARY CHESTER, PA.